D1337115

Great Songs of the Church

REVISED

A·C·U
PRESS
Abilene, Texas
1986

THE HYMNAL COMMITTEE

Forrest M. McCann, *Chairman and General Editor*

Jack Boyd, *Music Editor*

ASSOCIATE EDITORS

Rollie Blondeau   Milton Pullen

ADVISORY COMMITTEE

Bill W. Davis, *Honorary Chairman*

Kenneth Adams, Jr.
Fred Alexander
Tony Ash
Joe B. Baisden
Irma Lee Batey
Larry M. Bills
Marca Lee Bircher
Terry M. Blake
Nick Boone
Carl Brecheen
Marvin A. Brooker, Jr.
George E. Butterfield
Gerald Casey
Ralph A. Casey
H. Decker Clark, Jr.
Paul A. Clark
John Clovis
Bevan Collingwood
Charles E. Cox
Max E. Craddock
Robert M. Cronin
Dan G. Danner

Kenneth Davis, Jr.
Lloyd A. Deal
Enos E. Dowling
William E. Fowler
James Fulbright
Neil Fry
Clifton L. Ganus III
Andrew Gardiner
Ronald B. Hadfield
Jim Hawkins
Ken Helterbrand
L.D. (Bill) Hilton
Wayne Hinds
James L. Jackson
Dale A. Jorgenson
William T. King
Thomas A. Langford
Ernest E. Lyon
Gary Mabry
Bruce Mayhall
Larry McCommas
Patricia Burke McNicol

Timothy M. Meixner
Erle T. Moore
Anthony Mukitus
R Stafford North
Thomas H. Olbricht
Paul R. Piersall
Richard David Ramsey
Robert M. Randolph
H. Putnam Reeves, Jr.
Andy T. Richie III
Jerry Rushford
Leon B. Sanderson
Tommy Spain
Russel N. Squire
William J. Teague
Darryl Tippens
Bill B. Totty
Peggy Spoonts West
Bill Waugh
James Willett
John F. Wilson

Music Typography

Don Ellingson: Musictype, Omaha, Arkansas

Typography

Texas Photocomp, Abilene, Texas

Cover Design

Rubén Santiago

Book Design and Production

Ronald B. Hadfield

ISBN 0-915547-90-2

Library of Congress 85-82565

FOREWORD

This revised edition of **Great Songs of the Church** represents the fruits of many years of labor. No effort has been spared to collect into a single portable volume the choicest hymns and songs of all times. Our aim has been to provide for every age group, for every kind of public meeting, and for private devotions a suitable body of poems and tunes to satisfy the will to praise, to pray, and to exhort.

Great Songs of the Church, Revised represents an effort to preserve and to continue the work of its original compiler, Elmer Leon Jorgenson (1886-1968). **Great Songs** was first published in 1921. It was improved in 1922 with a **Supplement** of 50 songs which were amalgamated with the original collection in 1925. This Number One book continued until 1937, at which time **Great Songs of the Church, Number Two** appeared.

Since 1937, no major changes have been made in the collection, with the exception of the addition of a **Supplement** of 70 songs in 1975. Our aim in the **Supplement** and now in the revision is to work from the same principles which actuated the original compiler. He said: "Excellence alone has been the principle of inclusion . . . The standards followed were truth and soundness, first of all; then strength and clearness, poetic beauty and lyric quality—the music wedded to the words and fit to wing them to the heart."

The special features of this revised edition are these:

• *A topical arrangement:* The Table of Contents will indicate the divisions of the compilation. These divisions are not meant to be inflexible and are not indicated elsewhere in the book. They can be helpful in selecting materials suitable to various occasions and subjects.

• *Every song arranged for congregational use:* "Let all the people sing" has been our rule. To this end the musical editor has given special attention to the musical settings that these may be neither too difficult nor too demanding, while yet preserving the power of every hymn and song.

• *Scripture selections:* More than 100 passages from the Bible are distributed throughout the hymnal, and each has been assigned its own number. These scriptures may be employed devotionally or responsively, in either public worship or private praise. The scriptures included were chosen to reinforce the hymn poems with which they appear.

• *Revised indexes:* These include an Author-Composer Index, a much enlarged Tune Index (each selection having been assigned a tune name), a Topical Index which has been revised in connection with the topical arrangement of the hymns and songs, a First Line Index, and a Scripture Index of all passages either cited or quoted in full in the body of the hymnal.

• *A larger format:* The larger page size allows for a clearer note face and more readable typeface, and, at the same time, a cleaner look to every page.

In presenting this revised hymnal to the churches, the Executive Hymnal Committee desires to express thanks to the Advisory Committee from around the world which gave *gratis* a wealth of suggestions and evaluations resulting in the revisions contained in this book; to the Liaison Committee which worked untold hours in securing copyrights and in preparing copy for the press; and to the administration of Abilene Christian University for its interest and financial outlay in making this edition possible.

Chiefly we give thanks to the Lord whose mercy endures forever and who inhabits the praises of His people, asking that He may be pleased to accept our work in the name of Jesus the Lord.

Abilene, Texas • January, 1986

CONTENTS

MAKE A JOYFUL NOISE UNTO

GOD

ALL THE EARTH:

SING FORTH THE GLORY OF HIS NAME:

MAKE HIS PRAISE GLORIOUS

—Psalm 66:1,2

We Gather Together

1. We gather together to ask the Lord's blessing;
2. Beside us to guide us, our God with us joining,
3. We all do extol Thee, Thou King of the nation,

He chastens and hastens His will to make known;
Ordaining, maintaining His kingdom divine;
And pray that Thou still our Defender wilt be;

The wicked oppressing now cease from distressing:
So from the beginning the fight we were winning:
May Thy congregation escape tribulation:

Sing praises to His Name— He fails not His own!
Lord, Thine be all the glory—The vic't'ry is Thine!
Be Thou forever praised, Thou God of the free!

Romans 8:31. Words, from Adrianus Valerius' *Nederlandtsch Gedenckclanck*, 1626; trans. Theodore Baker, 1894, alt. Tune KREMSER, Netherlands Folk Tune; arr. Edward Kremser, 1877.

2 **O For a Thousand Tongues to Sing**

1. O for a thou - sand tongues to sing My
2. My gra - cious Mas - ter and my God, As -
3. Je - sus! the name that charms our fears, That
4. He breaks the power of can - celed sin, He

great Re - deem - er's praise, The glo - ries of my
sist me to pro - claim, To spread thro' all the
bids our sor - rows cease, 'Tis mu - sic in the
sets the pris - oner free; His blood can make the

God and King, The tri - umphs of His grace!
earth a - broad The hon - ors of Thy name.
sin - ners' ears, 'Tis life, and health, and peace.
foul - est clean; His blood a - vailed for me.

Psalm 35:28. Words, Charles Wesley, 1739. Tune AZMON, Carl G. Gläser, 1828; arr. Lowell Mason, 1839.

3 **Lord Jesus Christ, Be Present Now**

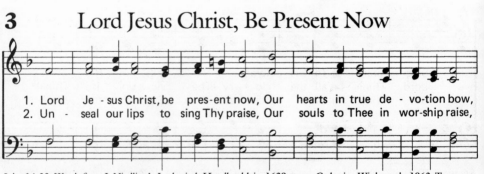

1. Lord Je - sus Christ, be pres - ent now, Our hearts in true de - vo - tion bow,
2. Un - seal our lips to sing Thy praise, Our souls to Thee in wor - ship raise,

John 14:23. Words from J. Niedling's *Lutherisch Handbuchlein*, 1638; trans. Catherine Winkworth, 1863. Tune HERR JESU CHRIST, in *Cantionale Sacrum*, 1651; harm. J. S. Bach.

Thy Spir-it send with grace di-vine, And let Thy truth with-in us shine.
Make strong our faith, in-crease our light That we may know Thy name a-right.

Lord, We Come Before Thee Now   4

Slowly

1. Lord, we come be-fore Thee now; At Thy feet we hum-bly
2. Lord, on Thee our souls de-pend: In com-pas-sion now de-
3. In Thine own ap-point-ed way, Now we seek Thee, here we
4. Grant that all may seek and find Thee a God su-preme-ly

bow: O do not our suit dis-dain; Shall we seek Thee,
scend; Fill our hearts with Thy rich grace, Tune our lips to
stay; Lord, we know not how to go, Till a bless-ing
kind; Heal the sick, the cap-tive free; Let us all re-

Lord, in vain? Shall we seek Thee, Lord, in vain?
sing Thy praise, Tune our lips to sing Thy praise.
Thou be-stow, Till a bless-ing Thou be-stow.
joice in Thee, Let us all re-joice in Thee.

Psalm 20:7. Words, William Hammond, 1745. Tune HENDON, Henri A. C. Malan, 1823.

5   Come, Let Us Join Our Cheerful Songs

1. Come let us join our cheer - ful songs With an - gels round the throne; Ten thou - sand thou - sand are their tongues, But all their joys are one.
2. "Wor - thy the Lamb that died," they cry, "To be ex - alt - ed thus!" "Wor - thy the Lamb," our lips re - ply, "For He was slain for us!"
3. Je - sus is wor - thy to re - ceive Hon - or and pow'r di - vine; And bless - ings, more than we can give, Be, Lord, for - ev - er Thine.
4. Let all cre - a - tion join in one To bless the sa - cred name Of him who sits up - on the throne, And to a - dore the Lamb.

Revelation 5:12. Words, Isaac Watts, 1707. Tune GRÄFENBURG, Johann Crüger's *Praxis Pietatis Melica*, 1653. Arr. J.B., Copyright 1986, ACU Press.

6   Revelation 5:11-13

I heard a voice of many angels round about the throne and the living creatures and the elders; and the number of them was ten thousand times ten thousand, and thousands of thousands; saying with a great voice,

    Worthy is the Lamb that has been slain to receive the power, and riches, and wisdom, and might, and honor, and glory, and blessing.

And every created thing which is in the heaven, and on the earth, and under the earth, and on the sea, and all things that are in them, heard I saying,

    Unto him that sitteth on the throne and unto the Lamb, be the blessing, and the honor, and the glory, and the dominion, for ever and ever.

1. God Him-self is with us: Let us now a - dore Him,
2. O Thou Fount of bless - ing, Pu - ri - fy my spir - it;

And with awe ap - pear be - fore Him. God is in His
Trust-ing on - ly in Thy mer - it, Like the ho - ly

tem - ple All with - in keep si - lence, Pros-trate lie with
an - gels Who be - hold Thy glo - ry, May I cease-less-

deep - est rev - erence, Him a - lone God we own,
ly a - dore Thee, And in all, Great and small,

Him, our God and Sav - ior; Praise His Name for - ev - er.
Seek to do most near - ly What Thou lov - est dear - ly. A-men.

Psalm 27:4. Words, Gerhardt Tersteegen, 1729; trans. composite. Tune ARNSBERG, Joachim Neander, 1680.

8 The Lord is in His Holy Temple

The Lord is in His ho-ly tem-ple: Let all the earth keep si-lence be-fore Him; Keep si-lence, keep si-lence, Keep si-lence be-fore Him.

Habakkuk 2:20. Words, paraphrase. Tune HIERON, William J. Kirkpatrick, 1900.

9   2 Corinthians 6:14-18

Be not unequally yoked with unbelievers: for what fellowship have righteousness and iniquity? Or what communion hath light with darkness? And what concord hath Christ with Belial? Or what portion hath a believer with an unbeliever? And what agreement hath a temple of God with idols? For we are a temple of the living God; even as God said,

I will dwell in them, and walk in them;
and I will be their God,
and they shall be my people.

Wherefore,

Come ye out from among them, and be ye separate,

saith the Lord,

And touch no unclean thing;
And I will receive you,
And will be to you a Father,
And ye shall be to me sons and daughters, saith the Lord Almighty.

Lord, Dismiss Us With Thy Blessing

1. Lord, dis - miss us with Thy bless - ing; Fill our hearts with joy and peace; Let us each, Thy love pos - sess - ing, Tri - umph in re - deem - ing grace. O re - fresh us, O re - fresh us, Trav - eling through this wil - der - ness.

2. Thanks we give and ad - o - ra - tion For Thy Gos - pel's joy - ful sound. May the fruits of Thy sal - va - tion In our hearts and lives a - bound; Ev - er faith - ful, ev - er faith - ful To the truth may we be found. A - men.

Hebrews 13:20,21. Words, John Fawcett, 1773. Tune SICILIAN MARINERS, in W. D. Tattersall's *Improved Psalmody*, 1794.

11   Savior, Again to Thy Dear Name

1. Sav - ior, a - gain to Thy dear name we raise, With one ac -
2. Grant us Thy peace up - on our home-ward way; With Thee be -
3. Grant us Thy peace through - out our earth - ly life, Our balm in

cord our part - ing hymn of praise; We stand to bless Thee ere our
gan, with Thee shall end the day; Guard Thou the lips from sin, the
sor - row, and our stay in strife; Then, when Thy voice shall bid our

wor - ship cease, Then, low - ly bow - ing, wait Thy word of peace.
hearts from shame, That in this house have called up - on Thy name.
con - flict cease, Call us, O Lord, to Thine e - ter - nal peace. A - men.

Matthew 26:30. Words, John Ellerton, 1868. Tune ELLERS, Edward J. Hopkins, 1869.

12   Hebrews 13:20,21

Now the God of peace, who brought again from the dead the great shepherd of the sheep with the blood of an eternal covenant, even our Lord Jesus, make you perfect in every good thing to do his will, working in us that which is well-pleasing in his sight, through Jesus Christ; to whom be the glory for ever and ever. Amen.

O Savior, Bless Us Ere We Go

13

1. O Savior, bless us ere we go; Thy word into our minds instill, And make our lukewarm hearts to glow With lowly love and fervent will.
2. Grant us, dear Lord, from evil ways True absolution and release; And bless us, more than in past days, With purity and inward peace.
3. Do more than pardon: give us joy, Sweet fear, and sober liberty, And loving hearts without alloy That only long to be like Thee.

Thro' life's long day, and death's dark night, O gentle Jesus, be our light.

John 1:9. Frederick W. Faber, 1849. Tune STELLA, English air; arr. Henri F. Hemy in *Easy Tunes for Catholic Schools*, 1852.

14   God Be With You Till We Meet Again

1. God be with you till we meet a - gain;
2. God be with you till we meet a - gain;
3. God be with you till we meet a - gain;
4. God be with you till we meet a - gain;

By His coun-sels guide, up - hold you, With His sheep se - cure-ly
'Neath His wings se -cure - ly hide you, Dai - ly man - na still pro-
When life's per - ils thick con - found you, Put His arms un - fail-ing
Keep love's ban-ner float-ing o'er you, Smite death's threat-ening wave be-

fold you: God be with you till we meet a - gain.
vide you: God be with you till we meet a - gain.
round you: God be with you till we meet a - gain.
fore you: God be with you till we meet a - gain. A-men.

Genesis 31:49. Words, Jeremiah E. Rankin, 1880. Tune GOD BE WITH YOU, William G. Tomer, 1880.

15   Psalm 73:23-25

I am continually with thee:
Thou hast holden my right hand.
Thou wilt guide me with thy counsel
And afterward receive me to glory.
My flesh and my heart faileth;
But God is the strength of my heart and my portion for ever.

Our Day of Praise is Done 16

1. Our day of praise is done, The eve-ning shad-ows fall;
2. A - round the throne on high, Where night can nev - er be,
3. 'Tis Thine each soul to calm, Each way - ward tho't re - claim,

But pass not from us with the sun, True light that light-est all.
The white-robed an - gels of the sky Bring cease-less hymns to Thee.
And make our life a dai - ly psalm Of glo - ry to Thy name.

Psalm 139:12. Words, John Ellerton, 1871. Tune ST. THOMAS, Aaron Williams, 1763.

May the Grace of Christ Our Savior 17

1. May the grace of Christ our Sav-ior And the Fa - ther's bound-less love,
2. Thus may we a - bide in un - ion With each oth -er and the Lord,

With the Ho - ly Spir-it's fa -vor, Rest up - on us from a - bove.
And pos-sess, in sweet com-mu-nion, Joys which earth can-not af-ford. A-men.

2 Corinthians 13:14. Words, John Newton, 1779. Tune STUTTGART, Ludwig and Witt's *Psalmodia Sacra*, 1715; adpt. Henry J. Gauntlett, 1861.

18 This is the Day the Lord Hath Made

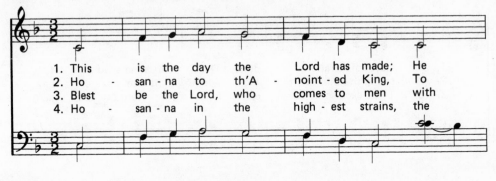

1. This is the day the Lord has made; He
2. Ho - san - na to th'A - noint - ed King, To
3. Blest be the Lord, who comes to men with
4. Ho - san - na in the high - est strains, the

calls the hours His own. Let heav'n re - joice, let
Da - vid's ho - ly Son. Help us, O Lord; de -
mes - sag - es of grace; Who comes, in God His
church on earth can raise; The high - est heav'ns, in

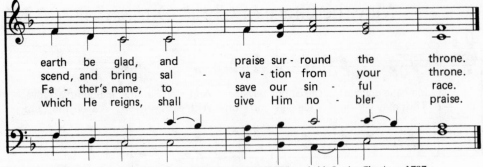

earth be glad, and praise sur - round the throne.
scend, and bring sal - va - tion from your throne.
Fa - ther's name, to save our sin - ful race.
which He reigns, shall give Him no - bler praise.

Psalm 118:24. Words, Isaac Watts, 1719. Tune TWENTY-FOURTH, probably Lucius Chapin, c. 1787.
Arr. J.B., Copyright 1986, ACU Press.

19 Psalm 118:24-26

This is the day which the Lord hath made;
We will rejoice and be glad in it.
Save now, we beseech thee, O Lord:
O Lord, we beseech thee, send now prosperity.
Blessed be he that cometh in the name of the Lord.

Welcome, Delightful Morn

1. Wel - come, de-light-ful morn, Thou day of sa - cred rest!
2. To spend one sa - cred day Where God and saints a - bide
3. Now may the King de - scend And fill His throne with grace;

I hail thy kind re - turn: Lord, make these mo-ments blest;
Af - fords di - vin - er joy Than thou-sand days be - side;
The scep - ter, Lord, ex - tend, While saints ad - dress Thy face;

From the low train of mor - tal toys, I soar to reach im -
I love it more where God re - sorts, To keep the door than
Let sin - ners feel Thy quick - 'ning word And learn to know and

mor - tal joys, I soar to reach im - mor - tal joys.
shine in courts, To keep the door than shine in courts.
fear the Lord, And learn to know and fear the Lord. A - men.

Matthew 18:20. Words, "Hayward," in John Dobell's *Selection*, 1806. Tune LISCHER, Friedrich Schneider, 1841.

21 Hail, Morning Known Among the Blest

1. Hail, morn-ing known a - mong the blest! This day of hope and joy and love, Of heav'n-ly peace and ho - ly rest, The pledge of end - less rest a - bove.
2. Blest be the Fa - ther of our Lord, Who from the dead has brought His Son! Hope to the lost was then re - stored, And ev - er - last - ing glo - ry won.
3. Scarce morn-ing twi - light had be - gun To chase the shades of night a - way, When Christ a - rose— un - set - ting Sun— The dawn of joy's e - ter - nal day!
4. God's good - ness let us bear in mind, Who to His saints this day has giv'n, For rest and se - rious joy de - signed, To fit us for the bliss of heav'n.

Matthew 28:1. Words, Ralph Wardlaw, 1803. Tune CANONBURY, from Robert Schumann's "Nachstücke," 1839; adpt. J. Ireland Tucker, 1872.

22   2 Corinthians 4:6

It is God that said, Light shall shine out of darkness, who shined in our hearts, to give the light of the knowledge of the glory of God in the face of Jesus Christ.

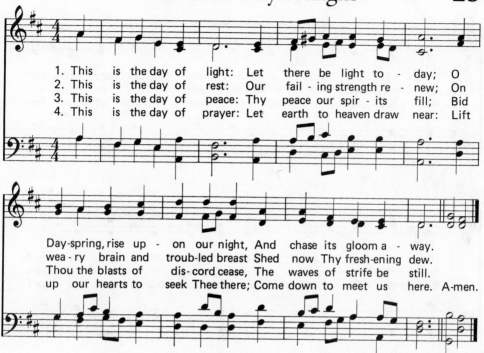

1. This is the day of light: Let there be light to - day; O
2. This is the day of rest: Our fail - ing strength re - new; On
3. This is the day of peace: Thy peace our spir - its fill; Bid
4. This is the day of prayer: Let earth to heaven draw near: Lift

Day-spring, rise up - on our night, And chase its gloom a - way.
wea - ry brain and troub-led breast Shed now Thy fresh-ening dew.
Thou the blasts of dis-cord cease, The waves of strife be still.
up our hearts to seek Thee there; Come down to meet us here. A-men.

2 Peter 1:19. Words, John Ellerton, 1867. Tune SWABIA, Johann M. Spiess, 1745; arr. W. H. Havergal, 1847.

Psalm 36:5-9

24

Thy lovingkindness, O Lord, is in the heavens;
Thy faithfulness reacheth unto the skies.
Thy righteousness is like the mountains of God;
Thy judgments are a great deep:
O Lord, thou preservest man and beast.
How precious is thy lovingkindness, O God!
And the children of men take refuge under the shadow of thy wings.
They shall be abundantly satisfied with the fatness of thy house;
And thou wilt make them drink of the river of thy pleasures.
For with thee is the fountain of life:
In thy light shall we see light.

25 # Blessed Jesus, at Thy Word

1. Bless - ed Je - sus, at Thy word We are gath - ered
2. All our knowl-edge, sense, and sight Lie in deep - est
3. Glo - rious Lord, Thy - self im - part! Light of light, from

all to hear Thee; Let our hearts and souls be stirred
dark - ness shroud - ed, Till Thy spir - it breaks our night
God pro - ceed - ing, O - pen Thou our ears and heart;

Now to seek and love and fear Thee, By Thy teach - ings
With the beams of truth un - cloud - ed. Thou a - lone to
Help us by Thy spir - it's plead - ing; Hear the cry Thy

sweet and ho - ly, Drawn from earth to love Thee sole - ly.
God canst win us; Thou must work all good with - in us.
peo - ple rais - es; Hear, and bless our prayers and prais - es. A - men.

Ephesians 1:17. Words, Tobias Clausnitzer, 1663; trans. Catherine Winkworth, 1858. Tune LIEBSTER JESU, Johann R. Ahle, 1664.

Father, We Praise Thee

1. Fa - ther, we praise Thee, now the night is o - ver;
2. Mon - arch of all things, fit us for Thy man - sions;
3. All ho - ly Fa - ther, Son, and e - qual Spir - it,

Ac - tive and watch - ful, stand we all be - fore Thee; Sing - ing, we
Ban - ish our weak - ness, health and whole-ness send - ing; Bring us to
Trin - i - ty bless - ed, send us Thy sal - va - tion; Thine is the

of - fer prayer and med - i - ta - tion; Thus we a - dore Thee.
heav-en, where Thy saints u - nit - ed Joy with-out end - ing.
glo - ry, gleam-ing and re - sound-ing Through all cre - a - tion. A-men.

Psalm 92:1,2. Words, attr. to Gregory the Great, 6th cent.; trans. Percy Dearmer, 1906. Tune CHRISTE
SANCTORUM, from Paris Antiphoner, 1681; arr. in La Veillee's *Nouvelle Methode de plain-chant*, 1782.
From *The English Hymnal* by permission of Oxford University.

Psalm 59:16,17

I will sing of thy strength;
Yea, I will sing aloud of thy lovingkindness in the morning:
For thou hast been my high tower,
And a refuge in the day of my distress.
Unto thee, O my strength, will I sing praises:
For God is my high tower, the God of my mercy.

28 Again the Lord of Light and Life

1. A - gain the Lord of light and life A - wakes the kin-dling ray,
2. O what a night was that which wrapt The hea-then world in gloom!
3. This day be grate-ful hom - age paid, And loud ho-san - nas sung;
4. Ten thou-sand dif - f'rent lips shall join To hail this wel - come morn,

Un - seals the eye - lids of the morn, And pours in-creas-ing day.
O what a Sun which rose this day Tri - um-phant from the tomb!
Let glad - ness dwell in ev - 'ry heart, And praise on ev - 'ry tongue.
Which scat-ters bless - ings from its wings To na - tions yet un - born.

1 John 1:5. Words, Anna L. Barbauld, 1772. Tune ARLINGTON, Thomas A. Arne, 1762; adpt. Ralph Harrison, 1784.

29 1 Corinthians 15:20,21,55,57

But now hath Christ been raised from the dead, the firstfruits of them that are asleep. For since by man came death, by man came also the resurrection of the dead . . . O death, where is thy victory? O death, where is thy sting? . . . Thanks be to God, who giveth us the victory through our Lord Jesus Christ.

All Praise to Thee, My God, This Night **30**

1. All praise to Thee, my God, this night, For
2. For-give me, Lord, for Thy dear Son, The
3. O may my soul on Thee re-pose, And
4. Praise God, from whom all bless-ings flow; Praise

all the bless-ings of the light! Keep me, O keep me,
ill that I this day have done, That with the world, my-
with sweet sleep mine eye-lids close, Sleep that may me more
Him, all crea-tures here be-low; Praise Him a-bove, ye

King of kings, Be-neath thine own al-might-y wings!
self, and thee, I, ere I sleep, at peace may be.
vig-orous make To serve my God when I a-wake.
heav-enly host; Praise Fa-ther, Son, and Ho-ly Ghost. A-men.

Psalm 42:8. Words, Thomas Ken, 1709. Tune TALLIS' CANON, Thomas Tallis, 1567.

Psalm 4:8 **31**

In peace will I both lay me down and sleep;
For thou, O Lord, alone makest me dwell in safety.

32

Hail, Gladdening Light

1. Hail, glad-dening Light, of His pure glo-ry poured,
2. Now are we come to the sun's hour of rest;
3. The lights of even-ing now a-round us shine;
4. By grate-ful hearts, with un-de-fil-ed tongue,

Who is th'im-mor-tal Fa-ther, heav'n-ly blest;
All times are or-dered in Thy word a-lone,
We hymn Thy blest hu-man-i-ty di-vine;
Son of our God, Giv-er of life a-lone!

High - est and ho - liest, Je - sus Christ, our Lord!
There - fore the day and night Thy glo - ries own.
Wor - thiest art Thou at all times to be sung.
There - fore shall all the worlds Thy glo - ries own.

Al - le - lu - ia! Al - le - lu - ia!
Al - le - lu - ia! Al - le - lu - ia!
Al - le - lu - ia! Al - le - lu - ia!
Al - le - lu - ia! Al - le - lu - ia!

2 Corinthians 4:6. Words, Greek Evening Hymn, φῶς ἱλαρον, 3rd cent.; trans. John Keble, 1834;
Tune SARUM, Joseph Barnby, 1868.

Abide With Me

33

Psalm 145:18. Words, Henry F. Lyte, 1847. Tune EVENTIDE, William H. Monk, 1861.

34   **Now the Day is Over**

1. Now the day is o - ver,   Night is draw-ing nigh;
2. Je - sus, give the wea - ry   Calm and sweet re - pose;
3. Grant to lit - tle chil - dren   Vi - sions bright of Thee;
4. Com-fort ev - 'ry suf - f'rer   Watch-ing late in pain;
5. When the morn-ing wak - ens,   Then may I a - rise

Shad - ows of the eve - ning   Steal a - cross the sky.
With Thy ten-d'rest bless - ing   May our eye - lids close.
Guard the sail - ors toss - ing   On the deep blue sea.
Those who plan some e - vil   From their sin re - strain.
Pure, and fresh, and sin - less   In Thy ho - ly eyes. A-men.

(1.) eve -ning Steal a - cross the sky.

Psalm 104:23. Words, Sabine Baring-Gould, 1865. Tune EVENING, Joseph Barnby, 1867.

35   **Softly Now the Light of Day**

1. Soft - ly now the light of day   Fades up - on our sight a - way;
2. Thou, whose all-per - vad-ing eye   Naught es-capes, with - out, with - in,
3. Soon for us the light of day   May for ev - er pass a - way;

Free from care, from la - bor free,   Lord, we would com-mune with Thee.
Par - don each in - firm - i - ty,   O - pen fault, and se - cret sin.
Then, from sin and sor - row free,   Take us Lord, to dwell with Thee. A-men.

Psalm 141:2. Words, George W. Doane, 1827. Tune SEYMOUR, Carl Maria von Weber, 1825.

At Even, When the Sun Was Set

1. At e - ven when the sun was set, The sick, O
2. Once more 'tis e - ven - tide, and we, Op - pressed with
3. O Sav - ior Christ, our woes dis - pel; For some are
4. And none, O Lord, have per - fect rest, For none are
5. O Sav - ior Christ, Thou too art man; Thou hast been
6. Thy touch has still its an - cient power; No word from

Lord, a - round Thee lay; O in what di - vers
va - rious ills, draw near; What if Thy form we
sick, and some are sad, And some have nev - er
whol - ly free from sin; And they who fain would
trou - bled, tempt - ed, tried; Thy kind but search - ing
Thee can fruit - less fall; Hear, in this sol - emn

pains they met! O with what joy they went a - way!
can - not see? We know and feel that Thou art here.
loved thee well, And some have lost the love they had;
serve thee best Are con-scious most of wrong with - in.
glance can scan The ver - y wounds that shame would hide.
eve - ning hour, And in thy mer - cy heal us all. A - men.

Mark 1:32. Words, Henry Twells, 1868. Tune ABENDS, Herbert S. Oakeley, 1874.

37   Day is Dying in the West

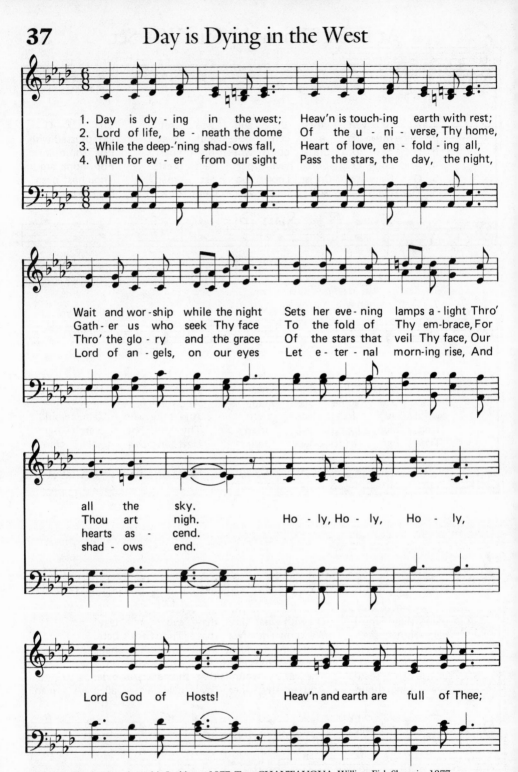

1. Day is dy - ing in the west; Heav'n is touch-ing earth with rest;
2. Lord of life, be - neath the dome Of the u - ni - verse, Thy home,
3. While the deep-'ning shad-ows fall, Heart of love, en - fold - ing all,
4. When for ev - er from our sight Pass the stars, the day, the night,

Wait and wor - ship while the night Sets her eve - ning lamps a - light Thro'
Gath - er us who seek Thy face To the fold of Thy em-brace, For
Thro' the glo - ry and the grace Of the stars that veil Thy face, Our
Lord of an - gels, on our eyes Let e - ter - nal morn-ing rise, And

all the sky.
Thou art nigh.
hearts as - cend.
shad - ows end.

Ho - ly, Ho - ly, Ho - ly,

Lord God of Hosts!   Heav'n and earth are full of Thee;

Isaiah 6:3. Words, Mary Artemisia Lathbury, 1877. Tune CHAUTAUQUA, William Fisk Sherwin, 1877.

Heav'n and earth are prais-ing Thee, O Lord Most High!

The Sun Declines   38

1. The sun de-clines: o'er land and sea Creeps on the night;
2. And when with morn-ing light we rise, Kept by Thy care,

The twin-kling stars come one by one to shed their light;
We'll lift to Thee with grate-ful hearts Our morn-ing prayer;

With Thee there is no dark-ness, Lord: With us a-bide;
Be Thou thro' life our Strength and Stay, Our Guard and Guide

Be-neath Thy wings we rest se-cure This e-ven-tide.
To that dear home where there will be no e-ven-tide.

Psalm 139:12. Words, Robert Walmsley, 1893. Tune WENTWORTH, Frederick C. Maker, 1876. Arr. J.B.,
Copyright 1986, ACU Press.

39 The Day Thou Gavest, Lord, is Ended

Unison, or with harmony

1. The day Thou gav - est, Lord, is end - ed,
2. We thank Thee that Thy church, un - sleep - ing,
3. The sun that bids us rest is wak - ing,
4. So be it, Lord: Thy throne shall nev - er,

The dark - ness falls at Thy be - hest;
While earth rolls on - ward in - to light,
Our breth - ren 'neath the west - ern sky;
Like earth's proud em - pires, pass a - way;

To Thee our morn - ing hymns as - cend - ed:
Thro' all the world her watch is keep - ing,
And hour by hour fresh lips are mak - ing
But stand and rule and grow for ev - er,

Thy praise shall hal - low now our rest.
And rests not now by day or night.
Thy won - drous do - ings heard on high.
Till all Thy crea - tures own Thy sway. A - men.

Psalm 113:2,3. Words, John Ellerton, 1870. Tune SHENG EN, Su Yin-Lan, 1934; arr. J.B., Copyright 1986, ACU Press.

Savior, Breathe an Evening Blessing

1. Sav - ior, breathe an eve - ning bless - ing Ere re -
2. Tho' de - struc - tion walk a - round us, Tho' the
3. Tho' the night be dark and drear - y, Dark - ness
4. Should swift death this night o'er - take us, And our

pose our spir - its seal; Sin and want we come con -
ar - rows past us fly, An - gel guards from Thee sur -
can - not hide from Thee; Thou art He who, nev - er
couch be - come our tomb, May the morn in heav'n a -

fess - ing: Thou canst save and Thou canst heal.
round us: We are safe if Thou art nigh.
wea - ry, Watch-est where Thy peo - ple be.
wake us, Clad in bright and death - less bloom. A - men.

Psalm 91:5. Words, James Edmeston, 1820. Tune EVENING PRAYER, George Coles Stebbins, 1878.

41 Walking Alone at Eve

1. Walk-ing a-lone at eve and view-ing the skies a-far, Bid-ding the
2. Sit-ting a-lone at eve and dream-ing the hours a-way, Watch-ing the
3. Clos-ing my eyes at eve and think-ing of heav-en's grace, Long-ing to

dark-ness come to wel-come each sil-ver star; I have a great de-light
shad-ows fall-ing now at the close of day; God in His mer-cy comes
see my Lord, yes, meet-ing Him face to face; Trust-ing Him as my all

in the won-der-ful scenes a-bove, God in His pow'r and might is
with His word He is draw-ing near, Spread-ing His love and truth a-
where-so-ev-er my foot-steps roam, Plead-ing with Him to guide me

show-ing His truth and love.
round me and ev-'ry-where. O! for a home with God, a place in His
on to the spir-it's home!

Psalm 141:2. Words, Thomas R. Sweatmon. Tune SLATER, William Washington Slater, 1917.

courts to rest. Sure in a safe a-bode with Je-sus and the blest;

Rest for a wea-ry soul once re-deemed by the Sav-ior's love

Where I'll be pure and whole and live with my God a-bove!

Sun of My Soul

42

1. Sun of my soul, Thou Sav-ior dear, It is not night if Thou be near;
2. When the soft dews of kind-ly sleep My wea-ried eye-lids gen-tly steep,
3. A-bide with me from morn till eve, For with-out Thee I can-not live;
4. Come near and bless us when we wake, Ere thro' the world our way we take;

O may no earth-born cloud a-rise To hide Thee from Thy ser-vant's eyes.
Be my last tho't, how sweet to rest For ev-er on my Sav-ior's breast.
A-bide with me when night is nigh, For with-out Thee I dare not die.
Till, in the o-cean of Thy love, We lose our-selves in heav'n a-bove.

Psalm 139:12. Words, John Keble, 1820. Tune HURSLEY, arr. from *Katholisches Gesangbuch*, Vienna, ca. 1774.

The God of Abraham Praise

1. The God of A - braham praise, Who reigns en-throned a - bove;
2. The God of A - braham praise, At whose su - preme com - mand
3. He by Him-self hath sworn: I on His oath de - pend;

An - cient of ev - er - last - ing days, And God of love;
From earth I rise and seek the joys At His right hand;
I shall, on an - gel wings up-borne, To heav'n as - cend;

Je - ho - vah, great I AM, By earth and heav'n con - fessed;
I all on earth for - sake, Its wis - dom, fame and pow'r;
I shall be - hold His face, I shall His pow'r a - dore,

I bow and bless the sa - cred name, For ev - er blest.
And Him my on - ly por - tion make, My shield and tow'r.
And sing the won-ders of His grace For ev - er - more.

Hebrews 13:8. Words, Daniel ben Judah Dayyan, c. 1400; tr. Thomas Olivers, 1770. Tune LEONI, Traditional
Hebrew Melody; transcribed Meyer Lyon, c. 1770.

We Praise Thee, O God, Our Redeemer **44**

1. We praise Thee, O God, our Re - deem - er, Cre - a - tor,
2. We wor - ship Thee, God of our fa - thers, we bless Thee;
3. With voi - ces u - nit - ed our prais - es we of - fer,

In grate - ful de - vo - tion our trib - ute we bring.
Through life's storm and tem - pest our Guide hast Thou been.
And glad - ly our an - thems of wor - ship we raise.

We lay it be - fore Thee, we kneel and a - dore Thee,
When per - ils o'er - take us, es - cape Thou wilt make us,
Thy strong arm will guide us, our God is be - side us,

We bless Thy ho - ly Name, glad prais - es we sing.
And with Thy help, O Lord, life's bat - tles we win.
To Thee, our great Re - deem - er, for - ev - er be praise. A - men.

Luke 1:68. Words, Julia Cady Cory, 1902. Tune KREMSER, Netherlands Folk Song; arr. Edward Kremser, 1877.

45 Praise to the Lord, the Almighty

1. Praise to the Lord, the Al - might-y, the King of cre - a - tion!
2. Praise to the Lord, who o'er all things so won-drous-ly reign - eth,
3. Praise to the Lord, who doth pros-per thy work and de - fend thee;
4. Praise to the Lord! O let all that is in me a - dore Him!

O my soul, praise Him, for He is thy health and sal - va - tion!
Shield-eth thee un - der His wings, yea, so gent - ly sus - tain - eth!
Sure - ly His good - ness and mer - cy here dai - ly at - tend thee.
All that hath life and breath, come now with prais - es be - fore Him!

All ye who hear, Now to His tem - ple draw near;
Hast thou not seen How thy de - sires e'er have been
Pon - der a - new What the Al - might - y can do,
Let the a - men Sound from His peo - ple a - gain;

Join me in glad ad - o - ra - - tion!
Grant-ed in what He or - dain - - eth?
If with His love He be - friend thee.
Glad - ly for - ev - er a - dore Him. A - men.

Psalm 103:1-6. Words, Joachim Neander, 1680; tr. Catherine Winkworth, 1863. Tune LOBE DEN HERREN, *Stralsund Gesangbuch*, 1665.

O praise the Lord, all ye na-tions; Praise Him, all ye peo-ple, praise Him, all ye peo-ple. O praise the Lord, Praise Him, all ye peo-ple, For His mer-ci-ful kind-ness is great tow'rd us, is great tow'rd us; and the truth of the Lord en-dur-eth for ev-er, for ev-er and ev-er, ev-er and ev-er: Praise ye the Lord.

Psalm 117. Words, paraphrase of Psalm 117. Tune HILL, Will Hill.

Psalm 100:1,2,5

47

Make a joyful noise unto the Lord, all ye lands.
Serve the Lord with gladness:
Come before his presence with singing.
For the Lord is good;
His mercy is everlasting;
And his truth endureth to all generations.

Holy God, We Praise Thy Name

1. Ho - ly God, we praise Thy name; Lord of all, we
2. Hark, the glad ce - les - tial hymn, An - gel choirs a -
3. Ho - ly Fa - ther, ho - ly Son, Ho - ly Spir - it:

bow be - fore Thee; All on earth Thy scep - ter claim,
bove are rais - ing; Cher - u - bim and ser - a - phim,
Three we name Thee, Though in es - sence on - ly One;

All in heaven a - bove a - dore Thee. In - fi - nite Thy
In un - ceas - ing cho - rus prais - ing, Fill the heavens with
Un - di - vid - ed God we claim Thee, And a - dor - ing

vast do - main, Ev - er - last - ing is Thy reign.
sweet ac - cord: Ho - ly, ho - ly, ho - ly Lord.
bend the knee While we own the mys - te - ry. A - men.

Isaiah 6:3. Words, from *Te Deum*, 4th cent.; attr. to Ignaz Franz, c. 1774; tr. Clarence A. Walworth, 1853.
Tune GROSSER GOTT, WIR LOBEN DICH, *Katholisches Gesangbuch*, Vienna, c. 1774.

Let Every Heart Rejoice and Sing

49

1. { Let ev - 'ry heart re - joice and sing, Let cho - ral an - thems rise; }
   { Ye a - ged men, and chil - dren bring To God your sac - ri - fice; }

2. { He bids the sun to rise and set; In heav'n His pow'r is known; }
   { And earth, sub - dued to Him, shall yet Bow low be - fore His throne; }

For He is good, the Lord is good, And kind are all His ways; With songs and

hon - ors sound - ing loud, The Lord Je - ho - vah praise; While the rocks and the rills,

While the vales and the hills A glo - rious an - them raise; Let each pro - long the

grate - ful song, And the God of our fa - thers praise, And the God of our fa - thers praise.

Psalm 136:1. Words, Henry S. Washburne. Tune WASHBURNE, George J. Webb.

50 Hallelujah, Praise Jehovah!

1. Hal - le - lu - jah, praise Je - ho - vah! From the heav-ens praise His name;
2. Let them prais-es give Je - ho - vah! They were made at His com - mand;
3. All ye fruit-ful trees and ce - dars, All ye hills and moun-tains high,

Praise Je - ho - vah in the high - est; All His an - gels praise pro-claim.
Them for - ev - er He es - tab - lished: His de - cree shall ev - er stand.
Creep-ing things and beasts and cat - tle, Birds that in the heav - ens fly,

All His hosts to - geth - er praise Him, Sun and moon and stars on high;
From the earth, O praise Je - ho - vah, All ye floods, ye drag - ons all,
Kings of earth, and all ye peo - ple, Princ-es great, earth's judg-es all;

Praise Him, O ye heav'n of heav - ens, And ye floods a-bove the sky.
Fire and hail and snow and va - pors, Storm-y winds that hear Him call.
Praise His name, young men and maid - ens, A - ged men, and chil-dren small.

Psalm 148. Words, paraphrase of Psalm 148. Tune AINOS, William J. Kirkpatrick, 1893.

Let them prais - - es give Je - ho - vah, For His name a - lone is high,
Let them prais-es

And His glo - - ry is ex - alt - ed, And His glo - - ry is ex - alt - ed,
And His glo-ry   And His glo-ry

And His glo - - ry is ex - alt - ed Far a - bove the earth and sky.
And His glo-ry

Psalm 148:1-5,13   **51**

Praise the Lord.
Praise the Lord from the heavens:
Praise him in the heights.
Praise him, all his angels:
Praise him, all his host.
Praise him, sun and moon:
Praise him, all you stars of light.
Praise him, you heaven of heavens,
And you waters that are above the heavens.
Let them praise the name of the Lord;
For his name alone is exalted;
His glory is above the earth and the heavens.

52 Through All the Changing Scenes

1. Through all the chang-ing scenes of life, In trou-ble and in joy, The prais-es of my God shall still My heart and tongue em-ploy.
2. O mag-ni-fy the Lord with me, With me ex-alt His name; When in dis-tress to Him I called, He to my res-cue came.
3. O make but tri-al of His love; Ex-pe-rience will de-cide How blest are they, and on-ly they, Who in His truth con-fide.
4. Fear Him, ye saints, and you will then Have noth-ing else to fear; Make you His serv-ice your de-light; Your wants shall be His care.
5. For God pre-serves the souls of those Who on His truth de-pend; To them and their pos-ter-i-ty His bless-ing shall de-scend. A-men.

Psalm 34:1. Words, *New Version*, Tate and Brady, 1696. Tune IRISH, *A Collection of Hymns and Sacred Poems*, 1749; prob. arr. John F. Lampe, c. 1749.

Praise, My Soul, the King of Heaven 53

1. Praise, my soul, the King of heav-en, To His feet thy
2. Praise Him for His grace and fa - vor To our fa - thers
3. Frail as sum - mer's flow'r we flour-ish; Blows the wind and
4. An - gels in the height, a - dore Him; Ye be - hold Him

trib - ute bring; Ran - somed, healed, re - stored, for -
in dis - tress; Praise Him, still the same as
it is gone; But, while mor - tals rise and
face to face; Saints tri - um - phant, bow be -

giv - en, Ev - er - more His prais-es sing; Al - le - lu - ia!
ev - er, Slow to chide, and swift to bless; Al - le - lu - ia!
per - ish, God en - dures un - chang-ing on: Al - le - lu - ia!
fore Him; Gath - ered in from ev - 'ry race; Al - le - lu - ia!

Al - le - lu - ia! Praise the ev - er - last - ing King.
Al - le - lu - ia! Glo - rious in His faith - ful - ness.
Al - le - lu - ia! Praise the high e - ter - nal one.
Al - le - lu - ia! Praise with us the God of grace. A - men.

Psalm 78:2-4. Words, Henry F. Lyte, 1834. Tune LAUDA ANIMA (Andrews), Mark Andrews, 1931.

O Lord, Our Lord

All voices or women only

O Lord, our Lord, how ex-cel-lent Thy name; How ex-cel-lent is Thy

Women

name in all the earth; Who has set Thy glo-ry a-

Men

bove the heav'ns! We'll praise Thy ho-ly name for-ev - er, ev-er-more.

All voices

O Lord, our Lord how ex - cel-lent Thy name; O
We will praise Thy name for evermore, how ex-cel-lent Thy glorious name;

Lord our Lord, how ex - cel-lent Thy name.
We will praise Thy name for evermore, how ex - cel-lent Thy name. We'll praise and

Psalm 8:1. Words, paraphrase Psalm 8:1. Tune PALMER, Horatio R. Palmer, 1874. Countermelody J.B., Copyright 1986, ACU Press.

55   Joyful, Joyful, We Adore Thee

1. Joy-ful, joy-ful, we a-dore Thee, God of glo-ry, Lord of love;
2. All Thy works with joy sur-round Thee, Earth and heav'n re-flect Thy rays,
3. Thou art giv-ing and for-giv-ing, Ev-er bless-ing, ev-er blest,
4. Mor-tals join the might-y cho-rus, Which the morn-ing stars be-gan;

Hearts un-fold like flowers be-fore Thee, Open-ing to the sun a-bove.
Stars and an-gels sing a-round Thee, Cen-ter of un-bro-ken praise;
Well-spring of the joy of liv-ing, O-cean-depth of hap-py rest!
Fa-ther love is reign-ing o'er us, Broth-er love binds man to man.

Melt the clouds of sin and sad-ness; Drive the dark of doubt a-way;
Field and for-est, vale and moun-tain, Flow-ery mead-ow, flash-ing sea,
Thou our Fa-ther, Christ our broth-er, All who live in love are Thine;
Ev-er sing-ing, march we on-ward, Vic-tors in the midst of strife;

Giv-er of im-mor-tal glad-ness, Fill us with the light of day!
Chant-ing bird and flow-ing foun-tain, Call us to re-joice in Thee.
Teach us how to love each oth-er, Lift us to the joy di-vine.
Joy-ful mu-sic leads us sun-ward In the tri-umph song of life. A-men.

Psalm 98:4. Words, Henry van Dyke, 1907. Used by permission of Charles Scribner's Sons from *The Poems of Henry van Dyke.* Copyright 1911 Charles Scribner's Sons; renewal Copyright 1939 Tertius van Dyke. Tune HYMN TO JOY, Ludwig van Beethoven, 1824.

Ancient of Days

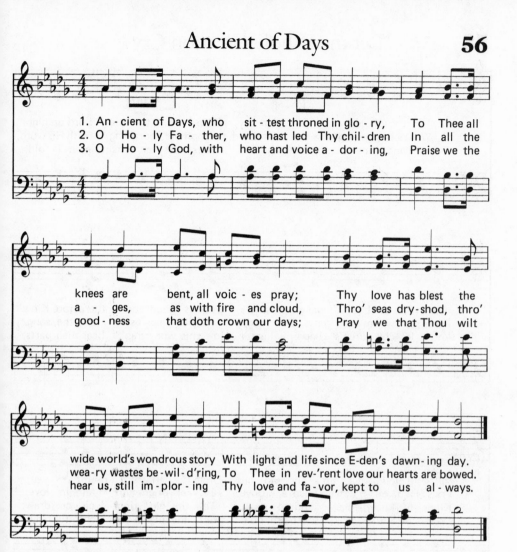

1. An-cient of Days, who sit-test throned in glo-ry, To Thee all
2. O Ho-ly Fa-ther, who hast led Thy chil-dren In all the
3. O Ho-ly God, with heart and voice a-dor-ing, Praise we the

knees are bent, all voic-es pray; Thy love has blest the
a-ges, as with fire and cloud, Thro' seas dry-shod, thro'
good-ness that doth crown our days; Pray we that Thou wilt

wide world's wondrous story With light and life since E-den's dawn-ing day.
wea-ry wastes be-wil-d'ring, To Thee in rev-'rent love our hearts are bowed.
hear us, still im-plor-ing Thy love and fa-vor, kept to us al-ways.

Lamentations 3:22. Words, William C. Doane, 1886, 1892. Tune ANCIENT OF DAYS, J. Albert Jeffrey, 1886.

Psalm 118:4-6,8,14

Let them now that fear the Lord say,
That his mercy endureth for ever.
Out of my distress I called upon the Lord:
The Lord answered me and set me in a large place.
The Lord is on my side; I will not fear:
What can man do unto me?
It is better to trust in the Lord
Than to put confidence in man.
The Lord is my strength and song;
And he is become my salvation.

58 Let the Whole Creation Cry

1. Let the whole cre - a - tion cry, "Glo - ry to the Lord on high."
2. War-riors fight-ing for the Lord, Proph-ets burn- ing with His word,
3. Men and wom - en, young and old, Raise the an - them man - i - fold;

Heaven and earth, a - wake and sing, "God is good and there-fore King."
Those to whom the arts be - long, Add their voic - es to the song.
And let chil - dren's hap - py hearts In this wor - ship bear their parts;

Praise Him, all ye hosts a - bove, Ev - er bright and fair in love;
Kings of knowl-edge and of law, To the glo - rious cir - cle draw;
From the north to south-ern pole Let the might - y cho - rus roll:

Sun and moon, up - lift your voice, Night and stars, in God re-joice!
All who work and all who wait, Sing, "The Lord is good and great!"
"Ho - ly, ho - ly, ho - ly One, Glo - ry be to God a - lone!" A-men.

Revelation 5:13. Words, Stopford A. Brooke, 1881. Tune SALZBURG, Jacob Hintze, 1678; harm. J. S. Bach.

Now Thank We All Our God

1. Now thank we all our God With heart and hands and voic - es,
2. O may this boun-teous God Through all our life be near us,
3. All praise and thanks to God The Fa - ther now be giv - en,

Who won-drous things hath done, In whom His world re - joic - es;
With ev - er joy - ful hearts And bless-ed peace to cheer us;
The Son, and Him who reigns With them in high-est heav - en,

Who, from our moth-ers' arms, Hath blessed us on our way
And keep us in His grace, And guide us when per - plexed,
The one e - ter - nal God Whom earth and heaven a - dore;

With count-less gifts of love, And still is ours to - day.
And free us from all ills In this world and the next.
For thus it was, is now, And shall be ev - er - more. A-men.

1 Thessalonians 5:18. Words, Martin Rinkart, 1636; trans. Catherine Winkworth, 1858. Tune NUN DANKET, Johann Crüger, 1647.

O Lord, My God

1. O Lord my God! When I in awe-some won-der Con-sid-er
2. When through the woods and for-est glades I wan-der And hear the
3. And when I think that God, His Son not spar-ing, Sent Him to
4. When Christ shall come with shout of ac-cla-ma-tion And take me

all the worlds Thy hands have made, I see the stars, I hear the roll-ing
birds sing sweet-ly in the trees; When I look down from loft-y moun-tain
die, I scarce can take it in; That on the cross, my bur-den glad-ly
home, what joy shall fill my heart! Then I shall bow in hum-ble ad-o-

thun-der, Thy pow'r through-out the un-i-verse dis-played.
gran-deur And hear the brook and feel the gen-tle breeze; Then sings my
bear-ing, He bled and died to take a-way my sin;
ra-tion And there pro-claim, my God, how great Thou art!

soul, my Sav-ior God to Thee; How great Thou art, how great Thou art! Then sings my

Acts 4:24. Words, Carl Boberg, 1886; trans. Stuart K. Hine, 1949. Tune O STORE GUD, Swedish Folk Melody; arr. Stuart K. Hine, 1949.

soul, my Sav-ior God to Thee; How great Thou art, how great Thou art!

We Praise Thee, O God 61

1. We praise Thee, O God, For the Son of Thy love, For Je - sus who
2. We praise Thee, O God, For Thy Spir - it of light, Who has shown us our
3. All glo - ry and praise To the Lamb that was slain, Who has borne all our
4. All glo - ry and praise To the God of all grace, Who has bought us, and
5. Re - vive us a - gain: Fill each heart with Thy love; May each soul be re -

died and is now gone a - bove.
Sav - ior, and scat - tered our night.
sins, and has cleansed ev - 'ry stain. Hal - le - lu - jah! Thine the glo - ry;
sought us, And guid - ed our ways.
kin - dled With fire from a - bove.

Hal - le - lu - jah! A - men! Hal - le - lu - jah! Thine the glo - ry; Re - vive us a - gain.

Psalm 85:6. Words, William P. Mackay, 1863. Tune REVIVE US AGAIN, John J. Husband, c. 1820.

62

Praise God

Praise God, ye heav'n-ly host a-bove; Praise Him, all crea-tures of His love;

Praise Him each morn-ing, noon, and night with sweet de-light. A-men.

Psalm 66:4. Words, William T. Moore, 1865. Tune TROYTE'S CHANT, No. 1, 1860.

63

We Praise Thee, God

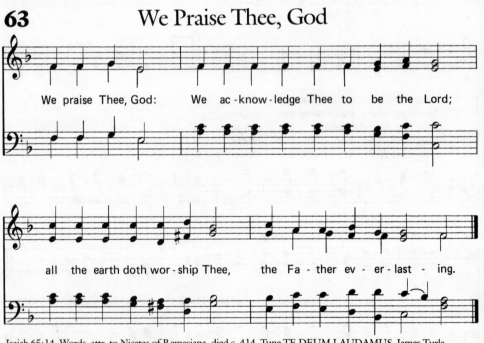

We praise Thee, God: We ac-know-ledge Thee to be the Lord;

all the earth doth wor-ship Thee, the Fa-ther ev-er-last-ing.

Isaiah 65:14. Words, attr. to Nicetas of Remesiana, died c. 414. Tune TE DEUM LAUDAMUS, James Turle, c. 1882; arr. Copyright 1986, ACU Press.

All Things Praise Thee

1. All things praise Thee, Lord most high, Heav'n and earth, and sea and sky;
2. All things praise Thee—night to night Sings in si - lent hymns of light;
3. All things praise Thee: heav'n's high shrine Rings with mel-o - dy di-vine;

All were for Thy glo - ry made, That Thy great-ness, thus dis-played,
All things praise Thee— day by day Chants Thy pow'r in burn-ing ray;
Low-ly bend-ing at Thy feet, Ser - aph and arch - an - gel meet;

Should all wor-ship bring to Thee; All things praise Thee—Lord, may we!
Time and space are prais-ing Thee; All things praise Thee—Lord, may we!
This their high-est bliss, to be Ev - er prais-ing— Lord, may we!

Psalm 145:10. Words, George W. Conder, 1853. Tune DIX, Conrad Kocher, 1838; adpt. William H. Monk, 1861.

Psalm 104:24,31,33

65

O Lord, how manifold are thy works!
In wisdom hast thou made them all:
The earth is full of thy riches.
Let the glory of the Lord endure for ever;
Let the Lord rejoice in his works:
I will sing unto the Lord as long as I live:
I will sing praise to my God while I have any being.

66 All Creatures of Our God and King

1. All creatures of our God and King, Lift
2. Thou flow-ing wa-ter, pure and clear, Make
3. And all ye men of ten-der heart, For-
4. Let all things their Cre-a-tor bless, And

1. All creatures of our God and
2., 3., 4.

up your voice and with us sing, Al - le - lu - ia! Al - le -
mu-sic for thy Lord to hear. Al - le - lu - ia! Al - le -
giv-ing oth-ers, take your part. O sing ye! Al - le -
wor-ship Him in hum-ble - ness. O praise Him! Al - le -

King, Lift up your voice and with us sing, Al - le -

lu - ia! Thou burn-ing sun with gold-en beam, Thou
lu - ia! Thou fire so mas-ter-ful and bright, Thou
lu - ia! Ye who long pain and sor-row bear, Praise
lu - ia! O praise the Fa-ther, praise the Son, And

lu - ia! Thou burn-ing sun with gold-en

sil - ver moon with soft-er gleam! O praise Him, O
giv - est man both warmth and light! O praise Him, O
God and on Him cast your care! O praise Him, O
praise the Spir-it, Three in One! O praise Him, O

beam, Thou sil - ver moon with soft-er gleam! O

Psalm 150:6. Words, Francis of Assisi, c. 1226; tr. William H. Draper, after 1899; pub. 1926. Tune LASST UNS ERFREUEN, *Geistliche Kirchengesang*, 1623. Arr. J.B., Copyright 1974, ACU Press.

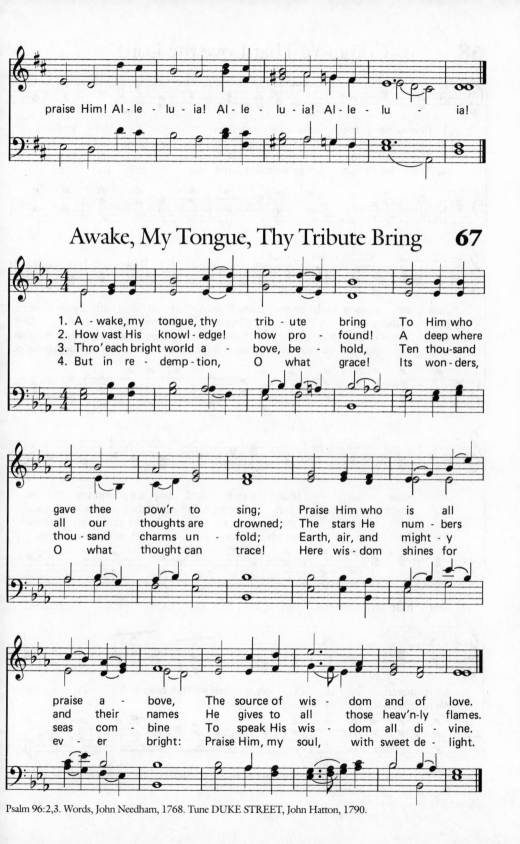

praise Him! Al - le - lu - ia! Al - le - lu - ia! Al - le - lu - ia!

Awake, My Tongue, Thy Tribute Bring 67

1. A - wake, my tongue, thy   trib - ute   bring To Him who
2. How vast His knowl - edge! how pro - found! A deep where
3. Thro' each bright world a - bove, be - hold, Ten thou-sand
4. But in re - demp - tion, O what grace! Its won - ders,

gave thee   pow'r to   sing; Praise Him who   is   all
all   our   thoughts are   drowned; The stars He   num - bers
thou - sand charms un - fold; Earth, air, and   might - y
O what   thought can   trace! Here wis - dom   shines for

praise a - bove, The source of wis - dom and of love.
and their names He gives to all those heav'n-ly flames.
seas com - bine To speak His wis - dom all di - vine.
ev - er bright: Praise Him, my soul, with sweet de - light.

Psalm 96:2,3. Words, John Needham, 1768. Tune DUKE STREET, John Hatton, 1790.

68 Come, Ye That Love the Lord

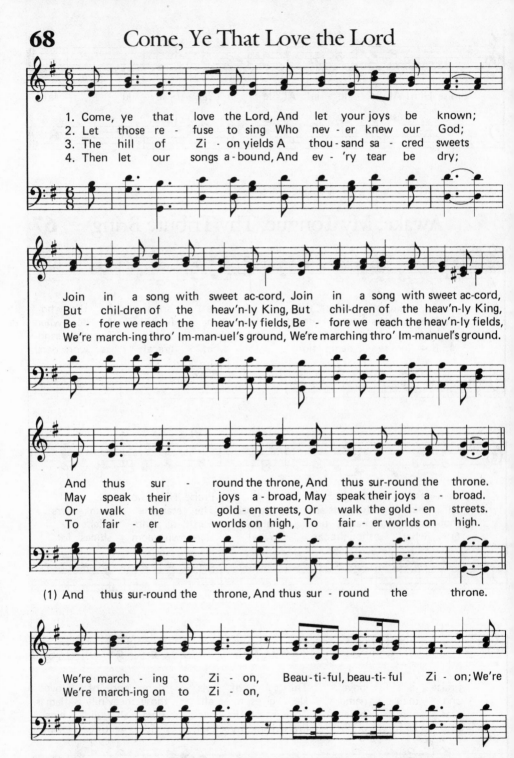

1. Come, ye that love the Lord, And let your joys be known;
2. Let those re-fuse to sing Who nev-er knew our God;
3. The hill of Zi-on yields A thou-sand sa-cred sweets
4. Then let our songs a-bound, And ev-'ry tear be dry;

Join in a song with sweet ac-cord, Join in a song with sweet ac-cord,
But chil-dren of the heav'n-ly King, But chil-dren of the heav'n-ly King,
Be - fore we reach the heav'n-ly fields, Be - fore we reach the heav'n-ly fields,
We're march-ing thro' Im-man-uel's ground, We're marching thro' Im-manuel's ground.

And thus sur - round the throne, And thus sur-round the throne.
May speak their joys a - broad, May speak their joys a - broad.
Or walk the gold - en streets, Or walk the gold - en streets.
To fair - er worlds on high, To fair - er worlds on high.

(1) And thus sur-round the throne, And thus sur - round the throne.

We're march - ing to Zi - on, Beau-ti-ful, beau-ti-ful Zi - on; We're
We're march-ing on to Zi - on,

Hebrews 13:14,15. Words, Isaac Watts, 1707. Tune MARCHING TO ZION and Refrain, Robert Lowry, 1867.

march-ing up-ward to Zi - on, The beau-ti-ful cit-y of God.
Zi - on, Zi - on,

Holy, Holy, Holy!

69

1. Ho-ly, ho-ly, ho - ly! Lord God Al - might-y! Ear-ly in the
2. Ho-ly, ho-ly, ho - ly! all the saints a - dore Thee, Cast-ing down their
3. Ho-ly, ho-ly, ho - ly! tho' the dark-ness hide Thee! Tho' the eye of
4. Ho-ly, ho-ly, ho - ly! Lord God Al - might-y! All Thy works shall

morn - ing our song shall rise to Thee; Ho - ly, ho - ly, ho - ly!
gold - en crowns a - round the crys - tal sea; Cher-u - bim and ser - a-phim
sin - ful man Thy glo - ry may not see; On - ly Thou art ho - ly!
praise Thy name, in earth, and sky, and sea; Ho - ly, ho - ly, ho - ly!

mer - ci - ful and might-y! God o - ver all, and blest e - ter - nal - ly.
fall - ing down be-fore Thee, Who wast, and art, and ev - er-more shall be.
there is none be - side Thee, Per - fect in pow'r, in love, and pu - ri - ty.
mer - ci - ful and might-y! God o - ver all, and blest e - ter - nal - ly.

Isaiah 6:3. Words, Reginald Heber, 1826. Tune NICAEA, John B. Dykes, 1861.

70 O God, We Praise Thee, and Confess

1. O God, we praise Thee, and con-fess That Thou the on-ly Lord
2. To Thee all an-gels cry a-loud; To Thee the powers on high,
3. O ho-ly, ho-ly, ho-ly Lord, Whom heaven-ly hosts o-bey,
4. The ho-ly Church through-out the world, O Lord, con-fess-es Thee,

And ev-er-last-ing Fa-ther art, By all the earth a-dored.
Both cher-u-bim and ser-a-phim, Con-tin-ual-ly do cry:
The world is with the glo-ry filled Of Thy ma-jes-tic sway!
That Thou e-ter-nal Fa-ther art, Of bound-less maj-es-ty. A-men.

Revelation 4:8. Words, based on *Te Deum*, 4th cent.; in *A Supplement to the New Version*, 1700; alt. Tune TALLIS' ORDINAL, Thomas Tallis, c. 1561.

71 Psalm 95:1-3,6,7

Oh come, let us sing unto the Lord;
Let us make a joyful noise to the rock of our salvation.
Let us come before his presence with thanksgiving;
Let us make a joyful noise unto him with psalms.
For the Lord is a great God,
And a great King above all gods.
O come, let us worship and bow down;
Let us kneel before the Lord our Maker:
For he is our God,
And we are the people of his pasture, and the sheep of his hand.

Praise the Lord, His Glories Show

1. Praise the Lord, His glo - ries show, Al - le - lu - ia!
2. Earth to heav'n and heav'n to earth, Al - le - lu - ia!
3. Praise the Lord, His mer - cies trace, Al - le - lu - ia!

Saints with - in His courts be - low, Al - le - lu - ia!
Tell His won - ders, sing His worth, Al - le - lu - ia!
Praise His prov - i - dence and grace, Al - le - lu - ia!

An - gels round His throne a - bove, Al - le - lu - ia!
Age to age and shore to shore, Al - le - lu - ia!
All that He for man hath done, Al - le - lu - ia!

All that see and share His love, Al - le - lu - ia!
Praise Him, praise Him ev - er - more! Al - le - lu - ia!
All He sends us through His Son. Al - le - lu - ia! A-men.

Psalm 148. Words, Henry F. Lyte, 1834. Tune GWALCHMAI, Joseph D. Jones, 1868.

73   Praise God From Whom All Blessings

Praise God from whom all bless-ings flow; Praise Him, all crea-tures here be-low;

Praise Him a-bove, ye heaven-ly host: Praise Fa-ther, Son, and Ho-ly Ghost. A-men.

Psalm 150:6. Words, Thomas Ken, 1695. Tune OLD HUNDREDTH; alt. *Genevan Psalter*, 1551.

74   All People That on Earth Do Dwell

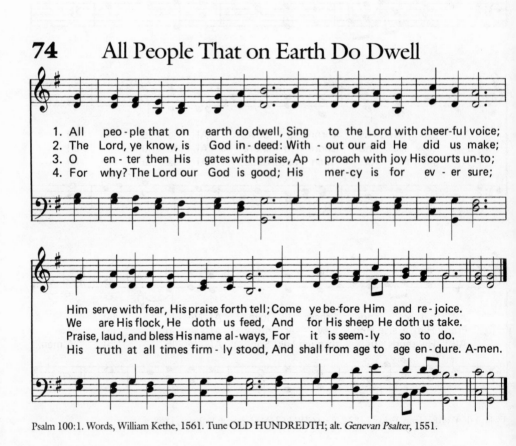

1. All peo-ple that on earth do dwell, Sing to the Lord with cheer-ful voice;
2. The Lord, ye know, is God in-deed: With-out our aid He did us make;
3. O en-ter then His gates with praise, Ap-proach with joy His courts un-to;
4. For why? The Lord our God is good; His mer-cy is for ev-er sure;

Him serve with fear, His praise forth tell; Come ye be-fore Him and re-joice.
We are His flock, He doth us feed, And for His sheep He doth us take.
Praise, laud, and bless His name al-ways, For it is seem-ly so to do.
His truth at all times firm-ly stood, And shall from age to age en-dure. A-men.

Psalm 100:1. Words, William Kethe, 1561. Tune OLD HUNDREDTH; alt. *Genevan Psalter*, 1551.

Immortal, Invisible, God Only Wise

1. Im - mor-tal, in - vis - i - ble, God on - ly wise,
2. Un - rest-ing, un - hast-ing, and si - lent as light,
3. To all, life Thou giv - est, to both great and small;
4. Great Fa - ther of Glo - ry, pure Fa - ther of Light,

In light in - ac - ces - si - ble hid from our eyes,
Nor want-ing, nor wast-ing, Thou rul - est in might;
In all life Thou liv - est, the true Life of all;
Thine an - gels a - dore Thee, all veil - ing their sight.

Most bless - ed, most glo - rious, the An - cient of Days,
Thy jus - tice like moun-tains high soar - ing a - bove
Thy wis - dom so bound-less, Thy mer - cy so free,
All laud we would ren - der. O help us to see

Al - might-y, vic - to - rious, Thy great name we praise.
Thy clouds which are foun-tains of good-ness and love.
E - ter - nal Thy good-ness, for naught chang-eth Thee.
'Tis on - ly the splen-dor of light hid - eth Thee.

1 Timothy 1:17. Words, Walter Chalmers Smith, 1867. Tune ST. DENIO, 1839.

Glory Be to the Father

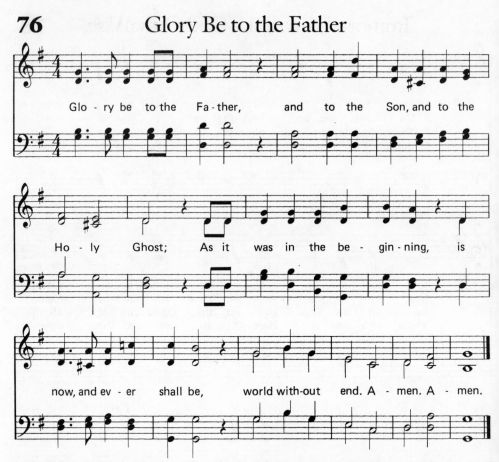

Glo - ry be to the Fa - ther, and to the Son, and to the Ho - ly Ghost; As it was in the be - gin - ning, is now, and ev - er shall be, world with-out end. A - men. A - men.

2 Corinthians 13:14. Words, Anonymous, 4th century. Tune GLORIA PATRI (Meinecke), Charles Meinecke, 1844.

77   # Romans 11:33-36

O the depth of the riches both of the wisdom and the knowledge of God! How unsearchable are his judgments, and his ways past tracing out! For who hath known the mind of the Lord? Or who hath been his counsellor? Or who hath first given to him, and it shall be recompensed unto him again? For of him, and through him, and unto him, are all things. To him be the glory for ever.

    Amen.

From All That Dwell Below the Skies

1. From all that dwell below the skies Let the Cre-a-tor's praise a-rise;
2. E - ter-nal are Thy mer-cies, Lord; E - ter-nal truth at-tends Thy Word:

Al-le-lu - ia! Al-le - lu - ia! Let the Re-deem-er's name be sung
Al-le-lu - ia! Al-le - lu - ia! Thy praise shall sound from shore to shore

Thro' ev - 'ry land, by ev - 'ry tongue. Al-le - lu - ia! Al-le - lu - ia!
Till suns shall rise and set no more. Al-le - lu - ia! Al-le - lu - ia!

Al - le - lu - ia! Al-le - lu - ia! Al - le - lu - ia!
Al - le - lu - ia! Al-le - lu - ia! Al - le - lu - ia! A - men.

Psalm 117:1,2. Words, Isaac Watts, 1719. Tune LASST UNS ERFREUEN, *Geistliche Kirchengesang*, 1623.

79   To God Be the Glory

1. To God be the glo - ry, great things He hath done; So
2. O per - fect re - demp-tion, the pur - chase of blood, To
3. Great things He hath taught us, great things He hath done, And

loved He the world that He gave us His Son, Who
ev - 'ry be - liev - er the prom - ise of God; The
great our re - joic - ing thro' Je - sus the Son; But

yield - ed His life an a - tone - ment for sin, And
vil - est of - fend - er who tru - ly be - lieves, Will
pur - er, and high - er, and great - er will be Our

o - pened the life - gate that all may go in.
sure - ly from Je - sus a par-don re - ceive. Praise the Lord, praise the
won - der, our trans-port, when Je - sus we see.

John 3:16. Words, Fanny J. Crosby, 1875. Tune TO GOD BE THE GLORY, William H. Doane, 1875.

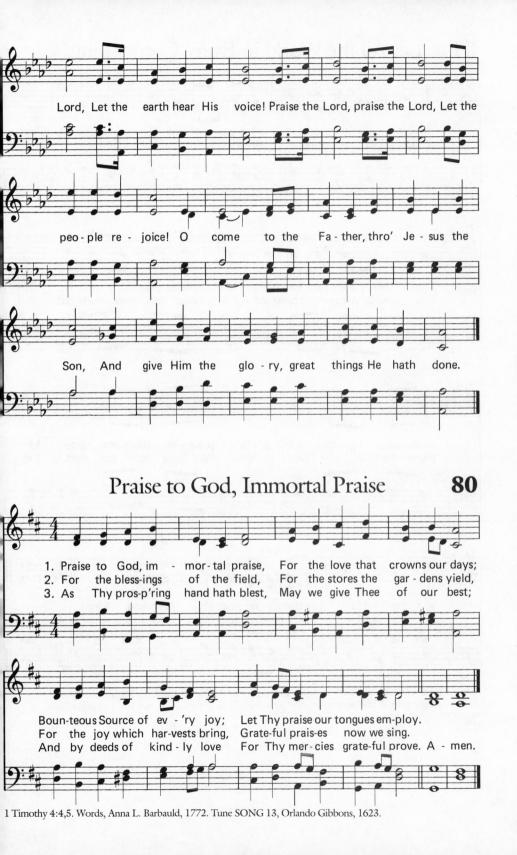

Lord, Let the earth hear His voice! Praise the Lord, praise the Lord, Let the

peo-ple re-joice! O come to the Fa-ther, thro' Je-sus the

Son, And give Him the glo-ry, great things He hath done.

Praise to God, Immortal Praise 80

1. Praise to God, im - mor-tal praise, For the love that crowns our days;
2. For the bless-ings of the field, For the stores the gar - dens yield,
3. As Thy pros-p'ring hand hath blest, May we give Thee of our best;

Boun-teous Source of ev - 'ry joy; Let Thy praise our tongues em-ploy.
For the joy which har-vests bring, Grate-ful prais-es now we sing.
And by deeds of kind - ly love For Thy mer-cies grate-ful prove. A - men.

1 Timothy 4:4,5. Words, Anna L. Barbauld, 1772. Tune SONG 13, Orlando Gibbons, 1623.

81 Let All the World in Every Corner Sing

1. Let all the world in ev-ery cor-ner sing: My God and King!
2. Let all the world in ev-ery cor-ner sing: My God and King!

The heavens are not too high, His praise may thith - er fly; The
The church with psalms must shout, No door can keep them out; But,

earth is not too low, His prais - es there may grow. Let
more than all, the heart Must bear the long - est part. Let

all the world in ev-ery cor-ner sing: My God and King!
all the world in ev-ery cor-ner sing: My God and King! A - men.

Hebrews 2:12. Words, George Herbert, 1633. Tune ALL THE WORLD, Robert G. McCutchan, 1934.
Music Copyright renewal 1962 assigned to Abingdon Press. Used by permission. Arr. J.B., Copyright 1986,
ACU Press.

Now Rest Beneath Night's Shadow
82

1. Now rest be-neath night's shad-ow The wood-land, field and
2. Lord Je-sus, who dost love me, O spread Thy wings a-

mead - ow: The world in slum - ber lies;
bove me, And shield me from a - larm;

But thou, my heart, a - wake thee, To prayer and song be-
Though Sa - tan would de - vour me, Let an - gel guards sing

take thee, Let praise to thy Cre - a - tor rise.
o'er me: "This child of God shall meet no harm."

Psalm 91:9-12. Words, Paul Gerhardt, 1653; trans. Hermann H. M. Brueckner, 1927, alt. Tune NUN RUHEN
ALLE WÄLDER, Henrich Isaac, c. 1450; arr. J. S. Bach.

83   # Open Now Thy Gates of Beauty

1. O - pen now thy gates of beau-ty, Zi - on, let me en-ter there,
2. Gra-cious God, I come be-fore Thee, Come Thou al - so un-to me;

Where my soul in joy-ful du - ty, Waits for Him who an-swers prayer.
Where we find Thee and a - dore Thee, There a heaven on earth must be.

O how bless-ed is this place, Filled with sol-ace, light, and grace!
To my heart O en - ter Thou, Let it be Thy tem-ple now.

1 John 3:24. Words, Benjamin Schmolck, 1732; trans. Catherine Winkworth, 1863. Tune NEANDER, Joachim Neander, 1680.

84   # Let Us With a Gladsome Mind

1. Let us, with a glad-some mind, Praise the Lord, for He is kind:
2. He with all - com - mand-ing might Filled the new-made world with light:
3. He the gold - en - tress - ed sun Caused all day his course to run:
4. All things liv - ing He doth feed, His full hand sup - plies their need:
5. Let us, with a glad-some mind, Praise the Lord, for He is kind:

Psalm 136. Words, John Milton, paraphrase Psalm 136, 1623. Tune MONKLAND, John Antes; arr. John B. Wilkes, 1861.

For His mer-cies aye en-dure, Ev-er faith-ful, ev-er sure. A-men.

Stand Up and Bless the Lord 85

1. Stand up and bless the Lord, Ye peo-ple of His choice;
2. Though high a-bove all praise, A-bove all bless-ing high,
3. God is our strength and song, And His sal-va-tion ours;
4. Stand up and bless the Lord; The Lord your God a-dore;

Stand up and bless the Lord your God, With heart and soul and voice.
Who would not fear His ho-ly name, And laud and mag-ni-fy?
Then be His love in Christ pro-claimed With all our ran-somed powers.
Stand up and bless His glo-rious name, Hence-forth for ev-er-more. A-men.

Psalm 63:4. Words, James Montgomery, 1825. Tune FESTAL SONG, William H. Walter, 1894.

Psalm 145:1,2 86

I will extol thee, my God, O King;
And I will bless thy name for ever and ever.
Every day will I bless thee;
And I will praise thy name for ever and ever.

87   # O Worship the King

1. O wor-ship the King, all - glo - rious a - bove, And grate-ful-ly
2. Thy boun-ti - ful care, what tongue can re - cite? It breathes in the
3. Frail chil-dren of dust, and fee - ble as frail, In Thee do we

sing His won - der - ful love; Our Shield and De - fend - er, the
air, it shines in the light; It streams from the hills, it de -
trust, nor find Thee to fail; Thy mer - cies, how ten - der! how

An - cient of Days, Pa - vil - ioned in splen-dor and gird - ed with praise.
scends to the plain, And sweet-ly dis - tills in the dew and the rain.
firm to the end! Our Mak - er, De - fend - er, Re - deem - er, and Friend!

1 Chronicles 29:11. Words, Robert Grant, 1833. Tune LYONS, attr. to Johann Michael Haydn in William Gardiner's *Sacred Melodies*, 1815.

88   # Come, Thou Almighty King

1. Come, Thou al - might - y King, Help us Thy name to sing.
2. Come, Thou In - car - nate Word, Gird on Thy might - y sword,
3. O Lord, our God, to Thee The high-est prais - es be,

Daniel 7:9,13,14. Words, Anonymous, 1757. Tune ITALIAN HYMN, Felice de Giardini, 1769.

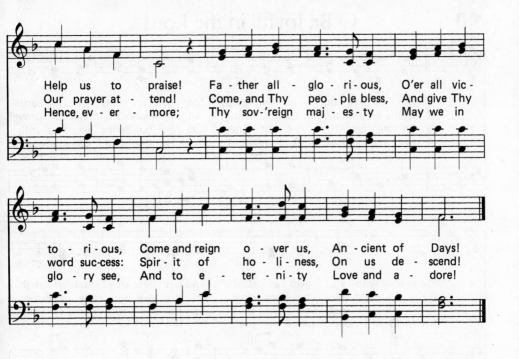

Help us to praise! Fa-ther all - glo - ri-ous, O'er all vic-
Our prayer at - tend! Come, and Thy peo -ple bless, And give Thy
Hence, ev - er - more; Thy sov-'reign maj - es - ty May we in

to - ri-ous, Come and reign o - ver us, An -cient of Days!
word suc-cess: Spir - it of ho - li - ness, On us de - scend!
glo - ry see, And to e - ter - ni - ty Love and a - dore!

Psalm 47:7,8; John 1:14; 2 Corinthians 13:14   **89**

For God is the King of all the earth:
Sing ye praises with understanding.
God reigneth over the nations:
God sitteth upon his holy throne.

And the Word became flesh and dwelt among us (and we beheld his glory, glory as of the only begotten from the Father), full of grace and truth.

The grace of the Lord Jesus Christ, and the love of God, and the communion of the Holy Spirit, be with you all.

O Be Joyful in the Lord

1. O be joy - ful   in the Lord!   Sing be - fore Him,   all the earth!
2. Know ye that the   Lord is King!   All His works His   wis-dom prove!
3. En - ter now His   ho - ly gate;   Let our bur-dened hearts be still;
4. For the Lord our   God is kind,   And His love shall   con-stant be;

Praise Him with a   glad ac - cord   And with lives of   no-blest worth.
By   His might the   heav-ens ring;   In His love we   live and move.
In   the sa - cred   si - lence wait,   As we seek to   know His will.
In   His will our   peace we find;   In His serv - ice,   lib - er - ty.

Sons of ev - ery   land,   Hum-bly now be - fore Him stand!
By Him we are   made,   So we trust Him   un - a - fraid.
Let our lives ex - press   Our a - bun-dant   thank-ful - ness;
Yea, His law is   sure;   In His light we   walk se - cure;

Raise your voice   and re-joice   In the boun-ty   of His   hand.
Stand-ing fast   to   the last,   By His hand our   lives are   stayed.
All   our days,   all   our ways,   Shall our Fa - ther's   love con - fess.
Ev - er-more,   as   of yore,   Shall His change-less truth en - dure.   A-men.

Psalm 100. Words, based on Psalm 100 by Curtis Beach. Tune ROCK OF AGES, Traditional Hebrew Melody.

1. The spa-cious fir-ma-ment on high, With all the blue, e-the-real sky,
2. Soon as the eve-ning shades pre-vail, The moon takes up the won-drous tale,
3. What tho' in sol-emn si-lence all Move round this dark ter-res-trial ball?

And span-gled heav'ns, a shin-ing frame, Their great O-rig-i-nal pro-claim:
And night-ly to the lis-t'ning earth Re-peats the sto-ry of her birth;
What tho' no re-al voice nor sound A-mid their ra-diant orbs be found?

Th'un-wea-ried sun from day to day Does his Cre-a-tor's pow'r dis-play,
While all the stars that round her burn, And all the plan-ets in their turn,
In rea-son's ear they all re-joice, And ut-ter forth a glo-rious voice,

And pub-lish-es to ev-'ry land The work of an al-might-y hand.
Con-firm the tid-ings as they roll, And spread the truth from pole to pole.
For ev-er sing-ing as they shine, "The hand that made us is di-vine."

Psalm 19:1-6. Words, Joseph Addison, 1812. Tune CREATION, Franz Joseph Haydn, 1798.

I Sing the Mighty Power of God

1. I sing the might-y power of God, That made the moun-tains rise,
2. I sing the good-ness of the Lord, That filled the earth with food;
3. There's not a plant or flower be-low, But makes thy glo-ries known;

That spread the flow-ing seas a-broad, And built the loft-y skies.
He formed the crea-tures with His word, And then pro-nounced them good.
And clouds a-rise, and tem-pests blow, By or-der from Thy throne,

I sing the wis-dom that or-dained The sun to rule the day;
Lord, how Thy won-ders are dis-played, Wher-e'er I turn my eye:
While all that bor-rows life from Thee Is ev-er in Thy care,

The moon shines full at His com-mand, And all the stars o-bey.
If I sur-vey the ground I tread, Or gaze up-on the sky!
And ev-'ry-where that man can be, Thou, God, art pres-ent there. A-men.

Genesis 1:31. Words, Isaac Watts, 1715. Tune ELLACOMBE, from *Gesangbuch der . . . Hofkapelle*, 1784.

Men and Children Everywhere

93

1. Men and chil-dren ev-ery-where, With sweet mu-sic fill the air!
2. Morn-ing, eve-ning, bless His name, Skies with crim-son clouds a-flame,
3. Storm and flood and o-cean's roar, Break-ers crash-ing on the shore,

Na-tions, come, your voic-es raise To the Lord in hymns of praise!
Rain-bow arch, His cov-enant sign, Count-less stars by night that shine!
Wa-ter-falls that nev-er sleep, Tow-er-ing moun-tain, can-yon deep,

Join the an-gel song, All the worlds to Him be-long!
Through His far do-main, Love is king where He doth reign!
Tell ye forth His might, Lord of life and truth and right!

Ho - ly, ho - ly, To our God all glo-ry be!
Ho - ly, ho - ly, To our God all glo-ry be!
Ho - ly, ho - ly, To our God all glo-ry be!

Psalm 150:6. Words, John J. Moment, 1930. Copyright 1941 by H.W. Gray Company, used by permission. Tune ROCK OF AGES, Traditional Hebrew Melody.

94   For the Beauty of the Earth

1. For the beau-ty   of the earth,   For the beau-ty   of the skies,
2. For the beau-ty   of each hour   Of the day and   of the night,
3. For the joy of   hu - man love,   Broth-er, sis - ter,   par - ent, child,
4. For Thy church that   ev - er - more   Lift-eth ho - ly   hands a - bove,

For the love which from our birth   O - ver and a - round us lies:
Hill and vale, and   tree, and flow'r,   Sun and moon, and stars of light:
Friends on earth, and   friends a - bove,   For all gen - tle thoughts and mild:
Of - f'ring up   on   ev - 'ry shore   Her pure sac - ri - fice of love:

Lord of all, to   Thee we raise   This, our sac - ri - fice of praise.

Psalm 107:21,22. Words, Folliott S. Pierpoint, 1864. Tune DIX, Conrad Kocher, 1838;
adpt. W. H. Monk, 1861.

95   Angels Holy, High and Lowly

1. An - gels ho - ly,   high and low - ly,   Sing the prais-es   of the Lord!
2. Rock and high-land, wood and is - land,   Crag where ea - gle's pride hath soared,
3. Roll - ing riv - er,   praise Him ev - er,   From the moun-tain's deep vein poured;
4. Praise Him ev - er,   boun-teous giv - er!   Praise Him, Fa - ther, Friend, and Lord!

Psalm 92:1,2. Words based on the *Benedicite*, John S. Blackie, b. 1908. Tune LLANHERNE, George
T. Thalben-Ball, 1926.

Earth and sky, all liv - ing na - ture, Man, the stamp of
Might - y moun - tains, pur - ple - breast - ed, Peaks cloud - cleav - ing,
Sil - ver foun - tain, clear - ly gush - ing, Trou - bled tor - rent,
Each glad soul its free course wing - ing, Each blithe voice its

thy Cre - a - tor. Praise ye, praise ye, God the Lord!
snow - y - crest - ed, Praise ye, praise ye, God the Lord!
mad - ly rush - ing, Praise ye, praise ye, God the Lord!
free song sing - ing, Praise the great and might - y Lord! A - men.

Psalm 97:1,2,6,10-12   96

The Lord reigneth; let the earth rejoice;
Let the multitude of isles be glad.
Clouds and darkness are round about him:
Righteousness and justice are the foundation of his throne.
The heavens declare his righteousness,
And all the peoples have seen his glory.
O ye that love the Lord, hate evil:
He preserveth the souls of his saints;
He delivereth them out of the hand of the wicked.
Light is sown for the righteous,
And gladness for the upright in heart.
Be glad in the Lord, ye righteous;
And give thanks to his holy memorial name.

97   God of the Earth, the Sky, the Sea

1. God of the earth, the sky, the sea, Mak-er of
2. Thy love is in the sun - shine's glow, Thy life is
3. We feel Thy calm at eve - ning's hour, Thy gran-deur
4. But high - er far, and far more clear, Thee in man's

all a - bove, be - low, Cre - a - tion lives and
in the quick-ening air; When light-nings flash and
in the march of night; And, when the morn - ing
spir - it we be - hold; Thine im - age and Thy-

moves in Thee, Thy pres-ent life through all doth flow.
storm-winds blow, There is Thy power; Thy law is there.
breaks in power, We hearThy word, "Let there be light!"
self are there, In - dwell-ing God, pro - claimed of old. A - men.

Acts 17:28. Words, Samuel Longfellow, b. 1819. Tune HERR JESU CHRIST, MEIN'S LEBENS LICHT, in *As Hymnodus Sacer*, 1625.

98   Isaiah 40:28-31

Hast thou not known? Hast thou not heard? The everlasting God, the Lord, the Creator of the ends of the earth, fainteth not, neither is weary; there is no searching of his understanding. He giveth power to the faint; and to him that hath no might he increaseth strength. Even the youths shall faint and be weary, and the young men shall utterly fall; but they that wait for the Lord shall renew their strength; they shall mount up with wings as eagles; they shall run, and not be weary; they shall walk, and not faint.

Praise the Lord! Ye Heavens Adore Him   99

1. Praise the Lord! ye heavens a-dore Him; Praise Him, an - gels, in the height;
2. Praise the Lord! for He is glo-rious; Nev - er shall His prom-ise fail;

Sun and moon, re - joice be-fore Him; Praise Him, all ye stars of light.
God hath made His saints vic - to - rious; Sin and death shall not pre-vail.

Praise the Lord! for He hath spo - ken; Worlds His might - y voice o-beyed;
Praise the God of our sal - va - tion! Hosts on high, His power pro-claim;

Laws which nev-er shall be bro-ken For their guid-ance hath He made.
Heaven and earth, and all cre-a - tion, Laud and mag-ni - fy His name. A-men.

Psalm 148. Words, from *The Foundling Hospital Collection*, 1796. Tune AUSTRIAN HYMN, Franz Joseph Haydn, 1797.

100 Praise the Lord! Ye Heavens Adore Him

1. Praise the Lord, ye heav'ns a-dore Him! Praise Him, an - gels, in the height;
2. Praise the Lord, for He hath spo-ken; Worlds His might-y voice o - beyed;
3. Praise the Lord, for He is glo-rious; Nev - er shall His prom-ise fail;
4. Praise the God of our sal - va - tion; Hosts on high, His pow'r pro-claim;

Sun and moon rejoice be-fore Him;   Praise Him, all ye stars of light.
Laws which never shall be bro- ken,   For their guidance He hath made.
God hath made His saints victorious;   Sin and death shall not prevail.
Heav'n and earth, and all cre-a-tion,   Laud and mag-ni-fy His name.

1. Sun and moon rejoice before Him; Praise Him, all ye stars of light.

Hal - le - lu-jah! A - men, Hal-le - lu-jah! A-men, A - men, A - men.

Psalm 148. Words, from *The Foundling Hospital Collection*, 1796. Tune PEREZ, Lowell Mason.

101 Thou, Whose Almighty Word

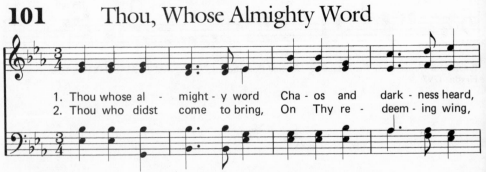

1. Thou whose al - might - y word Cha - os and dark - ness heard,
2. Thou who didst come to bring, On Thy re - deem - ing wing,

2 Corinthians 4:6. Words, John Marriott, 1813. Tune BRAINE, W. R. Braine.

And took their flight, Hear us, we hum - bly pray, And where the
Heal - ing and sight, Health to the sick in mind, Sight to the

gos - pel day Sheds not its glo - rious ray, Let there be light!
in - ly blind— O now to all man-kind Let there be light! A - men.

Genesis 1:1-3; 2 Corinthians 4:5,6   **102**

In the beginning God created the heaven and the earth. And the earth was without form, and void; and darkness was upon the face of the deep. And the Spirit of God moved upon the face of the waters. And God said, Let there be light; and there was light.

We preach not ourselves, but Christ Jesus the Lord; and ourselves your servants for Jesus' sake. For God who commanded the light to shine out of darkness, hath shined in our hearts, to give the light of the knowledge of the glory of God in the face of Jesus Christ.

103 This is My Father's World

1. This is my Fa-ther's world, And to my list-ening ears All
2. This is my Fa-ther's world, The birds their car-ols raise, The
3. This is my Fa-ther's world, O let me ne'er for-get That

na-ture sings, and round me rings The mu-sic of the spheres.
morn-ing light, the lil-y white, De-clare their mak-er's praise.
though the wrong seems oft so strong, God is the rul-er yet.

This is my Fa-ther's world: I rest me in the thought Of
This is my Fa-ther's world: He shines in all that's fair; In the
This is my Fa-ther's world: Why should my heart be sad? The

rocks and trees, of skies and seas; His hand the won-ders wrought.
rust-ling grass I hear Him pass, He speaks to me ev-ery-where.
Lord is King: let the heav-ens ring! God reigns: let the earth be glad!

Amos 4:13. Words, Maltbie D. Babcock, 1901. Tune TERRA BEATA, Franklin L. Sheppard, 1915.

A Mighty Fortress is Our God **104**

1. A might-y for-tress is our God, A bul-wark nev-er fail - ing;
2. Did we in our own strength con-fide, Our striv-ing would be los - ing,
3. And though this world, with de-mons filled, Should threat-en to un - do us,
4. That word a-bove all earth-ly powers, No thanks to them, a - bid-eth;

Our help-er He a - mid the flood Of mor-tal ills pre - vail - ing:
Were not the right man on our side, The man of God's own choos - ing:
We will not fear, for God hath willed His truth to tri-umph through us:
The Spir-it and the gifts are ours Through Him who with us sid - eth:

For still our an-cient foe Doth seek to work us woe; His craft and power are
Dost ask who that may be? Christ Je - sus, it is He; Lord Sa - ba-oth, His
The Prince of Dark-ness grim, We trem-ble not for him; His rage we can en-
Let goods and kin-dred go, This mor-tal life al - so; The bod - y they may

great, And, armed with cru-el hate, On earth is not his e - qual.
name, From age to age the same, And He must win the bat - tle.
dure, For lo, his doom is sure; One lit - tle word shall fell him.
kill: God's truth a - bid-eth still; His king-dom is for - ev - er. A-men.

Psalm 46. Words, Martin Luther, 1529; trans. Frederick H. Hedge, 1853. Tune EIN' FESTE BURG, Martin Luther, 1529. Arr. J.B., Copyright 1986, ACU Press.

105   The Lord Jehovah Reigns

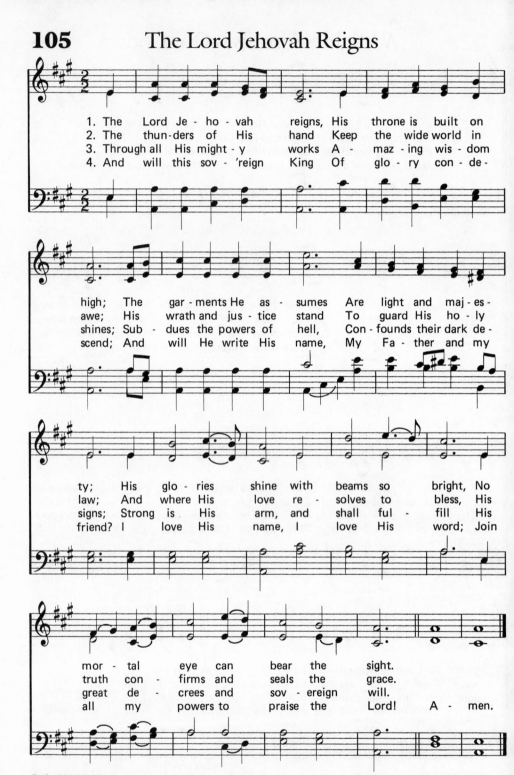

1. The Lord Jehovah reigns, His throne is built on high; The garments He assumes Are light and majesty; His glories shine with beams so bright, No mortal eye can bear the sight.

2. The thunders of His hand Keep the wide world in awe; His wrath and justice stand To guard His holy law; And where His love resolves to bless, His truth confirms and seals the grace.

3. Through all His mighty works Amazing wisdom shines; Subdues the powers of hell, Confounds their dark designs; Strong is His arm, and shall fulfill His great decrees and sovereign will.

4. And will this sov'reign King Of glory condescend; And will He write His name, My Father and my friend? I love His name, I love His word; Join all my powers to praise the Lord! A-men.

Psalm 103:19. Words, Isaac Watts, 1707. Tune MILLENNIUM, from *Plymouth Collection*, 1855.

Thou Art Merciful, O Father

106

1. Thou art mer-ci-ful, O Fa-ther, Full of pit-y, love and grace;
2. Like a Fa-ther's ten-der pit-y, Is God mer-cy tow'rd His own;
3. In the heav-ens, well es-tab-lished, Is His u-ni-ver-sal throne;

Thou wilt not for-ev-er chas-ten, Nor in an-ger hide Thy face.
For He knows our frame, re-mem-b'ring We are dust, our days soon gone.
For His king-dom rul-eth ev-er, And His sway all kings shall own.

High as heav-en vast and bound-less, Hath Thy lov-ing-kind-ness been;
Like a flow-er, bloom-ing, fad-ing, Like the grass, we pass a-way;
Bless Je-ho-vah, ye, His an-gels, Bless Him, hosts of His con-trol,

Far as east from west is dis-tant Hast Thou put a-way our sin.
But God's right-eous-ness and mer-cy On His chil-dren rest al-way.
Bless Je-ho-vah all His crea-tures, Bless Je-ho-vah, O my soul!

Psalm 103:8-22. Words, paraphrase by Elmer Leon Jorgenson, 1921. Tune JORGENSON, Wolfgang Amadeus Mozart, arr. from K. 331.

107 There is Beyond the Azure Blue

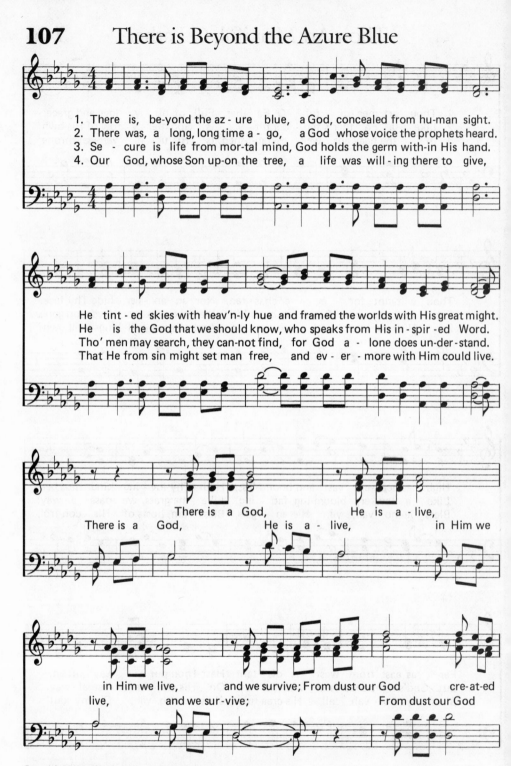

1. There is, be-yond the az - ure blue, a God, concealed from hu-man sight.
2. There was, a long, long time a - go, a God whose voice the prophets heard.
3. Se - cure is life from mor-tal mind, God holds the germ with-in His hand.
4. Our God, whose Son up-on the tree, a life was will - ing there to give,

He tint - ed skies with heav'n-ly hue and framed the worlds with His great might.
He is the God that we should know, who speaks from His in - spir -ed Word.
Tho' men may search, they can-not find, for God a - lone does un-der-stand.
That He from sin might set man free, and ev - er - more with Him could live.

There is a God, He is a - live,
There is a God, He is a - live, in Him we

in Him we live, and we survive; From dust our God cre-at-ed
live, and we sur-vive; From dust our God

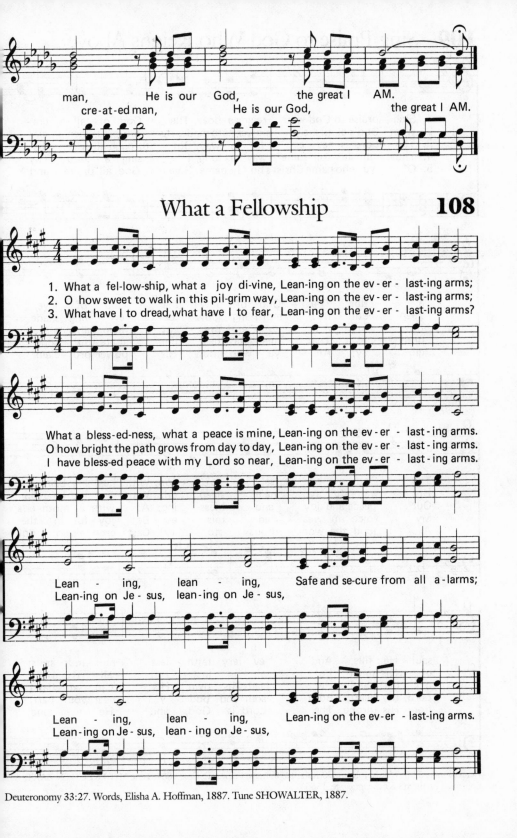

man, He is our God, the great I AM.
cre-at-ed man, He is our God, the great I AM.

What a Fellowship 108

1. What a fel-low-ship, what a joy di-vine, Lean-ing on the ev-er-last-ing arms;
2. O how sweet to walk in this pil-grim way, Lean-ing on the ev-er-last-ing arms;
3. What have I to dread, what have I to fear, Lean-ing on the ev-er-last-ing arms?

What a bless-ed-ness, what a peace is mine, Lean-ing on the ev-er-last-ing arms.
O how bright the path grows from day to day, Lean-ing on the ev-er-last-ing arms.
I have bless-ed peace with my Lord so near, Lean-ing on the ev-er-last-ing arms.

Lean - ing, lean - ing, Safe and se-cure from all a-larms;
Lean-ing on Je - sus, lean-ing on Je - sus,

Lean - ing, lean - ing, Lean-ing on the ev-er-last-ing arms.
Lean-ing on Je - sus, lean - ing on Je - sus,

Deuteronomy 33:27. Words, Elisha A. Hoffman, 1887. Tune SHOWALTER, 1887.

109 Sing Praise to God Who Reigns Above

1. Sing praise to God who reigns a - bove, The God of all cre -
2. What God's al - might - y power hath made, His gra - cious mer - cy
3. The Lord is nev - er far a - way, But through all grief dis -
4. Thus, all my toil - some way a - long, I sing a - loud Thy
5. O ye who name Christ's ho - ly name, Give God all praise and

a - tion, The God of pow'r, the God of love,
keep - eth; By morn - ing glow or eve - ning shade
tress - ing, An ev - er pres - ent help and stay,
prais - es, That men may hear the grate - ful song
glo - ry; All ye who know His power pro - claim

The God of our sal - va - tion; With heal - ing balm my
His watch - ful eye ne'er sleep - eth; With - in the king - dom
Our peace and joy and bless - ing; As with a moth - er's
My voice un - wea - ried rais - es; Be joy - ful in the
A - loud the won - drous sto - ry! Cast each false i - dol

soul He fills, And ev - ery faith - less mur - mur stills:
of His might, Lo! all is just and all is right:
ten - der hand, He leads His own, His cho - sen band:
Lord, my heart, Both soul and bod - y bear your part:
from His throne, The Lord is God, and He a - lone:

Deuteronomy 32:3. Words, Johann J. Schütz, 1675; trans. Frances E. Cox, 1864. Tune MIT FREUDEN ZART, Bohemian Brethren's *Kirchengesänge*, 1566.

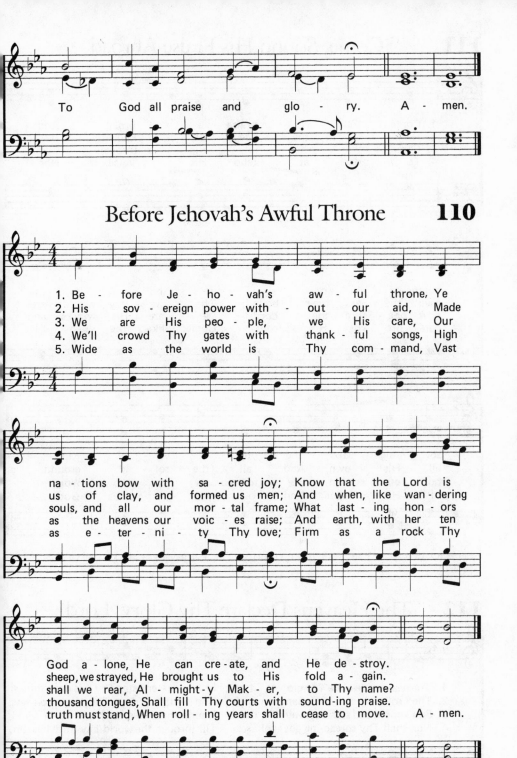

To God all praise and glo - ry. A - men.

Before Jehovah's Awful Throne **110**

1. Be - fore Je - ho - vah's aw - ful throne, Ye
2. His sov - ereign power with - out our aid, Made
3. We are His peo - ple, we His care, Our
4. We'll crowd Thy gates with thank - ful songs, High
5. Wide as the world is Thy com - mand, Vast

na - tions bow with sa - cred joy; Know that the Lord is
us of clay, and formed us men; And when, like wan - dering
souls, and all our mor - tal frame; What last - ing hon - ors
as the heavens our voic - es raise; And earth, with her ten
as e - ter - ni - ty Thy love; Firm as a rock Thy

God a - lone, He can cre - ate, and He de - stroy.
sheep, we strayed, He brought us to His fold a - gain.
shall we rear, Al - might - y Mak - er, to Thy name?
thousand tongues, Shall fill Thy courts with sound - ing praise.
truth must stand, When roll - ing years shall cease to move. A - men.

Psalm 100. Words, Isaac Watts, 1706. Tune WINCHESTER, NEW, from *Musikalisches Handbuch*, 1690; arr.
W. H. Havergal, 1847.

111   # Come, Sound His Praise Abroad

1. Come, sound His praise a - broad And hymns of glo - ry sing: Je - ho - vah is the sov - ereign God, The u - ni - ver - sal King.
2. He formed the deeps un - known; He gave the seas their bound; The wa - tery worlds are all His own, And all the sol - id ground.
3. Come, wor - ship at His throne; Come, bow be - fore the Lord: We are His works and not our own; He formed us by His Word.
4. To - day at - tend His voice, Nor dare pro - voke His rod; Come, like the peo - ple of His choice, And own your gra - cious God.

Psalm 95:6,7. Words, Isaac Watts, 1719. Tune CAMBRIDGE, arr. from Ralph Harrison, 1784, by Samuel S. Wesley, 1872.

112   # The Heavens Declare Thy Glory, Lord

1. The heavens de-clare Thy glo - ry, Lord; In ev - ery star Thy wis-dom shines;
2. The roll - ing sun, the chang-ing light, And nights and days, Thy power con-fess;
3. Sun, moon, and stars con-vey Thy praise Round the whole earth and nev-er stand,
4. Nor shall Thy spread-ing gos - pel rest Till through the world Thy truth has run,

Psalm 19. Words, Isaac Watts, 1719. Tune UXBRIDGE, Lowell Mason, 1830.

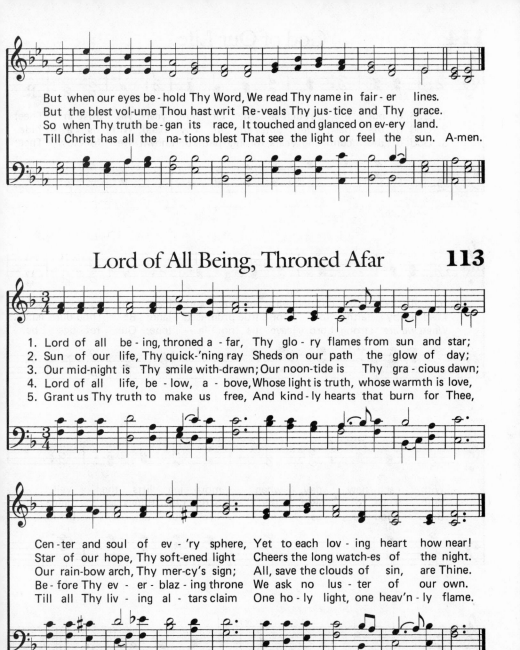

But when our eyes be - hold Thy Word, We read Thy name in fair - er   lines.
But the blest vol-ume Thou hast writ Re - veals Thy jus-tice and Thy   grace.
So when Thy truth be - gan its   race, It touched and glanced on ev-ery   land.
Till Christ has all the   na-tions blest That see the light or feel the   sun. A-men.

Lord of All Being, Throned Afar   113

1. Lord of all   be - ing, throned a - far, Thy glo - ry flames from sun and star;
2. Sun   of our life, Thy quick-'ning ray Sheds on our path   the glow of day;
3. Our mid-night is Thy smile with-drawn; Our noon-tide is   Thy gra - cious dawn;
4. Lord of all   life, be - low, a - bove, Whose light is truth, whose warmth is love,
5. Grant us Thy truth to make us   free, And kind - ly hearts that burn for Thee,

Cen - ter and soul of ev - 'ry sphere, Yet to each lov - ing heart   how near!
Star of our hope, Thy soft-ened light   Cheers the long watch-es of   the night.
Our rain-bow arch, Thy mer-cy's sign;   All, save the clouds of   sin,   are Thine.
Be - fore Thy ev - er - blaz - ing throne   We ask no lus - ter of   our own.
Till all Thy liv - ing al - tars claim   One ho - ly light, one heav'n - ly flame.

John 14:23. Words, Oliver Wendell Holmes, 1848. Tune ARIZONA, Robert H. Earnshaw.

114 God of Our Life

1. God of our life, through all the cir-cling years, We trust in Thee;
2. God of the past, our times are in Thy hand; With us a-bide.
3. God of the com-ing years, through paths un-known We fol-low Thee;

In all the past, through all our hopes and fears, Thy hand we see.
Lead us by faith to hope's true prom-ised land; Be Thou our guide.
When we are strong, Lord, leave us not a-lone; Our ref-uge be.

With each new day, when morn-ing lifts the veil,
With Thee to bless, the dark-ness shines as light,
Be Thou for us in life our dai-ly bread,

We own Thy mer-cies, Lord, which nev-er fail.
And faith's fair vi-sion chan-ges in-to sight.
Our heart's true home when all our years have sped. A-men.

Psalm 90:1,2. Words, Hugh T. Kerr, 1916. Copyright *The Church School Hymnal for Youth*, 1928, renewed
1956 by Board of Christian Education of the Presbyterian Church in the U.S.A.; used by permission of The
Westminster Press. Tune SANDON, Charles H. Purday, 1860.

Father and Friend, Thy Light, Thy Love 115

1. Fa - ther and Friend, Thy light, Thy love, Beam - ing thro'
2. Thy voice we hear, Thy pres - ence feel, While Thou, too
3. Thy chil - dren shall not faint nor fear, Sus - tained by

all Thy works we see; Thy glo - ry gilds the
pure for mor - tal sight, En - wrapt in clouds, in -
this de - light - ful thought; Since Thou, their God, art

heav'ns a - bove, And all the earth is full of Thee.
vis - i - ble, Reign-est the Lord of life and light.
ev - 'ry - where, They can-not be where Thou art not.

Psalm 139:17,18. Words, John Bowring, 1824. Tune HESPERUS, Henry Baker, 1866.

John 3:16,17   116

For God so loved the world, that he gave his only begotten Son, that whosoever believeth in him should not perish, but have everlasting life. For God sent not his Son into the world to condemn the world; but that the world through him might be saved.

117 Through the Love of God, Our Savior

1. Through the love of God, our Sav - ior, All will be well;
2. Though we pass through trib - u - la - tion, All will be well;
3. We ex - pect a bright to - mor - row, All will be well;

Free and change-less is His fa - vor— All will be well.
Ours is such a full sal - va - tion— All will be well.
Faith can sing through days of sor - row, All will be well.

Pre - cious is the blood that healed us, Per - fect is the grace that
Hap - py when in God con - fid - ing, Fruit - ful if in Christ a -
On our Fa - ther's love re - ly - ing, Je - sus ev - ery need sup -

sealed us, Strong the hand stretched out to shield us— All will be well.
bid - ing, Ho - ly through the Spir - it's guid-ing— All will be well.
ply - ing In our liv - ing, in our dy - ing, All will be well.

Philippians 4:13. Words, Mary Peters. Tune AR HYD Y NOS, Traditional Welsh Melody.

The King of Love My Shepherd Is **118**

1. The King of love my shep - herd is, Whose good - ness
2. Where streams of liv - ing wa - ter flow, My ran - somed
3. Per - verse and fool - ish oft I strayed, But yet in
4. In death's dark vale I fear no ill, With Thee, dear
5. Thou spreadst a ta - ble in my sight; A - noint - ing
6. And so through all the length of days, Thy good - ness

fail - eth nev - er; I noth - ing lack if
soul He lead - eth And, where the ver - dant
love He sought me, And on His shoul - der
Lord, be - side me, Thy rod and staff my
grace be - stow - eth; And, oh, what trans - port
fail - eth nev - er. Good Shep - herd, may I

I am His And He is mine for - ev - er.
pas - tures grow, With food ce - les - tial feed - eth.
gen - tly laid, And home, re - joic - ing, brought me.
com - fort still; Thy cross be - fore to guide me.
of de - light From Thy pure chal - ice flow - eth!
sing Thy praise With - in Thy house for - ev - er.

Psalm 23. Words, Henry W. Baker, 1868. Tune ST. COLUMBA, Traditional Irish Melody.

119   God is Love; His Mercy Brightens

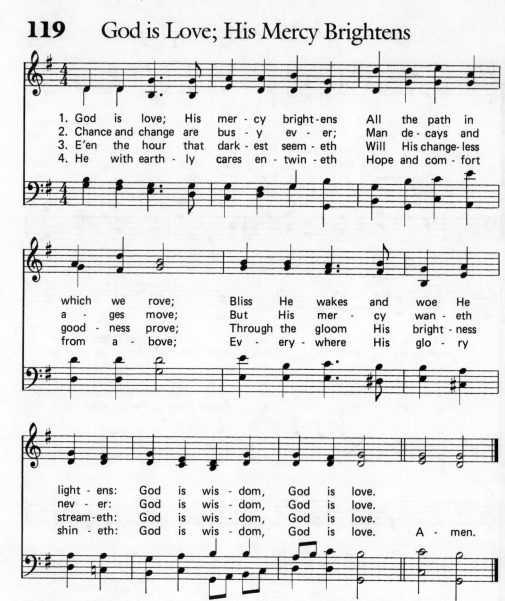

1. God is love; His mer - cy bright-ens All the path in
2. Chance and change are bus - y ev - er; Man de - cays and
3. E'en the hour that dark - est seem - eth Will His change-less
4. He with earth - ly cares en - twin - eth Hope and com - fort

which we rove; Bliss He wakes and woe He
a - ges move; But His mer - cy wan - eth
good - ness prove; Through the gloom His bright - ness
from a - bove; Ev - ery - where His glo - ry

light - ens: God is wis - dom, God is love.
nev - er: God is wis - dom, God is love.
stream-eth: God is wis - dom, God is love.
shin - eth: God is wis - dom, God is love. A - men.

1 John 4:4. Words, John Bowring, 1853. Tune STUTTGART, from *Psalmodia Sacra*, 1715; adpt. Henry J. Gauntlett, 1861.

120   1 John 1:5,7

This is the message which we have heard from him and announce to you, that God is light, and in him is no darkness at all . . . If we walk in the light, as he is in the light, we have fellowship one with another, and the blood of Jesus his Son cleanses us from all sin . . . Behold what manner of love the Father has bestowed upon us, that we should be called children of God; and such we are.

Amazing Grace

121

1. A - maz - ing grace! how sweet the sound, That
2. 'Twas grace that taught my heart to fear, And
3. Thro' man - y dan - gers, toils, and snares, I
4. The Lord has prom - ised good to me, His
5. And when this flesh and heart shall fail, And
6. When we've been there ten thou - sand years, Bright

saved a wretch like me! I once was lost,
grace my fears re - lieved; How pre - cious did
have al - read - y come; 'Tis grace hath brought
word my hope se - cures; He will my shield
mor - tal life shall cease, I shall pos - sess
shin - ing as the sun, We've no less days

but now am found, Was blind, but now I see.
that grace ap - pear The hour I first be - lieved!
me safe thus far, And grace will lead me home.
and por - tion be As long as life en - dures.
with - in the veil A life of joy and peace.
to sing God's praise Than when we've first be - gun.

2 Corinthians 9:8. Words st. 1-5, John Newton, 1779; st. 6, Anonymous. Tune AMAZING GRACE, *Virginia Harmony*, 1831. Arr. J.B., Copyright 1986, ACU Press.

122 Amazing Grace

1. A - maz - ing grace! how sweet the sound, That saved a wretch like me! I once was lost, but now am found, Was blind, but now I see.

2. 'Twas grace that taught my heart to fear, And grace my fears re - lieved; How pre - cious did that grace ap - pear The hour I first be - lieved!

3. Thro' man - y dan - gers, toils, and snares, I have al - read - y come; 'Tis grace hath brought me safe thus far, And grace will lead me home.

4. The Lord has prom - ised good to me, His word my hope se - cures; He will my shield and por - tion be As long as life en - dures.

5. And when this flesh and heart shall fail, And mor - tal life shall cease, I shall pos - sess with - in the veil A life of joy and peace.

6. When we've been there ten thou - sand years, Bright shin - ing as the sun, We've no less days to sing God's praise Than when we've first be - gun.

2 Corinthians 9:8. Words, st. 1-5, John Newton, 1779; st. 6, Anonymous. Tune AMAZING GRACE, *Virginia Harmony*, 1831. Arr. Edwin O. Excell, 1900.

O My Soul, Bless God the Father   123

1. O my soul, bless God the Father; All with-
2. Who for - giv - eth thy trans - gres - sions, Thy dis -
3. Far as east from west is dis - tant, He hath
4. As it was with - out be - gin - ning, So it
5. Un - to such as keep His cove - nant And are
6. Bless the Fa - ther, all His crea - tures, Ev - er

in me bless His name; Bless the Fa - ther, and for - get not
eas - es all who heals; Who re - deems thee from de - struc-tion,
put a - way our sin; Like the pit - y of a fa - ther
lasts with - out an end; To their chil - dren's chil - dren ev - er
stead-fast in His way; Un - to those who still re - mem - ber
un - der His con - trol; All through-out His vast do - min - ion

All His mer - cies to pro - claim.
Who with thee so kind - ly deals.
Hath the Lord's com - pas - sion been.
Shall His righ - teous - ness ex - tend:
His com - mand - ments, and o - bey.
Bless the Fa - ther, O my soul. A - men.

Psalm 103:1-22. Words, paraphrase in *The Book of Psalms*, 1871. Tune STUTTGART, from *Psalmodia Sacra*, 1715; adpt. Henry J. Gauntlett, 1861.

124 Marvelous Grace of Our Loving Lord

1. Mar-vel-ous grace of our lov-ing Lord, Grace that ex-ceeds our
2. Dark is the stain that we can-not hide, What can a-vail to
3. Mar-vel-ous, in-fi-nite, match-less grace, Free-ly be-stowed on

sin and our guilt, Yon-der on Cal-va-ry's mount out-poured,
wash it a-way? Look! there is flow-ing a crim-son tide;
all who be-lieve; All who are long-ing to see His face,

There where the blood of the Lamb was spilt. Grace, grace,
Whit-er than snow you may be to-day.
Will you this mo-ment His grace re-ceive? Mar-vel-ous grace,

God's grace, Grace that will par-don and cleanse with-in; Grace,
in-fi-nite grace, Mar-vel-ous

Romans 3:14-16. Words, Julia H. Johnston, 1910. Tune MOODY, Daniel B. Towner, 1910. Copyright 1910.
Renewal 1938 by Hope Publishing Co., Carol Stream, IL 60188. All rights reserved. Used by permission.

grace, God's grace, Grace that is great-er than all our sin.
grace, in - fi-nite grace,

Father of Mercies   **125**

1. Fa - ther of mer - cies, day by day My love to Thee grows
2. Fa - ther of mer - cies, God of love, Whose gen - tle gifts all
3. Fa - ther of mer - cies, may our hearts Ne'er o - ver - look Thy

more and more; Thy gifts are strewn up - on my way Like sands up-
crea - tures share, The roll - ing sea - sons as they move Pro - claim to
boun - teous care; But what our Fa - ther's hand im - parts Still own in

on the great sea - shore, Like sands up - on the great sea - shore.
all Thy con - stant care, Pro - claim to all Thy con - stant care.
grate - ful praise and prayer, Still own in grate - ful praise and prayer.

2 Corinthians 1:3,4. Words, st. 1, Frederick W. Faber, 1849; st. 2 and 3, Alice Flowerdew, 1803.
Tune ELEOS, Traditional English Melody.

126 **Can You Count the Stars?**

1. Can you count the stars of eve-ning That are shin-ing in the sky?
2. Can you count the birds that war-ble In the sun-shine all the day?
3. Can you count the man-y chil-dren In their lit-tle beds at night?

Can you count the clouds that dai-ly O-ver all the world go by?
Can you count the lit-tle fish-es That in spark-ling wa-ters play?
Who with-out a thought of sor-row Rise a-gain at morn-ing light?

God the Lord, who doth not slum-ber, Keep-eth all the bound-less num-ber,
God the Lord their num-ber know-eth, For each one His care He show-eth:
God the Lord, who dwells in heav-en, Lov-ing care to each has giv-en:

But He car-eth more for thee, But He car-eth more for thee.
Shall He not re-mem-ber thee? Shall He not re-mem-ber thee?
He hath not for-got-ten thee, He hath not for-got-ten thee.

Deuteronomy 31:6. Words, Johann Hey, 1837; trans. Elmer Leon Jorgenson, 1921. Tune WEISST DU WIE
VIEL STERNLEIN STEHEN, German Folk Tune, 16th century.

Be Not Dismayed Whate'er Betide

127

1. Be not dismayed what-e'er betide, God will take care of you;
2. Thro' days of toil when heart doth fail God will take care of you;
3. All you may need He will pro-vide, God will take care of you;
4. No mat-ter what may be the test, God will take care of you;

Be - neath His wings of love a - bide, God will take care of you.
When dan-gers fierce your path as - sail, God will take care of you.
Noth - ing you ask will be de - nied, God will take care of you.
Lean, wea - ry one, up - on His breast, God will take care of you.

God will take care of you, Thro' ev - 'ry day, O'er all the way;

He will take care of you, God will take care of you.
take care of you.

Luke 12:6,7. Words, Civilla D. Martin, 1904. Tune GOD WILL TAKE CARE OF YOU, Walter Stillman Martin, 1904.

128 Come, Come, Ye Saints

1. Come, come, ye saints, no toil nor la-bor fear; But with joy
2. The world of care is with us ev-'ry day; Let it not
3. We'll find the rest which God for us pre-pared, When at last

wend your way. Tho' hard to you the jour-ney may ap-pear,
this ob-scure: Here we can serve the Mas-ter on the way,
He will call; Where none will come to hurt or make a-fraid,

Grace shall be as your day. We have a liv-ing
And in Him be se-cure. Gird up your loins; fresh
He will reign o-ver all. We will make the air with

Lord to guide, And we can trust Him to pro-vide; Do
cour-age take; Our God will nev-er us for-sake; And
mu-sic ring, Shout prais-es to our God and King; O

1 Peter 1:13. Words, William Clayton, 1846; alt. Joseph F. Green, 1960. Copyright 1960, Broadman Press. All rights reserved. Tune ALL IS WELL, adpt. from J. F. White, *The Sacred Harp*, 1844.

this, and joy your hearts will swell: All is well! All is well!
so our song no fear can quell: All is well! All is well!
how we'll make the cho - rus swell: All is well! All is well!

God is the Fountain Whence 129

1. God is the foun-tain whence Ten thou - sand bless-ings flow; To Him my
2. The com-forts He af - fords Are nei - ther few nor small; He is the
3. He fills my heart with joy, My lips at - tunes for praise; And to His

life, my health, and friends, And ev - 'ry good I owe.
source of fresh de - lights, My por - tion and my all.
glo - ry I'll de - vote The rem - nant of my days.

Psalm 36:9. Words, Benjamin Beddome, pub. 1817. Tune GERAR, Lowell Mason, 1839.

James 1:17,18 130

Every good gift and every perfect gift is from above, coming down from the Father
of lights, with whom can be no variation, neither shadow that is cast by turning.
Of his own will he brought us forth by the word of truth, that we should be a kind
of firstfruits of his creatures.

131   When All Thy Mercies, O My God

1. When all Thy mer-cies, O my God, My ris-ing soul sur-veys, Trans-
2. Un-num-bered com-forts to my soul Thy ten-der care be-stowed, Be-
3. Ten thou-sand, thou-sand pre-cious gifts My dai-ly thanks em-ploy Nor
4. Thro' all e-ter-ni-ty, to Thee A joy-ful song I'll raise; But

port-ed with the view, I'm lost In won-der, love, and praise.
fore my in-fant heart could know From whom those comforts flowed.
is the least a cheer-ful heart That tastes those gifts with joy.
O e-ter-ni-ty's too short To ut-ter all Thy praise. A-men.

Psalm 33:1. Words, Joseph Addison, 1712. Tune WINCHESTER, OLD, Thomas Est's *Whole Book of Psalms*, 1592.

132   Father, Lead Me Day by Day

1. Fa-ther, lead me day by day, Ev-er in Your own strong way;
2. When, in dan-ger, make me brave, Make me know that You can save;
3. When I'm tempt-ed to do wrong, Make me stead-fast, wise and strong;

Teach me to be pure and true, Show me what I ought to do.
Keep me safe-ly by Your side; Let me in Your love a-bide.
And when all a-lone I stand, Shield me with Your might-y hand. A-men.

Psalm 27:9. Words, John P. Hopps. Tune ORIENTIS PARTIBUS, from the Office of Pierre de Corbeil; harm. Richard Redhead, 1853.

He Leadeth Me

1. He lead-eth me: O bless-ed tho't! O words with heav'nly comfort fraught!
2. Sometimes 'mid scenes of deep-est gloom, Some-times where Eden's bowers bloom,
3. Lord, I would clasp Thy hand in mine, Nor ev-er mur-mur nor re-pine;
4. And when my task on earth is done, When by Thy grace the vic-t'ry's won,

What-e'er I do, wher-e'er I be, Still 'tis God's hand that lead-eth me.
By wa-ters still, o'er trou-bled sea— Still 'tis God's hand that lead-eth me.
Con-tent, what-ev-er lot I see, Since 'tis God's hand that lead-eth me.
E'en death's cold wave I will not flee, Since God thro' Jor-dan lead-eth me.

He lead-eth me, He lead-eth me, By His own hand He lead-eth me.

His faith-ful fol-low'r I would be, For by His hand He lead-eth me.

Isaiah 48:17. Words, Joseph H. Gilmore, 1862. Tune HE LEADETH ME, William B. Bradbury, 1864.

134   Day by Day

1. Day by day and with each passing moment, Strength I find to meet my trials here; Trusting in my Father's wise bestowment, I've no cause for worry or for fear. He whose heart is kind beyond all measure Gives un-

2. Ev-'ry day the Lord Himself is near me With a special mercy for each hour; All my cares He fain would bear, and cheer me, He whose name is Counsel-lor and Pow'r. The protection of His child and treasure Is a-

3. Help me then in ev'ry tribulation So to trust Thy promises, O Lord, That I lose not faith's sweet consolation Offered me within Thy holy Word. Help me, Lord, when toil and trouble meeting, E'er to

Isaiah 41:10. Words, Carolina V. Sandell-Berg, 1865; trans. A. L. Skoog, d. 1934. Tune BLOTT EN DAG, Oscar Ahnfelt, d. 1882.

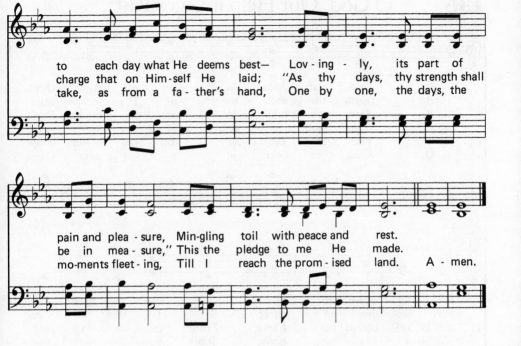

to each day what He deems best— Lov-ing-ly, its part of
charge that on Him-self He laid; "As thy days, thy strength shall
take, as from a fa-ther's hand, One by one, the days, the

pain and plea - sure, Min-gling toil with peace and rest.
be in mea - sure," This the pledge to me He made.
mo-ments fleet - ing, Till I reach the prom - ised land. A - men.

Deuteronomy 33:25-27; John 9:4   **135**

As thy days, so shall thy strength be.
There is none like unto God,
Who rideth upon the heavens for thy help,
And in his excellency on the skies.
The Eternal God is thy dwelling-place,
And underneath are the everlasting arms.

We must work the works of him that sent me, while it is day: the night cometh,
when no man can work.

136   O God, Our Help in Ages Past

1. O God, our help in a - ges past, Our hope for years to come, Our shel - ter from the storm - y blast, And our e - ter - nal home!

2. Be - neath the shad - ow of Thy throne Still may we dwell se - cure; Suf - fi - cient is Thine arm a - lone, And our de - fense is sure.

3. Be - fore the hills in or - der stood, Or earth re - ceived her frame, From ev - er - last - ing Thou art God, To end - less years the same.

4. A thou - sand a - ges, in Thy sight, Are like an eve - ning gone; Short as the watch that ends the night, Be - fore the ris - ing sun.

5. Time, like an ev - er - roll - ing stream, Bears all its sons a - way; They fly for - got - ten, as a dream Dies at the open - ing day.

6. O God, our help in a - ges past, Our hope for years to come; Be Thou our guide while life shall last, And our e - ter - nal home! A - men.

Psalm 90:1-5. Words, Isaac Watts, 1719. Tune ST. ANNE, William Croft, 1708.

Eternal Father, Strong to Save
137

1. E - ter - nal Fa - ther, strong to save, Whose arm hath bound the rest-less wave,
2. O Christ, whose voice the waters heard, And hushed their rag - ing at Thy word,
3. O Trin - i - ty of love and pow'r Our breth - ren shield in dan-ger's hour;

Who bidd'st the might-y o - cean deep Its own ap - point-ed lim - its keep:
Who walk-edst on the foam-ing deep, And calm a - mid the storm didst sleep:
From rock and tem-pest, fire and foe, Pro - tect them, where-so - e'er they go:

O hear us when we cry to Thee For those in per - il on the sea.
O hear us when we cry to Thee For those in per - il on the sea.
Thus ev - er-more shall rise to Thee Glad hymns of praise from land and sea.

Psalm 107:26-32. Words, William Whiting, 1860. Tune MELITA, John B. Dykes, 1861.

Psalm 90:1,2,12   **138**

Lord, thou hast been our dwelling-place
In all generations.
Before the mountains were brought forth,
Or ever thou hadst formed the earth and the world
Even from everlasting to everlasting, thou art God.
So teach us to number our days,
That we may get us a heart of wisdom.

139 God Moves in a Mysterious Way

1. God moves in a mys - te - rious way His won-ders to per - form;
2. Deep in un-fath-om - a - ble mines Of nev-er-fail-ing skill,
3. Ye fear-ful saints, fresh cour-age take; The clouds ye so much dread
4. Judge not the Lord by fee-ble sense, But trust Him for His grace;
5. His pur-pos-es will rip-en fast, Un-fold-ing ev-'ry hour;
6. Blind un-be-lief is sure to err, and scan His work in vain;

He plants His foot-steps in the sea And rides up-on the storm.
He treas-ures up His bright de-signs And works His gra-cious will.
Are big with mer-cy, and shall break In bless-ings on your head.
Be-hind a frown-ing prov-i-dence He hides a smil-ing face.
The bud may have a bit-ter taste, But sweet will be the flow'r.
God is His own in - ter-pret-er, And He will make it plain.

Romans 11:33. Words, William Cowper, 1774. Tune DUNDEE, *Scottish Psalter*, 1615.

140 O God of Bethel, by Whose Hand

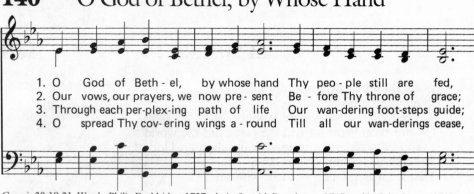

1. O God of Beth-el, by whose hand Thy peo-ple still are fed,
2. Our vows, our prayers, we now pre-sent Be-fore Thy throne of grace;
3. Through each per-plex-ing path of life Our wan-dering foot-steps guide;
4. O spread Thy cov-ering wings a-round Till all our wan-derings cease,

Genesis 28:19-21. Words, Philip Doddridge, 1737; alt. in *Scottish Paraphrases*, 1745, and by John Logan, 1781.
Tune DUNDEE, *Scottish Psalter*, 1615.

Who through this wea-ry pil-grim-age Hast all our fa-thers led.
God of our fa-thers, be the God Of their suc-ceed-ing race.
Give us each day our dai-ly bread, And rai-ment fit pro-vide.
And at our Fa-ther's loved a-bode Our souls ar-rive in peace. A-men.

Great God, We Sing That Mighty Hand 141

1. Great God, we sing that might-y hand By which sup-
2. By day, by night, at home, a-broad, Still are we
3. With grate-ful hearts the past we own; The fu-ture,
4. In scenes ex-alt-ed or de-pressed Thou art our
5. When death shall in-ter-rupt our songs And seal in

port-ed still we stand; The o-pening year Thy
guard-ed by our God: By His in-ces-sant
all to us un-known, We to Thy guard-ian
joy, and Thou our rest; Thy good-ness all our
si-lence mor-tal tongues, Our help-er, God, in

mer-cy shows, That mer-cy crowns it till it close.
boun-ty fed, By His un-err-ing coun-sel led.
care com-mit And, peace-ful, leave be-fore Thy feet.
hopes shall raise, A-dored through all our chang-ing days.
whom we trust, In bet-ter worlds our souls shall boast. A-men.

Psalm 65:9-13. Words, Philip Doddridge, 1755. Tune WAREHAM, William Knapp, 1738.

142　O How Kindly Hast Thou Led Me

1. O how kind-ly hast Thou led me, Heav'n-ly Fa - ther, day by day;
2. O how slow-ly have I oft - en Followed where Thy hand would draw!

Found my dwell-ing clothed and fed me, Fur - nished friends to cheer my way!
How Thy kind-ness failed to soft - en! How Thy chas - t'ning failed to awe!

Didst Thou bless me, didst Thou chas-ten, With Thy smile or with Thy rod,
Make me for Thy rest more read - y, As Thy path is long - er trod;

'Twas that still my step might has - ten Homeward, heav'nward, to my God.
Keep me in Thy friend-ship stead - y, Till Thou call me home, my God.

Hebrews 12:7-11. Words, Thomas Grinfield, 1836. Tune MIDDLETOWN, Traditional English Melody.

The Lord's My Shepherd 143

1. The Lord's my Shep - herd, I'll not want. He makes me
2. My soul He doth re - store a - gain; And me to
3. Yea, though I walk in death's dark vale, Yet will I
4. My ta - ble Thou hast fur - nish - ed In pres - ence
5. Good - ness and mer - cy all my life Shall sure - ly

down to lie In pas - tures green; He lead - eth
walk doth make With - in the paths of right - eous -
fear none ill: For Thou art with me; and Thy
of my foes; My head Thou dost with oil a -
fol - low me: And in God's house for - ev - er -

me The qui - et wa - ters by.
ness, E'en for His own name's sake.
rod And staff me com - fort still.
noint, And my cup o - ver - flows.
more My dwell - ing place shall be. A - men.

Psalm 23. Words, metrical version from the *Scottish Psalter*, 1650. Tune CRIMOND, Jessie Seymour Irvine, 1872.

Psalm 23 144

The Lord is my shepherd; I shall not want. He maketh me to lie down in green pastures; He leadeth me beside the still waters. He restoreth my soul: He leadeth me in the paths of righteousness for his name's sake. Yea, though I walk through the valley of the shadow of death, I will fear no evil: For thou art with me; thy rod and thy staff they comfort me. Thou preparest a table before me in the presence of mine enemies: Thou anointest my head with oil; my cup runneth over. Surely goodness and mercy shall follow me all the days of my life: And I will dwell in the house of the Lord for ever.

145 The Lord My Shepherd Is

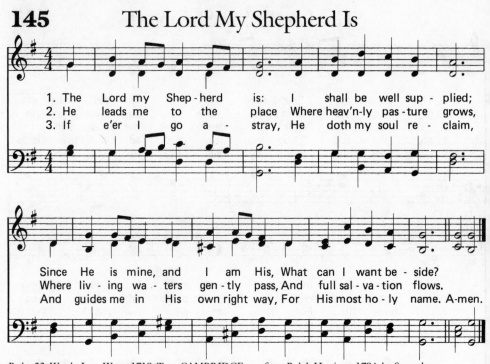

1. The Lord my Shep-herd is: I shall be well sup-plied;
2. He leads me to the place Where heav'n-ly pas-ture grows,
3. If e'er I go a-stray, He doth my soul re-claim,

Since He is mine, and I am His, What can I want be-side?
Where liv-ing wa-ters gen-tly pass, And full sal-va-tion flows.
And guides me in His own right way, For His most ho-ly name. A-men.

Psalm 23. Words, Isaac Watts, 1719. Tune CAMBRIDGE, arr. from Ralph Harrison, 1784, by Samuel S. Wesley, 1872.

146 Shepherd of Souls, Refresh

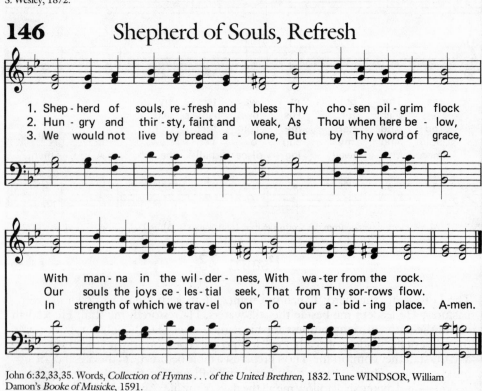

1. Shep-herd of souls, re-fresh and bless Thy cho-sen pil-grim flock
2. Hun-gry and thir-sty, faint and weak, As Thou when here be-low,
3. We would not live by bread a-lone, But by Thy word of grace,

With man-na in the wil-der-ness, With wa-ter from the rock.
Our souls the joys ce-les-tial seek, That from Thy sor-rows flow.
In strength of which we trav-el on To our a-bid-ing place. A-men.

John 6:32,33,35. Words, *Collection of Hymns . . . of the United Brethren*, 1832. Tune WINDSOR, William Damon's *Booke of Musicke*, 1591.

Great is Thy Faithfulness

147

1. Great is Thy faith-ful-ness, O God my Fa-ther, There is no shad-ow of
2. Sum-mer and win-ter, and spring-time and har-vest, Sun, moon, and stars in their
3. Par-don for sin and a peace that en-dur-eth, Thine own dear presence to

turn-ing with Thee; Thou changest not, Thy compassions, they fail not: As Thou hast
cours-es a-bove Join with all na-ture in man-i-fold wit-ness To Thy great
cheer and to guide; Strength for to-day and bright hope for to-mor-row, Blessings all

been Thou for-ev-er wilt be.
faith-ful-ness, mer-cy, and love. Great is Thy faith-ful-ness! Great is Thy
mine, with ten thou-sand be-side!

faith-ful-ness! Morn-ing by morn-ing new mer-cies I see; All I have need-ed Thy

hand hath pro-vid-ed; Great is Thy faith-ful-ness, Lord, un-to me! A-men.

Lamentations 3:22-24. Words, Thomas O. Chisholm, 1923. Tune FAITHFULNESS, William M. Runyan, 1923.
Copyright 1923. Renewal 1951 extended by Hope Publishing Co., Carol Stream, IL 60188. All rights reserved.
Used by permission.

148 Unto the Hills

1. Un - to the hills a - round do I lift up My long - ing eyes;
2. He will not suf - fer that thy foot be moved: Safe shalt thou be;
3. Je - ho - vah is Him - self thy keep - er true: Thy change-less shade,
4. From ev - 'ry e - vil shall He keep thy soul, From ev - 'ry sin;

O whence for me shall my sal - va - tion come, From whence a - rise?
No care - less slum - ber shall His eye - lids close, Who keep - eth thee;
Je - ho - vah ev - er - more on thy right hand Him - self hath made;
Je - ho - vah shall pre - serve thy go - ing out, Thy com - ing in;

From God the Lord doth come my cer - tain aid, From
Be - hold, He sleep - eth not, He slum - b'reth ne'er, Who
And thee no sun by day shall ev - er smite, No
A - bove thee watch - ing, He whom we a - dore Shall

God the Lord, who heav'n and earth hath made.
keep - eth Is - rael in His ho - ly care.
moon shall harm thee in the si - lent night.
keep thee hence - forth, yea, for ev - er - more.

Psalm 121. Words, paraphrase by John Campbell, 1866. Tune SANDON, Charles Purday, 1860.

O Lord of Heaven and Earth and Sea **149**

1. O Lord of heav'n and earth and sea, To Thee all
2. For peace - ful homes and health - ful days, For all the
3. Thou didst not spare Thine on - ly Son, But gav'st Him
4. Thou giv'st the Spir - it's bless - ed dower, Spir - it of
5. For souls re - deemed, for sins for - given, For means of

praise and glo - ry be; How shall we show our
bless - ings earth dis - plays, We owe Thee thank - ful -
for a world un - done, And free - ly with that
life and love and power, And dost His seven - fold
grace and hopes of heaven, Our Fa - ther, praise to

love to Thee, Who giv - est all?
ness and praise, Who giv - est all.
bless - ed One, Thou giv - est all.
grac - es shower Up - on us all.
Thee be given, Who giv - est all. A - men.

Acts 14:15-17. Words, Christopher Wordsworth, 1863. Tune MEYER, J. D. Meyer's *Geistliche Seelenfreud*, 1692.

Romans 8:28 **150**

We know that all things work together for good to them that love God, to them who are the called according to his purpose.

151 **Come, Christians, Join to Sing**

1. Come, Chris-tians, join to sing Al - le - lu - ia! A - men!
2. Come, lift your hearts on high; Al - le - lu - ia! A - men!
3. Praise yet the Lord a - gain; Al - le - lu - ia! A - men!

Loud praise to Christ our King; Al - le - lu - ia! A - men!
Let prais - es fill the sky; Al - le - lu - ia! A - men!
Life shall not end the strain; Al - le - lu - ia! A - men!

Let all, with heart and voice, Be - fore His throne re - joice;
He is our guide and friend; To us He'll con - des - cend,
On heav - en's bliss - ful shore His good - ness we'll a - dore,

Praise is His gra-cious choice: Al - le - lu - ia! A - men!
His love shall nev - er end: Al - le - lu - ia! A - men!
Sing - ing for - ev - er - more Al - le - lu - ia! A - men! A - men.

Colossians 3:4. Words, Christian Henry Bateman, 1843. Tune SPANISH HYMN; arr. Benjamin Carr, 1826.

When Morning Gilds the Skies **152**

1. When morning gilds the skies My heart a-wak-ing cries, May Je-sus Christ be praised;
2. In heav'n's e - ter - nal bliss The sweet-est strain is this, May Je-sus Christ be praised;
3. Be this, while life is mine, My can - ti - cle di - vine, May Je-sus Christ be praised;

A - like at work and prayer To Je-sus I re-pair: May Je-sus Christ be praised.
Let earth and sea and sky From depth to height reply, May Je-sus Christ be praised!
Be this th'e-ter - nal song Thro' all the a - ges on, May Je-sus Christ be praised!

2 Peter 1:19. Words, *Katholisches Gesangbuch*, 1828; trans. Edward Caswall, 1854. Tune LAUDES DOMINI,
Joseph Barnby, 1868.

Awake, and Sing the Song **153**

1. A - wake, and sing the song Of Mos - es and the Lamb;
2. Sing of His dy - ing love; Sing of His ris - ing pow'r;
3. Sing on your heav'n-ly way, Ye ran-somed sin - ners, sing;
4. Soon shall you hear Him say, "Ye bless - ed chil - dren, come!"

Wake, ev - 'ry heart and ev - 'ry tongue,To praise the Sav - ior's name.
Sing how He in - ter - cedes a - bove For those whose sins He bore.
Sing on, re - joic - ing ev - 'ry day In Christ, the glo - rious King.
Soon will He call you hence a - way, And take His pil - grims home.

Revelation 15:3,4. Words, William Hammond, 1745. Tune ST. THOMAS, Aaron Williams, 1763.

154 **Blessed Savior, We Adore Thee**

1. Bless-ed Sav - ior, we a - dore Thee, We Thy love and grace pro-claim;
2. Great Re-deem-er, Lord and Mas - ter, Light of all e - ter - nal days;
3. From the throne of heav-en's glo - ry To the cross of sin and shame,

Thou art might-y, Thou art ho - ly, Glo - rious is Thy match-less name!
Let the saints of ev - 'ry na - tion Sing Thy just and end - less praise!
Thou didst come to die a ran - som, Guilt - y sin - ners to re - claim!

Glo - - - ri-ous, Glo - - - ri - ous,

Glo - rious is Thy name, O Lord! Glo - rious is Thy name, O Lord!

Glo - rious is Thy name, O Lord! Glo - - - ri - ous,

Glo - rious is Thy name, O Lord!

Philippians 2:9-11. Words and tune GLORIOUS NAME, B. B. McKinney, 1942. Copyright 1942. Renewal 1970, Broadman Press. All rights reserved. International Copyright secured. Used by permission.

Glo - - ri-ous, Glo-rious is Thy name, O Lord! A - men.

Christ, We do All Adore Thee   155

Christ, we do all a - dore Thee, and do we praise Thee for-ev - er; Christ, we do

cresc.

all a - dore Thee, and we do praise Thee for - ev - er, for on the ho - ly

mf   *p*   *pp*

cross hast Thou the world from sin re - deem - ed; Christ, we do all a - dore Thee,

pp   *p* > *pp*

and we do praise Thee for ev - er: Christ, we do all a - dore Thee!

Revelation 5:9. Words, Theodore Baker, 1927. Tune ADORAMUS TE CHRISTE, Theodore Dubois, 1867.
Copyright 1927, renewal, G. Schirmer, Inc.

1. Fair - est Lord Je - sus! Rul - er of all na - ture!
2. Fair are the mead - ows, Fair - er still the wood - lands,
3. Fair is the sun - shine, Fair - er still the moon - light,
4. Beau - ti - ful Sav - ior! Lord of all na - tions!

O Thou of God and man the Son! Thee will I cher - ish,
Robed in the bloom-ing garb of spring; Je - sus is fair - er,
And all the twin-kling star - ry host: Je - sus shines bright - er,
Son of God and Son of Man. Glo - ry and hon - or,

Thee will I hon - or, Thou, my soul's glo - ry, joy, and crown.
Je - sus is pur - er, Who makes the woe-ful heart to sing.
Je - sus shines pur - er, Than all the an - gels heav'n can boast.
Praise, ad - o - ra - tion Now and for - ev - er - more be Thine.

Colossians 1:17. Words, Anonymous German Hymn in *Münster Gesangbuch*, 1677; st. 1 and 3, Heinrich von Fallersleben, 1842; st. 2, trans. Richard S. Willis, 1850. Tune SCHÖNSTER HERR JESU, Heinrich von Fallersleben's *Schlesische Volkslieder*, 1842; arr. Richard S. Willis, 1850.

157   Colossians 1:15-17

He is the image of the invisible God, the firstborn of every creature: for by him were all things created, that are in heaven, and that are in earth, visible and invisible, whether they be thrones, or dominions, or principalities, or powers: all things were created by him, and for him: and he is before all things, and by him all things consist.

O Splendor of God's Glory Bright

1. O splen - dor of God's glo - ry bright,
2. Come, ver - y Sun of truth and love,
3. Teach us to work with all our might;
4. All praise to God the Fa - ther be,

Who bring - est forth the light from Light;
Come in Thy ra - diance from a - bove,
Put Sa - tan's fierce as - saults to flight;
All praise, be - lov - ed Son, to Thee,

O Light of light, the foun - tain spring;
And shed the Ho - ly Spir - it's ray
Turn all to good that seems most ill;
Whom with the Spir - it we a - dore,

O Day, our days il - lu - min - ing.
On all we think or do to - day.
Help us our call - ing to ful - fill.
For ev - er and for ev - er - more. A - men.

Hebrews 1:3. Words, Ambrose of Milan, d. 397; trans. Compilers of *Hymns Ancient and Modern*, 1904. Tune
SOLEMNIS HAEC FESTIVITAS, from *Paris Gradual*, 1689. Arr. J.B., Copyright 1986, ACU Press.

159   Jesus is Lord

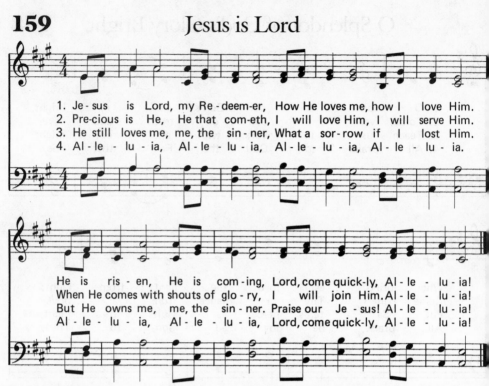

1. Je - sus is Lord, my Re - deem-er, How He loves me, how I love Him.
2. Pre-cious is He, He that com-eth, I will love Him, I will serve Him.
3. He still loves me, me, the sin - ner, What a sor-row if I lost Him.
4. Al - le - lu - ia, Al - le - lu - ia, Al - le - lu - ia, Al - le - lu - ia.

He is ris - en, He is com-ing, Lord, come quick-ly, Al - le - lu - ia!
When He comes with shouts of glo - ry, I will join Him. Al - le - lu - ia!
But He owns me, me, the sin - ner. Praise our Je - sus! Al - le - lu - ia!
Al - le - lu - ia, Al - le - lu - ia, Lord, come quick-ly, Al - le - lu - ia!

Romans 10:9. Words, st. 1, Anonymous; st. 2, Larry Simpson, 1974; st. 3, Jack Boyd, 1974. Tune EGERTHE, arr. Copyright 1974, ACU Press.

160   Creator of the Stars of Night

All voices

1. Cre - a - tor of the stars of night, Thy peo - ple's ev - er -
2. At the great name of Je - sus, now All knees must bend, all
3. Come in Thy ho - ly might, we pray; Re - deem us for e -

last - ing light, O Christ, Thou Sav - ior of us all,
hearts must bow; And things ce - les - tial Thee shall own,
ter - nal day From ev - ery power of dark - ness when

                            *

We pray Thee, hear us when we call.   A - men.
And things ter - res - trial, Lord a - lone.   A - men.
Thou judg - est all the sons of men.   A - men.

*The amen may be used after each stanza.

John 1:1-3. Words, Anonymous Latin, 9th cent.; adpt. from John M. Neale, 1852, in *The Hymnal*, 1940. Used by permission of the Church Pension Fund. Tune CONDITOR ALME, Sarum Plainsong, Mode IV.

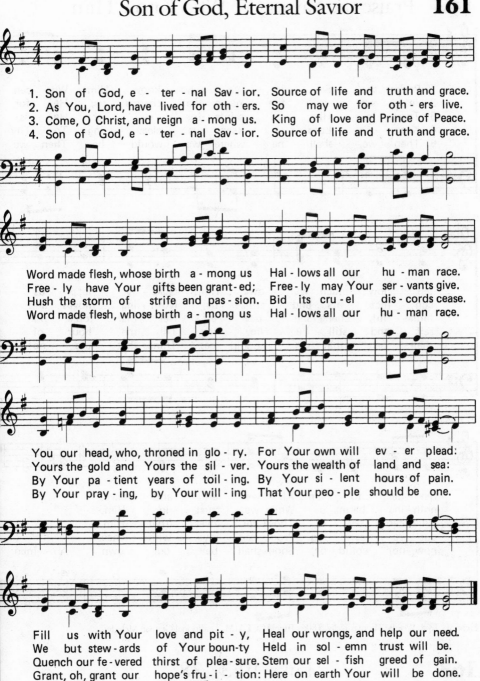

1. Son of God, e - ter - nal Sav - ior. Source of life and truth and grace.
2. As You, Lord, have lived for oth - ers. So may we for oth - ers live.
3. Come, O Christ, and reign a - mong us. King of love and Prince of Peace.
4. Son of God, e - ter - nal Sav - ior. Source of life and truth and grace.

Word made flesh, whose birth a - mong us   Hal - lows all our   hu - man race.
Free - ly have Your gifts been grant - ed;   Free - ly may Your   ser - vants give.
Hush the storm of strife and pas - sion.   Bid its cru - el   dis - cords cease.
Word made flesh, whose birth a - mong us   Hal - lows all our   hu - man race.

You our head, who, throned in glo - ry.   For Your own will   ev - er plead:
Yours the gold and Yours the sil - ver.   Yours the wealth of   land and sea:
By Your pa - tient years of toil - ing.   By Your si - lent   hours of pain.
By Your pray - ing, by Your will - ing   That Your peo - ple   should be one.

Fill us with Your love and pit - y,   Heal our wrongs, and help our need.
We but stew - ards of Your boun - ty   Held in sol - emn   trust will be.
Quench our fe - vered thirst of plea - sure. Stem our sel - fish   greed of gain.
Grant, oh, grant our hope's fru - i - tion: Here on earth Your   will be done.

John 1:14. Words, Somerset C. Lowry, 1893. Copyright Oxford University Press. Tune IN BABILONE, Amsterdam, 1710. Setting Julius Röntgen, 1912.

162   Praise the Savior, Ye Who Know Him

1. Praise the Sav - ior, ye who know Him! Who can
2. Je - sus is the name that charms us; He for
3. Trust in Him, ye saints, for - ev - er; He is
4. Keep us, Lord, O keep us cleav - ing To Thy -
5. Then we shall be where we would be, Then we

tell how much we owe Him? Glad - ly let us
con - flict fits and arms us; Noth - ing moves and
faith - ful, chang - ing nev - er; Nei - ther force nor
self and still be - liev - ing, Till the hour of
shall be what we should be; Things that are not

ren - der to Him All we are and have.
noth - ing harms us While we trust in Him.
guile can sev - er Those He loves from Him.
our re - ceiv - ing Prom - ised joys with Thee.
now, nor could be, Soon shall be our own. A - men.

Hebrews 13:8. Words, Thomas Kelly, 1806. Tune ACCLAIM, Traditional German Melody.

163   Luke 19:37,38

And as he was now drawing nigh, even at the descent of the mount of Olives, the whole multitude of the disciples began to rejoice and praise God with a loud voice for all the mighty works which they had seen; saying, "Blessed is the King that cometh in the name of the Lord: peace in heaven, and glory in the highest."

Hosanna, Loud Hosanna 164

1. Ho - san - na, loud ho - san - na The lit - tle chil - dren sang;
2. From Ol - i - vet they fol - lowed Mid an ex - ult - ant crowd,
3. "Ho - san - na in the high - est!" That an - cient song we sing,

Through pil - lared court and tem - ple The love - ly an - them rang;
The vic - tor palm branch wav - ing, And chant - ing clear and loud;
For Christ is our Re - deem - er, The Lord of heaven our King.

To Je - sus, who had blessed them Close fold - ed to His breast,
The Lord of men and an - gels Rode on in low - ly state,
O may we ev - er praise Him With heart and life and voice,

The chil - dren sang their prais - es, The sim - plest and the best.
Nor scorned that lit - tle chil - dren Should on His bid - ding wait.
And in His bliss - ful pres - ence E - ter - nal - ly re - joice! A - men.

Mark 11:1-10. Words, Jeannette Threlfall, 1856. Tune ELLACOMBE, *Gesangbuch der H. W. K. Hofkapelle*, 1784.

165   I Will Sing the Wondrous Story

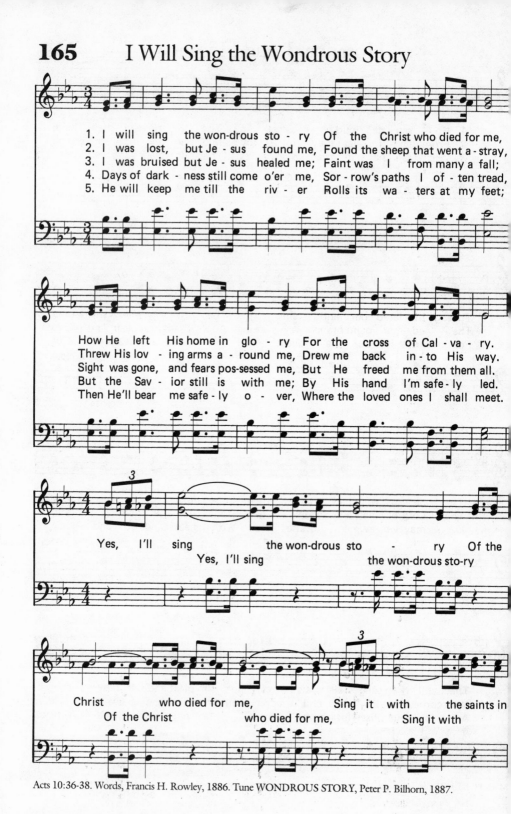

1. I will sing the won-drous sto - ry Of the Christ who died for me,
2. I was lost, but Je - sus found me, Found the sheep that went a - stray,
3. I was bruised but Je - sus healed me; Faint was I from many a fall;
4. Days of dark - ness still come o'er me, Sor - row's paths I of - ten tread,
5. He will keep me till the riv - er Rolls its wa - ters at my feet;

How He left His home in glo - ry For the cross of Cal - va - ry.
Threw His lov - ing arms a - round me, Drew me back in - to His way.
Sight was gone, and fears pos-sessed me, But He freed me from them all.
But the Sav - ior still is with me; By His hand I'm safe - ly led.
Then He'll bear me safe - ly o - ver, Where the loved ones I shall meet.

Yes, I'll sing the won-drous sto - ry Of the
Yes, I'll sing the won-drous sto-ry

Christ who died for me, Sing it with the saints in
Of the Christ who died for me, Sing it with

Acts 10:36-38. Words, Francis H. Rowley, 1886. Tune WONDROUS STORY, Peter P. Bilhorn, 1887.

glo - ry, Gath-ered by the crys-tal sea.
the saints in glo-ry, Gath-ered by the crys-tal sea.

Shepherd of Tender Youth 166

1. Shep - herd of ten - der youth, Guid - ing in love and truth,
2. Thou art the great High Priest; Thou hast pre-pared the feast
3. Ev - er be Thou our guide, Our shep-herd and our pride,
4. So now, and till we die, Sound we Thy prais - es high,

Thro' de - vious ways; Christ, our tri - um - phant King, We come Thy
Of heav'n-ly love; While in our mor - tal pain None call on
Our staff and song; Je - sus, Thou Christ of God, By Thy per-
And joy - ful sing; Let all the ho - ly throng, Who to Thy

name to sing, Hith - er our chil - dren bring To shout Thy praise.
Thee in vain; Help Thou dost not dis - dain, Help from a - bove.
en - nial word, Lead us where Thou hast trod, Make our faith strong.
church be - long, U - nite to swell the song To Christ, our King!

Romans 14:9. Words, Clement of Alexandria, ca. 200; trans. Henry M. Dexter, 1846. Tune KIRBY BEDON,
Edward Bunnett, 1887.

167 All Glory, Laud, and Honor

1. All glo-ry, laud, and hon-or To Thee, Re-deem-er King,
2. The com-pa-ny of an-gels Are prais-ing Thee on high,
3. To Thee, be-fore Thy pas-sion They sang their hymns of praise;

To whom the lips of chil-dren Made sweet ho-san-nas ring.
And mor-tal men and all things Cre-a-ted make re-ply.
To Thee, now high ex-alt-ed, Our mel-o-dy we raise.

Thou art the King of Is-ra-el, Thou Da-vid's roy-al Son,
The peo-ple of the He-brews With palms be-fore Thee went;
Thou didst ac-cept their prais-es; Ac-cept the prayers we bring,

Who in the Lord's name com-est, The King and bless-ed One.
Our praise and prayer and an-thems Be-fore Thee we pre-sent.
Who in all good de-light-est, Thou good and gra-cious King. A-men.

Matthew 21:1-11. Words, Theodulph of Orleans, d. 821; trans. John M. Neale, 1851. Tune ST. THEODULPH, Melchior Teschner, 1615.

Worthy of Praise

168

1. Wor-thy of praise is Christ our Re - deem - er; Wor - thy of glo - ry,
2. Lift up the voice in praise and de - vo - tion, Saints of all earth be -
3. Lord, may we come be - fore Thee with sing - ing, Filled with Thy Spir - it,

hon - or and pow'r! Wor - thy of all our soul's ad - o - ra - tion,
fore Him should bow; An - gels in heav - en wor - ship Him, say - ing,
wis - dom and pow'r: May we as - cribe Thee glo - ry and hon - or,

Wor-thy art Thou! Wor-thy art Thou! Wor-thy of rich-es, bless-ings and
Wor-thy art Thou!

hon - or, Wor-thy of wis-dom, glo-ry and pow'r! Wor-thy of earth and

heav-en's thanks-giv - ing, Wor-thy art Thou! Wor-thy art Thou!
Wor-thy art Thou! art Thou!

Revelation 5:12. Words and tune WORTHY ART THOU, Tillit S. Teddlie, 1930.

169 Praise Him! Praise Him!

1. Praise Him! praise Him! Je - sus our bless-ed Re - deem - er! Sing, O
2. Praise Him! praise Him! Je - sus our bless-ed Re - deem - er! For our
3. Praise Him! praise Him! Je - sus our bless-ed Re - deem - er! Heav'n-ly

Earth, His won-der - ful love pro - claim! Hail Him! hail Him! high-est arch-
sins He suf-fered and bled and died; He, our Rock, our hope of e -
por - tals loud with ho-san - nas ring! Je - sus, Sav - ior, reign-eth for

an - gels in glo - ry; Strength and hon - or give to His ho - ly name!
ter - nal sal - va - tion; Hail Him! hail Him! Je - sus the Cru - ci - fied!
ev - er and ev - er; Crown Him! crown Him! Prophet and Priest and King!

Like a shep - herd, Je - sus will guard His chil - dren; In His arms He
Sound His prais - es! Je - sus who bore our sor - rows, Love un - bound-ed,
Christ is com - ing! o - ver the world vic - to - rious, Pow'r and glo - ry

Revelation 1:5. Words, Fanny J. Crosby, 1869. Tune JOYFUL SONG, Chester G. Allen, 1869.

Come Now, O Lord of Victory **170**

1. Come, now O Lord of vic-to-ry, Your mer-cy here dis-close,
2. Your moth-er's kin-dred now we are, Your Fa-ther's kin-dred we,
3. The gates of heav-en, long de-nied To us through Sa-tan's guile,
4. O Sav-ior, Heal-er, Shap-er, Lord, A-rise, Your works de-fend

Great Mea-sur-er of all man-kind And Con-quor-er of foes.
Down to this mid-dle-earth You came To set Your broth-ers free.
Stand o-pen now, for by Your blood We are no more de-filed.
From that foul, dark, se-duc-ing fiend, And work Your king-dom's end.

Hebrews 2:13. Words, Cynewulf, *Christ*, 8th cent.; trans. Forrest M. McCann, 1984. Tune SIGOR, M. L. Daniels, 1984.

171   Is it for Me?

1. Is it for me, dear Sav-ior, Thy glo-ry and Thy rest— For me, so
2. Is it for me, Thy wel-come, Thy gra-cious "En-ter in"— For me Thy
3. O Sav-ior, pre-cious Sav-ior, My heart is at Thy feet; I bless Thee,
4. I'll be with Thee for ev-er, And nev-er grieve Thee more; Dear Sav-ior,

weak and sin - ful? O shall I be so blest?
"Come, ye bless-ed," For me so full of sin? O Sav-ior, my Re-deem-er,
and I love Thee, And Thee I long to meet.
I must praise Thee, And love Thee ev-er-more.

What can I but a - dore, And mag-ni-fy and praise Thee, And love Thee ev-er-more?

Galatians 2:20. Words, Frances R. Havergal. Tune O'KANE, Tullius C. O'Kane.

172   Matthew 11:28-30

Come unto me, all ye that labor and are heavy laden, and I will give you rest. Take my yoke upon you, and learn of me; for I am meek and lowly in heart: and ye shall find rest unto your souls. For my yoke is easy, and my burden is light.

The Great Physician

1. The great Phy-si - cian now is near, The sym - pa - thiz - ing Je - sus;
2. All glo - ry to the dy-ing Lamb! I now be - lieve in Je - sus;
3. His name dis-pels my guilt and fear, No oth - er name but Je - sus;
4. And when to that bright world a-bove, We rise to see our Je - sus,

He speaks the droop-ing heart to cheer: O hear the voice of Je - sus.
I love the bless - ed Sav - ior's name, I love the name of Je - sus.
O how my soul de - lights to hear The charm-ing name of Je - sus.
We'll sing a - round the throne of love His name, the name of Je - sus.

Sweet-est note in ser - aph song, Sweet-est name on mor - tal tongue,

Sweet-est car - ol ev - er sung, Je - sus, bless - ed Je - sus.

Luke 4:18. Words, William Hunter, 1859. Tune GREAT PHYSICIAN, John H. Stockton, 1869.

174 Blessing and Honor

1. Bless - ing and hon - or and glo - ry and power,
2. Sound - eth the heav'n of the heav'ns with His name;
3. Ev - er as - cend - eth the song and the joy;
4. Give we the glo - ry and praise to the Lamb;

Wis - dom and rich - es and strength ev - er - more
Ring - eth the earth with His glo - ry and fame;
Ev - er de - scend - eth the love from on high;
Take we the robe and the harp and the palm;

Give ye to Him who our bat - tle hath won,
O - cean and moun - tain, stream, for - est, and flower
Bless - ing and hon - or and glo - ry and praise—
Sing we the song of the Lamb that was slain,

Whose are the King - dom, the crown, and the throne.
Ech - o His prais - es and tell of His power.
This is the theme of the hymns that we raise.
Dy - ing in weak - ness, but ris - ing to reign. A - men.

Revelation 5:12. Words, Horatius Bonar, 1866. Tune O QUANTA QUALIA, *Paris Antiphoner*, 1681; adpt. in LaFeillée's *Methode de Plain Chant*, 1808.

Ye Servants of God

175

1. Ye ser - vants of God, your Mas - ter pro - claim,
2. God rul - eth on high, al - might - y to save;
3. "Sal - va - tion to God, who sits on the throne!"
4. Then let us a - dore and give Him His right,

And pub - lish a - broad His won - der - ful name;
And still He is nigh, His pres - ence we have;
Let all cry a - loud and hon - or the Son:
All glo - ry and power, all wis - dom and might,

The name all - vic - to - rious of Je - sus ex - tol;
The great con - gre - ga - tion His tri - umph shall sing,
The prais - es of Je - sus the an - gels pro - claim,
All hon - or and bless - ing, with an - gels a - bove,

His king - dom is glo - rious and rules o - ver all.
As - crib - ing sal - va - tion to Je - sus, our King.
Fall down on their fac - es and wor - ship the Lamb.
And thanks nev - er ceas - ing and in - fi - nite love. A - men.

Revelation 7:9-12. Words, Charles Wesley, 1744. Tune HANOVER, prob. by William Croft, in *Supplement to the New Version*, 1708.

I saw as it were a sea of glass mingled with fire; and them that come off victorious
. . . and they sing the song of Moses the servant of God, and the song of the Lamb,
saying,

> Great and marvelous are thy works, O Lord God, the Almighty; righteous and
> true are thy ways, thou King of the ages. Who shall not fear, O Lord, and
> glorify thy name? For thou only art holy.

177 On Zion's Glorious Summit

1. On Zi-on's glo-rious sum-mit stood A nu-m'rous host re-
2. Here all who suf-fered sword or flame For truth, or Je-sus'
3. While ev-er-last-ing a-ges roll, E-ter-nal love shall

deemed by blood! They hymned their King in strains di-vine; I heard the
love-ly name, Shout vic-t'ry now and hail the Lamb, And bow be-
feast their soul, And scenes of bliss, for ev-er new, Rise in suc-

song and strove to join, I heard the song and strove to join.
fore the great I AM, And bow be-fore the great I AM.
ces-sion to their view, Rise in suc-ces-sion to their view.

Revelation 14:1-3. Words, John Kent, 1803. Tune SKENE, Robert Skene, 1869.

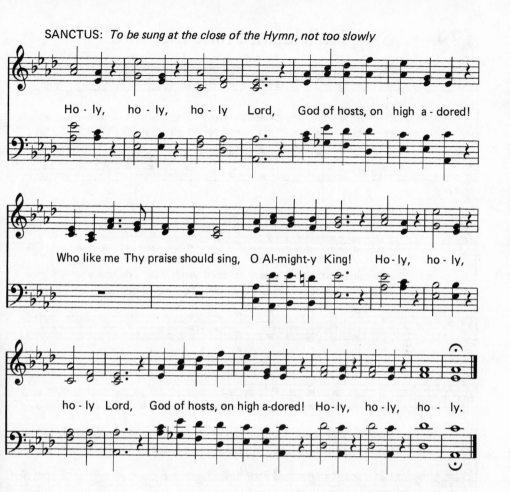

Ho - ly, ho - ly, ho - ly Lord, God of hosts, on high a - dored!

Who like me Thy praise should sing, O Al - might - y King! Ho - ly, ho - ly,

ho - ly Lord, God of hosts, on high a-dored! Ho - ly, ho - ly, ho - ly.

Romans 7:24,25; Ephesians 3:20,21 **178**

Wretched man that I am! Who shall deliver me out of the body of this death? I thank God through Jesus Christ our Lord.

Now unto him that is able to do exceeding abundantly above all that we ask or think, according to the power that worketh in us, unto him be the glory in the church and in Christ Jesus unto all generations for ever and ever. Amen.

179 Sing Hallelujah, Praise the Lord!

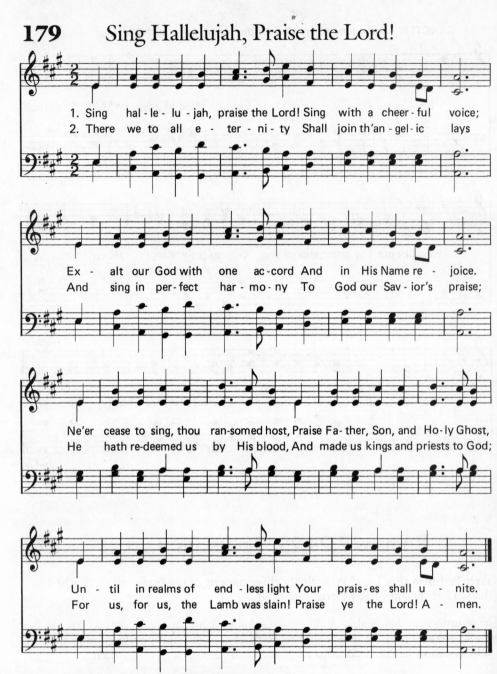

1. Sing hal-le-lu-jah, praise the Lord! Sing with a cheer-ful voice;
2. There we to all e-ter-ni-ty Shall join th'an-gel-ic lays

Ex - alt our God with one ac-cord And in His Name re - joice.
And sing in per-fect har-mo-ny To God our Sav-ior's praise;

Ne'er cease to sing, thou ran-somed host, Praise Fa-ther, Son, and Ho-ly Ghost,
He hath re-deemed us by His blood, And made us kings and priests to God;

Un - til in realms of end - less light Your prais-es shall u - nite.
For us, for us, the Lamb was slain! Praise ye the Lord! A - men.

Ephesians 3:21. Words, John Swertner, 1789. Tune BECHLER, John C. Bechler.

Lo, How a Rose E'er Blooming 180

1. Lo, how a rose e'er bloom - ing From ten - der stem hath sprung,
2. I - sai - ah 'twas fore-told it, The rose I have in mind,
3. This flow'r, whose fragrance ten - der With sweet-ness fills the air,

Of Jes - se's lin - eage com - ing, As men of old have sung.
With Ma - ry we be - hold it, The vir - gin moth - er kind.
Dis - pels with glo - rious splen - dor The dark-ness ev - 'ry - where.

It came, a flow - 'ret bright, A - mid the cold
To show God's love a - right, She bore to them
True Man, yet ver - y God, From sin and death

of win - ter, When half - spent was the night.
a Sav - ior, When half - spent was the night.
He saves us And light - ens ev - ery load.

Isaiah 11:1-9. Words, st. 1 and 2, *Alte Catholische Geistliche Kirchengesäng*, 1599, trans. Theodore Baker, 1894; st. 3, Berlin, 1844, trans. Harriet Spaeth, 1875. Tune ES IST EIN ROS', *Alte Catholische Geistliche Kirchengesäng*, 1599.

181 Watchman, Tell Us of the Night

1. Watch-men, tell us of the night, What its signs of prom-ise are.
2. Watch-men, tell us of the night; High-er yet that star as-cends.
3. Watch-men, tell us of the night, For the morn-ing seems to dawn.

Trav - 'ler, o'er yon moun-tain's height, See that glo - ry - beam-ing star.
Trav - 'ler, bless-ed - ness and light, Peace and truth its course por-tends.
Trav - 'ler, dark - ness takes its flight, Doubt and ter - ror are with-drawn.

Watch-man, does its beau-teous ray Aught of joy or hope fore - tell?
Watch-man, will its beams a - lone Gild the spot that gave them birth?
Watch-man, let thy wan-d'rings cease; Hie thee to thy qui - et home.

Trav-'ler, yes; it brings the day, Prom-ised day of Is - ra - el.
Trav-'ler, a - ges are its own; See, it bursts o'er all the earth.
Trav-'ler, lo! the Prince of Peace, Lo! the Son of God is come!

Numbers 24:17. Words, John Bowring, 1825. Tune ABERYSTWYTH, Joseph Parry, 1879. Arr. J.B., Copyright 1986, ACU Press.

O Come, O Come, Emmanuel 182

1. O come, O come, Em - man - u - el, And ran - som
2. O come, Thou Day - spring, come and cheer Our spir - its
3. O come, Thou Wis - dom from on high, And or - der
4. O come, De - sire of na - tions, bind All peo - ples

cap - tive Is - ra - el. That mourns in lone - ly
by Thine ad - vent here; Dis - perse the gloom - y
all things, far and nigh; To us the path of
in one heart and mind; Bid en - vy, strife and

ex - ile here, Un - til the Son of God ap - pear.
clouds of night, And death's dark shad-ows put to flight.
knowl - edge show, And cause us in her ways to go.
quar - rels cease; Fill the whole world with heav - en's peace.

Re - joice, re - joice! Em - man - u - el

Shall come to thee, O Is - ra - el!

Isaiah 7:14; 9:6,7. Words, based on ancient Antiphons; *Psalteriolum Cantionum Catholicarum*, 1710; st. 1 and 2, trans. John M. Neale, 1851; st. 3 and 4, Henry Sloan Coffin, 1916. Tune VENI EMMANUEL, adpt. from Plainsong, Mode I by Thomas Helmore, 1854. Arr. J.B., Copyright 1986, ACU Press.

183 Comfort, Comfort Now My People

1. "Com-fort, com-fort now my peo - ple; Tell of peace!" So says our God.
2. For the her - ald's voice is cry - ing In the des - ert far and near,
3. Straight shall be what long was crook - ed, And the rough - er plac - es plain!

Com-fort those who sit in dark - ness, Mourn-ing un - der sor - row's load.
Call - ing us to true re - pen - tance, Since the King-dom now is here.
Let your hearts be true and hum - ble, As be - fits His ho - ly reign!

To God's peo - ple now pro - claim That God's par - don waits for them!
Oh, that warn - ing cry o - bey! Now pre - pare for God a way!
For the glo - ry of the Lord Now on earth is shed a - broad,

Tell them that their war is o - ver, God will reign in peace for - ev - er!
Let the val - leys rise to meet Him, And the hills bow down to greet Him!
And all flesh shall see the to - ken That God's word is nev - er bro - ken.

Isaiah 40:1,2. Words, Johann Olearius, 1671; trans. Catherine Winkworth, 1863. Tune FREU DICH SEHR, *Trente quatre Pseaumes de David*, 1551.

Come, Give Now to Christ All Honor **184**

1. Come, give now to Christ all hon - or, Heart and
2. See what God in love has giv - en, Life e -
3. Hal - lowed be that hour re - deem - ing, When Thee
4. Ra - diant Child with - in the stall, Thou, be -

mind bend to His pow - er; Sing with joy, make
ter - nal, His Son ris - en, Who shall free us
in our hearts re - ceiv - ing, Prais - ing Thee with
friend and bring us all There - in where fair

heard the hour, Sing, ye folk of Chris - ten - dom.
from our pris - on, Lift from pain to Heav - en's joy.
lips be - liev - ing, We con - fess Thee, Je - sus Christ.
sounds en - thrall— An - gel hosts sing prais - ing Thee.

Luke 2:7-14. Words, Paul Gerhardt, 1667; trans. Copyright The Plough Pub. House. Tune from Hohenfurth Manuscript, 1410.

Isaiah 40:1,3-5 **185**

Comfort ye, comfort ye my people, saith your God.
The voice of him that crieth in the wilderness,
Prepare ye the way of the Lord, make straight in the desert a highway
    for our God.
Every valley shall be exalted, and every mountain and hill shall be made low:
    and the crooked shall be made straight, and the rough places plain:
And the glory of the Lord shall be revealed, and all flesh shall see it together:
for the mouth of the Lord hath spoken it.

186 How Brightly Beams the Morning Star

1. How bright-ly beams the morn-ing star! What sud-den ra-diance
2. Through Thee a-lone can we be blest; Then deep be on our
3. All praise to Him who came to save, Who con-quered death and

from a-far Doth cheer us with its shin-ing?
hearts im-prest The love that Thou hast borne us;
scorned the grave; Each day new praise re-sound-eth

Bright-ness of God, that breaks our night And fills the dark-ened
So make us read-y to ful-fill With ar-dent zeal Thy
To Him, the Life who once was slain, The friend whom none shall

souls with light, Who long for truth were pin-ing!
ho-ly will, Though men may vex or scorn us;
trust in vain, Whose grace for aye a-bound-eth;

Matthew 2:1,2. Words, Philipp Nicolai, 1597; trans. from *The Lutheran Service Book and Hymnal*, 1955, by permission of the Commission on the Liturgy and Hymnal. Tune WIE SCHÖN LEUCHTET DER MORGENSTERN, Philipp Nicolai, 1599; Arr. J.B., Copyright 1986, ACU Press.

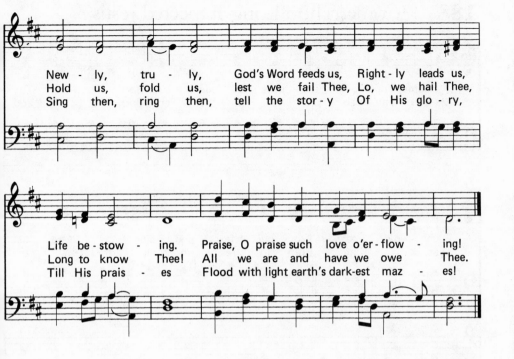

New - ly, tru - ly, God's Word feeds us, Right - ly leads us,
Hold us, fold us, lest we fail Thee, Lo, we hail Thee,
Sing then, ring then, tell the stor - y Of His glo - ry,

Life be - stow - ing. Praise, O praise such love o'er - flow - ing!
Long to know Thee! All we are and have we owe Thee.
Till His prais - es Flood with light earth's dark-est maz - es!

Matthew 2:1-6   **187**

Now when Jesus was born in Bethlehem of Judea in the days of Herod the king, behold, wise men from the east came to Jerusalem, saying, "Where is he that is born King of the Jews? For we saw his star in the east, and are come to worship him." And when Herod the king heard it, he was troubled, and all Jerusalem with him. And gathering together all the chief priests and scribes of the people, he inquired of them where the Christ should be born. And they said unto him, "In Bethlehem of Judea: for thus it is written through the prophet,

'And thou Bethlehem, land of Judah,
Art in no wise least among the princes of Judah:
For out of thee shall come forth a governor,
Who shall be shepherd of my people Israel.' "

188 Come, Thou Long-Expected Jesus

1. Come, Thou long - ex - pect - ed Je - sus, Born to set Thy
2. Born Thy peo - ple to de - liv - er, Born a child, and

peo - ple free; From our fears and sins re - lease us;
yet a King, Born to reign in us for - ev - er,

Let us find our rest in Thee. Is - rael's strength and con - so -
Now Thy gra - cious king - dom bring. By Thine own e - ter - nal

la - tion, Hope of all the earth Thou art; Dear de - sire of
spir - it Rule in all our hearts a - lone; By Thine all - suf -

ev - 'ry na - tion, Joy of ev - 'ry long - ing heart.
fi - cient mer - it, Raise us to Thy glo - rious throne. A - men.

Haggai 2:6-9. Words, Charles Wesley, 1744. Tune HYFRYDOL, Rowland H. Prichard, c. 1830.

O How Shall I Receive Thee?

189

1. O how shall I re - ceive Thee, How meet Thee on Thy way,
2. Thy Zi - on palms is strew - ing, And branch-es fresh and fair;
3. Love caused Thy in - car - na - tion; Love brought Thee down to me.
4. Thou com - est, Lord, with glad - ness, In mer - cy and good will,

Blest hope of ev - ery na - tion, My soul's de - light and stay?
My soul, to praise a - wak - ing, Her an - them shall pre - pare.
Thy thirst for my sal - va - tion Pro - cured my lib - er - ty.
To bring an end to sad - ness And bid our fears be still.

O Je - sus, Je - sus, give me Now by Thy own pure light
Un - end - ing thanks and prais - es From my glad heart shall spring;
O love be - yond all tell - ing, That led Thee to em - brace,
We wel - come Thee, our Sav - ior; Come gath - er us to Thee,

To know what-e'er is pleas - ing And wel-come in Thy sight.
And to Thy name the serv - ice Of all my powers I bring.
In love all love ex - cell - ing, Our lost and trou - bled race.
That in Thy light e - ter - nal Our joy - ous home may be.

Psalm 118:25,26. Words, Paul Gerhardt, 1653; trans. Arthur Tozer Russell, 1851. Tune VALET WILL ICH DIR GEBEN, Melchior Teschner, 1613.

190 The Greatness of God

1. The great-ness of God in His love has been shown,
2. He rolls the grim dark-ness and sor-row a - way
3. And, though we have sinned like the Prod-i-gal Son,
4. The Light of the World is more clear to our sight

The light of His life on the na - tions is shown; And
And brings all our fears to the light of the day; The
His love to our suc - cour and wel - come will run. His
As er - rors dis - perse and men see Him a - right: In

that which the Jews and the Greeks did di - vine
i - dols are fall - en of an - ger and blood,
gos - pel of par - don, of love and ac - cord,
lands long in shad - ow, His Church - es a - rise

Is come in the full - ness of Je - sus to shine:
And God is re - vealed as the lov - ing and good;
Will mas - ter op - pres - sion and shat - ter the sword:
And blaze for their neigh - bors the Way of the Wise:

1 John 2:8. Words, Traditional English Carol. Tune INFINITE LIGHT, Traditional English Carol.

The Light of the World in the dark-ness has shone,

And grows in our sight as the a-ges flow on.

Lift Up Your Heads, Ye Mighty Gates **191**

1. Lift up your heads, ye might-y gates; Be-hold, the King
2. Fling wide the por-tals of your heart; Make it a tem-
3. Re-deem-er, come, with us a-bide; Our hearts to Thee

of glo-ry waits; The King of kings is draw-ing
ple, set a-part From earth-ly use for heaven's em-
we o-pen wide; Let us Thy in-ner pres-ence

near; The Sav-ior of the world is here!
ploy, A-dorned with prayer and love and joy.
feel; Thy grace and love in us re-veal. A-men.

Psalm 24:7-9. Words, Georg Weissel, 1642; trans. Catherine Winkworth, 1855. Tune TRURO, from Thomas
Williams' *Psalmodia Evangelica*, 1789.

192 Let All Together Praise Our God

1. Let all to-geth-er praise our God Up-on His loft-y throne;
2. He lays a-side His maj-es-ty And seems as noth-ing worth,
3. Be-hold the won-der-ful ex-change Our Lord with us does make!
4. The glo-rious gates of par-a-dise The an-gel guards no more;

For He un-clos-es heav'n to-day And gives to us His
And takes on Him a serv-ant's form, Who made the heav'n and
Lo, He as-sumes our flesh and blood, And we of heav'n par-
This day a-gain those gates un-fold. With praise our God a-

Son, And gives to us His Son.
earth, Who made the heav'n and earth.
take, And we of heav'n par-take.
dore, With praise our God a-dore! A-men.

Philippians 2:5-7. Words, Nicolaus Herman, c. 1554; trans. Arthur Tozer Russell, 1851. Tune LOBT GOTT, IHR CHRISTEN, Nicolaus Herman, 1554.

O Little Town of Bethlehem 193

1. O   lit - tle town of   Beth - le - hem, How   still   we   see thee   lie!
2. For   Christ is born of   Ma —   ry, And   gath -ered   all   a -   bove,
3. How   si - lent - ly, how   si - lent - ly, The   won-drous gift   is   giv'n!
4. O   ho - ly Child of   Beth - le - hem, De - scend   to   us, we   pray,

A - bove thy deep and   dream - less sleep The   si - lent stars go   by;
While   mor - tals sleep, the   an - gels keep Their   watch of won-d'ring love;
So   God im - parts to   hu - man hearts The   bless - ings of His heav'n;
Cast   out our sin, and   en - ter in— Be   born in us   to - day;

Yet   in   thy dark streets shin - eth The   ev - er - last - ing   Light;
O   morn - ing stars, to - geth - er Pro - claim the ho - ly   birth;
No   ear may hear His   com - ing; But   in this world of   sin,
We   hear the ho - ly   an - gels The   great glad ti - dings   tell;

The   hopes and fears of   all   the years Are   met   in   thee   to - night.
And   prais - es sing to   God the King, And   peace   to   men   on   earth.
Where meek souls will re - ceive Him, still The   dear Christ en - ters   in.
O   come to us, a - bide with us, Our   Lord Em - man - u - el!

Matthew 2:6. Words, Philips Brooks, 1868. Tune ST. LOUIS, Lewis H. Redner, 1868.

194 Angels, From the Realms of Glory

1. An - gels, from the realms of glo - ry, Wing your flight o'er
2. Shep - herds, in the field a - bid - ing, Watch - ing o'er your
3. Sa - ges, leave your con - tem - pla - tions; Bright - er vi - sions
4. Saints, be - fore the al - tar bend - ing, Watch - ing long in

all the earth; Ye who sang cre - a - tion's sto - ry
flocks by night, God with man is now re - sid - ing;
beam a - far; Seek the great De - sire of na - tions;
hope and fear, Sud - den - ly the Lord, de - scend - ing,

Now pro - claim Mes - si - ah's birth: Come and wor - ship,
Yon - der shines the in - fant light: Come and wor - ship,
Ye have seen His na - tal star: Come and wor - ship,
In His tem - ple shall ap - pear: Come and wor - ship,

Come and wor - ship, Wor - ship Christ, the new - born King.
Come and wor - ship, Wor - ship Christ, the new - born King.
Come and wor - ship, Wor - ship Christ, the new - born King.
Come and wor - ship, Wor - ship Christ, the new - born King. A - men.

Matthew 2:1,2. Words, James Montgomery, 1816. Tune REGENT SQUARE, Henry Smart, 1867.

It Came Upon the Midnight Clear **195**

1. It came up-on the mid-night clear, That glo-rious song of old,
2. Still through the clo-ven skies they come With peace-ful wings un-furled,
3. Yet with the woes of sin and strife The world has suf-fered long;
4. For lo! the days are has-tening on, By proph-ets seen of old,

From an-gels bend-ing near the earth, To touch their harps of gold:
And still their heaven-ly mu-sic floats O'er all the wea-ry world;
Be-neath the an-gel-strain have rolled Two thou-sand years of wrong;
When with the ev-er-cir-cling years Shall come the time fore-told

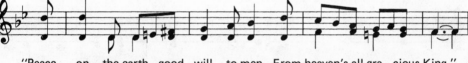

"Peace on the earth, good will to men, From heaven's all-gra-cious King."
A-bove its sad and low-ly plains They bend on hov-ering wing,
And men, at war with men, hear not The love-song which they bring:
When the whole heav'n and earth shall own The Prince of Peace their King,

The world in sol-emn still-ness lay, To hear the an-gels sing.
And ev-er o'er its Ba-bel sounds The bless-ed an-gels sing.
O hush the noise, ye men of strife, And hear the an-gels sing.
And the whole world send back the song Which now the an-gels sing.

Isaiah 9:6,7. Words, Edmund H. Sears, 1849. Tune CAROL, Richard S. Willis, 1850.

196 ## Gentle Mary Laid Her Child

1. Gen - tle Ma - ry laid her child Low - ly in a man - ger;
2. An - gels sang a - bout His birth; Wise men sought and found Him;
3. Gen - tle Ma - ry laid her child Low - ly in a man - ger;

There He lay, the un - de - filed, To the world a stran - ger.
Heav - en's star shone bright - ly forth, Glo - ry all a - round Him.
He is still the un - de - filed, But no more a stran - ger.

Such a babe in such a place, Can He be the Sav - ior?
Shep - herds saw the won - drous sight, Heard the an - gels sing - ing:
Son of God, of hum - ble birth, Beau - ti - ful the sto - ry;

Ask the saved of all the race Who have found His fa - vor.
All the plains were lit that night; All the hills were ring - ing.
Praise His name in all the earth; Hail the King of glo - ry!

Luke 2:7. Words, Joseph S. Cook, 1919. Copyright 1956, 1958, by Gordon V. Thompson, Ltd., Toronto. Used by permission of Carl Fischer, Inc., New York. Tune TEMPUS ADEST FLORIDUM, from Theodoricus Petrus' *Piae Cantiones*, 1582.

While Shepherds Watched

1. While shep-herds watched their flocks by night, All seat-ed
2. "Fear not!" said he; for might-y dread Had seized their
3. "To you, in Da-vid's town, this day Is born, of
4. "All glo-ry be to God on high, And to the

on the ground, The an-gel of the Lord came down.
trou-bled mind; "Glad ti-dings of great joy I bring
Da-vid's line, The Sav-ior who is Christ the Lord,
earth be peace: Good will hence-forth from heav'n to men

And glo-ry shone a-round, And glo-ry shone a-round.
To you and all man-kind, To you and all man-kind.
And this shall be the sign: And this shall be the sign:
Be-gin and nev-er cease! Be-gin and nev-er cease!"

Luke 2:8-14. Words, Nahum Tate, 1700. Tune CHRISTMAS; arr. from George F. Handel, 1728, in James Hewitt's *Harmonia Sacra*, 1812.

Luke 2:8-11

And there were in the same country shepherds abiding in the field, keeping watch over their flock by night. And, lo, the angel of the Lord came upon them, and the glory of the Lord shone round about them: and they were sore afraid. And the angel said unto them, "Fear not: for, behold, I bring you good tidings of great joy, which shall be to all people. For unto you is born this day in the city of David a Savior, which is Christ the Lord."

199 From Heaven Above

1. From heav'n a - bove to earth I come To bring good news to ev - 'ry - one! Glad tid - ings of great joy I bring To all the world and glad - ly sing.
2. To you this night is born a child Of Ma - ry, cho - sen vir - gin mild; This new - born child of low - ly birth Shall be the joy of all the earth.
3. This is the Christ, God's Son most high, Who hears your sad and bit - ter cry; He will Him - self your Sav - ior be And from all sin will set you free.
4. The bless - ing which the Fa - ther planned The Son holds in His in - fant hand, That in His king - dom, bright and fair, You may with us His glo - ry share.
5. My heart for ver - y joy now leaps; My voice no long - er si - lence keeps; I too must join the an - gel throng To sing with joy His cra - dle - song.
6. "Glo - ry to God in high - est heav'n, Who un - to us His Son has giv'n." With an - gels sing in pi - ous mirth: A glad new year to all the earth! A - men.

Luke 2:11-14. Words, Martin Luther, 1535; trans. Copyright Inter-Lutheran Commission on Worship in *Lutheran Book of Worship*, 1978. Tune VOM HIMMEL HOCH, Martin Luther, 1539.

1. Break forth, O beau-teous heaven-ly light, And ush-er in the morn - ing; Ye shep-herds, shrink not with af - fright, But hear the an - gel's warn - ing. This child, now weak in in - fan-cy, Our con - fi - dence and joy shall be, The power of Sa - tan break - ing, Our peace e - ter - nal mak - ing.

John 1:4,5. Words, Johann Rist, 1641; trans. John Troutbeck, ca. 1880. Tune ERMUNTRE DICH, Johann Schop, 1641.

201 Angels We Have Heard on High

1. An - gels we have heard on high Sweet - ly sing - ing o'er the plains
2. Shep - herds, why this ju - bi - lee? Why your joy - ous strains pro - long?
3. Come to Beth - le - hem and see Him whose birth the an - gels sing;

And the moun - tains in re - ply Ech - o - ing their joy - ous strains.
What the glad - some tid - ings be Which in - spire your heaven - ly song?
Come, a - dore on bend - ed knee Christ, the Lord, the new - born King.

Glo - - - - - - - ri - a

in ex - cel - sis De - o, Glo - - - -

Luke 2:14. Words, Traditional French Carol, *Nouveau recueil de cantiques*, 1855; trans. *Crown of Jesus*, 1862.
Tune GLORIA, Traditional French Carol, *Nouveau recueil de cantiques*, 1855.

ri - a   in ex - cel - sis De -   o.

Silent Night, Holy Night   202

1. Si - lent night,   ho - ly night,   All   is   calm,   all   is bright
2. Si - lent night,   ho - ly night,   Shep-herds quake   at   the sight,
3. Si - lent night,   ho - ly night,   Son   of   God,   love's pure light
4. Si - lent night,   ho - ly night,   Won-drous star,   lend thy light;

Round yon vir - gin moth-er and child.   Ho - ly in-fant so   ten-der and mild,
Glo - ries stream from heav-en a - far,   Heav'n-ly hosts sing   Al - le - lu - ia;
Ra - diant beams from Thy ho - ly face,   With the dawn of re - deem - ing grace,
With the an - gels let   us sing,   Al - le - lu - ia   to   our King;

Sleep   in heav -en - ly   peace,   Sleep   in heav - en - ly   peace.
Christ the Sav - ior is   born!   Christ   the Sav - ior is   born!
Je - sus, Lord, at Thy   birth,   Je - sus, Lord, at Thy   birth.
Christ the Sav - ior is   born,   Christ   the Sav - ior is   born.

Luke 2:8-11. Words, Joseph Mohr, 1818; trans. John F. Young, 1863. Tune STILLE NACHT,
Franz Gruber, 1818.

203 Hark! The Herald Angels Sing

1. Hark! the her - ald an - gels sing, "Glo - ry to the new-born King;
2. Mild He lays His glo - ry by, Born that man no more may die,
3. Hail the heaven-born Prince of Peace! Hail the Sun of Righ-teous-ness!

Peace on earth, and mer - cy mild, God and sin - ners rec - on - ciled!"
Born to raise the sons of earth, Born to give them sec - ond birth.
Light and life to all He brings, Risen with heal - ing in His wings,

Joy - ful, all ye na - tions rise, Join the tri - umph of the skies;
Veiled in flesh the God - head see; Hail th'in - car - nate De - i - ty,
Christ, by high - est heaven a - dored; Christ, the ev - er - last - ing Lord!

With th'an - gel - ic hosts pro - claim, "Christ is born in Beth - le - hem!"
Pleased as man with men to dwell, Je - sus, our Em - man - u - el.
Come, De - sire of na - tions come, Fix in us Thy hum - ble home.

Malachi 4:2. Words, Charles Wesley, 1739. Tune MENDELSSOHN, Felix Mendelssohn, 1840; arr. William H. Cummings, 1855.

Hark! the her - ald an - gels sing, "Glo - ry to the new-born King!"

Away in a Manger

204

1. A - way in a man-ger, no crib for a bed, The lit - tle Lord
2. The cat - tle are low - ing, the ba - by a - wakes, But lit - tle Lord
3. Be near me, Lord Je - sus, I ask Thee to stay Close by me for -

Je - sus laid down His sweet head. The stars in the sky looked
Je - sus, no cry - ing He makes. I love Thee, Lord Je - sus, look
ev - er, and love me, I pray; Bless all the dear chil-dren in

down where He lay, The lit - tle Lord Je - sus, a - sleep on the hay.
down from the sky, And stay by my cra - dle till morn-ing is nigh.
Thy ten - der care, And take us to glo - ry to live with Thee there.

Luke 2:7. Words, st. 1,2, Anonymous, c. 1884; st. 3, John T. McFarland, c. 1892. Tune AWAY IN A MANGER, James R. Murray, 1887.

2 Corinthians 8:9

205

For ye know the grace of our Lord Jesus Christ, that, though he was rich, yet for your sakes he became poor, that ye through his poverty might become rich.

206 ## Good Christian Men, Rejoice

1. Good Chris-tian men, re - joice With heart and soul and voice!
2. Good Chris-tian men, re - joice With heart and soul and voice!
3. Good Chris-tian men, re - joice With heart and soul and voice!

Give ye heed to what we say: Je - sus Christ is born to - day.
Now ye hear of end - less bliss: Je - sus Christ was born for this.
Now ye need not fear the grave: Je - sus Christ was born to save:

Man and beast be - fore Him bow, And He is in the man - ger now:
He hath o - pened heav - en's door, And man is blest for - ev - er - more.
Calls you one and calls you all, To gain His ev - er - last - ing hall.

Christ is born to - day, Christ is born to - day!
Christ was born for this, Christ was born for this!
Christ was born to save, Christ was born to save!

John 18:37. Words, Medieval Latin Carol, 14th cent.; trans. John Mason Neale, 1853. Tune IN DULCI JUBILO, Traditional German Carol, 14th cent.

What Child is This?

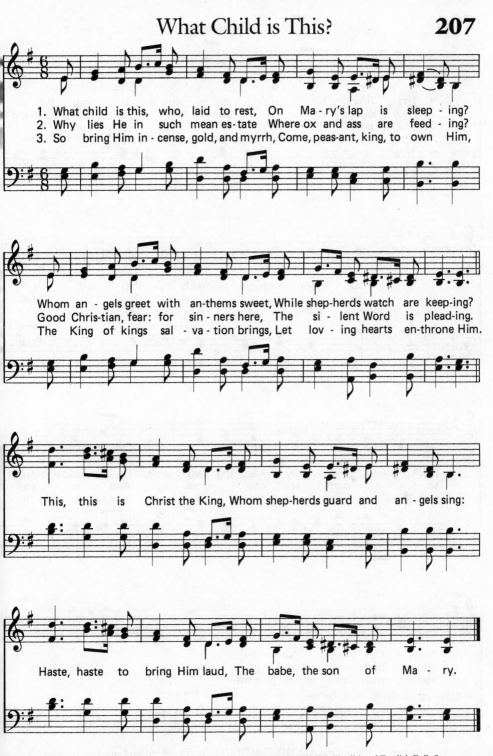

1. What child is this, who, laid to rest, On Ma-ry's lap is sleep-ing?
2. Why lies He in such mean es-tate Where ox and ass are feed-ing?
3. So bring Him in-cense, gold, and myrrh, Come, peas-ant, king, to own Him,

Whom an-gels greet with an-thems sweet, While shep-herds watch are keep-ing?
Good Chris-tian, fear: for sin-ners here, The si-lent Word is plead-ing.
The King of kings sal-va-tion brings, Let lov-ing hearts en-throne Him.

This, this is Christ the King, Whom shep-herds guard and an-gels sing:

Haste, haste to bring Him laud, The babe, the son of Ma-ry.

Matthew 2:11. Words, William Chatterton Dix, 1865. Tune GREENSLEEVES, Traditional English Folk Song, 16th cent.

The First Noel

1. The first No - el, the an - gel did say, Was to cer - tain poor shep - herds in fields as they lay; In fields where they lay keep - ing their sheep, On a cold win - ter's night that was so deep. No - el, No - el, No -

2. They look - ed up and saw a star Shin - ing in the east, be - yond them far; And to the earth it gave great light, And so it con - tin - ued both day and night. No - el, No - el, No -

3. And by the light of that same star The wise men came from coun - try far; To seek for a king was their in - tent, And to fol - low the star wher - ev - er it went.

Luke 2:8-11; Matthew 2:12. Words and tune THE FIRST NOEL, Traditional English Carol; tune arr. John Stainer, 1871.

el, No - el, Born is the King of Is - ra - el.

Infant Holy, Infant Lowly 209

1. In - fant ho - ly, In - fant low - ly, For His bed a
2. Flocks were sleep - ing; Shep-herds keep - ing Vig - il till the

cat - tle stall; Ox - en low - ing, Lit - tle know - ing
morn-ing new Saw the glo - ry, Heard the sto - ry,

Christ the babe is Lord of all. Swift are wing - ing An - gels sing - ing,
Tid - ings of a Gos-pel true. Thus re - joic - ing, Free from sor - row,

No - els ring - ing, Tid - ings bring - ing: Christ the babe is Lord of all.
Prais-es voic - ing Greet the mor - row: Christ the babe was born for you.

Luke 2:8-11. Words, Polish Carol; paraphrase Edith M. G. Reed, c. 1925. Used by permission of Evans Brothers, Ltd. Tune W ZLOBIE LEZY, Polish Carol; arr. J.B., Copyright 1986, ACU Press.

210   O Come, All Ye Faithful

1. O come, all ye faith-ful, Joy-ful and tri-um-phant, O come ye, O
2. Sing choirs of an-gels, Sing in ex-ul-ta-tion, O sing, all ye
3. Yea, Lord, we bless Thee, Born for our sal-va-tion; O Je-sus, for

come ye, to Beth - le - hem; Come and a - dore Him,
cit - i - zens of heav - en a - bove! Glo - ry to God, all
ev - er be Thy Name a - dored; Word of the Fa - ther,

Born the King of an - gels;
glo - ry in the high - est; O come, let us a - dore Him, O come, let
Now in flesh ap - pear - ing;

us a - dore Him, O come, let us a - dore Him, Christ, the Lord.

Luke 2:15. Words, Latin Hymn; attr. to John Francis Wade, ca. 1743; trans. Frederick Oakeley, 1841, and others.
Tune ADESTE FIDELES, John Francis Wade, 1743.

Brightest and Best

1. Bright - est and best of the sons of the morn - ing,
Dawn on our dark - ness and lend us Thine aid;
Star of the East, the ho - ri - zon a - dorn - ing,
Guide where our in - fant Re - deem - er is laid.

2. Cold on His cra - dle the dew - drops are shin - ing;
Low lies His head with the beasts of the stall;
An - gels a - dore Him in slum - ber re - clin - ing,
Mak - er and Mon - arch and Sav - ior of all.

3. Vain - ly we of - fer each am - ple ob - la - tion;
Vain - ly with gifts would His fa - vor se - cure;
Rich - er by far is the heart's ad - o - ra - tion;
Dear - er to God are the prayers of the poor.

4. Bright - est and best of the sons of the morn - ing,
Dawn on our dark - ness and lend us Thine aid;
Star of the East, the ho - ri - zon a - dorn - ing,
Guide where our in - fant Re - deem - er is laid.

Luke 1:46,47. Words, Reginald Heber, 1827. Tune MORNING STAR, James P. Harding, 1892.

212 Night With Ebon Pinion

1. Night with eb - on pin - ion, Brood - ed o'er the vale;
2. Smit - ten for of - fen - ses Which were not His own,
3. "Ab - ba Fa - ther, Fa - ther, If in - deed it may,

All a - round was si - lent, Save the night wind's wail,
He, for our trans - gres - sions, Had to weep a - lone;
Let this cup of an - guish Pass from Me, I pray;

When Christ, the Man of Sor - rows, In tears and sweat and blood,
No friend with words to com - fort, Nor hand to help was there,
Yet, if it must be suf - fered, By Me, Thine on - ly Son,

Pros - trate in the gar - den, Raised His voice to God.
When the Meek and Low - ly Hum - bly bowed in prayer.
Ab - ba, Fa - ther, Fa - ther, Let Thy will be done."

Luke 22:44. Words, Love H. Jameson, d. 1892. Tune EBON PINION, Joseph P. Powell, 1883. *Note: "ebon pinion" (st. 1) i.e. "black wing," a metaphor for the deepest darkness.*

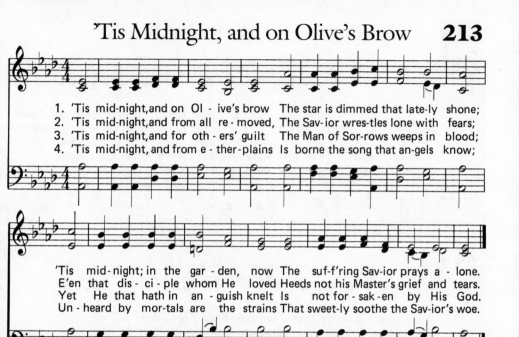

1. 'Tis mid-night, and on Ol - ive's brow   The star is dimmed that late-ly shone;
2. 'Tis mid-night, and from all re - moved,   The Sav-ior wres-tles lone with fears;
3. 'Tis mid-night, and for oth - ers' guilt   The Man of Sor-rows weeps in blood;
4. 'Tis mid-night, and from e - ther-plains   Is borne the song that an-gels know;

'Tis   mid-night; in the gar - den, now   The suf-f'ring Sav-ior prays a - lone.
E'en   that dis - ci - ple whom He   loved Heeds not his Master's grief and tears.
Yet   He that hath in   an - guish knelt   Is   not for - sak - en   by His God.
Un - heard by   mor-tals are   the strains   That sweet-ly soothe the Sav-ior's woe.

Mark 14:32-38. Words, William B. Tappan, 1822. Tune OLIVE'S BROW, William B. Bradbury, 1853.

Mark 14:26, 32-36   **214**

And when they had sung a hymn, they went out into the mount of Olives . . . And they came to a place which was named Gethsemane: and he saith to his disciples, "Sit ye here, while I shall pray." And he taketh with him Peter and James and John, and began to be sore amazed, and to grow very heavy; and saith unto them, "My soul is exceedingly sorrowful unto death: tarry ye here, and watch." And he went forward a little, and fell on the ground, and prayed that, if it were possible, the hour might pass from him. And he said, "Abba, Father, all things are possible unto thee; take away this cup from me: nevertheless not what I will, but what thou wilt."

215 ## Alas! And Did My Savior Bleed?

1. A - las! and did my Sav - ior bleed? And did my Sov - 'reign die?
2. Was it for crimes that I have done He groaned up - on the tree?
3. Well might the sun in dark - ness hide, And shut his glo - ries in,
4. Thus might I hide my blush - ing face While His dear cross ap - pears;
5. But drops of grief can ne'er re - pay The debt of love I owe:

Would He de - vote that sa - cred head For such a one as I?
A - maz - ing pit - y! grace un - known! And love be - yond de - gree!
When Christ, the might - y Mak - er, died For man, the crea - ture's sin.
Dis - solve my heart in thank - ful - ness, And melt mine eyes to tears.
Here, Lord, I give my - self a - way, 'Tis all that I can do!

Chorus following the final stanza only

At the cross, at the cross where I first saw the light, And the

bur - den of my heart rolled a - way (rolled a - way), It was there by faith

Isaiah 53:4. Words, Isaac Watts, 1707; refrain, Ralph E. Hudson, 1885. Tune HUDSON,
Ralph E. Hudson, 1885.

I re-ceived my sight, And now I am hap-py all the day!

Ride On! Ride On in Majesty! 216

1. Ride on! ride on in ma-jes-ty! Hark! all the tribes ho-
2. Ride on! ride on in ma-jes-ty! In low-ly pomp ride
3. Ride on! ride on in ma-jes-ty! The an-gel ar-mies

san - na cry; Thy hum-ble beast pur - sues his road
on to die: O Christ, Thy tri - umphs now be - gin
of the sky Look down with sad and won - d'ring eyes

With palms and scat - ter'd gar - ments strowed.
O'er cap - tive death and con - quer'd sin.
To see the ap - proach - ing sac - ri - fice. A - men.

Matthew 21:1-11. Words, Henry H. Milman, 1827. Tune WINCHESTER, NEW, Georg Rebenlein's *Musicalische Handbuch*, 1690; arr. William H. Havergal, 1847.

217 There is a Fountain Filled With Blood

1. There is a foun - tain filled with blood Drawn
2. The dy - ing thief re - joiced to see That
3. Dear dy - ing Lamb, Thy pre - cious blood Shall
4. E'er since, by faith, I saw that stream Thy
5. Then in a no - bler, sweet - er song, I'll

from Em - man - uel's veins; And sin - ners, plunged be -
foun - tain in his day; And there may I, though
nev - er lose its power, Till all the ran - somed
flow - ing wounds sup - ply, Re - deem - ing love has
sing Thy power to save, When this poor lisp - ing,

neath that flood, Lose all their guilt - y stains, Lose
vile as he, Wash all my sins a - way, Wash
Church of God Be saved, to sin no more, Be
been my theme, And shall be till I die, And
stam - mering tongue Lies si - lent in the grave, Lies

all their guilt - y stains, Lose all their guilt - y stains;
all my sins a - way, Wash all my sins a - way;
saved, to sin no more, Be saved to sin no more;
shall be till I die, And shall be till I die;
si - lent in the grave, Lies si - lent in the grave;

Zechariah 13:1. William Cowper, 1771. Tune CLEANSING FOUNTAIN, Traditional American Melody;
arr. Lowell Mason, 1830.

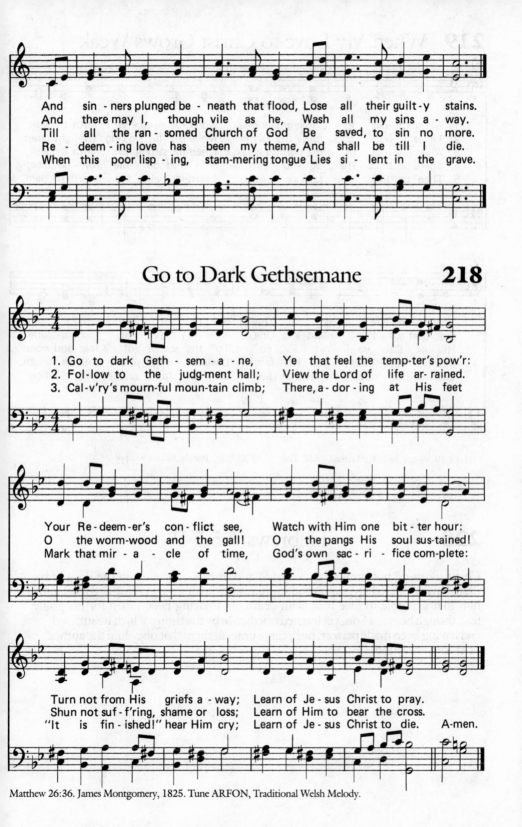

And   sin - ners plunged be - neath that flood, Lose all   their guilt - y stains.
And   there may I,   though vile   as he, Wash all   my sins a - way.
Till   all   the ran - somed Church of God Be saved, to sin no more.
Re - deem - ing love has   been my theme, And shall be till I die.
When this poor lisp - ing, stam - mering tongue Lies si - lent in the grave.

Go to Dark Gethsemane   **218**

1. Go to dark Geth - sem - a - ne,   Ye that feel the temp - ter's pow'r:
2. Fol - low to   the   judg - ment hall; View the Lord of life ar - rained.
3. Cal - v'ry's mourn - ful moun - tain climb; There, a - dor - ing at His feet

Your Re - deem - er's con - flict see,   Watch with Him one bit - ter hour:
O   the worm - wood and the gall!   O   the pangs His soul sus - tained!
Mark that mir - a - cle of time,   God's own sac - ri - fice com - plete:

Turn not from His   griefs a - way; Learn of Je - sus Christ to pray.
Shun not suf - f'ring, shame or loss; Learn of Him to bear the cross.
"It   is fin - ished!" hear Him cry; Learn of Je - sus Christ to die.   A - men.

Matthew 26:36. James Montgomery, 1825. Tune ARFON, Traditional Welsh Melody.

219 When My Love to Christ Grows Weak

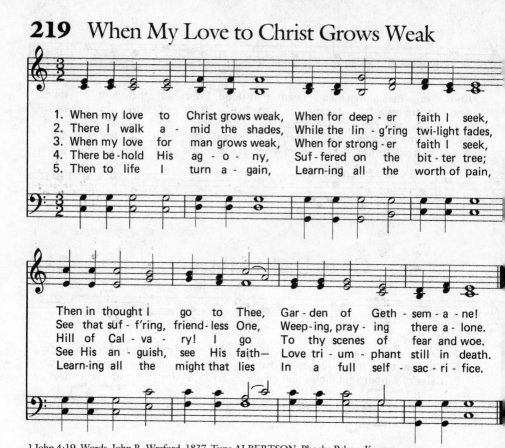

1. When my love to Christ grows weak, When for deep - er faith I seek,
2. There I walk a - mid the shades, While the lin - g'ring twi-light fades,
3. When my love for man grows weak, When for strong - er faith I seek,
4. There be-hold His ag - o - ny, Suf - fered on the bit - ter tree;
5. Then to life I turn a - gain, Learn-ing all the worth of pain,

Then in thought I go to Thee, Gar - den of Geth - sem - a - ne!
See that suf - f'ring, friend - less One, Weep-ing, pray - ing there a - lone.
Hill of Cal - va - ry! I go To thy scenes of fear and woe.
See His an - guish, see His faith— Love tri - um - phant still in death.
Learn-ing all the might that lies In a full self - sac - ri - fice.

1 John 4:19. Words, John R. Wreford, 1837. Tune ALBERTSON, Phoebe Palmer Knapp.

220   Hebrews 5:5,7-9

Christ glorified not himself to be made a high priest, but . . . in the days of his flesh, having offered up prayers and supplications with strong crying and tears unto him that was able to save him from death, and having been heard for his godly fear, though he was a Son, yet learned obedience by the things which he suffered; and having been made perfect, he became unto all them that obey him the author of eternal salvation.

O Sacred Head

1. O sa-cred head, now wound-ed, With grief and shame weighed down;
2. What lan-guage shall I bor-row To thank Thee, dear-est Friend,

Now scorn-ful-ly sur-round-ed With thorns, Thine on-ly crown;
For this Thy dy-ing sor-row, Thy pit-y with-out end?

How art Thou pale with an-guish, With sore a-buse and scorn;
O make me Thine for ev-er; And, should I faint-ing be,

How doth that vis-age lan-guish, Which once was bright as morn!
Lord, let me nev-er, nev-er Out-live my love to Thee.

Matthew 27:29. Words, attr. to Bernard of Clairvaux, d. 1153; trans. Paul Gerhardt, 1656 (German); trans. James W. Alexander, 1830 (English). Tune PASSION CHORALE, Hans Leo Hassler, 1601; harm. J. S. Bach, 1729.

222

Ah, Holy Jesus

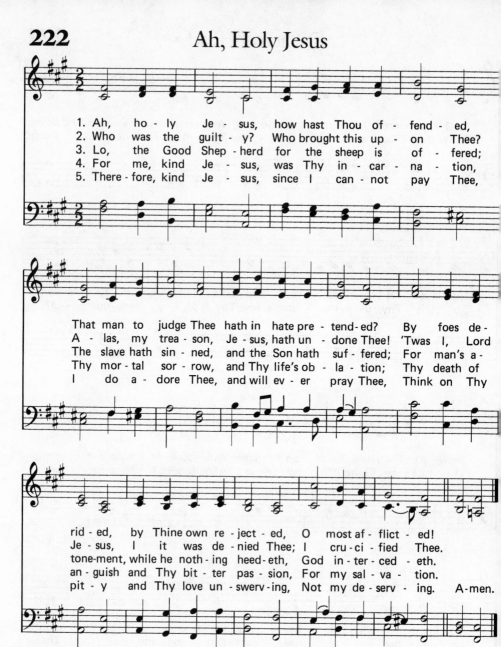

1. Ah, ho - ly Je - sus, how hast Thou of - fend - ed,
2. Who was the guilt - y? Who brought this up - on Thee?
3. Lo, the Good Shep - herd for the sheep is of - fered;
4. For me, kind Je - sus, was Thy in - car - na - tion,
5. There - fore, kind Je - sus, since I can - not pay Thee,

That man to judge Thee hath in hate pre - tend - ed? By foes de -
A - las, my trea - son, Je - sus, hath un - done Thee! 'Twas I, Lord
The slave hath sin - ned, and the Son hath suf - fered; For man's a -
Thy mor - tal sor - row, and Thy life's ob - la - tion; Thy death of
I do a - dore Thee, and will ev - er pray Thee, Think on Thy

rid - ed, by Thine own re - ject - ed, O most af - flict - ed!
Je - sus, I it was de - nied Thee; I cru - ci - fied Thee.
tone - ment, while he noth - ing heed - eth, God in - ter - ced - eth.
an - guish and Thy bit - ter pas - sion, For my sal - va - tion.
pit - y and Thy love un - swerv - ing, Not my de - serv - ing. A - men.

Isaiah 53:3. Words, Johann Heermann, c. 1630; trans. Robert S. Bridges, 1899. Tune HERZLIEBSTER JESU, Johann Crüger, 1640.

223

John 10:11,14,15

I am the good shepherd: the good shepherd layeth down his life for the sheep . . .
I am the good shepherd; and I know mine own, and mine own know me, even as
the Father knoweth me, and I know the Father; and I lay down my life for the sheep.

Lift High the Cross

Lift high the Cross, the love of Christ pro - claim, Till

all the world a - dore His sa - cred name. *Fine*

all the world a - dore His sa - cred name.

1. Come, breth - ren, fol - low where our Sav - ior trod, Our
2. Led on their way by this tri - um - phant sign, The
3. O Lord, once lift - ed on the glo - rious Tree, As
4. Set up Thy throne, that earth's de - spair may cease, Be -
5. For Thy blest Cross which doth for all a - tone, Cre -

D.C.

King vic - to - rious, Christ, the Son of God.
hosts of God in con - qu'ring ranks com - bine.
Thou hast prom - ised, draw men un - to Thee.
neath the shad - ow of its heal - ing peace.
a - tion's prais - es rise be - fore Thy throne.

John 12:32. Words, George W. Kitchin and Michael R. Newbolt, 1916. Tune CRUCIFER, Sydney H. Nicholson, 1916. Words and music by permission of Hymns Ancient & Modern, Ltd.

225   What Wondrous Love is This?

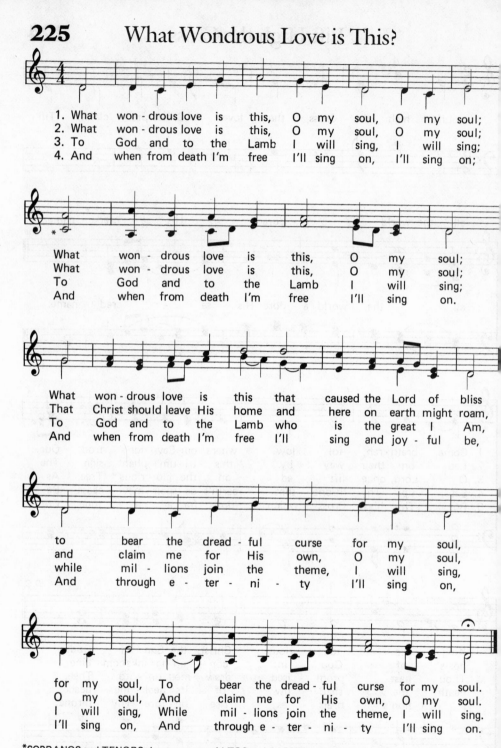

1. What won - drous love is this, O my soul, O my soul;
2. What won - drous love is this, O my soul, O my soul;
3. To God and to the Lamb I will sing, I will sing;
4. And when from death I'm free I'll sing on, I'll sing on;

What won - drous love is this, O my soul;
What won - drous love is this, O my soul;
To God and to the Lamb I will sing;
And when from death I'm free I'll sing on.

What won - drous love is this that caused the Lord of bliss
That Christ should leave His home and here on earth might roam,
To God and to the Lamb who is the great I Am,
And when from death I'm free I'll sing and joy - ful be,

to bear the dread - ful curse for my soul,
and claim me for His own, O my soul,
while mil - lions join the theme, I will sing,
And through e - ter - ni - ty I'll sing on,

for my soul, To bear the dread - ful curse for my soul.
O my soul, And claim me for His own, O my soul.
I will sing, While mil - lions join the theme, I will sing.
I'll sing on, And through e - ter - ni - ty I'll sing on.

*SOPRANOS and TENORS sing top notes, ALTOS and BASSES sing bottom notes.

1 John 3:1. Words, American Folk Hymn; attr. to Alexander Means. Tune WONDROUS LOVE, "Christopher" in William Walker's *Southern Harmony*, 1835. Arr. J.B., Copyright 1986, ACU Press.

There is a Green Hill Far Away 226

1. There is a green hill far a-way, With-out a cit-y wall,
2. We may not know, we can-not tell What pains He had to bear,
3. He died that we may be for-given, He died to make us good,
4. O dear-ly, dear-ly has He loved! And we must love Him too,

Where the dear Lord was cru-ci-fied, Who died to save us all.
But we be-lieve it was for us He hung and suf-fered there.
That we might go at last to heaven, Saved by His pre-cious blood.
And trust in His re-deem-ing blood, And try His works to do. A-men.

John 19:17,18. Words, Cecil Francis Alexander, 1848. Tune MEDITATION, John H. Gower, 1890.

Hebrews 13:10-14 227

We have an altar, whereof they have no right to eat that serve the tabernacle. For the bodies of those beasts whose blood is brought into the holy place by the high priest as an offering for sin, are burned without the camp. Where Jesus also, that he might sanctify the people through his own blood, suffered without the gate. Let us therefore go forth unto him without the camp, bearing his reproach. For we have not here an abiding city, but we seek after the city which is to come.

228

Were You There

1. Were you there when they cru - ci - fied my Lord? (Were you there?
2. Were you there when the sun re - fused to shine? (Were you there?
3. Were you there when they nailed Him to the tree? (Were you there?
4. Were you there when they laid Him in the tomb? (Were you there?

Were you there when they cru - ci - fied my Lord? (Were you there?)
Were you there when the sun re - fused to shine? (Were you there?)
Were you there when they nailed Him to the tree? (Were you there?)
Were you there when they laid Him in the tomb? (Were you there?)

Oh!   Some-times it caus - es me to trem-ble,
Oh!   Some-times it caus - es me to trem-ble,
Oh!   Some-times it caus - es me to trem-ble,
Oh!   Some-times it caus - es me to trem-ble,

trem-ble, trem-ble. Were you there when they cru - ci - fied my Lord?
trem-ble, trem-ble. Were you there when the sun re - fused to shine?
trem-ble, trem-ble. Were you there when they nailed Him to the tree?
trem-ble, trem-ble. Were you there when they laid Him in the tomb?

Mark 15:25. Words, Traditional Negro Spiritual; adapted, John W. Work, Jr., and Frederick J. Work, 1907. Tune WERE YOU THERE, arr. J.B., Copyright 1974, ACU Press.

Beneath the Cross of Jesus

229

1. Be - neath the cross of Je - sus I fain would take my stand,
2. O safe and hap - py shel - ter, O ref - uge tried and sweet,
3. Up - on that cross of Je - sus, Mine eye at times can see
4. I take, O cross, thy shad - ow For my a - bid - ing place;

The shad - ow of a might - y rock With - in a wea - ry land,
O tryst - ing-place where heav - en's love And heav - en's jus - tice meet!
The ver - y dy - ing form of One Who suf - fered there for me;
I ask no oth - er sun - shine than The sun - shine of His face;

A home with - in the wil - der - ness, A rest up - on the way,
As to the ho - ly pa - tri - arch That wondrous dream was giv'n,
And from my smit - ten heart with tears Two won - ders I con - fess:
Con - tent to let the world go by, To know no gain nor loss,

From the burn - ing of the noon - tide heat And the bur - den of the day.
So seems my Sav - ior's cross to me, A lad - der up to heav'n.
The won - ders of His glo - rious love, And my own worth - less - ness.
My sin - ful self my on - ly shame, My glo - ry all the cross!

Galatians 6:14. Words, Elizabeth C. Clephane, 1872. Tune ST. CHRISTOPHER, Frederick C. Maker, 1881.

230   I Stand Amazed

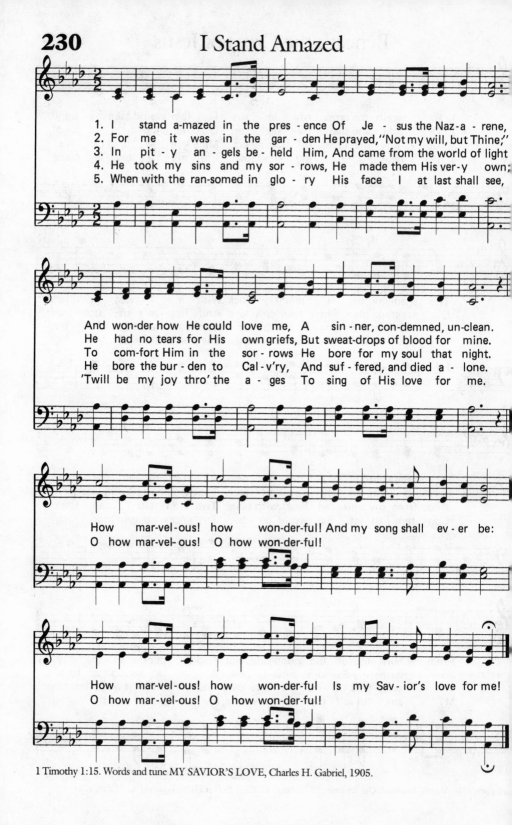

1. I stand a-mazed in the pres - ence Of Je - sus the Naz-a - rene,
2. For me it was in the gar - den He prayed, "Not my will, but Thine;"
3. In pit - y an - gels be - held Him, And came from the world of light
4. He took my sins and my sor - rows, He made them His ver-y own;
5. When with the ran-somed in glo - ry His face I at last shall see,

And won-der how He could love me, A sin - ner, con-demned, un-clean.
He had no tears for His own griefs, But sweat-drops of blood for mine.
To com-fort Him in the sor - rows He bore for my soul that night.
He bore the bur - den to Cal - v'ry, And suf - fered, and died a - lone.
'Twill be my joy thro' the a - ges To sing of His love for me.

How mar-vel-ous! how won-der-ful! And my song shall ev - er be:
O how mar-vel- ous! O how won-der-ful!

How mar-vel-ous! how won-der-ful Is my Sav - ior's love for me!
O how mar-vel-ous! O how won-der-ful!

1 Timothy 1:15. Words and tune MY SAVIOR'S LOVE, Charles H. Gabriel, 1905.

King of My Life

1. King of my life I crown Thee now— Thine shall the glo - ry be;
2. Show me the tomb where Thou wast laid, Ten - der - ly mourned and wept;
3. Let me like Ma - ry, through the gloom, Come with a gift to Thee;
4. May I be will - ing, Lord, to bear Dai - ly my cross for Thee;

Lest I for - get Thy thorn-crowned brow, Lead me to Cal - va - ry.
An - gels in robes of light ar - rayed, Guard-ed Thee whilst Thou slept.
Show to me now the emp - ty tomb— Lead me to Cal - va - ry.
E - ven Thy cup of grief to share Thou hast borne all for me.

Lest I for - get Geth - sem - a - ne, Lest I for - get Thine ag - o - ny,

Lest I for - get Thy love for me, Lead me to Cal - va - ry.

1 Peter 2:24. Words, Jennie Evelyn Hussey, 1921. Tune LEAD ME TO CALVARY, William J. Kirkpatrick, 1921. Copyright 1921. Renewal 1949 extended by Hope Publishing Co., Carol Stream, Illinois, 60188. All rights reserved. Used by permission.

232 O How He Loves You and Me

1. Oh, how He loves you and me,
   Oh, how He loves you and me. He gave His life, what more could He give; Oh, how He loves you, Oh, how He loves me, Oh, how He loves you and me.

2. Je - sus to Cal - v'ry did go,
   His love for man - kind to show. What He did there brought hope from de - spair. Oh, how He loves you, Oh, how He loves me, Oh, how He loves you and me.

John 3:16. Words and tune KAISER, Kurt Kaiser.

When I Survey the Wondrous Cross   **233**

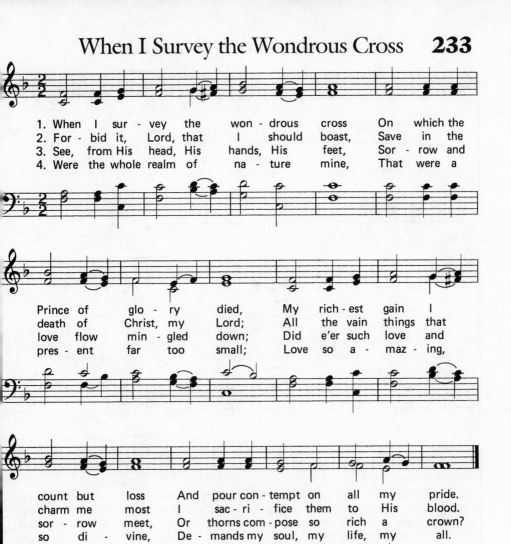

1. When I sur-vey the won-drous cross On which the Prince of glo-ry died, My rich-est gain I count but loss And pour con-tempt on all my pride.
2. For-bid it, Lord, that I should boast, Save in the death of Christ, my Lord; All the vain things that charm me most I sac-ri-fice them to His blood.
3. See, from His head, His hands, His feet, Sor-row and love flow min-gled down; Did e'er such love and sor-row meet, Or thorns com-pose so rich a crown?
4. Were the whole realm of na-ture mine, That were a pres-ent far too small; Love so a-maz-ing, so di-vine, De-mands my soul, my life, my all.

Philippians 3:7. Words, Isaac Watts, 1707. Tune HAMBURG, based on Gregorian Psalm Tone, Mode I, Lowell Mason, 1824.

Galatians 6:14   **234**

Far be it from me to glory, save in the cross of our Lord Jesus Christ, through which the world hath been crucified unto me, and I unto the world.

235 Christ, the Lord, is Risen Today

1. Christ, the Lord, is ris'n to - day, Hal - le - lu - jah!
2. Love's re - deem - ing work is done, Hal - le - lu - jah!
3. Vain the stone, the watch, the seal, Hal - le - lu - jah!
4. Lives a - gain our glo - rious King, Hal - le - lu - jah!

Sons of men and an - gels say, Hal - le - lu - jah!
Fought the fight, the bat - tle won, Hal - le - lu - jah!
Christ hath burst the gates of hell, Hal - le - lu - jah!
Where, O death, is now thy sting? Hal - le - lu - jah!

Raise your joys and tri - umphs high, Hal - le - lu - jah!
Lo! our sun's e - clipse is o'er, Hal - le - lu - jah!
Death in vain for - bids His rise, Hal - le - lu - jah!
Once He died our souls to save, Hal - le - lu - jah!

Sing, ye heav'ns; thou earth, re - ply, Hal - le - lu - jah!
Lo! He sets in blood no more, Hal - le - lu - jah!
Christ hath o - pened par - a - dise, Hal - le - lu - jah!
Where's thy vic - t'ry, boast - ing grave? Hal - le - lu - jah!

Matthew 28:1-8. Words, Charles Wesley, 1739. Tune EASTER HYMN, *Lyra Davidica*, 1708.

Hail the Day That Sees Him Rise **236**

1. Hail the day that sees Him rise,
2. There the glo-rious tri-umph waits; Al - le - lu - ia!
3. See! He lifts His hands a - bove;
4. Lord be-yond our mor-tal sight,

Glo-rious to His na-tive skies;
Lift your heads, e - ter - nal gates! A - le - lu - ia!
See! He shows the prints of love:
Raise our hearts to reach Thy height,

Christ, a - while to mor-tals giv'n,
Wide un-fold the ra-diant scene; Al - le - lu - ia!
Hark! His gra-cious lips be-stow,
There Thy face un-cloud-ed see,

En - ters now the high-est heav'n!
Take the King of glo-ry in! Al - le - lu - ia! A-men.
Bless-ings on His Church be-low.
Find our heav'n of heav'ns in Thee.

Luke 24:50-53. Words, Charles Wesley, 1739. Tune LLANFAIR, Robert Williams, 1817; harm. John Roberts, 1837.

237 Christ Jesus Lay in Death's Strong Bands

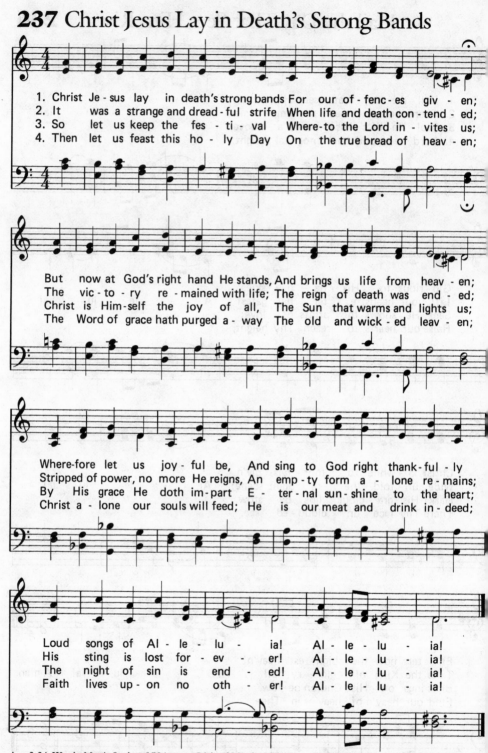

1. Christ Jesus lay in death's strong bands For our of-fenc-es giv-en;
2. It was a strange and dread-ful strife When life and death con-tend-ed;
3. So let us keep the fes-ti-val Where-to the Lord in-vites us;
4. Then let us feast this ho-ly Day On the true bread of heav-en;

But now at God's right hand He stands, And brings us life from heav-en;
The vic-to-ry re-mained with life; The reign of death was end-ed;
Christ is Him-self the joy of all, The Sun that warms and lights us;
The Word of grace hath purged a-way The old and wick-ed leav-en;

Where-fore let us joy-ful be, And sing to God right thank-ful-ly
Stripped of power, no more He reigns, An emp-ty form a-lone re-mains;
By His grace He doth im-part E-ter-nal sun-shine to the heart;
Christ a-lone our souls will feed; He is our meat and drink in-deed;

Loud songs of Al-le-lu-ia! Al-le-lu-ia!
His sting is lost for-ev-er! Al-le-lu-ia!
The night of sin is end-ed! Al-le-lu-ia!
Faith lives up-on no oth-er! Al-le-lu-ia!

Acts 2:24. Words, Martin Luther, 1524; trans. Richard Massie, 1854. Tune CHRIST LAG IN TODESBANDEN, Johann Walther's *Geistliches Gesangbüchlein*, 1524.

The Strife is O'er, the Battle Done
238

1. The strife is o'er, the bat - tle done; The vic - to - ry of
2. The powers of death have done their worst, But Christ their le - gions
3. The three sad days have quick - ly sped; He ris - es glo - rious
4. Lord, by the stripes which wound - ed Thee, From death's dread sting Thy

life is won; The song of tri - umph has be - gun: Al - le - lu - ia!
hath dis - persed; Let shouts of ho - ly joy out - burst: Al - le - lu - ia!
from the dead; All glo - ry to our ris - en Head! Al - le - lu - ia!
ser - vants free, That we may live and sing to Thee: Al - le - lu - ia!

Hebrews 2:14,15. Words, Latin Hymn, *Finita jam sunt praelia*, c. 1695; trans. Francis Pott, 1859.
Tune VICTORY; arr. from *Giovanni P. da Palestrina* by William H. Monk, 1861.

Matthew 28:1-6   239

Now late on the sabbath day, as it began to dawn toward the first day of the week, came Mary Magdalene and the other Mary to see the sepulcher. And behold, there was a great earthquake; for an angel of the Lord descended from heaven, and came and rolled away the stone, and sat upon it. His appearance was as lightning, and his raiment white as snow: and for fear of him the watchers did quake, and became as dead men. And the angel answered and said unto the women, "Fear not ye; for I know that ye seek Jesus, who hath been crucified. He is not here; for he is risen, even as he said. Come, see the place where the Lord lay."

240   Thine is the Glory

1. Thine is the glo - ry, Ris - en, con - qu'ring Son;
2. Lo! Je - sus meets thee, Ris - en from the tomb;
3. No more we doubt thee, Glo - rious Prince of life!

End - less is the vic - t'ry Thou o'er death hast won.
Lov - ing - ly He greets thee, Scat - ters fear and gloom;
Life is naught with - out Thee; Aid us in our strife;

An - gels in bright rai - ment Rolled the stone a - way,
Let His church with glad - ness Hymns of tri - umph sing,
Make us more than con - querors, Through Thy death - less love;

Kept the fold - ed grave - clothes Where Thy bod - y lay.
For her Lord now liv - eth; Death hath lost its sting.
Bring us safe through Jor - dan To Thy home a - bove.

Matthew 28:6. Words, Edmond L. Budry, 1884; trans. R. Birch Hoyle, 1923. Tune JUDAS MACCABEUS, George Frederick Handel, 1745. Copyright World Student Christian Federation. Used by permission.

Thine is the glo - ry, Ris - en, con - quering Son;

End - less is the vic - t'ry Thou o'er death hast won. A-men.

Revelation 1:17,18; Romans 6:8,9 **241**

He laid his right hand upon me, saying, "Fear not; I am the first and the last, and the Living one; and I was dead, and behold, I am alive for evermore, and I have the keys of death and of Hades."

But if we died with Christ, we believe that we shall also live with him; knowing that Christ being raised from the dead dieth no more; death no more hath dominion over him.

242 The Day of Resurrection

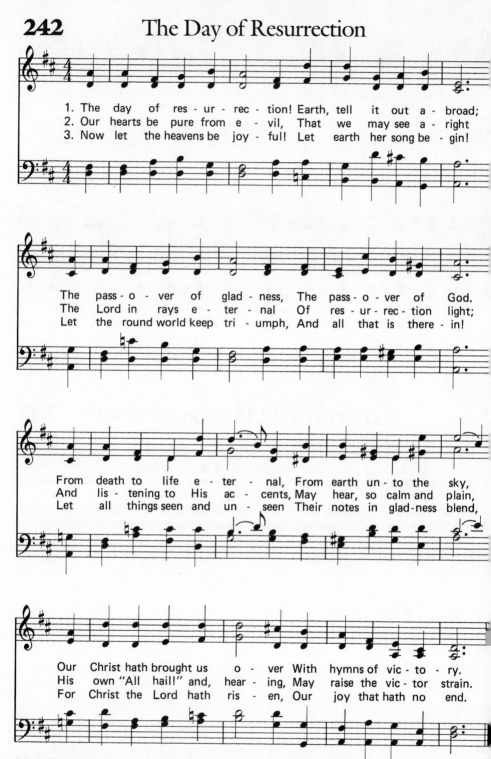

1. The day of res - ur - rec - tion! Earth, tell it out a - broad;
2. Our hearts be pure from e - vil, That we may see a - right
3. Now let the heavens be joy - ful! Let earth her song be - gin!

The pass - o - ver of glad - ness, The pass - o - ver of God.
The Lord in rays e - ter - nal Of res - ur - rec - tion light;
Let the round world keep tri - umph, And all that is there - in!

From death to life e - ter - nal, From earth un - to the sky,
And lis - tening to His ac - cents, May hear, so calm and plain,
Let all things seen and un - seen Their notes in glad - ness blend,

Our Christ hath brought us o - ver With hymns of vic - to - ry.
His own "All hail!" and, hear - ing, May raise the vic - tor strain.
For Christ the Lord hath ris - en, Our joy that hath no end.

1 Corinthians 15:20. Words, John of Damascus, 8th cent.; trans. John Mason Neale, 1862.
Tune LANCASHIRE, Henry Smart, 1835.

Now the Green Blade Riseth

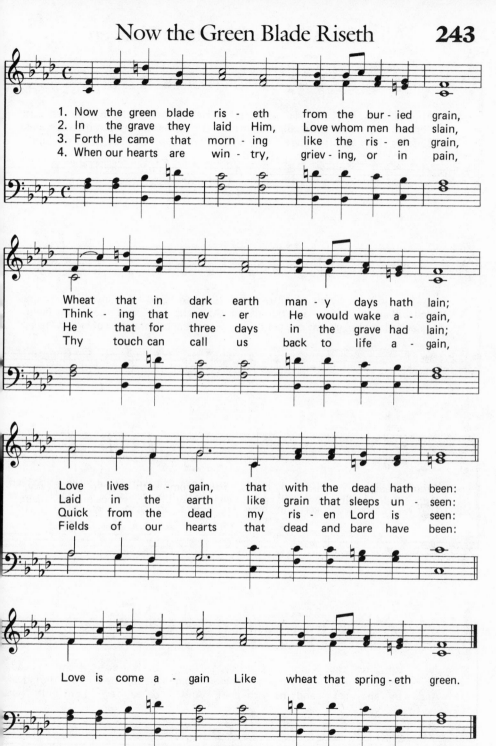

1. Now the green blade ris - eth   from the bur - ied grain,
2. In   the grave they laid Him,   Love whom men had slain,
3. Forth He came that   morn - ing like the ris - en grain,
4. When our hearts are win - try, griev - ing, or in pain,

Wheat that in dark earth man - y days hath lain;
Think - ing that nev - er He would wake a - gain,
He that for three days in the grave had lain;
Thy touch can call us back to life a - gain,

Love lives a - gain, that with the dead hath been:
Laid in the earth like grain that sleeps un - seen:
Quick from the dead my ris - en Lord is seen:
Fields of our hearts that dead and bare have been:

Love is come a - gain Like wheat that spring - eth green.

John 12:24. Words, John M. C. Crum, 1928. Tune FRENCH CAROL, Traditional French Carol; arr. Martin Shaw, 1928. From *The Oxford Book of Carols*, by permission of Oxford University Press.

244 Alleluia! Alleluia! Hearts to Heaven

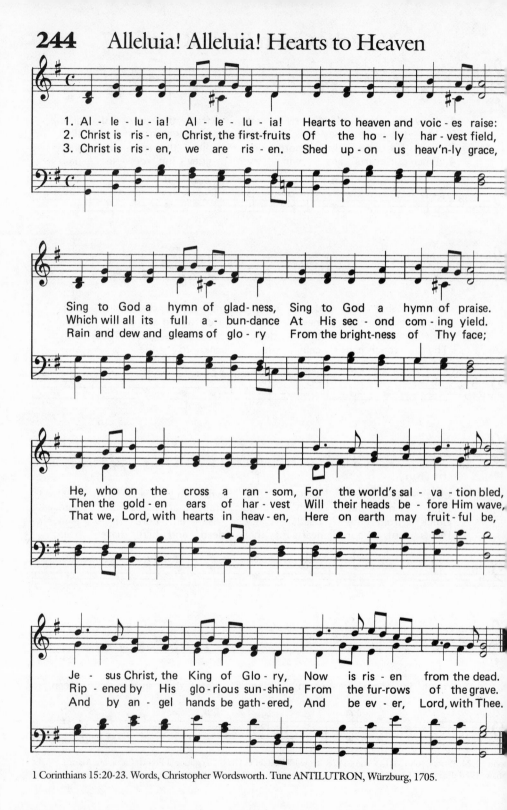

1. Al - le - lu - ia! Al - le - lu - ia! Hearts to heaven and voic - es raise:
2. Christ is ris - en, Christ, the first-fruits Of the ho - ly har - vest field,
3. Christ is ris - en, we are ris - en. Shed up - on us heav'n-ly grace,

Sing to God a hymn of glad - ness, Sing to God a hymn of praise.
Which will all its full a - bun-dance At His sec - ond com - ing yield.
Rain and dew and gleams of glo - ry From the bright-ness of Thy face;

He, who on the cross a ran - som, For the world's sal - va - tion bled,
Then the gold - en ears of har - vest Will their heads be - fore Him wave,
That we, Lord, with hearts in heav - en, Here on earth may fruit - ful be,

Je - sus Christ, the King of Glo - ry, Now is ris - en from the dead.
Rip - ened by His glo - rious sun-shine From the fur-rows of the grave.
And by an - gel hands be gath - ered, And be ev - er, Lord, with Thee.

1 Corinthians 15:20-23. Words, Christopher Wordsworth. Tune ANTILUTRON, Würzburg, 1705.

Low in the Grave He Lay

1. Low in the grave He lay— Je - sus, my Sav - ior! Wait - ing the com-ing day—
2. Vain - ly they watch His bed— Je - sus, my Sav - ior! Vain - ly they seal the dead—
3. Death can-not keep his prey— Je - sus, my Sav - ior! He tore the bars a - way—

Chorus after third stanza only

Je - sus, my Lord! Up from the grave He a - rose With a mighty triumph o'er His
He a-rose

foes; He a - rose a Vic-tor from the dark domain, And He lives for ever with His
He a-rose,

saints to reign: He a - rose! He a - rose! Hal-le - lu-jah! Christ a-rose!
He a-rose! He a-rose!

Matthew 28:2. Words and tune CHRIST AROSE, Robert Lowry, 1874.

246   O Sons and Daughters, Let Us Sing

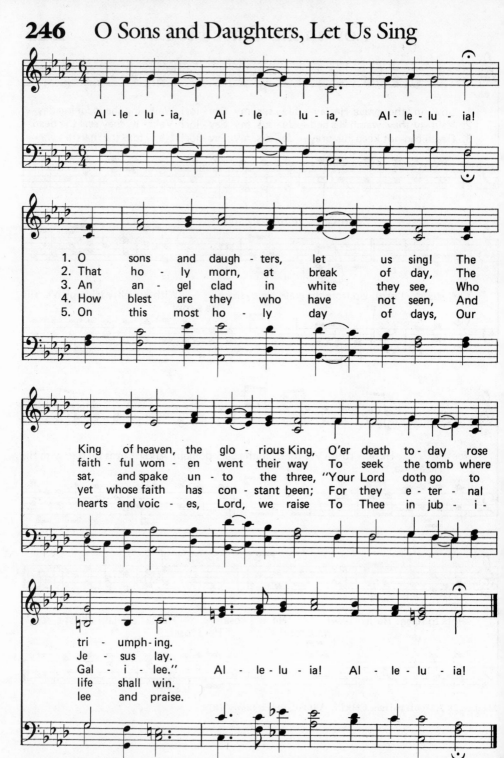

Al - le - lu - ia,   Al - le - lu - ia,   Al - le - lu - ia!

1. O sons and daugh - ters, let us sing! The
2. That ho - ly morn, at break of day, The
3. An an - gel clad in white they see, Who
4. How blest are they who have not seen, And
5. On this most ho - ly day of days, Our

King of heaven, the glo - rious King, O'er death to - day rose
faith - ful wom - en went their way To seek the tomb where
sat, and spake un - to the three, "Your Lord doth go to
yet whose faith has con - stant been; For they e - ter - nal
hearts and voic - es, Lord, we raise To Thee in jub - i -

tri - umph - ing.
Je - sus lay.
Gal - i - lee."   Al - le - lu - ia!   Al - le - lu - ia!
life shall win.
lee and praise.

Luke 24:6. Words, Jean Tisserand, c. 1490; trans. John Mason Neale, 1851. Tune O FILII ET FILIAE, Traditional French Melody, 17th century.

Christos the Lord is Risen Again   **247**

1. Christ the Lord is   risen a - gain,   Christ hath bro - ken   ev - ery chain,
2. He who bore all   pain and loss   Com - fort - less up - on the cross,
3. He who slum-bered in   the grave Is   ex - alt - ed   now to save;

Hark, the   an - gels shout for joy,   Sing - ing ev - er - more on high:
Lives in   glo - ry   now on high,   Pleads for us and   hears our cry:
Now through Chris-ten - dom it rings   That   the Lamb is   King of kings:

Al - le - lu - ia!   A - men.

Philippians 2:9. Words, based on *Victimae Paschali laudes*, Wipo, d. 1050; trans. Michael Weisse (German), 1531; trans. Catherine Winkworth (English), 1858. Tune CHRIST IST ERSTANDEN, Plainsong Melody, 12th century.

1 Corinthians 15:1-4   **248**

Now I make known unto you, brethren, the gospel which I preached unto you, which also ye receive, wherein also ye stand, by which also ye are saved, if ye hold fast the word which I preached unto you, except ye believed in vain. For I delivered unto you first of all that which I also received: that Christ died for our sins according to the scriptures; and that he was buried; and that he hath been raised on the third day according to the Scriptures.

249   Sing With All the Sons of Glory

1. Sing with all the sons of glo - ry, Sing the res - ur - rec - tion song!
2. O what glo - ry, far ex - ceed - ing All that eye has yet per-ceived!
3. Life e - ter - nal! heaven re - joic - es: Je - sus lives who once was dead;
4. Life e - ter - nal! O what won - ders Crowd on faith; what joy un - known,

Death and sor - row, earth's dark sto - ry, To the for - mer
Ho - liest hearts for a - ges plead - ing, Nev - er that full
Join, O man, the death - less voic - es; Child of God, lift
When, a - midst earth's clos - ing thun - ders, Saints shall stand be -

days be - long. All a - round the clouds are break - ing,
joy con - ceived. God has prom - ised, Christ pre - pares it,
up thy head! Pa - triarchs from the dis - tant a - ges,
fore the throne! O to en - ter that bright por - tal,

Soon the storms of time shall cease; In God's like - ness,
There on high our wel - come waits; Ev - ery hum - ble
Saints all long - ing for their heav'n, Proph - ets, psalm - ists,
See that glow - ing fir - ma - ment, Know, with Thee, O

1 Corinthians 15:20. Words, William J. Irons, 1873. Tune HYMN TO JOY, Ludwig van Beethoven, 1826; arr. Edward Hodges, 1864.

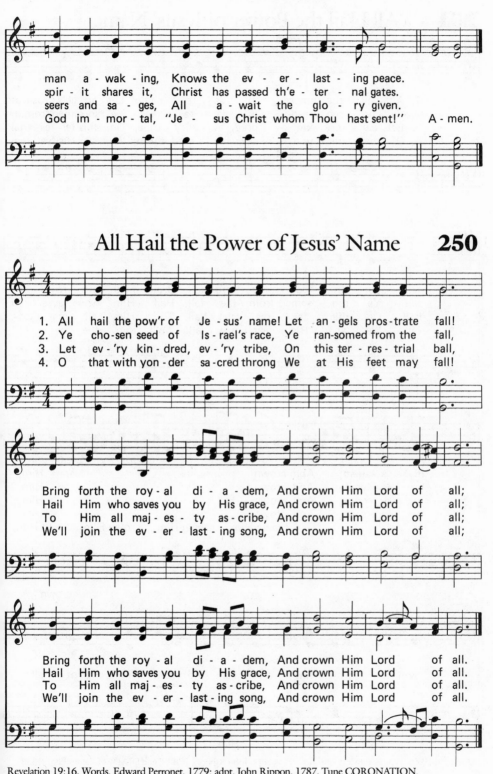

man a - wak - ing, Knows the ev - er - last - ing peace.
spir - it shares it, Christ has passed th'e - ter - nal gates.
seers and sa - ges, All a - wait the glo - ry given.
God im - mor - tal, "Je - sus Christ whom Thou hast sent!" A - men.

All Hail the Power of Jesus' Name   250

1. All hail the pow'r of Je - sus' name! Let an-gels pros-trate fall!
2. Ye cho-sen seed of Is - rael's race, Ye ran-somed from the fall,
3. Let ev - 'ry kin - dred, ev - 'ry tribe, On this ter - res - trial ball,
4. O that with yon - der sa -cred throng We at His feet may fall!

Bring forth the roy - al di - a - dem, And crown Him Lord of all;
Hail Him who saves you by His grace, And crown Him Lord of all;
To Him all maj - es - ty as - cribe, And crown Him Lord of all;
We'll join the ev - er - last - ing song, And crown Him Lord of all;

Bring forth the roy - al di - a - dem, And crown Him Lord of all.
Hail Him who saves you by His grace, And crown Him Lord of all.
To Him all maj - es - ty as - cribe, And crown Him Lord of all.
We'll join the ev - er - last - ing song, And crown Him Lord of all.

Revelation 19:16. Words, Edward Perronet, 1779; adpt. John Rippon, 1787. Tune CORONATION, Oliver Holden, 1792.

251　All Hail the Power of Jesus' Name

1. All hail the power of Je - sus' name! Let an - gels pros-trate
2. Ye cho - sen seed of Is - rael's race, Ye ran-somed from the
3. Let ev - ery kin - dred, ev - 'ry tribe, On this ter - res - trial
4. O that with yon - der sa - cred throng We at His feet may

fall, Let an - gels pros - trate fall; Bring forth the roy - al
fall, Ye ran - somed from the fall, Hail Him who saves you
ball, On this ter - res - trial ball, To Him all maj - es -
fall, We at His feet may fall! We'll join the ev - er -

di - a - dem, And crown ... Him,
by His grace, And crown ... Him,
ty as - cribe, And crown ... Him,
last - ing song, And crown ... Him
crown Him, crown Him, crown Him, crown Him,

crown

crown Him, crown Him, crown Him, And crown Him Lord of all.

Him,

Revelation 19:16. Words, Edward Perronet, 1779; adpt. John Rippon, 1787. Tune DIADEM, James Ellor, 1838.

Look, Ye Saints! The Sight is Glorious 252

1. Look, ye saints! the sight is glo - rious; See the Man of
2. Crown the Sav - ior! an - gels, crown Him! Rich the tro - phies
3. Sin - ners in de - ri - sion crowned Him, Mock - ing thus the
4. Hark! those bursts of ac - cla - ma - tion! Hark! those loud tri -

Sor - rows now; From the fight re - turned vic - to - rious,
Je - sus brings; In the seat of pow'r en - throne Him,
Sav - ior's claim; Saints and an - gels crowd a - round Him,
um - phant chords! Je - sus takes the high - est sta - tion—

Ev - 'ry knee to Him shall bow: Crown Him!
While the vault of heav - en rings: Crown Him!
Own His ti - tle, praise His name: Crown Him!
O what joy the sight af - fords! Crown Him!

crown Him! Crowns be - come the Vic - tor's brow.
crown Him! Crown the Sav - ior King of kings.
crown Him! Spread a - broad the Vic - tor's fame!
crown Him! King of kings and Lord of lords!

Revelation 11:15. Words, Thomas Kelly, 1809. Tune BRYN CALFARIA, William Owen, 1886.

253 Alleluia! Sing to Jesus

1. Al - le - lu - ia! sing to Je - sus, His the
2. Al - le - lu - ia! not as or - phans We are
3. Al - le - lu - ia! Bread of Heav - en, Thou on

scep - tre, His the throne: Al - le - lu - ia! His the
left in sor - row now: Al - le - lu - ia! He is
earth our food and stay; Al - le - lu - ia! here the

tri - umph, His the vic - to - ry a - lone.
near us, Faith be - lieves, nor ques - tions how;
sin - ful Flee to Thee from day to day;

Hark! the songs of peace - ful Zi - on Thun - der
Though the cloud from sight re - ceived Him When the
In - ter - ces - sor, friend of sin - ners, Earth's Re -

1 Timothy 2:5. Words, William Chatterton Dix, 1866. Tune HYFRYDOL, Rowland H. Prichard, c. 1830.

like a might - y flood, "Je - sus out of ev - ery
for - ty days were o'er, Shall our hearts for - get His
deem - er, plead for me, Where the songs of all the

na - tion Hath re - deemed us by His blood."
prom - ise, "I am with you ev - er - more"?
sin - less Sweep a - cross the crys - tal sea. A - men.

Acts 5:29-32   254

Peter and the apostles answered and said, "We must obey God rather than men.
The God of our fathers raised up Jesus, whom ye slew, hanging him on a tree. Him
did God exalt with his right hand to be a Prince and a Savior, to give repentance
to Israel, and remission of sins. And we are witnesses of these things; and so is the
Holy Spirit, whom God hath given to them that obey him."

255 **Crown Him With Many Crowns**

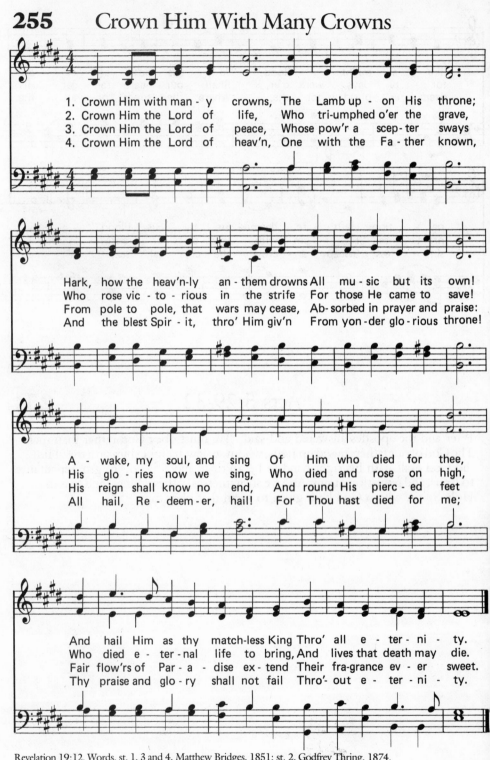

1. Crown Him with man-y crowns, The Lamb up-on His throne;
2. Crown Him the Lord of life, Who tri-umphed o'er the grave,
3. Crown Him the Lord of peace, Whose pow'r a scep-ter sways
4. Crown Him the Lord of heav'n, One with the Fa-ther known,

Hark, how the heav'n-ly an-them drowns All mu-sic but its own!
Who rose vic-to-rious in the strife For those He came to save!
From pole to pole, that wars may cease, Ab-sorbed in prayer and praise:
And the blest Spir-it, thro' Him giv'n From yon-der glo-rious throne!

A-wake, my soul, and sing Of Him who died for thee,
His glo-ries now we sing, Who died and rose on high,
His reign shall know no end, And round His pierc-ed feet
All hail, Re-deem-er, hail! For Thou hast died for me;

And hail Him as thy match-less King Thro' all e-ter-ni-ty.
Who died e-ter-nal life to bring, And lives that death may die.
Fair flow'rs of Par-a-dise ex-tend Their fra-grance ev-er sweet.
Thy praise and glo-ry shall not fail Thro'-out e-ter-ni-ty.

Revelation 19:12. Words, st. 1, 3 and 4, Matthew Bridges, 1851; st. 2, Godfrey Thring, 1874.
Tune DIADEMATA, George J. Elvey, 1868.

Joy to the World

1. Joy to the world, the Lord is come! Let earth re-
2. Joy to the earth, the Sav-ior reigns! Let men their
3. No more let sins and sor-rows grow, Nor thorns in-
4. He rules the world with truth and grace, And makes the

ceive her King; Let ev-'ry heart pre-pare Him
songs em-ploy, While fields, and floods, rocks, hills, and
fest the ground; He comes to make His bless-ings
na-tions prove The glo-ries of His right-eous-

room, And heav'n and na-ture sing, And heav'n and na-ture
plains Re-peat the sound-ing joy, Re-peat the sound-ing
flow Far as the curse is found, Far as the curse is
ness, And won-ders of His love, And won-ders of His
1. And heav'n and na-ture sing, And

sing, And heav'n, and heav'n and na-ture sing.
joy, Re-peat, re-peat the sound-ing joy.
found, Far as, far as the curse is found.
love, And won-ders, won-ders of His love.
heav'n and na-ture sing,

Isaiah 35:1-10. Words, Isaac Watts, 1719. Tune ANTIOCH, George Frederick Handel; arr. Lowell Mason, 1836.

257 The Head That Once Was Crowned

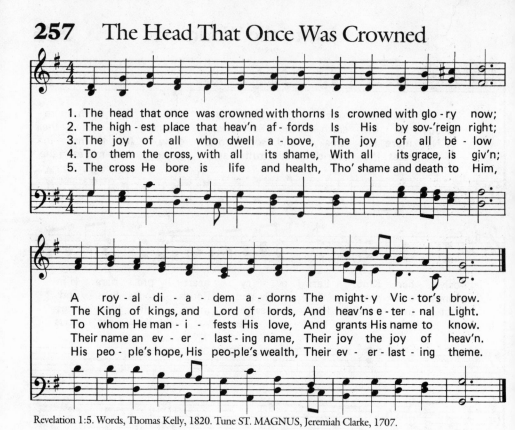

1. The head that once was crowned with thorns Is crowned with glo-ry now;
2. The high-est place that heav'n af-fords Is His by sov-'reign right;
3. The joy of all who dwell a-bove, The joy of all be-low
4. To them the cross, with all its shame, With all its grace, is giv'n;
5. The cross He bore is life and health, Tho' shame and death to Him,

A roy-al di-a-dem a-dorns The might-y Vic-tor's brow.
The King of kings, and Lord of lords, And heav'ns e-ter-nal Light.
To whom He man-i-fests His love, And grants His name to know.
Their name an ev-er-last-ing name, Their joy the joy of heav'n.
His peo-ple's hope, His peo-ple's wealth, Their ev-er-last-ing theme.

Revelation 1:5. Words, Thomas Kelly, 1820. Tune ST. MAGNUS, Jeremiah Clarke, 1707.

258 Hebrews 2:9,10

We behold him who hath been made a little lower than the angels, even Jesus, because of the suffering of death crowned with glory and honor, that by the grace of God he should taste of death for every man. For it became him, for whom are all things, in bringing many sons unto glory, to make the author of their salvation perfect through sufferings.

Lead On, O King Eternal

1. Lead on, O King E - ter - nal, The day of march has come;
2. Lead on, O King E - ter - nal, Till sin's fierce war shall cease,
3. Lead on, O King E - ter - nal, We fol - low, not with fear;

Hence - forth in fields of con - quest Thy tents shall be our home;
And ho - li - ness shall whis - per The sweet A - men of peace;
For glad - ness breaks like morn - ing Wher - e'er Thy face ap - pears;

Thro' days of prep - a - ra - tion Thy grace has made us strong,
For not with swords loud clash - ing, Nor roll of stir - ring drums:
Thy cross is lift - ed o'er us: We jour - ney in its light;

And now, O King E - ter - nal, We lift our bat - tle song.
With deeds of love and mer - cy, The heav'n - ly king - dom comes.
The crown a - waits the con - quest: Lead on, O God of might!

2 Timothy 2:4. Words, Ernest W. Shurtleff, 1887. Tune LANCASHIRE, Henry Smart, 1835.

260   Majestic Sweetness

1. Ma - jes - tic sweet - ness sits en - throned Up - on the Sav - ior's brow; His head with ra - diant glo - ries crowned, His lips with grace o'er flow.

2. No mor - tal can with Him com - pare A - mong the sons of men; Fair - er is He than all the fair Who fill the heav'n - ly train.

3. He saw me plunged in deep dis - tress, And flew to my re - lief; For me He bore the shame - ful cross, And car - ried all my grief.

4. To Him I owe my life and breath, And all the joys I have; He makes me tri - umph o - ver death, And saves me from the grave.

5. Since from Thy boun - ty I re - ceive Such proofs of love di - vine, Had I a thou - sand hearts to give, Lord, they should all be Thine.

Hebrews 2:9. Words, Samuel Stennett, 1787. Tune MANOAH, Henry W. Greatorex's *Collection*, 1851.

Jesus Shall Reign

1. Je - sus shall reign wher - e'er the sun Does his suc -
2. To Him shall end - less prayer be made, And end - less
3. Bless - ings a - bound wher - e'er He reigns; The pris - oner
4. Where He dis - plays His heal - ing pow'r Death and the
5. Let ev - ery crea - ture rise and bring His grate - ful

ces - sive jour - neys run; His king - dom spread from
prais - es crown His head; His name like sweet per -
leaps to loose his chains; The wea - ry find e -
curse are known no more; In Him the tribes of
hon - ors to our King; An - gels de - scend with

shore to shore, Till moons shall wax and wane no more.
fume shall rise With ev - ery morn - ing sac - ri - fice.
ter - nal rest, And all the sons of want are blest.
A - dam boast More bless - ings than their fa - ther lost.
songs a - gain, And earth re - peat the loud a - men!

Psalm 72:8. Words, Isaac Watts, 1719. Tune DUKE STREET, John Hatton, 1793.

262 I Am the Vine

1. "I am the vine and ye are the branch-es:" Bear pre-cious fruit for
2. "Now ye are clean thro' words I have spo-ken; Liv-ing in me, much
3. Yes, by your fruits the world is to know you, Walk-ing in love as

Je - sus to - day; Branch-es in Him no fruit ev - er bear - ing,
fruit ye shall bear; Dwell-ing in you, my prom-ise un - bro - ken,
chil-dren of day; Fol - low your Guide: He pass-eth be - fore you,

Je - sus hath said, "He tak-eth a - way."
Glo-ry in heav'n with me ye shall share." "I am the vine and ye are the
Lead-ing to realms of glo-ri-ous day.

branch-es; I am the vine, be faith-ful and true; Ask what ye will, your

John 15:5. Words and tune AMPELOS, Knowles Shaw, d. 1878.

prayer shall be grant-ed; The Fa-ther loved me, so I have loved you."

Jesus, Thou Joy of Loving Hearts 263

1. Je - sus, Thou joy of lov - ing hearts, Thou fount of life, Thou light of men, From all the bliss that earth im - parts We turn un - filled to Thee a - gain.

2. Thy truth un - changed hath ev - er stood; Thou sav - est those that on Thee call; To them that seek Thee Thou art good; To them that find Thee, all in all.

3. On Thee we feed, Thou liv - ing bread, And long to feast up - on Thee still; We drink of Thee, Thou foun - tain - head, Whose streams each thirst - ing soul can fill.

4. Our rest - less spir - its yearn for Thee, Wher - e'er our change - ful lot is cast— Glad when Thy gra - cious smile we see, Blest when our faith can hold Thee fast.

5. O Je - sus, ev - er with us stay, Make all our mo - ments calm and bright; Chase the dark night of sin a - way, Shed o'er the world Thy ho - ly light.

Ephesians 3:17-19. Words, attr. to Bernard of Clairvaux, c. 1150; trans. Ray Palmer, 1858. Tune MARYTON, Henry P. Smith, 1874.

In Loving-Kindness Jesus Came

1. In lov-ing-kind-ness Je-sus came, My soul in mer-cy to re-claim;
2. He called me long be-fore I heard, Be-fore my sin-ful heart was stirred,
3. His brow was pierced with man-y a thorn, His hands by cru-el nails were torn,
4. Now on a high-er plane I dwell, And with my soul I know 'tis well;

And from the depths of sin and shame Thro' grace He lift-ed me.
But when I took Him at His word, For-giv'n He lift-ed me.
When from my guilt and grief, for-lorn, In love He lift-ed me
Yet how or why, I can-not tell, He should have lift-ed me.

From sink-ing sand He lift-ed me, With ten-der hand He lift-ed me;

From shades of night to plains of light, O praise His name, He lift-ed me!

Psalm 40:1-3. Words and tune HE LIFTED ME, Charles H. Gabriel, 1905.

Jesus, the Very Thought of Thee

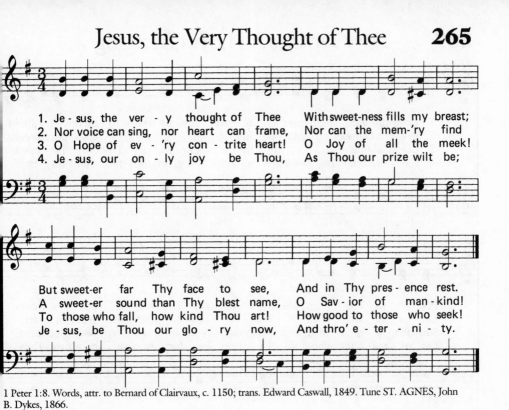

1. Je - sus, the ver - y thought of Thee   With sweet-ness fills my breast;
2. Nor voice can sing, nor heart can frame,   Nor can the mem-'ry find
3. O Hope of ev - 'ry con - trite heart!   O Joy of all the meek!
4. Je - sus, our on - ly joy be Thou,   As Thou our prize wilt be;

But sweet-er far Thy face to see,   And in Thy pres - ence rest.
A sweet-er sound than Thy blest name,   O Sav - ior of man - kind!
To those who fall, how kind Thou art!   How good to those who seek!
Je - sus, be Thou our glo - ry now,   And thro' e - ter - ni - ty.

1 Peter 1:8. Words, attr. to Bernard of Clairvaux, c. 1150; trans. Edward Caswall, 1849. Tune ST. AGNES, John B. Dykes, 1866.

Hebrews 12:1-3

Therefore let us also, seeing we are compassed about with so great a cloud of witnesses, lay aside every weight, and the sin which doth so easily beset us, and let us run with patience the race that is set before us, looking unto Jesus the author and perfecter of our faith, who for the joy that was set before him endured the cross, despising shame, and hath sat down at the right hand of the throne of God.

267 Love Divine, All Loves Excelling

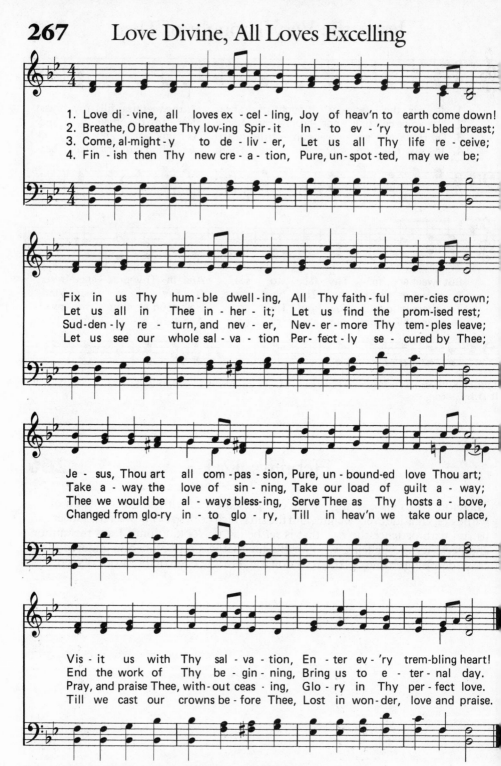

1. Love di - vine, all loves ex - cel - ling, Joy of heav'n to earth come down!
2. Breathe, O breathe Thy lov-ing Spir-it In - to ev - 'ry trou-bled breast;
3. Come, al-might-y to de - liv - er, Let us all Thy life re - ceive;
4. Fin - ish then Thy new cre - a - tion, Pure, un-spot-ted, may we be;

Fix in us Thy hum - ble dwell-ing, All Thy faith-ful mer-cies crown;
Let us all in Thee in - her - it; Let us find the prom-ised rest;
Sud-den-ly re - turn, and nev - er, Nev - er-more Thy tem-ples leave;
Let us see our whole sal - va - tion Per - fect-ly se - cured by Thee;

Je - sus, Thou art all com - pas - sion, Pure, un - bound-ed love Thou art;
Take a - way the love of sin - ning, Take our load of guilt a - way;
Thee we would be al - ways bless-ing, Serve Thee as Thy hosts a - bove,
Changed from glo-ry in - to glo - ry, Till in heav'n we take our place,

Vis - it us with Thy sal - va - tion, En - ter ev - 'ry trem-bling heart!
End the work of Thy be - gin - ning, Bring us to e - ter - nal day;
Pray, and praise Thee, with-out ceas - ing, Glo - ry in Thy per - fect love.
Till we cast our crowns be - fore Thee, Lost in won - der, love and praise.

Colossians 3:14. Words, Charles Wesley, 1747. Tune BEECHER, John Zundel, 1870.

Years I Spent in Vanity

1. Years I spent in van - i - ty and pride, Car - ing not my Lord was
2. By God's word at last my sin I learned; Then I trem-bled at the
3. Now I've giv'n to Je - sus ev - 'ry - thing; Now I glad - ly own Him
4. O the love that drew sal - va - tion's plan! O the grace that bro't it

cru - ci - fied, Know-ing not it was for me He died On Cal - va - ry.
law I spurned, Till my guilt-y soul im - plor-ing turned To Cal - va - ry.
as my King; Now my rap-tured soul can on - ly sing Of Cal - va - ry.
down to man! O the might-y gulf that God did span At Cal - va - ry!

Mer - cy there was great, and grace was free; Par - don there was mul - ti -

plied to me; There my bur-dened soul found lib - er - ty, At Cal - va - ry.

Isaiah 53:10,11. Words, William R. Newell, 1895. Tune CALVARY, Daniel B. Towner, 1895.

269 Shall I Crucify My Savior

1. Shall I cru-ci-fy my Sav - ior, When for me He bore such loss?
2. Are temp-ta-tions so al - lur - ing? Do earth's pleasures so en - thrall
3. O the kind-ly hands of Je - sus, Pour-ing bless-ings on all men,

Shall I put to shame my Sav - ior? Can I nail Him to the cross?
That I can-not love my Sav - ior Well e-nough to leave them all?
Bleed-ing, nail-scarred hands of Je - sus! Can I nail them once a - gain?

Shall I cru-ci-fy my Sav - ior? Cru-ci-fy my Lord a - gain?

Once, O once I cru-ci-fied Him: Shall I cru-ci-fy a - gain?

Hebrews 6:6. Words, Carrie E. Breck, c. 1896. Tune TULLAR, Grant Colfax Tullar, 1896.

Thou Art the Way

1. Thou art the Way: to Thee a - lone From sin and death we flee;
2. Thou art the Truth: Thy word a - lone True wis-dom can im - part;
3. Thou art the Life: the rend - ing tomb Pro-claims Thy con - qu'ring arm;

And he who would the Fa - ther seek, Must seek Him, Lord, by Thee.
Thou on - ly canst in - struct the mind, And pu - ri - fy the heart.
And those who put their trust in Thee Nor death nor hell shall harm.

John 14:6. Words, George W. Doane, 1824. Tune SAWLEY, James Welch, 1860.

John 14:1-6; Hebrews 10:19-22   **271**

Let not your heart be troubled: believe in God, believe also in me. In my Father's house are many mansions; if it were not so I would have told you; for I go to prepare a place for you. And if I go and prepare a place for you, I will come again, and will receive you to myself; that where I am, there you may be also. And where I am going, you know the way . . . I am the way, and the truth, and the life: no one cometh unto the Father, but by me.

Having therefore, brethren, boldness to enter into the holy place by the blood of Jesus, by the way which he dedicated for us, a new and living way, through the veil, that is to say, his flesh; let us draw near with a true heart in fulness of faith.

272   Like a Shepherd, Tender, True

1. Like a shep-herd, ten-der, true, Je-sus leads,   Je-sus leads,
2. All a - long life's rug-ged road Je-sus leads,   Je-sus leads,
3. Thro' the sun - lit ways of life Je-sus leads,   Je-sus leads,

Je - sus leads,   Je - sus leads;

Dai - ly finds us pas-tures new, Je-sus leads,   Je-sus leads;
Till we reach that blest a - bode, Je-sus leads,   Je-sus leads;
Thro' the war - rings and the strife Je-sus leads,   Je-sus leads;

Je - sus leads,   Je-sus leads;

If thick mists are o'er the way, Or the flock 'mid dan-ger feeds,
All the way be-fore He's trod, And He now the flock pre-ceeds,
When we reach the Jor-dan's tide, Where life's bound - 'ry-line re - cedes,
(1) If thick mists are o'er the way, Or the flock 'mid dan-ger feeds,

He will watch them lest they stray: Je-sus leads,   Je-sus leads.
Safe in - to the fold of God: Je-sus leads,   Je-sus leads.
He will spread the waves a - side: Je-sus leads,   Je-sus leads.

Je-sus leads,

Revelation 7:17. Words, John R. Clements, 1893. Tune JESUS LEADS, John R. Sweney, 1893.

In Vain in High and Holy Lays

273

1. In vain in high and ho - ly lays, My soul her grate-ful voice would raise;
2. A joy by day, a peace by night; In storms a calm, in dark - ness light;
3. My hope for par - don when I call, My trust for lift - ing when I fall;

For who can sing the wor - thy praise Of the won-der-ful love of Je - sus!
In pain a balm, in weakness might, Is the won-der-ful love of Je - sus.
In life, in death, my all in all, Is the won-der-ful love of Je - sus.

Won-der-ful love! Won-der-ful love! Won-der-ful love of Je - sus!

Won-der-ful love! Won - der-ful love! Won-der-ful love of Je - sus!

John 10:11. Words, E.D. Mund. Tune WONDERFUL LOVE. Edmund S. Lorenz. *Note: "lays" (st. 1), i.e. songs or ballads.*

274 In the Hush of Early Morning

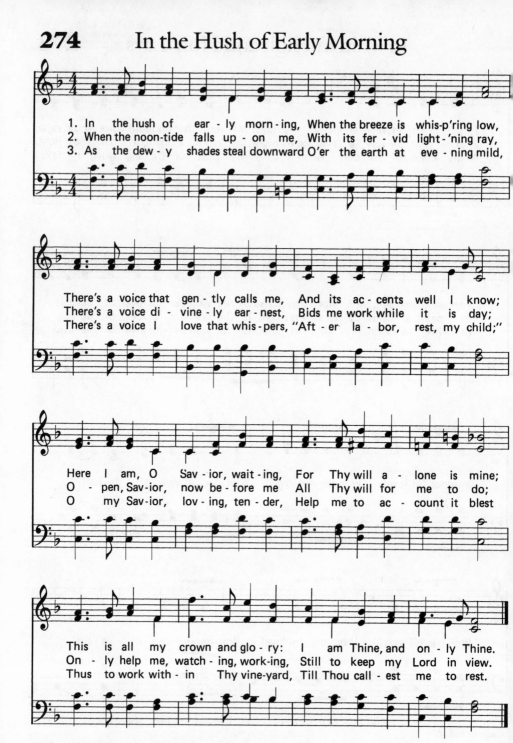

1. In the hush of ear - ly morn - ing, When the breeze is whis - p'ring low,
2. When the noon-tide falls up - on me, With its fer - vid light - 'ning ray,
3. As the dew - y shades steal downward O'er the earth at eve - ning mild,

There's a voice that gen - tly calls me, And its ac - cents well I know;
There's a voice di - vine - ly ear - nest, Bids me work while it is day;
There's a voice I love that whis - pers, "Aft - er la - bor, rest, my child;"

Here I am, O Sav - ior, wait - ing, For Thy will a - lone is mine;
O - pen, Sav - ior, now be - fore me All Thy will for me to do;
O my Sav - ior, lov - ing, ten - der, Help me to ac - count it blest

This is all my crown and glo - ry: I am Thine, and on - ly Thine.
On - ly help me, watch - ing, work-ing, Still to keep my Lord in view.
Thus to work with - in Thy vine-yard, Till Thou call - est me to rest.

Matthew 28:20. Words, Mrs. R.N. Turner, 1890. Tune PROIOS, William J. Kirkpatrick, 1890.

Flee as a Bird

275

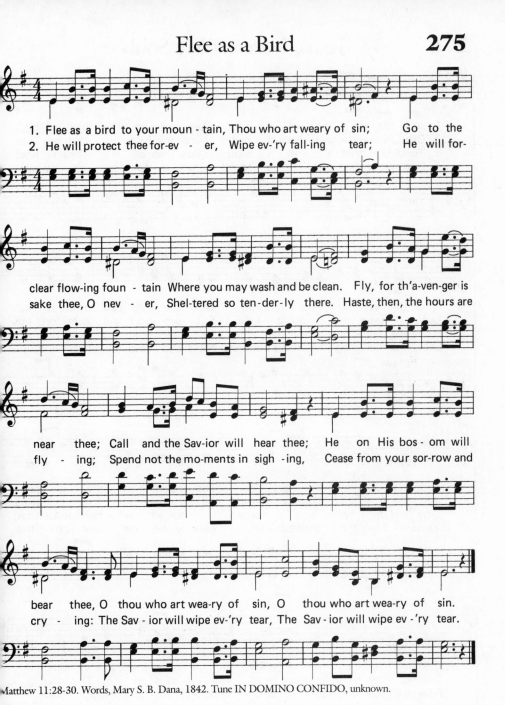

1. Flee as a bird to your moun - tain, Thou who art weary of sin; Go to the
2. He will protect thee for-ev - er, Wipe ev-'ry fall-ing tear; He will for-

clear flow-ing foun - tain Where you may wash and be clean. Fly, for th'a-ven-ger is
sake thee, O nev - er, Shel-tered so ten-der-ly there. Haste, then, the hours are

near thee; Call and the Sav-ior will hear thee; He on His bos - om will
fly - ing; Spend not the mo-ments in sigh -ing, Cease from your sor-row and

bear thee, O thou who art wea-ry of sin, O thou who art wea-ry of sin.
cry - ing: The Sav - ior will wipe ev-'ry tear, The Sav-ior will wipe ev -'ry tear.

Matthew 11:28-30. Words, Mary S. B. Dana, 1842. Tune IN DOMINO CONFIDO, unknown.

276 Jesus, Lover of My Soul

1. Je - sus, lov - er   of my soul,   Let me to Thy bos - om fly,
2. Oth - er ref - uge have I none; Hangs my help - less soul on Thee;
3. Thou, O Christ, art all I want; More than all in Thee I find;
4. Plen - teous grace with Thee is found, Grace to cov - er   all my sin;

While the near - er wa - ters roll, While the tem - pest still is high:
Leave, O leave me not a - lone, Still sup - port and com - fort me.
Raise the fall - en, cheer the faint, Heal the sick, and lead the blind.
Let the heal - ing streams a - bound; Make and keep me pure with - in.

Hide me, O my Sav - ior, hide, Till the storm of life is past;
All my trust on Thee is stayed; All my help from Thee I bring;
Just and ho - ly is Thy name; I am all un - righ - teous - ness;
Thou of life the foun - tain art; Free - ly let me take of Thee:

Safe un - to the ha - ven guide; O re - ceive my soul at last!
Cov - er my de - fense - less head With the shad - ow of Thy wing.
False and full of sin I am; Thou art full of truth and grace.
Spring Thou up with - in my heart; Rise to all e - ter - ni - ty. A - men

Isaiah 25:4. Words, Charles Wesley, 1740. Tune ABERYSTWYTH, Joseph Parry, 1879. Arr. J.B., Copyright 1986, ACU Press.

My Lord Has Garments

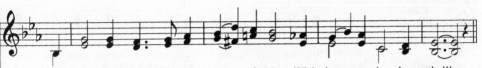

1. My Lord has gar-ments so won-drous fine, And myrrh their tex-ture fills;
2. His life had al - so its sor - rows sore, For al - oes had a part;
3. His gar-ments too were in cas-sia dipped, With heal - ing in a touch;
4. In gar-ments glo - ri - ous He will come, To o - pen wide the door;

Its fra-grance reached to this heart of mine, With joy my be - ing thrills.
And when I think of the cross He bore, My eyes with tear-drops start.
Each time my feet in some sin have slipped, He took me from its clutch.
And I shall en - ter my heav'n-ly home, To dwell for - ev - er - more.

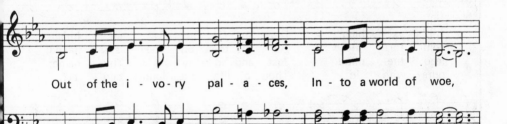

Out of the i - vo-ry pal - a - ces, In - to a world of woe,

On - ly His great, e - ter - nal love Made my Sav-ior go.

Psalm 45:8. Words and tune MONTREAT, Henry Barraclough, 1915. Arr. chorus, J.B., Copyright 1986, ACU Press.

278   Jesus, Lover of My Soul

1. Je - sus, lov - er   of   my soul,   Let   me to Thy   bos - om
2. Oth - er ref - uge   have I none;   Hangs my help - less soul   on
3. Thou, O Christ, art   all   I want;   More than all in   Thee   I
4. Plen - teous grace with Thee is found, Grace to cov - er   all   my

fly,   While the near - er   wa - ters roll,   While the tem - pest
Thee;   Leave, ah! leave me not a - lone,   Still sup-port and
find: Raise the fall - en, cheer the faint, Heal the sick, and
sin;   Let   the heal - ing streams a - bound; Make and keep me

still   is   high: Hide me, O   my Sav - ior,   hide,
com - fort me.   All   my trust on Thee is   stayed;
lead   the blind.   Just and ho - ly is   Thy   name;
pure with - in.   Thou of life the foun - tain   art;

Till   the storm of life   is   past;   Safe in - to the
All   my help from Thee   I   bring;   Cov - er my de -
I   am all   un - righ - teous - ness; False and full of
Free - ly let   me take   of   Thee: Spring Thou up with -

Isaiah 25:4. Words, Charles Wesley, 1740. Tune MARTYN, Simeon Butler Marsh, 1834.

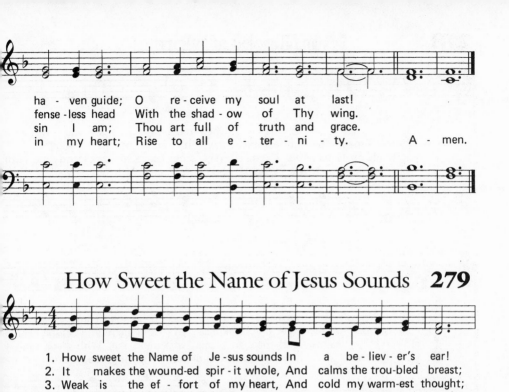

ha - ven guide; O re - ceive my soul at last!
fense - less head With the shad - ow of Thy wing.
sin I am; Thou art full of truth and grace.
in my heart; Rise to all e - ter - ni - ty. A - men.

How Sweet the Name of Jesus Sounds 279

1. How sweet the Name of Je - sus sounds In a be - liev - er's ear!
2. It makes the wound - ed spir - it whole, And calms the trou - bled breast;
3. Weak is the ef - fort of my heart, And cold my warm - est thought;
4. Till then I would Thy love pro - claim With ev - ery fleet - ing breath;

It sooths his sor - rows, heals his wounds, And drives a - way his fear.
'Tis man - na to the hun - gry soul, And to the wea - ry rest.
But when I see Thee as Thou art, I'll praise Thee as I ought.
And may the mu - sic of Thy Name Re - fresh my soul in death. A - men.

Matthew 1:21. Words, John Newton, 1779. Tune ST. PETER, Alexander R. Reinagle, c. 1836.

Acts 4:12 280

In none other is there salvation: for neither is there any other name under heaven, that is given among men, wherein we must be saved.

281 It May be at Morn

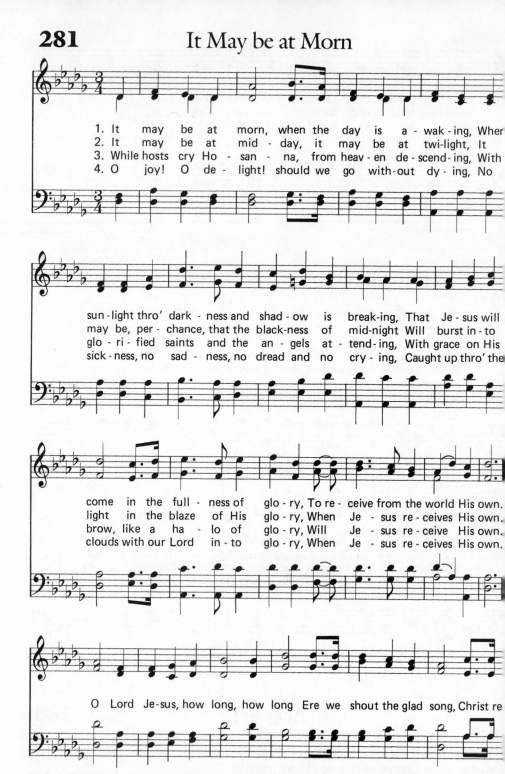

1. It may be at morn, when the day is a-wak-ing, When sun-light thro' dark-ness and shad-ow is break-ing, That Je-sus will come in the full-ness of glo-ry, To re-ceive from the world His own.

2. It may be at mid-day, it may be at twi-light, It may be, per-chance, that the black-ness of mid-night Will burst in-to light in the blaze of His glo-ry, When Je-sus re-ceives His own.

3. While hosts cry Ho-san-na, from heav-en de-scend-ing, With glo-ri-fied saints and the an-gels at-tend-ing, With grace on His brow, like a ha-lo of glo-ry, Will Je-sus re-ceive His own.

4. O joy! O de-light! should we go with-out dy-ing, No sick-ness, no sad-ness, no dread and no cry-ing, Caught up thro' the clouds with our Lord in-to glo-ry, When Je-sus re-ceives His own.

O Lord Je-sus, how long, how long Ere we shout the glad song, Christ re

Mark 13:35,37. Words, H.L. Turner, 1878. Tune CHRIST RETURNETH, James McGranahan, 1878.

turn-eth! Hal-le - lu-jah! Hal-le - lu-jah! A-men, Hal-le - lu-jah! A-men.

The Lord Will Come and Not be Slow 282

1. The Lord will come and not be slow, His
2. Truth from the earth, like to a flower, Shall
3. Rise, God, judge Thou the earth in might, This
4. The na - tions all whom Thou hast made Shall
5. For great Thou art, and won - ders great By

foot - steps can - not err; Be - fore Him righ - teous-
bud and blos - som then; And jus - tice, from her
wick - ed earth re - dress; For Thou art He who
come, and all shall frame To bow them low be -
Thy strong hand are done: Thou in Thy ev - er -

ness shall go, His roy - al har - bin - ger.
heaven - ly bower, Look down on mor - tal men.
shalt by right The na - tions all pos - sess.
fore Thee, Lord, And glo - ri - fy Thy name.
last - ing seat Re - main - est God a - lone. A - men.

Psalm 82:1. Words, John Milton, 1648; paraphrase of Psalms 85 and 86. Tune ST. STEPHEN,
William Jones, 1789.

283 One Day

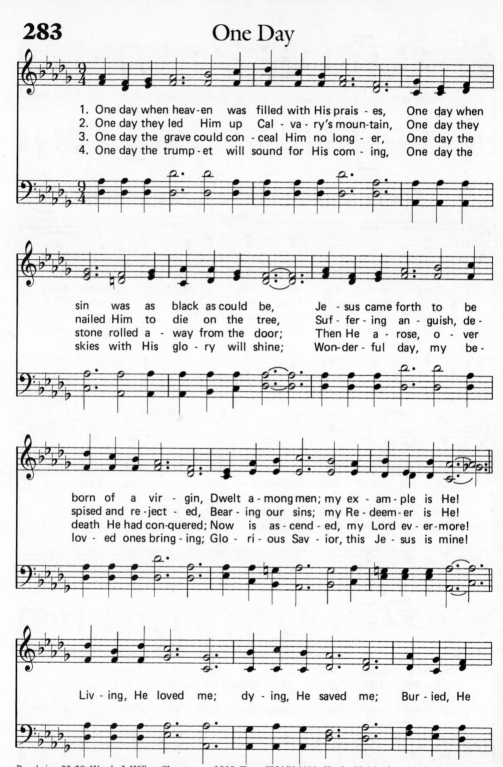

1. One day when heav-en was filled with His prais-es, One day when
2. One day they led Him up Cal - va - ry's moun-tain, One day they
3. One day the grave could con - ceal Him no long - er, One day the
4. One day the trump - et will sound for His com - ing, One day the

sin was as black as could be, Je - sus came forth to be
nailed Him to die on the tree, Suf - fer - ing an - guish, de -
stone rolled a - way from the door; Then He a - rose, o - ver
skies with His glo - ry will shine; Won - der - ful day, my be -

born of a vir - gin, Dwelt a - mong men; my ex - am - ple is He!
spised and re - ject - ed, Bear - ing our sins; my Re - deem - er is He!
death He had con-quered; Now is as - cend - ed, my Lord ev - er-more!
lov - ed ones bring - ing; Glo - ri - ous Sav - ior, this Je - sus is mine!

Liv - ing, He loved me; dy - ing, He saved me; Bur - ied, He

Revelation 22:20. Words, J. Wilbur Chapman, c. 1909. Tune CHAPMAN, Charles H. Marsh, c. 1909. Copyright 1910 by Charles H. Marsh. Renewal 1938. Used by permission of Word Music, Winona Lake, Indiana.

car - ried my sins far a - way; Ris - ing, He jus - ti - fied

free - ly for - ev - er; One day He's com - ing, O glo - ri - ous day!

The King Shall Come

284

1. The King shall come when morn-ing dawns And light tri - um - phant breaks,
2. Not as of old a lit - tle child, To bear and fight and die,
3. Oh, bright-er than the ris - ing morn When Christ, vic-to - rious rose
4. Oh, bright-er than that glo - rious morn Shall dawn up - on our race
5. The King shall come when morn-ing dawns And light and beau - ty brings.

When beau - ty gilds the east - ern hills And life to joy a - wakes.
But crowned with glo - ry like the sun That lights the morn-ing sky.
And left the lone - some place of death, De - spite the rage of foes.
The day when Christ in splen-dor comes, And we shall see His face.
Hail, Christ, the Lord! Your peo - ple pray: Come quick-ly, King of kings.

1 John 3:2. Words, John Brownlie, 1907; prob. based on Greek hymns. Tune CONSOLATION, in John Wyeth's *Repository of Sacred Music; Part Second*, 1813; arr. Copyright ACU Press, 1985.

Watch therefore: for ye know not when the lord of the house cometh, whether at even, or at midnight, or at cockcrowing, or in the morning: lest coming suddenly he find you sleeping. And what I say unto you I say unto all: Watch.

286   Wake, Awake, For Night is Flying

1. Wake, a-wake, for night is fly - ing: The watch-men on the heights are cry - ing, A - wake, Je - ru - sa - lem, a - rise! Mid - night's sol - emn hour is toll - ing; His char - iot wheels are

2. Zi - on hears the watch-men sing - ing; Her heart with deep de - light is spring - ing, She wakes, she ris - es from her gloom, For her Lord comes down all glo - rious, In grace ar - rayed, by

3. Now let all the heavens a - dore Thee, And men and an - gels sing be - fore Thee With harp and cym - bal's clear - est tone; Of one pearl each shin - ing por - tal, Where we shall join the

Matthew 25:6. Words, Philip Nocolai, 1597; trans. Catherine Winkworth, 1858. Tune WACHET AUF, Philip Nicolai, 1599; harm. J. S. Bach, 1731.

near - er roll - ing; He comes! O church, lift up thine eyes!
truth vic - to - rious; Her star is ris'n, her light is come!
choirs im - mor - tal In prais - es round Thy glo - rious throne;

Rise up, with will - ing feet Go forth, the Bride - groom meet:
Ah, come Thou bless - ed One, God's own be - lov - ed Son,
No vi - sion ev - er brought, No ear hath ev - er caught

Hal - le - lu - jah! Lo, great and small, We an - swer all;
Hal - le - lu - jah! We haste a - long, An ea - ger throng,
Such great glo - ry! There - fore will we, e - ter - nal - ly,

We fol - low where Thy voice shall call.
And glad - some join the ad - vent song.
Sing hymns of joy and praise to Thee. A - men.

1 Thessalonians 5:4-6   **287**

But ye, brethren, are not in darkness, that that day should overtake you as a thief:
for ye are all sons of light, and sons of the day: we are not of the night, nor of
darkness; so then let us not sleep, as do the rest, but let us watch and be sober.

288   Lord Christ, When First Thou Cam'st

1. Lord Christ, when first Thou cam'st to men, Up - on a cross
2. O awe - ful love, which found no room In life where sin
3. New ad - vent of the love of Christ, Shall we a - gain
4. O wound - ed hands of Je - sus, build In us Thy new

they bound Thee, And mocked Thy sav - ing
de - nied Thee, And, doomed to death, must
re - fuse Thee, Till in the night of
cre - a - tion; Our pride is dust; our

king - ship then By thorns with which they crowned Thee; And
bring to doom The power which cru - ci - fied Thee; Till
hate and war We per - ish as we lose Thee? From
vaunt is stilled; We wait Thy rev - e - la - tion. O

still our wrongs may weave Thee now New thorns to pierce that
not a stone was left on stone, And all a na - tion's
old un - faith our souls re - lease To seek the king - dom
love that tri - umphs o - ver loss, We bring our hearts be -

Colossians 3:1-4. Words, Walter Russell Bowie, 1928. By permission of Walter Russell Bowie. Tune MIT
FREUDEN ZART, Bohemian Brethren's *Kirchengesänge*, 1566; adpt. from *Geneva 138, Pseaumes*, 1547.

stead - y brow, And   robe of sor - row   round   Thee.
pride o'er-thrown, Went   down to dust be - side   Thee!
of Thy peace, By   which a - lone we   choose   Thee.
fore Thy cross, To   fin - ish Thy sal - va - tion.

Lo! He Comes With Clouds Descending 289

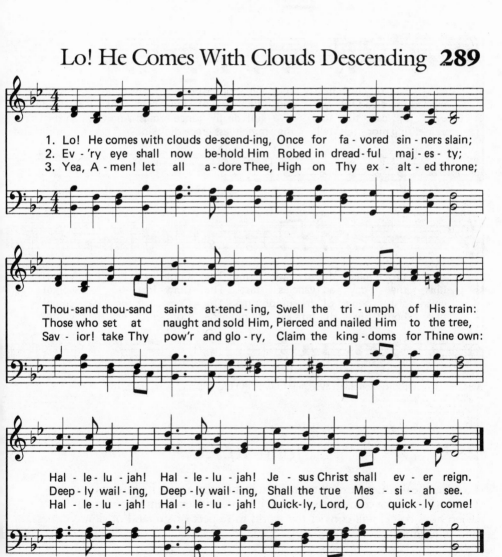

1. Lo! He comes with clouds de-scend-ing, Once for fa - vored sin - ners slain;
2. Ev - 'ry eye shall now be-hold Him Robed in dread-ful maj - es - ty;
3. Yea, A - men! let all a-dore Thee, High on Thy ex - alt - ed throne;

Thou-sand thou-sand saints at-tend - ing, Swell the tri - umph of His train:
Those who set at naught and sold Him, Pierced and nailed Him to the tree,
Sav - ior! take Thy pow'r and glo - ry, Claim the king - doms for Thine own:

Hal - le - lu - jah! Hal - le - lu - jah! Je - sus Christ shall ev - er reign.
Deep - ly wail - ing, Deep - ly wail - ing, Shall the true Mes - si - ah see.
Hal - le - lu - jah! Hal - le - lu - jah! Quick-ly, Lord, O quick-ly come!

Revelation 1:7. Words, John Cennick, 1752; alt. John Wesley, 1758, and Martin Madan, 1760. Tune REGENT SQUARE, Henry Smart, 1867.

290   O Spread the Tidings Round

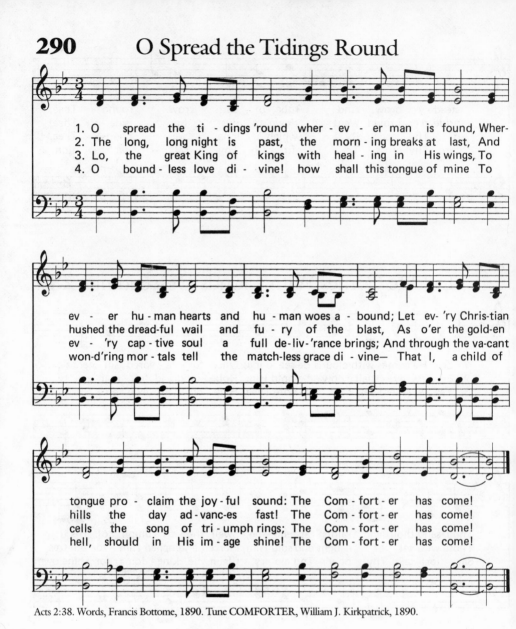

1. O spread the ti-dings 'round wher-ev-er man is found, Wher-
2. The long, long night is past, the morn-ing breaks at last, And
3. Lo, the great King of kings with heal-ing in His wings, To
4. O bound-less love di-vine! how shall this tongue of mine To

ev - er hu-man hearts and hu-man woes a-bound; Let ev-'ry Chris-tian
hushed the dread-ful wail and fu-ry of the blast, As o'er the gold-en
ev - 'ry cap-tive soul a full de-liv-'rance brings; And through the va-cant
won-d'ring mor-tals tell the match-less grace di-vine— That I, a child of

tongue pro - claim the joy-ful sound: The Com - fort - er has come!
hills the day ad-vanc-es fast! The Com - fort - er has come!
cells the song of tri - umph rings; The Com - fort - er has come!
hell, should in His im - age shine! The Com - fort - er has come!

Acts 2:38. Words, Francis Bottome, 1890. Tune COMFORTER, William J. Kirkpatrick, 1890.

291   John 16:7,8

I tell you the truth: it is expedient for you that I go away; for if I go not away, the
Comforter will not come unto you; but if I go, I will send him unto you. And he,
when he is come, will convict the world in respect of sin, and of righteousness,
and of judgment.

Come, Holy Spirit, God and Lord! 292

1. Come, Ho - ly Spir - it, God and Lord!
2. Lord, by the bright - ness of Thy light,
3. Thou strong De - fense, Thou ho - ly Light,

Be all Thy gra - ces now out - poured
Thou in the faith dost men u - nite
Teach us to know our God a - right,

On the be - liev - er's mind and soul,
Of ev - 'ry land and ev - 'ry tongue;
And call Him Fa - ther from the heart.

To strength-en, save, and make us whole.
This to Thy praise, O Lord, be sung.
The Word of life and truth im - part. A - men.

Romans 8:26. Words, Martin Luther, 1524; trans. Catherine Winkworth, 1855, alt. Tune DAS NEUGEBORNE
KINDELEIN, Melchior Vulpius, 1609; harm. J. S. Bach.

293   # Holy Spirit, Light Divine

1. Ho - ly Spir - it, Light di - vine, Shine up-
2. Ho - ly Spir - it, Power di - vine, Cleanse this
3. Ho - ly Spir - it, Joy di - vine, Cheer this
4. Ho - ly Spir - it, all di - vine, Dwell with-

on this heart of mine; Chase the shades of
guilt - y heart of mine; Long hath sin with-
sad - dened heart of mine; Bid my man - y
in this heart of mine; Cast down ev - 'ry

night a - way, Turn my dark - ness in - to day.
out con - trol Held do - min - ion o'er my soul.
woes de - part, Heal my wound - ed, bleed - ing heart.
i - dol throne, Reign su - preme, and reign a - lone. A - men.

Romans 8:11. Words, Andrew Reed, 1817, alt. Tune MERCY, Louis M. Gottschalk, 1854; arr. Edwin P. Parker, c. 1880.

294   # Romans 8:26

The Spirit also helpeth our infirmity: for we know not how to pray as we ought; but the Spirit himself maketh intercession for us with groanings which cannot be uttered.

Breathe on Me, Breath of God

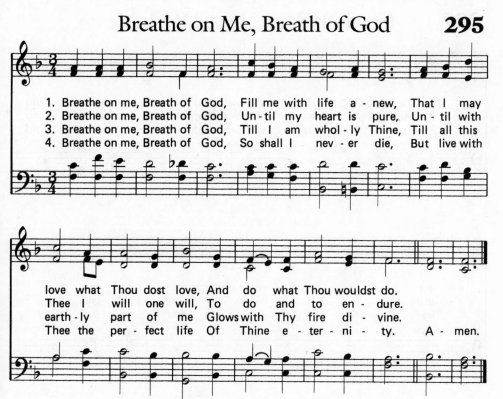

1. Breathe on me, Breath of God, Fill me with life a - new, That I may
2. Breathe on me, Breath of God, Un - til my heart is pure, Un - til with
3. Breathe on me, Breath of God, Till I am whol - ly Thine, Till all this
4. Breathe on me, Breath of God, So shall I nev - er die, But live with

love what Thou dost love, And do what Thou wouldst do.
Thee I will one will, To do and to en - dure.
earth - ly part of me Glows with Thy fire di - vine.
Thee the per - fect life Of Thine e - ter - ni - ty. A - men.

Ephesians 3:16. Words, Edwin Hatch, 1878. Tune TRENTHAM, Robert Jackson, 1888.

Ephesians 3:14-19

For this cause I bow my knees unto the Father from whom every family in heaven and on earth is named, that he would grant you, according to the riches of his glory, that ye may be strengthened with power through his Spirit in the inward man; that Christ may dwell in your hearts through faith; to the end that ye, being rooted and grounded in love, may be strong to apprehend with all the saints what is the breadth and length and height and depth, and to know the love of Christ which passeth knowledge, that ye may be filled unto all the fulness of God.

297 Gracious Spirit, Dwell With Me

1. Gra-cious Spir-it, dwell with me; I my-self would gra-cious be; And with words that help and heal Would Thy life in mine re-veal; And with ac-tions bold and meek Would for Christ my Sav-ior speak.

2. Truth-ful Spir-it, dwell with me; I my-self would truth-ful be; And with wis-dom kind and clear Let Thy life in mine ap-pear; And with ac-tions broth-er-ly Speak my Lord's sin-cer-i-ty.

3. Ho-ly Spir-it, dwell with me; I my-self would ho-ly be; Sep-a-rate from sin, I would Choose and cher-ish all things good, And what-ev-er I can be Give to Him who gave me Thee! A-men.

Romans 8:9. Words, Thomas Toke Lynch, 1855. Tune REDHEAD NO. 76, Richard Redhead, 1853.

O Word of God Incarnate 298

1. O Word of God in-car-nate, O Wis-dom from on high,
2. The Church from Thee, her Mas-ter, Re-ceived the gift di-vine,
3. It float-eth like a ban-ner Be-fore God's host un-furled;
4. O make Thy Church, dear Sav-ior, A lamp of pur-est gold,

O Truth un-changed, un-chang-ing, O Light of our dark sky:
And still that light she lift-eth O'er all the earth to shine.
It shin-eth like a bea-con A-bove the dark-ling world.
To bear be-fore the na-tions Thy true light as of old.

We praise Thee for the ra-diance That from the hal-lowed page,
It is the sa-cred ves-sel, Where gems of truth are stored;
It is the chart and com-pass That o'er life's surg-ing sea,
O teach Thy wan-dering pil-grims By this their path to trace,

A lan-tern to our foot-steps, Shines on from age to age.
It is the heaven-drawn pic-ture Of Thee, the liv-ing Word.
Mid mists and rocks and quick-sands, Still guides, O Christ, to Thee.
Till, clouds and dark-ness end-ed, They see Thee face to face. A-men.

2 Timothy 3:16,17. Words, William W. How, 1867. Tune MUNICH, *Neuvermehrtes Gesangbuch*, 1694; harm.
Felix Mendelssohn, 1847.

299 Give Me the Bible

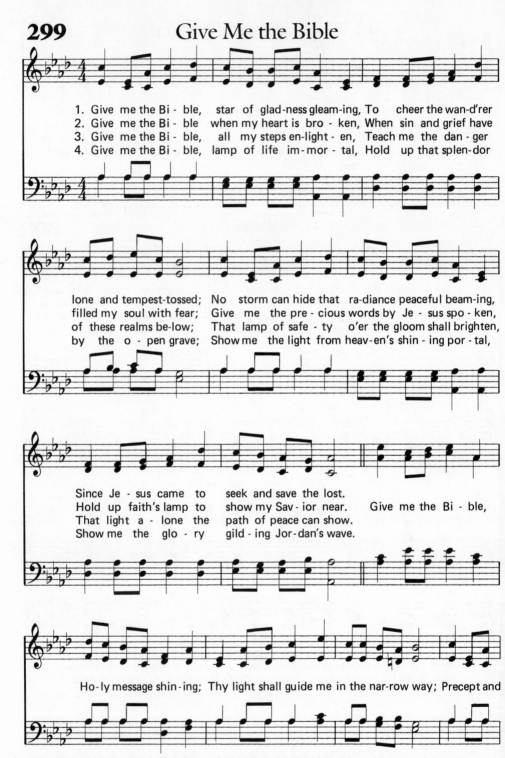

1. Give me the Bi - ble, star of glad-ness gleam-ing, To cheer the wan-d'rer
2. Give me the Bi - ble when my heart is bro - ken, When sin and grief have
3. Give me the Bi - ble, all my steps en-light - en, Teach me the dan - ger
4. Give me the Bi - ble, lamp of life im-mor - tal, Hold up that splen-dor

lone and tempest-tossed; No storm can hide that ra-diance peaceful beam-ing,
filled my soul with fear; Give me the pre - cious words by Je - sus spo - ken,
of these realms be-low; That lamp of safe - ty o'er the gloom shall brighten,
by the o - pen grave; Show me the light from heav-en's shin - ing por - tal,

Since Je - sus came to seek and save the lost.
Hold up faith's lamp to show my Sav - ior near. Give me the Bi - ble,
That light a - lone the path of peace can show.
Show me the glo - ry gild - ing Jor-dan's wave.

Ho-ly message shin-ing; Thy light shall guide me in the nar-row way; Precept and

2 Timothy 3:14,15. Words, Priscilla J. Owens, d. 1907. Tune GRAMMATA, Edmund S. Lorenz, d. 1942.

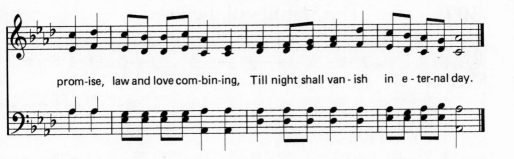

prom-ise, law and love com-bin-ing, Till night shall van - ish in e - ter-nal day.

2 Timothy 3:14-17

300

Psalm 119:105,130,160,172
2 Timothy 4:2

Abide in the things which you have learned and have been assured of, knowing of whom you have learned them; and that from a babe you have known the sacred writings which are able to make you wise in order to salvation through faith which is in Christ Jesus. Every scripture inspired of God is also profitable for teaching, for reproof, for correction, for instruction which is in righteousness: that the man of God may be complete, furnished completely unto every good work.

> Your word is a lamp to my feet,
> And light to my path.
> The opening of your words gives light;
> It gives understanding to the simple.
> The sum of your word is truth;
> And every one of your righteous ordinances endures for ever.
> Let my tongue sing of your word;
> For all your commandments are righteousness.

Preach the word; be urgent in season, out of season; reprove, rebuke, exhort, with all longsuffering and teaching.

301 The Statutes of the Lord

1. The stat-utes of the Lord are right, And do re-joice the heart;
2. Un-spot-ted is the fear of God, And ev-er doth en-dure;
3. They more than gold, yea, much fine gold, To be de-sir-ed are;
4. More-o-ver, they Thy serv-ant warn How he his life should frame;
5. O do not suf-fer sin to have Do-min-ion o-ver me;

The Lord's com-mand is pure, and doth Light to the eyes im-part.
The judg-ments of the Lord are truth, And right-eous-ness most pure.
Than hon-ey from the hon-ey-comb That drop-peth—sweet-er far.
A great re-ward pro-vid-ed is For them that keep the same.
I shall be right-eous, then, and from The great trans-gres-sion free.

"O how love I Thy law, O how love I Thy law! It is my med-i-

ta-tion all the day; O how love I Thy law, O how

Psalm 119:97. Words, paraphrase of Psalm 19:7-13. Tune O HOW LOVE I THY LAW, James McGranahan, 1897.

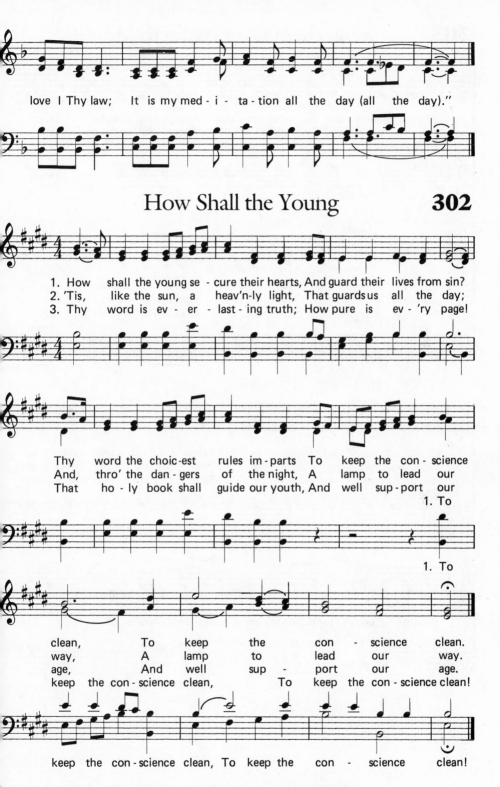

love I Thy law; It is my med - i - ta - tion all the day (all the day)."

How Shall the Young 302

1. How shall the young se - cure their hearts, And guard their lives from sin?
2. 'Tis, like the sun, a heav'n-ly light, That guards us all the day;
3. Thy word is ev - er - last-ing truth; How pure is ev - 'ry page!

Thy word the choic-est rules im-parts To keep the con - science
And, thro' the dan - gers of the night, A lamp to lead our
That ho - ly book shall guide our youth, And well sup-port our

1. To

clean, To keep the con - science clean.
way, A lamp to lead our way.
age, And well sup - port our age.
keep the con - science clean, To keep the con - science clean!

keep the con - science clean, To keep the con - science clean!

salm 119:9. Words, Isaac Watts, 1719. Tune NEANISKOI; attr. to Ludwig van Beethoven.

303 Sing Them Over Again to Me

1. Sing them o-ver a-gain to me, Won-der-ful words of Life;
2. Christ, the bless-ed One, gives to all, Won-der-ful words of Life;
3. Sweet-ly ech-o the gos-pel call, Won-der-ful words of Life;

Let me more of their beau-ty see, Won-der-ful words of Life.
Sin-ner, list to the lov-ing call, Won-der-ful words of Life.
Of-fer par-don and peace to all, Won-der-ful words of Life.

Words of life and beau-ty, Teach me faith and du-ty,
All so free-ly giv-en, Woo-ing us to heav-en,
Je-sus, on-ly Sav-ior, Sanc-ti-fy for-ev-er:

Beau-ti-ful words, won-der-ful words, Won-der-ful words of Life;

John 6:63. Words and tune WORDS OF LIFE, Philip P. Bliss, 1874.

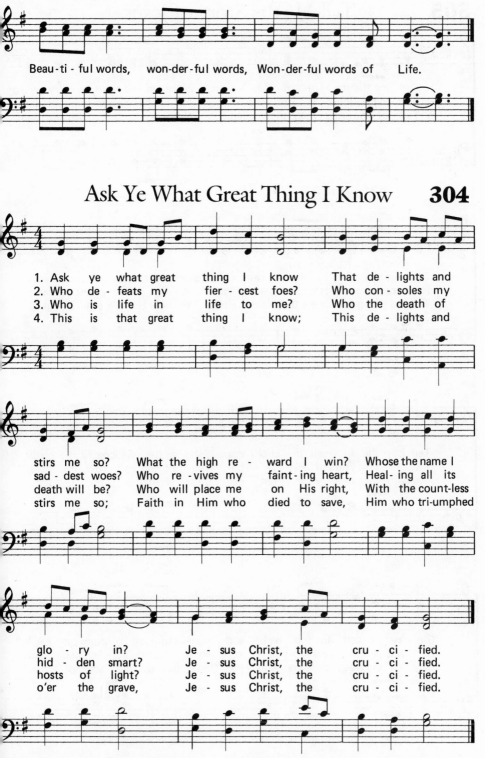

Beau-ti-ful words, won-der-ful words, Won-der-ful words of Life.

Ask Ye What Great Thing I Know 304

1. Ask ye what great thing I know That de-lights and
2. Who de-feats my fier-cest foes? Who con-soles my
3. Who is life in life to me? Who the death of
4. This is that great thing I know; This de-lights and

stirs me so? What the high re-ward I win? Whose the name I
sad-dest woes? Who re-vives my faint-ing heart, Heal-ing all its
death will be? Who will place me on His right, With the count-less
stirs me so; Faith in Him who died to save, Him who tri-umphed

glo-ry in? Je-sus Christ, the cru-ci-fied.
hid-den smart? Je-sus Christ, the cru-ci-fied.
hosts of light? Je-sus Christ, the cru-ci-fied.
o'er the grave, Je-sus Christ, the cru-ci-fied.

Corinthians 2:2. Words, John C. Schwedler, 1741; trans. Benjamin H. Kennedy, 1863. Tune HENDON, H. A. César Malan, 1823; arr. Lowell Mason, 1841.

305 Tell Me the Story of Jesus

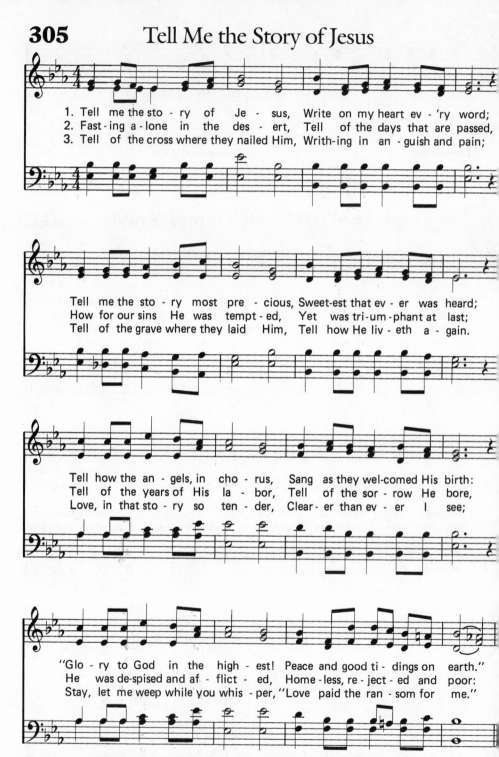

1. Tell me the sto - ry of Je - sus, Write on my heart ev - 'ry word;
2. Fast - ing a - lone in the des - ert, Tell of the days that are passed,
3. Tell of the cross where they nailed Him, Writh-ing in an - guish and pain;

Tell me the sto - ry most pre - cious, Sweet-est that ev - er was heard;
How for our sins He was tempt - ed, Yet was tri - um -phant at last;
Tell of the grave where they laid Him, Tell how He liv - eth a - gain.

Tell how the an - gels, in cho - rus, Sang as they wel-comed His birth:
Tell of the years of His la - bor, Tell of the sor - row He bore,
Love, in that sto - ry so ten - der, Clear - er than ev - er I see;

"Glo - ry to God in the high - est! Peace and good ti - dings on earth."
He was de-spised and af - flict - ed, Home - less, re - ject - ed and poor:
Stay, let me weep while you whis - per, "Love paid the ran - som for me."

Acts 10:36. Words, Fanny J. Crosby, 1880. Tune STORY OF JESUS, John R. Sweney, 1880.

Tell me the sto - ry of Je - sus, Write on my heart ev - 'ry word:

Tell me the sto - ry most pre - cious, Sweet-est that ev - er was heard.

Matthew 28:18-20; John 20:21-23   **306**

Jesus came to them and spake unto them, saying, "All authority hath been given unto me in heaven and on earth. Go ye therefore, and make disciples of all nations, baptizing them into the name of the Father and of the Son and of the Holy Spirit: teaching them to observe all things whatsoever I commanded you; and lo, I am with you always, even unto the end of the world."

Jesus therefore said to them again, "Peace be unto you: as the Father hath sent me, even so send I you." And when he had said this, he breathed on them, and said unto them, "Receive ye the Holy Spirit: whosoever sins ye forgive, they are forgiven unto them; whosoever sins ye retain, they are retained."

307 We Have Heard the Joyful Sound

1. We have heard the joy-ful sound: Je - sus saves! Je - sus saves!
2. Waft it on the roll - ing tide: Je - sus saves! Je - sus saves!
3. Sing a - bove the bat - tle strife: Je - sus saves! Je - sus saves!
4. Give the winds a might - y voice: Je - sus saves! Je - sus saves!

Spread the ti - dings all a - round: Je - sus saves! Je - sus saves!
Tell to sin - ners far and wide: Je - sus saves! Je - sus saves!
By His death and end - less life, Je - sus saves! Je - sus saves!
Let the na - tions now re - joice: Je - sus saves! Je - sus saves!

Bear the news to ev - 'ry land, Climb the steeps and cross the waves;
Sing, ye is - lands of the sea; Ech - o back, ye o - cean caves;
Sing it soft - ly thro' the gloom, When the heart for mer - cy craves;
Shout sal - va - tion full and free, High - est hills and deep - est caves;

On - ward! 'tis our Lord's com - mand: Je - sus saves! Je - sus saves!
Earth shall keep her ju - bi - lee: Je - sus saves! Je - sus saves!
Sing in tri - umph o'er the tomb: Je - sus saves! Je - sus saves!
This our song of vic - to - ry: Je - sus saves! Je - sus saves!

Acts 4:12. Words, Priscilla J. Owens, c. 1882. Tune JESUS SAVES, William J. Kirkpatrick, 1882.

There's a Wideness in God's Mercy   **308**

1. There's a wide-ness in God's mer-cy, Like the wide-ness of the sea;
2. For the love of God is broad-er Than the meas-ure of man's mind:

There's a kind-ness in His jus-tice, Which is more than lib-er-ty.
And the heart of the E-ter-nal Is most won-der-ful-ly kind.

There is wel-come for the sin-ner, And more grac-es for the good;
If our love were but more sim-ple, We should take Him at His word;

There is mer-cy with the Sav-ior; There is heal-ing in His blood.
And our lives would be all sun-shine In the sweet-ness of our Lord.

Mark 16:15. Words, Frederick W. Faber, 1862. Tune IN BABILONE, Traditional Dutch Melody; arr. Julius Röntgen, 1912.

309   I Love to Tell the Story

1. I love to tell the sto-ry Of un-seen things a-bove, Of
2. I love to tell the sto-ry: More won-der-ful it seems Than
3. I love to tell the sto-ry: 'Tis pleas-ant to re-peat What
4. I love to tell the sto-ry, For those who know it best Seem

Je - sus and His glo - ry, Of Je - sus and His love; I
all the gold-en fan - cies Of all my gold-en dreams; I
seems, each time I tell it, More won-der-ful-ly sweet; I
hun - ger-ing and thirst-ing To hear it like the rest; And

love to tell the sto-ry Be - cause I know 'tis true; It
love to tell the sto-ry: It did so much for me; And
love to tell the sto-ry, For some have nev - er heard The
when, in scenes of glo-ry, I sing the new, new song, 'Twill

sat - is-fies my long-ings As noth-ing else can do.
that is just the rea - son I tell it now to thee.
mes - sage of sal - va - tion From God's own ho - ly word.
be the old, old sto-ry That I have loved so long.

Acts 18:9,10. Words, Catherine Hankey, 1866. Tune HANKEY, William G. Fischer, 1869.

I love to tell the sto-ry! 'Twill be my theme in glo-ry

To tell the old, old sto-ry Of Je-sus and His love.

Acts 2:22-24,32,33,36; 3:17,18   **310**

Jesus of Nazareth, a man approved of God unto you by mighty works and wonders and signs which God did by him in the midst of you, even as ye yourselves know; him, being delivered up by the determinate counsel and foreknowledge of God, ye by the hand of lawless men did crucify and slay: whom God raised up, having loosed the pangs of death; because it was not possible that he should be held by it. . . This Jesus did God raise up, whereof we all are witnesses . . . Being therefore by the right hand of God exalted, and having received of the Father the promise of the Holy Spirit, he hath poured forth this, which ye see and hear. Let all the house of Israel therefore know assuredly, that God hath made him both Lord and Christ, this Jesus whom ye crucified . . . And now, brethren, I know that in ignorance ye did it, as did also your rulers. But the things God foreshowed by the mouth of all the prophets, that his Christ should suffer, he thus fulfilled.

311 O Soul, Are You Weary

1. O soul, are you wea-ry and trou - bled? No light in the
2. Through death in - to life ev - er - last - ing He passed, and we
3. His word shall not fail you—He prom - ised; Be - lieve Him, and

dark-ness you see? There's a light for a look at the Sav - ior, And
fol - low Him there; O - ver us sin no more hath do - min - ion—For
all will be well: Then go to a world that is dy - ing, His

life more a - bun-dant and free!
more than con-querors we are!   Turn your eyes up-on Je - sus,
per - fect sal - va - tion to tell!

Look full in His won-der-ful face,   And the things of

1 John 1:7. Words and tune LEMMEL, Helen H. Lemmel, 1922. Copyright 1922. Renewal 1950 by H. H. Lemmel. Assigned to Singspiration, Inc. All rights reserved. Used by permission.

earth will grow strange-ly dim In the light of His glo-ry and grace.

Break Thou the Bread of Life 312

1. Break Thou the bread of life, Dear Lord, to me, As Thou didst
2. Bless Thou the truth, dear Lord, To me, to me, As Thou didst

break the loaves Be - side the sea; Be - yond the sa - cred page
bless the bread By Gal - i - lee; Then shall all bond-age cease,

I seek Thee, Lord; My spir - it pants for Thee, O liv - ing Word!
All fet - ters fall, And I shall find my peace, My All in all.

John 6:35. Words, Mary Artemisia Lathbury, 1877. Tune BREAD OF LIFE, William F. Sherwin, 1877.

313   Free From the Law

1. Free from the law, O hap-py con - di - tion, Je - sus hath
2. Now are we free, there's no con-dem - na - tion, Je - sus pro -
3. "Chil - dren of God," O glo - ri - ous call - ing, Sure - ly His

bled, and there is re - mis - sion; Cursed by the law and bruised by the
vides a per - fect sal - va - tion; "Come un - to me," O hear His sweet
grace will keep us from fall - ing; Pass - ing from death to life at His

fall, Grace hath re-deemed us once for all.
call, Come, and He saves us once for all. Once for all, O
call, Bless - ed sal - va - tion once for all.

sin - ner, re - ceive it, Once for all, O friend, now be-lieve it; Cling to the

Galatians 3:13. Words and tune ONCE FOR ALL, Philip P. Bliss, 1873.

cross, the bur-den will fall, Christ hath re-deemed us once for all.

There is a Balm in Gilead 314

There is a balm in Gil-e-ad to make the wound-ed whole;

Fine

There is a balm in Gil-e-ad to heal the sin - sick soul.

1. Some - times I feel dis - cour-aged, and think my work's in vain,
2. If you can - not sing like an - gels, If you can - not preach like Paul,

D.C.

But then the Ho - ly Spir - it re - vives my soul a - gain.
You can tell the love of Je - sus and say He died for all.

Jeremiah 8:22. Words, Traditional American Spiritual. Tune BALM IN GILEAD, Traditional Spiritual in Frederick J. Work's *Folk Songs of the American Negro*, 1907. Arr. J.B., Copyright 1986, ACU Press.

315 I Gave My Life for Thee

1. I gave My life for thee, My pre-cious blood I shed,
2. My Fa-ther's house of light, My glo-ry-cir-cled throne
3. And I have brought to thee, Down from My home a-bove,

That thou might'st ran-somed be, And quick-ened from the dead;
I left for earth-ly night, For wan-drings sad and lone;
Sal-va-tion full and free, My par-don and My love;

I gave, I gave My life for thee: What hast thou giv'n for Me?
I left, I left it all for thee: Hast thou left aught for Me?
I bring, I bring rich gifts to thee: What hast thou brought to Me?

I gave, I gave My life for thee: What hast thou giv'n for Me?
I left, I left it all for thee: Hast thou left aught for Me?
I bring, I bring rich gifts to thee: What hast thou brought to Me?

Philippians 2:5-8. Words, Frances R. Havergal, 1858. Tune KENOSIS, Philip P. Bliss, 1873.

God Calling Yet! Shall I Not Hear? **316**

1. God call - ing yet! Shall I not hear? Earth's plea - sures
2. God call - ing yet! Shall I not rise? Can I His
3. God call - ing yet! And shall He knock, And I my
4. God call - ing yet! And shall I give No heed, but
5. God call - ing yet! I can - not stay; My heart I

shall I still hold dear? Shall life's swift pass - ing
lov - ing voice de - spise, And base - ly His kind
heart the clos - er lock? He still is wait - ing
still in bond - age live? I wait, but He does
yield with - out de - lay; Vain world, fare - well, from

years all fly, And still my soul in slum - ber lie?
care re - pay? He calls me still; can I de - lay?
to re - ceive, And shall I dare His Spir - it grieve?
not for - sake; He calls me still; my heart, a - wake!
thee I part; The voice of God hath reached my heart.

Psalm 95:7,8. Words, Gerhard Tersteegen, 1735; trans. Jane Borthwick, 1855. Tune FEDERAL STREET, Henry K. Oliver, 1832.

317 If You Are Tired of the Load

1. If you are tired of the load of your sin, Let Jesus come into your heart; If you desire a new life to begin,
2. If there's a tempest your voice cannot still, Let Jesus come into your heart; If there's a void this world never can fill,
3. If you would join the glad songs of the blest, Let Jesus come into your heart; If you would enter the mansions of rest,

Let Jesus come into your heart. Just now, your doubtings give o'er; Just now, reject Him no more; Just now, throw

Mark 11:23. Words and tune McCONNELSVLLE, Leila N. Morris, 1898.

o - pen the door; Let Je - sus come in - to your heart.

Ephesians 2:1-10
Romans 4:4,5,16,24,25

318

And you did he make alive, when ye were dead through your trespasses and sins, wherein ye once walked according to the course of this world, according to the prince of the powers of the air, of the spirit that now works in the sons of disobedience; among whom we also all once lived in the lusts of our flesh, doing the desires of the flesh and the mind, and were by nature children of wrath, even as the rest: but God, being rich in mercy, for his great love with which he loved us, even when we were dead through our trespasses, made us alive together with Christ (by grace have ye been saved), and raised us up with him, and made us to sit with him in the heavenly places, in Christ Jesus: that in the ages to come, he might show the exceeding riches of his grace in kindness toward us in Christ Jesus: for by grace have ye been saved through faith; and that not of yourselves, it is the gift of God; not of works, that no man should glory. For we are his workmanship, created in Christ Jesus for good works, which God before prepared that we should walk in them.

Now to him that works, the reward is not reckoned as of grace, but as of debt. But to him that does not work, but believes on him that justified the ungodly, his faith is reckoned for righteousness. It is of faith, that it may be according to grace; to the end that the promise may be sure to all . . . for our sake also, to whom it shall be reckoned, who believe on him that raised Jesus our Lord from the dead, who was delivered up for our trespasses, and was raised for our justification.

319 **Hear the Sweet Voice**

1. Hear the sweet voice of Je - sus say, "Come un-to me, I am the way;"
2. Cast-ing your heav - y bur-den down, Come to the cross, the world may frown;
3. O - pen, for you, the pearl-y gate; Loved ones for you now watch and wait;

Heark-en, the lov - ing call o - bey; Come, for He loves you so.
Yet you shall wear a glo-rious crown, When He makes up His own.
Ter - ri - ble tho't, to cry, "too late"—"Je - sus, I come to Thee."

On-ly a step, on - ly a step; Come, for He bled for you and died;

He's the same lov - ing Sav - ior yet, Je - sus the Cru - ci - fied.

John 6:37. Words and tune ONLY A STEP, Charles H. Gabriel, d. 1932.

Hark! the Gentle Voice

320

1. Hark! the gen - tle voice of Je - sus fall - eth Ten-der-ly up - on your ear;
2. Take His yoke, for He is meek and low-ly; Bear His bur-den, to Him turn;
3. Then, His lov - ing, ten-der voice o - bey-ing, Bear His yoke, His bur-den take;

Sweet His cry of love and pit - y call-eth: Turn and lis - ten, stay and hear.
He who call-eth is the Mas-ter ho - ly: He will teach if you will learn.
Find the yoke His hand is on you lay-ing, Light and eas - y for His sake.

Ye that la - bor and are heav-y - la-den, Lean up-on your dear Lord's breast;

Ye that la - bor and are heav-y - la-den, Come, and I will give you rest.

Matthew 11:28-30. Words, Mary B.C. Slade. Tune EVERETT, Asa Brooks Everett.

321   # Jesus is Tenderly Calling

1. Je-sus is ten-der-ly call-ing thee home, Call-ing to-day, call-ing to-day;
2. Je-sus is call-ing the wea-ry to rest, Call-ing to-day, call-ing to-day;
3. Je-sus is wait-ing, O come to Him now, Waiting to-day, wait-ing to-day;
4. Je-sus is plead-ing, O list to His voice: Hear Him to-day, hear Him to-day;

Why from the sun-shine of love wilt thou roam Far-ther and far-ther a-way?
Bring Him thy bur-den and thou shalt be blest; He will not turn thee a-way:
Come with thy sins, at His feet low-ly bow; Come, and no long-er de-lay:
They who be-lieve on His name shall re-joice; Quick-ly a-rise and a-way:

Call - ing to-day! Call - ing to-day!
Call-ing, call-ing to-day, to-day! Call-ing, call-ing to-day, to-day!

Je - sus is call - ing, Is ten-der-ly call-ing to-day.
Je-sus is ten-der-ly call-ing to-day,

2 Corinthians 6:2. Words, Fanny J. Crosby, 1883. Tune CALLING TODAY, George C. Stebbins, 1883.

God is Calling the Prodigal

322

1. God is call - ing the prod - i - gal, come with-out de - lay;
2. Pa - tient, lov - ing and ten-der - ly still the Fa - ther pleads;

Though you've wan-dered so far from home, hear His lov-ing voice to-day.
O re - turn to thy Fa-ther's house, now the Spir-it in -ter - cedes.

Call - ing now for thee; Wear - y soul, now come.

Pro - di - gal, O hear this call to-day; O pro - di - gal, now come.

Luke 15:20. Words, Charles H. Gabriel, 1889; arr. J.B., 1985. Tune ORR, Jack Boyd, 1985. Word arr. and tune Copyright 1986, ACU Press.

323   ## Softly and Tenderly

1. Soft-ly and ten-der-ly, Je-sus is call-ing, Call-ing for you and for me;
2. Why should we tarry when Jesus is pleading, Pleading for you and for me?
3. O for the won-der-ful love He has promised, Promised for you and for me;

See   on the por - tals He's waiting and watching, Watching for you and for me.
Why should we lin-ger and heed not His mercies, Mer-cies for you and for me?
Tho' we have sinned, He has mer-cy and par-don, Par-don for you and for me.

Come home,   come home,   Ye who are wea-ry, come home;
Come home,   come home,

Ear-nest-ly, ten-der-ly, Je-sus is call-ing, Call-ing, O sin-ner, come home!

Isaiah 42:1-4. Words and tune THOMPSON, Will L. Thompson, 1880.

Sinners Jesus Will Receive

324

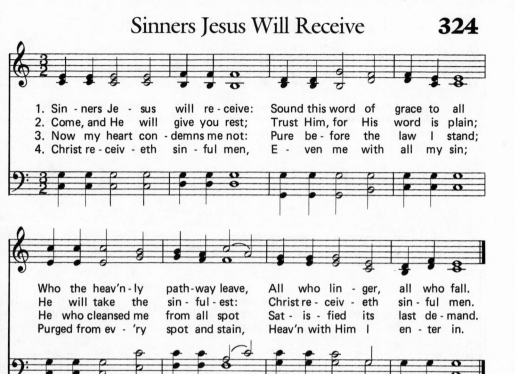

1. Sin - ners Je - sus   will re - ceive: Sound this word of   grace to   all
2. Come, and He   will   give you rest;   Trust Him, for   His   word is   plain;
3. Now my heart con - demns me not: Pure be - fore   the   law I   stand;
4. Christ re - ceiv - eth   sin - ful men,   E - ven me   with   all   my sin;

Who the heav'n - ly   path-way leave,   All who lin - ger,   all who fall.
He   will take   the   sin - ful - est: Christ re - ceiv - eth   sin - ful men.
He   who cleansed me   from all spot   Sat - is - fied   its   last de - mand.
Purged from ev - 'ry   spot and stain,   Heav'n with Him I   en - ter in.

1 Timothy 1:15. Words, Erdmann Neumeister, 1718; trans. Emma Frances Bevan, 1858. Tune ALBERTSON, Phoebe P. Knapp.

Luke 15:1-7

325

Now all the publicans and sinners were drawing near to him to hear him. And both the Pharisees and the scribes murmured, saying, "This man receives sinners, and eats with them." And he spoke this parable to them, saying, "What man of you, having a hundred sheep, and having lost one of them, does not leave the ninety-nine in the wilderness, and go after that which is lost, until he finds it? And when he has found it, he lays it on his shoulders, rejoicing. And when he comes home, he calls together his friends and his neighbors, saying to them, 'Rejoice with me, for I have found my sheep which was lost.' I say to you, that even so there shall be joy in heaven over one sinner that repents, more than over ninety-nine righteous persons, who need no repentance."

326 Bring Christ Your Broken Life

1. Bring Christ your bro-ken life, So marred by sin,
2. Bring Him your ev-'ry care If great or small—
3. Bring Him your wea-ri-ness, Re-ceive His rest;
4. Blest Sav-ior of us all! Al-might-y Friend!

He will cre-ate a-new, Make whole a-gain;
What-ev-er trou-bles you— O bring it all!
Weep out your blind-ing tears Up-on His breast;
His pres-ence shall be ours Un-to the end;

Your emp-ty, wast-ed years He will re-store,
Bring Him the haunt-ing fears, The name-less dread,
His love is won-der-ful, His pow'r is great,
With-out Him life would be How dark, how drear!

And your in-i-qui-ties Re-mem-ber no more.
Thy heart He will re-lieve, And lift up thy head.
"And none that trust in Him Shall be des-o-late."
But with Him morn-ing breaks And heav-en is near!

Titus 3:4-7. Words, Thomas O. Chisholm, 1935. Tune BROKEN LIFE, Lloyd O. Sanderson, 1935.

Come, Every Soul

327

1. Come, ev - 'ry soul by sin op-pressed, There's mer-cy with the Lord,
2. For Je - sus shed His pre-cious blood, Rich bless-ings to be - stow;
3. Come then, and join this ho - ly band, And on to glo - ry go,

And He will sure - ly give you rest By trust-ing in His word.
Plunge now in - to the crim - son flood That wash - es white as snow.
To dwell in that ce - les - tial land, Where joys im - mor - tal flow.

On - ly trust Him, on - ly trust Him, On - ly trust Him now;

He will save you, He will save you, He will save you now.

John 1:12,13. Words and tune STOCKSTON, John H. Stockton, c. 1873.

328 I Have a Savior

1. I have a Savior, He's pleading in glory, A dear loving Savior, tho' earth-friends be few; And now He is watching in tenderness o'er me, But O that my Savior were your Savior too!

2. I have a Father: to me He has given A hope for eternity, blessed and true; And soon He will call me to meet Him in heaven, But O that He'd let me bring you with me too!

3. I have a robe: 'tis resplendent in whiteness, Awaiting in glory my wondering view; O when I receive it all shining in brightness, Dear friend, could I see you receiving one too!

4. I have a peace: it is calm as a river, A peace that the friends of this world never knew; My Savior alone is its Author and Giver, And O could I know it was given to you!

1 John 2:1. Words, Samuel O'Malley Cluff, 1860. Tune INTERCESSION, Ira D. Sankey, 1875.

Chorus following final stanza only

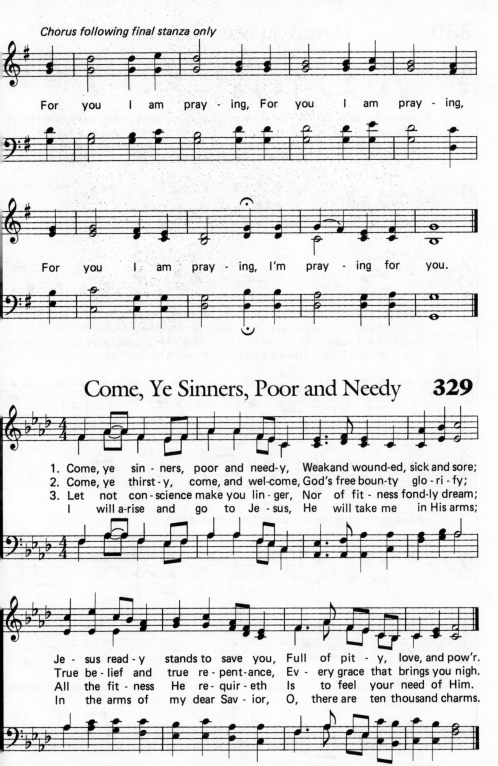

For you I am pray - ing, For you I am pray - ing,

For you I am pray - ing, I'm pray - ing for you.

Come, Ye Sinners, Poor and Needy   329

1. Come, ye sin - ners, poor and need - y, Weak and wound-ed, sick and sore;
2. Come, ye thirst - y, come, and wel-come, God's free boun-ty glo - ri - fy;
3. Let not con - science make you lin - ger, Nor of fit - ness fond-ly dream;
   I will a-rise and go to Je - sus, He will take me in His arms;

Je - sus read - y stands to save you, Full of pit - y, love, and pow'r.
True be - lief and true re - pent-ance, Ev - ery grace that brings you nigh.
All the fit - ness He re - quir - eth Is to feel your need of Him.
In the arms of my dear Sav - ior, O, there are ten thousand charms.

Luke 15:18. Words, Joseph Hart, 1759. Tune ARISE, Traditional American Melody. Arr. J.B., Copyright 1986, ACU Press.

330   Have You Been to Jesus?

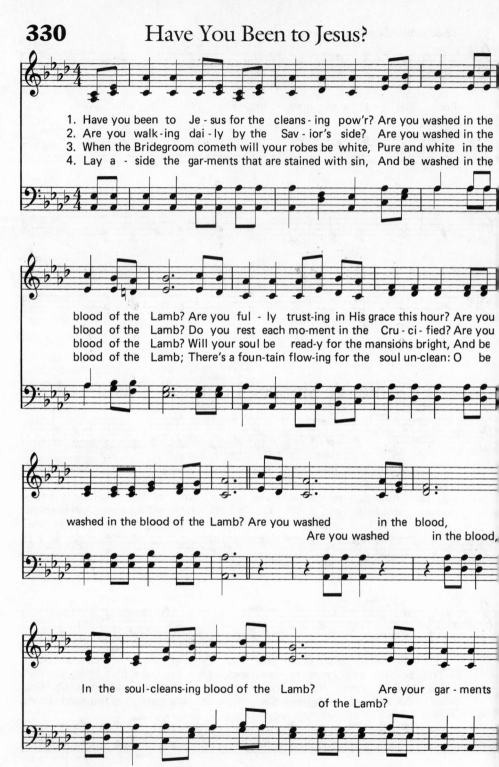

1. Have you been to Je - sus for the cleans - ing pow'r? Are you washed in the
2. Are you walk - ing dai - ly by the Sav - ior's side? Are you washed in the
3. When the Bridegroom cometh will your robes be white, Pure and white in the
4. Lay a - side the gar - ments that are stained with sin, And be washed in the

blood of the Lamb? Are you ful - ly trust-ing in His grace this hour? Are you
blood of the Lamb? Do you rest each mo-ment in the Cru - ci - fied? Are you
blood of the Lamb? Will your soul be read-y for the mansions bright, And be
blood of the Lamb; There's a foun-tain flow-ing for the soul un-clean: O be

washed in the blood of the Lamb? Are you washed   in the blood,
    Are you washed   in the blood,

In the soul-cleans-ing blood of the Lamb?   Are your gar - ments
of the Lamb?

Ephesians 1:7. Words and tune WASHED IN THE BLOOD, Elisha A. Hoffman, 1878.

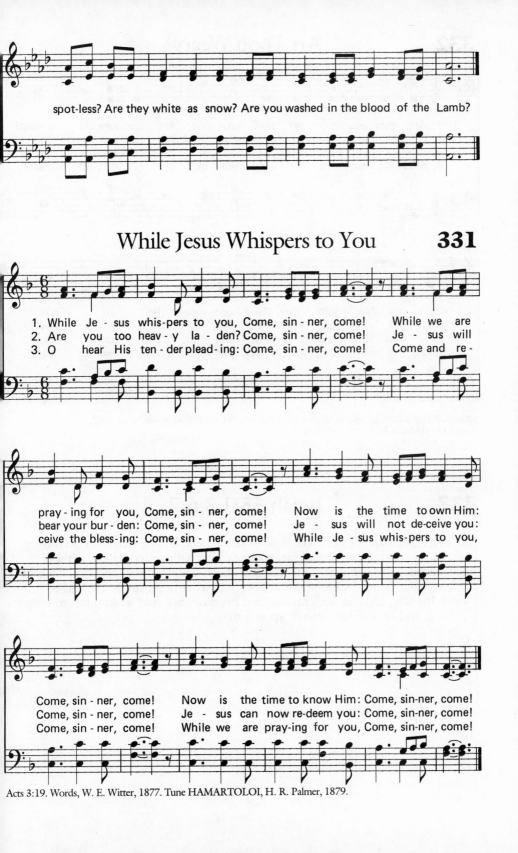

spot-less? Are they white as snow? Are you washed in the blood of the Lamb?

While Jesus Whispers to You 331

1. While Je - sus whis-pers to you, Come, sin - ner, come! While we are
2. Are you too heav - y la - den? Come, sin - ner, come! Je - sus will
3. O hear His ten - der plead-ing: Come, sin - ner, come! Come and re -

pray - ing for you, Come, sin - ner, come! Now is the time to own Him:
bear your bur - den: Come, sin - ner, come! Je - sus will not de-ceive you:
ceive the bless-ing: Come, sin - ner, come! While Je - sus whis-pers to you,

Come, sin - ner, come! Now is the time to know Him: Come, sin-ner, come!
Come, sin - ner, come! Je - sus can now re-deem you: Come, sin-ner, come!
Come, sin - ner, come! While we are pray-ing for you, Come, sin-ner, come!

Acts 3:19. Words, W. E. Witter, 1877. Tune HAMARTOLOI, H. R. Palmer, 1879.

332   Art Thou Weary?

1. Art thou wea-ry, art thou lan-guid; Art thou sore dis-tressed?
2. If I ask Him to re-ceive me, Will He say me nay!
3. If I still hold close-ly to Him, What hath He at last?
4. Find-ing Him, and fol-l'wing, keep-ing, Is He sure to bless?

"Come to Me," saith One, "and com-ing, Be at rest."
"Not till earth and not till heav-en Pass a-way."
"Sor-row van-quished, la-bor end-ed, Jor-dan passed."
Saints, a-pos-tles, proph-ets, mar-tyrs, An-swer "Yes!"

Matthew 11:28-30. Words, attr. to Stephen the Sabaite, d. 794; trans. John Mason Neale, 1862.
Tune STEPHANOS, Henry W. Baker, 1868.

333   Isaiah 55:1,3,6,7

Ho, every one that thirsteth, come ye to the waters, and he that hath no money; come ye, buy, and eat; yea, come, buy wine and milk without money and without price. Incline your ear, and come unto me: hear, and your soul will live. Seek ye the Lord while he may be found, call ye upon him while he is near: let the wicked forsake his way, and the unrighteous man his thoughts: and let him return unto the Lord, and he will have mercy upon him.

Come to the Savior Now

334

1. Come to the Sav - ior now, He gen - tly calls to you;
2. Come to the Sav - ior now, You who have wan - dered far;
3. Bring to the Sav - ior Ev - 'ry bur - den there may be;

In true re - pent - ance bow, In full com - mit - ment, too;
Re - new your sol - emn vow, For His by right you are;
Hear now His lov - ing call, "Cast all your care on Me."

His word has prom - ised us Sal - va - tion, peace, and love,
Come, like poor wan - dering sheep Re - turn - ing to the fold;
Come, and for ev - ery grief In Je - sus you will find

True joy on earth be - low, A home in heav'n a - bove.
His arm will safe - ly keep, His love will not grow cold.
Help, com - fort and re - lief, A lov - ing friend and kind.

John 10:16. Words, John M. Wigner, 1871. Tune INVITATION, Frederick C. Maker, 1881.

335 **Whosoever Heareth**

1. Who - so - ev - er hear - eth, shout, shout the sound! Spread the blessed ti - dings
2. Who - so - ev - er com - eth need not de - lay; Now the door is o - pen,
3. "Who - so - ev - er will"—the prom - ise se - cure— "Who - so - ev - er will" for

all the world a - round; Spread the joyful news wher - ev - er man is found:
en - ter while you may; Je - sus is the true, the on - ly Liv - ing Way:
ev - er must en - dure; "Who - so - ev - er will"—tis life for ev - er - more:

"Who - so - ev - er will may come."
"Who - so - ev - er will may come." "Who - so - ev - er will, who - so - ev - er
"Who - so - ev - er will may come."

will!" Send the pro - cla - ma - tion o - ver vale and hill; 'Tis a lov - ing

Fa - ther calls the wand'rer home: "Who - so - ev - er will may come."

Revelation 22:17. Words and tune WHOSOEVER, Philip P. Bliss, 1870.

Come to the Savior

336

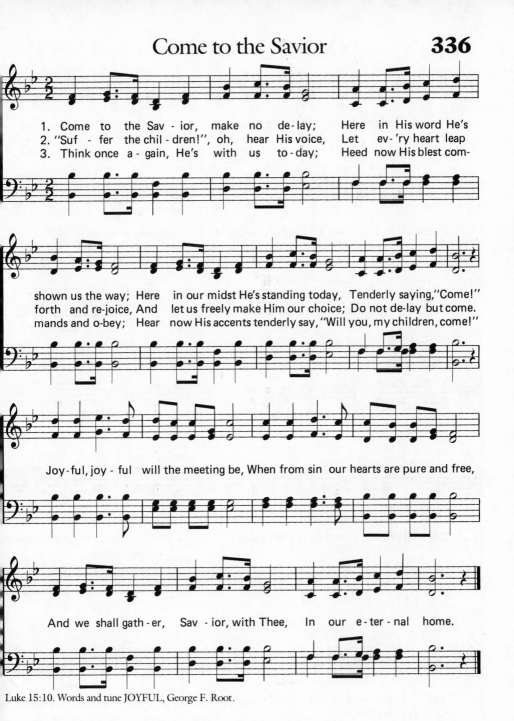

1. Come to the Sav - ior, make no de - lay; Here in His word He's
2. "Suf - fer the chil - dren!", oh, hear His voice, Let ev - 'ry heart leap
3. Think once a - gain, He's with us to - day; Heed now His blest com-

shown us the way; Here in our midst He's standing today, Tenderly saying, "Come!"
forth and re-joice, And let us freely make Him our choice; Do not de-lay but come.
mands and o-bey; Hear now His accents tenderly say, "Will you, my children, come!"

Joy - ful, joy - ful will the meeting be, When from sin our hearts are pure and free,

And we shall gath - er, Sav - ior, with Thee, In our e - ter - nal home.

Luke 15:10. Words and tune JOYFUL, George F. Root.

337 O Heart Bowed Down

1. O heart bowed down with sor - row! O eyes that long for sight!
2. Di - vin - est con - so - la - tion Doth Christ the Heal - er give;
3. His peace is like a riv - er, His love is like a song;

There's glad - ness in be - liev - ing; In Je - sus there is light.
Art thou in con - dem - na - tion? Be - lieve, re - pent and live.
His yoke's a bur - den nev - er; 'Tis eas - y all day long.

"Come un - to me, all ye that la - bor
"Come, O come, come un - to me, Come, O come, all ye that la - bor

and are heav - y - la - den, and I will give you rest.
Come, O come, la - den souls, I will give you rest.

Take my yoke up - on you and learn of me; for
Come, O come, Come, take my yoke, Come, O come, come learn of me;

Matthew 11:28-30. Words and tune BELDEN, Franklin E. Belden, 1895.

I am meek and low-ly in heart: and ye shall find rest un-to your souls."
I am meek and low-ly in heart:

Come, Ye Disconsolate   **338**

1. Come, ye dis - con - so-late, wher - e'er ye lan - guish, Come to the
2. Joy of the des - o - late, light of the stray - ing, Hope of the
3. Here see the Bread of Life; see wa - ters flow - ing Forth from the

mer - cy seat, fer - vent-ly kneel; Here bring your wound-ed hearts,
pen - i - tent, fade - less and pure! Here speaks the Com - fort-er,
throne of God, pure from a - bove: Come to the feast of love;

here tell your an - guish: Earth has no sor - row that heav'n can-not heal.
ten - der - ly say - ing, "Earth has no sor - row that heav'n can-not cure."
come, ev - er know - ing Earth has no sor - row but heav'n can re - move.

Romans 3:21-26. Words, st. 1 and 2, Thomas Moore, 1818; st. 3, Thomas Hastings, 1832. Tune CONSOLATOR,
from *A Collection of Motets and Antiphons*, 1792; arr. from Samuel Webbe, Sr., 1831.

339 Would You be Free?

1. Would you be free from your bur - den of sin? There's pow'r in the blood,
2. Would you be free from your pas - sion and pride? There's pow'r in the blood,
3. Would you be whit - er, much whit-er than snow? There's pow'r in the blood,
4. Would you do serv - ice for Je - sus your King? There's pow'r in the blood,

pow'r in the blood; Would you o'er e - vil a vic - to-ry win?
pow'r in the blood; Come for a cleans- ing to Cal - va-ry's tide;
pow'r in the blood; Sin - stains are lost in its life - giv-ing flow?
pow'r in the blood; Would you live dai - ly His prais - es to sing?

There's won - der - ful pow'r in the blood. There is pow'r, pow'r,
there is pow'r,

Won-der-work-ing pow'r in the blood of the Lamb; There is
in the blood of the Lamb;

Revelation 1:5. Words and tune POWER IN THE BLOOD, Lewis E. Jones, 1899.

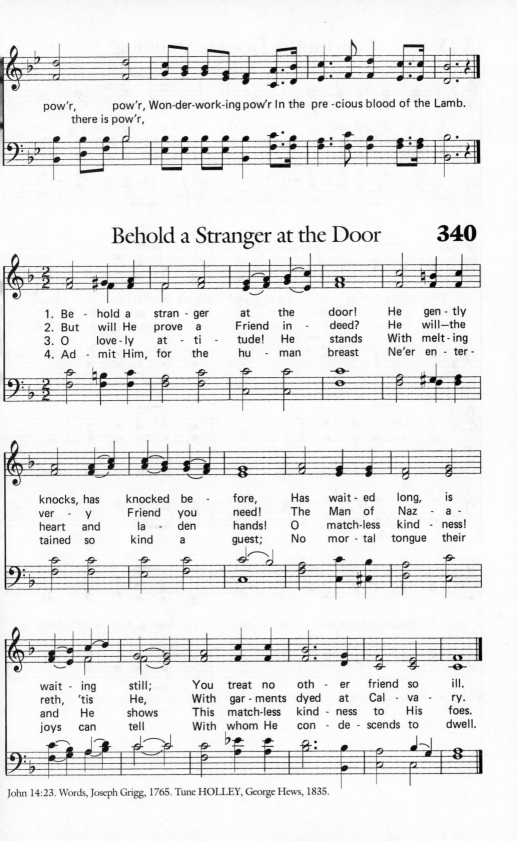

pow'r,   pow'r, Won-der-work-ing pow'r In the pre-cious blood of the Lamb.
there is pow'r,

Behold a Stranger at the Door   340

1. Be - hold a stran - ger at the door! He gen - tly
2. But will He prove a Friend in - deed? He will—the
3. O love - ly at - ti - tude! He stands With melt - ing
4. Ad - mit Him, for the hu - man breast Ne'er en - ter-

knocks, has knocked be - fore, Has wait - ed long, is
ver - y Friend you need! The Man of Naz - a -
heart and la - den hands! O match-less kind - ness!
tained so kind a guest; No mor - tal tongue their

wait - ing still; You treat no oth - er friend so ill.
reth, 'tis He, With gar - ments dyed at Cal - va - ry.
and He shows This match-less kind - ness to His foes.
joys can tell With whom He con - de - scends to dwell.

John 14:23. Words, Joseph Grigg, 1765. Tune HOLLEY, George Hews, 1835.

341 Who at the Door is Standing

1. Who at the door is stand - ing, Pa - tient - ly draw - ing near,
2. All thro' the dark hours drear - y, Knock-ing a - gain is He;
3. Door of my heart, I has - ten! Thee will I o - pen wide;

En - trance with-in de - mand - ing? Whose is the voice I hear?
Je - sus, art Thou not wea - ry, Wait - ing so long for me?
Tho' He re - buke and chas - ten, He shall with me a - bide.

Sweet - ly the tones are fall - ing: "O - pen the door for Me!

If thou wilt heed My call - ing, I will a - bide with thee."

Revelation 3:20. Words, Mary B. C. Slade, c. 1875. Tune EVERETT, Asa Brooks Everett, c. 1875.

Arise, My Soul, Arise

1. A - rise, my soul, a - rise, Shake off your guilt - y fears;
2. He ev - er lives a - bove, For me to in - ter - cede;
3. To God I'm rec - on - ciled, His par - d'ning voice I hear;

The bleed - ing Sac - ri - fice In your be - half ap - pears;
His all - re - deem - ing love, His pre - cious blood to plead;
He owns me for His child, I can no lon - ger fear;

Be - fore the throne my Sure - ty stands, My name is writ - ten
His blood a - toned for all our race, And sprin - kles now the
With con - fi - dence I now draw nigh, And "Fa - ther, Ab - ba,

on His hands, My name is writ - ten on His hands.
throne of grace, And sprin - kles now the throne of grace.
Fa - ther," cry, And "Fa - ther, Ab - ba, Fa - ther," cry.

Galatians 4:4-7. Words, Charles Wesley, 1742. Tune TOWNER, Traditional American Melody; arr. Daniel B. Towner, 1909.

343   I Heard the Voice of Jesus Say

1. I heard the voice of Je - sus say, "Come un - to me and rest;
2. I heard the voice of Je - sus say, "Be - hold I free - ly give
3. I heard the voice of Je - sus say, "I am this dark world's light;

Lay down, thou wea - ry one, lay down Thy head up - on my breast."
The liv - ing wa - ter: thirst - y one, Stoop down and drink, and live."
Look un - to me, thy morn shall rise, And all thy day be bright!"

I came to Je - sus as I was, Wea - ry and worn and sad;
I came to Je - sus and I drank Of that life - giv - ing stream:
I looked to Je - sus and I found In Him my Star, my Sun;

I found Him in a rest - ing place, And He has made me glad.
My thirst was quenched, my soul revived, And now I live in Him.
And in that light of life I'll walk Till trav-'ling days are done.

John 8:12. Words, Horatius Bonar, 1846. Tune SPOHR, Ludwig Spohr, 1834.

What Can Wash Away My Sin? **344**

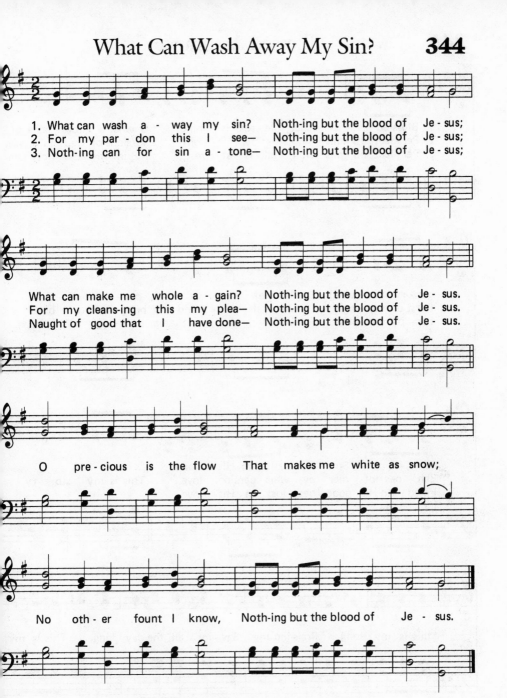

1. What can wash a - way my sin? Noth-ing but the blood of Je - sus;
2. For my par - don this I see— Noth-ing but the blood of Je - sus;
3. Noth-ing can for sin a - tone— Noth-ing but the blood of Je - sus;

What can make me whole a - gain? Noth-ing but the blood of Je - sus.
For my cleans-ing this my plea— Noth-ing but the blood of Je - sus.
Naught of good that I have done— Noth-ing but the blood of Je - sus.

O pre - cious is the flow That makes me white as snow;

No oth - er fount I know, Noth-ing but the blood of Je - sus.

Revelation 1:5. Words and tune NOTHING BUT THE BLOOD, Robert Lowry, 1876.

345 Blessed Assurance

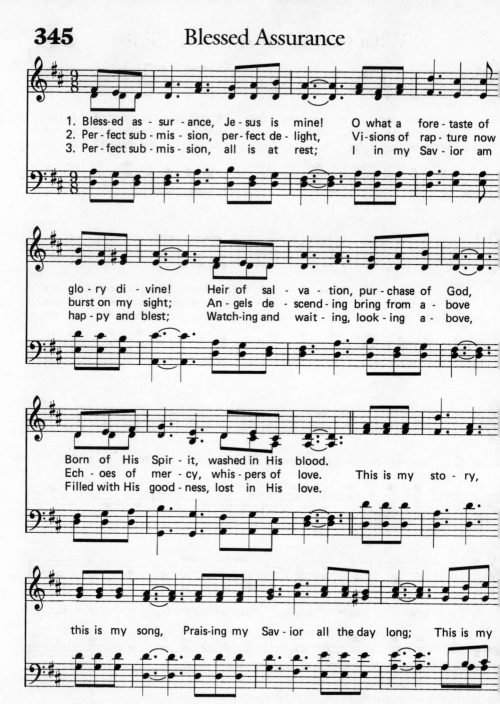

1. Bless-ed as-sur-ance, Je-sus is mine! O what a fore-taste of
2. Per-fect sub-mis-sion, per-fect de-light, Vi-sions of rap-ture now
3. Per-fect sub-mis-sion, all is at rest; I in my Sav-ior am

glo-ry di-vine! Heir of sal-va-tion, pur-chase of God,
burst on my sight; An-gels de-scend-ing bring from a-bove
hap-py and blest; Watch-ing and wait-ing, look-ing a-bove,

Born of His Spir-it, washed in His blood.
Ech-oes of mer-cy, whis-pers of love. This is my sto-ry,
Filled with His good-ness, lost in His love.

this is my song, Prais-ing my Sav-ior all the day long; This is my

Hebrews 7:25. Words, Fanny J. Crosby, 1873. Tune ASSURANCE, Phoebe P. Knapp, 1873.

sto - ry, this is my song, Prais - ing my Sav - ior all the day long.

Just as I Am

346

1. Just as I am! with-out one plea, But that Thy blood was shed for me,
2. Just as I am! and wait - ing not To rid my soul of one dark blot,
3. Just as I am! tho' tossed a - bout With many a con - flict, many a doubt,
4. Just as I am! poor, wretched, blind— Sight, rich - es, heal - ing of the mind,
5. Just as I am! Thou wilt re - ceive, Wilt wel - come, par - don, cleanse, re - lieve;
6. Just as I am! Thy love unknown Has bro - ken ev - 'ry bar - rier down;

And that Thou bidd'st me come to Thee, O Lamb of God, I come! I come!
To Thee, whose blood can cleanse each spot, O Lamb of God, I come! I come!
With fears with - in, and foes with - out, O Lamb of God, I come! I come!
Yea, all I need, in Thee to find,— O Lamb of God, I come! I come!
Be - cause Thy prom - ise I be - lieve, O Lamb of God, I come! I come!
Now to be Thine, yea, Thine a - lone, O Lamb of God, I come! I come!

Isaiah 1:18. Words, Charlotte Elliott, 1834. Tune WOODWORTH, William B. Bradbury, 1849.

I Bring My Sins to Thee

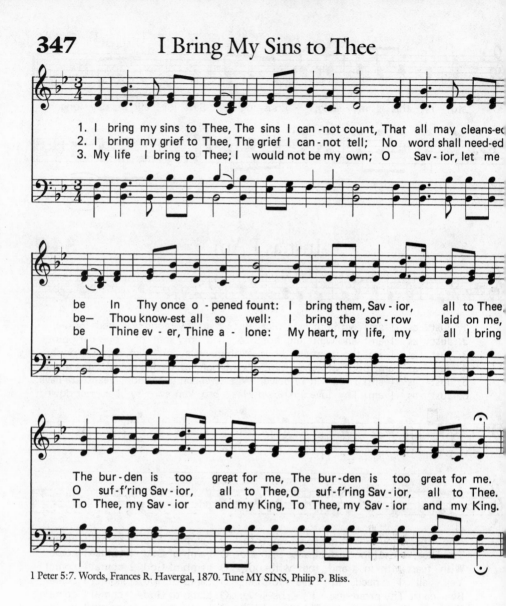

1. I bring my sins to Thee, The sins I can-not count, That all may cleans-ed
2. I bring my grief to Thee, The grief I can-not tell; No word shall need-ed
3. My life I bring to Thee; I would not be my own; O Sav-ior, let me

be In Thy once o-pened fount: I bring them, Sav-ior, all to Thee,
be— Thou know-est all so well: I bring the sor-row laid on me,
be Thine ev-er, Thine a-lone: My heart, my life, my all I bring

The bur-den is too great for me, The bur-den is too great for me.
O suf-f'ring Sav-ior, all to Thee, O suf-f'ring Sav-ior, all to Thee.
To Thee, my Sav-ior and my King, To Thee, my Sav-ior and my King.

1 Peter 5:7. Words, Frances R. Havergal, 1870. Tune MY SINS, Philip P. Bliss.

348 ## Luke 15:17-20

When he came to himself he said, "How many hired servants of my father's have bread enough and to spare, and I perish here with hunger! I will arise and go to my father, and will say to him, 'Father, I have sinned against heaven and in your sight: I am no more worthy to be called your son: make me as one of your hired servants.'" And he arose and came to his father. But while he was yet afar off, his father saw him, and was moved with compassion, and ran and fell on his neck and kissed him.

My Stubborn Will at Last Hath Yielded **349**

1. My stub-born will at last hath yield - ed; I would be
2. I'm tired of sin, foot-sore and wea - ry; The dark-some
3. Thy pre - cious will, O con - qu'ring Sav - ior, Doth now em -
4. Shut in with Thee, O Lord, for ev - er, My way - ward

Thine and Thine a - lone; And this the prayer
path hath drear - y grown; But now a light
brace and com - pass me; All dis - cords hushed,
feet no more to roam; What pow'r from Thee

my lips are bring - ing, "Lord, let in me Thy will be done."
has ris'n to cheer me: I find in Thee my Star, my Sun.
my peace a riv - er, My soul a pris-oned bird set free.
my soul can sev - er? The cen-ter of God's will my home.

Sweet will of God, still fold me clos - er, Till I am

whol - ly lost in Thee; Sweet will of God, still

fold me clos - er, Till I am whol - ly lost in Thee.

Galatians 2:20. Words and tune SWEET WILL OF GOD, Leila N. Morris, 1900.

350   Jesus, Priceless Treasure

1. Je - sus, price - less Treas - ure, Source of pur - est pleas - ure,
2. In thine arm I rest me; Foes who would mo - lest me
3. Hence, all thoughts of sad - ness! For the Lord of glad - ness,

Tru - est friend to me; Long my heart hath pant - ed, Till it al - most
Can - not reach me here. Though the earth be shak - ing, Ev - 'ry heart be
Je - sus, en - ters in. Those who love the Fa - ther, Tho' the storms ma

faint - ed, Thirst - ing af - ter Thee. Thine I am, O spot - less Lamb
quak - ing, God dis - pels our fear; Sin and hell in con - flict fell;
gath - er, Still have peace with - in; Yea, what-e'er we here must bear,

I will suf - fer nought to hide Thee, Ask for nought be - side Thee.
With their heav - iest storms as - sail us: Je - sus will not fail us.
Still in Thee lies pur - est pleas - ure, Je - sus, price - less Treas - ure.

*May be sung a half tone or full tone lower.

John 10:27-29. Words, Johann Franck, 1641; trans. Catherine Winkworth, 1863. Tune JESU, MEINE FREUDE,
Johann Crüger, 1653; harm. J. S. Bach.

I've Wandered Far

351

1. I've wan - dered far a - way from God: Now I'm com-ing home;
2. I've wast - ed man - y pre - cious years: Now I'm com-ing home;
3. I'm tired of sin and stray - ing, Lord: Now I'm com-ing home;

The paths of sin too long I've trod; Lord, I'm com-ing home.
I now re-pent with bit - ter tears: Lord, I'm com-ing home.
I'll trust Thy love, be - lieve Thy word: Lord, I'm com-ing home.

Com-ing home, com-ing home, Nev - er - more to roam;

O - pen wide Thine arms of love; Lord, I'm com-ing home.

Luke 15:17,18. Words and tune COMING HOME, William J. Kirkpatrick, 1892.

352　Out of My Bondage

1. Out of my bond - age, sor - row and night, Je - sus, I come,
2. Out of my shame - ful fail - ure and loss, Je - sus, I come,
3. Out of un - rest and ar - ro - gant pride, Je - sus, I come,
4. Out of the fear and dread of the tomb, Je - sus, I come,

Je - sus, I come; In - to Thy free - dom, glad - ness and light,
Je - sus, I come; In - to the glo - rious gain of Thy cross,
Je - sus, I come; In - to Thy bless - ed will to a - bide,
Je - sus, I come; In - to the joy and light of Thy home,

Je - sus, I come to Thee; Out of my sick - ness
Je - sus, I come to Thee; Out of earth's sor - rows
Je - sus, I come to Thee; Out of my - self to
Je - sus, I come to Thee; Out of the depths of

in - to Thy health, Out of my want and in - to Thy wealth,
in - to Thy balm, Out of life's storms and in - to Thy calm,
dwell in Thy love, Out of de - spair in - to rap - tures a - bove,
ru - in un - told, In - to the peace of Thy shel - ter - ing fold,

Titus 3:3-5. Words, William T. Sleeper, c. 1887. Tune JESUS, I COME, George C. Stebbins, c. 1887.

Out of my sin and in - to Thy -self, Je - sus, I come to Thee.
Out of dis - tress to ju - bi-lant psalm, Je - sus, I come to Thee.
Up - ward for aye on wings of a dove, Je - sus, I come to Thee.
Ev - er Thy glo - rious face to be - hold, Je - sus, I come to Thee.

Love for All 353

1. Love for all— and can it be? Can I hope it is for me—
2. I, the dis - o - be - dient child, Way-ward, ob - sti - nate and wild—
3. I, who spurned His lov - ing hold; I, who would not be con-trolled—
4. To my Fa - ther can I go? At His feet my - self I'll throw;
5. See! my Fa - ther wait - ing stands; See! He reach-es out His hands:

I, who strayed so long a - go, Strayed so far, and fell so low?
I, who left my Fa - ther's home, In for - bid - den ways to roam.
I, who would not hear His call; I, the will - ful prod - i - gal.
In His house there yet may be Place — a serv - ant's place—for me.
God is love, I know, I see, Love for me— yes, e - ven me.

Luke 15:17-20. Words, Samuel Longfellow, 1864. Tune HORTON, Xavier Schnyder von Wartensee, 1786.

Romans 5:8 354

God commendeth his own love toward us, in that, while we were yet sinners, Christ died for us.

355 Buried With Christ

1. Bur-ied with Christ, my bless-ed Re-deem-er, Dead to the
2. Dead un-to sin, a-live through the Spir-it, Ris-en with
3. Sin hath no more its cru-el do-min-ion, Walk-ing "in

old life of fol-ly and sin; Sa-tan may call, the world may en-
Him from the gloom of the grave, All things are new, and I am re-
new-ness of life, "I am free— Glo-ri-ous life of Christ, my Re-

treat me, There is no voice that an-swers with-in.
joic-ing In His great love, His pow-er to save. Dead to the world, to
deem-er, Which He so rich-ly shar-eth with me.

voic-es that call me, Liv-ing a-new, o-be-dient but free; Dead to the

Romans 6:4. Words, Thomas O. Chisholm, 1935. Tune BURIED WITH CHRIST, Lloyd O. Sanderson, 1935. Copyright 1963, renewal. L. O. Sanderson, owner. All rights reserved.

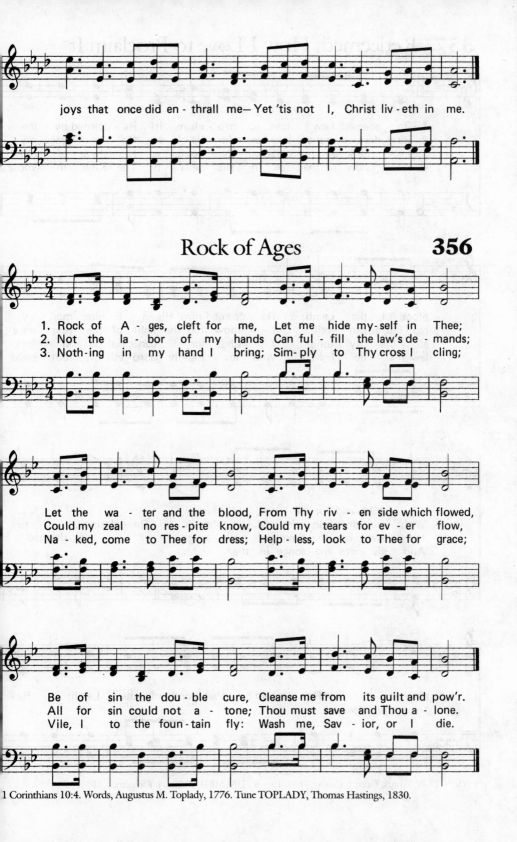

joys that once did en - thrall me— Yet 'tis not I, Christ liv - eth in me.

Rock of Ages

356

1. Rock of A - ges, cleft for me, Let me hide my - self in Thee;
2. Not the la - bor of my hands Can ful - fill the law's de - mands;
3. Noth - ing in my hand I bring; Sim - ply to Thy cross I cling;

Let the wa - ter and the blood, From Thy riv - en side which flowed,
Could my zeal no res - pite know, Could my tears for ev - er flow,
Na - ked, come to Thee for dress; Help - less, look to Thee for grace;

Be of sin the dou - ble cure, Cleanse me from its guilt and pow'r.
All for sin could not a - tone; Thou must save and Thou a - lone.
Vile, I to the foun - tain fly: Wash me, Sav - ior, or I die.

1 Corinthians 10:4. Words, Augustus M. Toplady, 1776. Tune TOPLADY, Thomas Hastings, 1830.

357 Redeemed, How I Love to Proclaim It

1. Re - deemed, how I love to pro - claim it! Re - deemed by the
2. Re - deemed, and so hap - py in Je - sus, No lan - guage my
3. I think of my bless - ed Re - deem - er, I think of Him
4. I know I shall see in His beau - ty The King in whose

blood of the Lamb; Re - deemed thro' His in - fi - nite mer - cy,
rap - ture can tell; I know that the light of His pres - ence
all the day long; I sing, for I can - not be si - lent;
law I de - light; Who lov - ing - ly guard - eth my foot - steps

His child, and for - ev - er, I am.
With me doth con - tin - ual - ly dwell. Re - deemed, re -
His love is the theme of my song. re - deemed,
And giv - eth me songs in the night.

deemed, Re - deemed by the blood of the Lamb; Re -
re - deemed,

1 Peter 1:18,19. Words, Fanny J. Crosby, 1882. Tune REDEEMED, William J. Kirkpatrick, 1882.

deemed, re-deemed, His child, and for-ev-er, I am.
re-deemed, re-deemed,

We Bless the Name of Christ the Lord **358**

1. We bless the name of Christ the Lord, We bless Him
2. We fol-low Him with pure de-light To sanc-ti-
3. Bap-tized in God— the Fa-ther, Son, And Ho-ly
4. By grace we "Ab-ba, Fa-ther" cry; By grace the

for His ho-ly Word, Who loved to do His Fa-ther's will,
fy His sa-cred rite; And thus our faith with wa-ter seal,
Spir-it— Three in One, With con-science free, we rest in God,
Com-fort-er comes nigh; And for Thy grace our love shall be

And all His right-eous-ness ful-fill.
To prove o-be-dience that we feel.
In love and peace thro' Je-sus' blood.
For-ev-er, on-ly, Lord, for Thee. A-men.

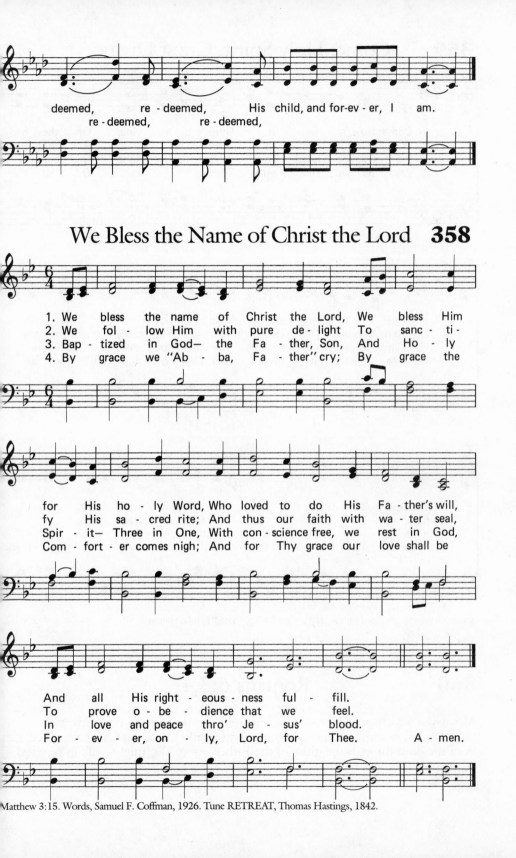

Matthew 3:15. Words, Samuel F. Coffman, 1926. Tune RETREAT, Thomas Hastings, 1842.

359   Come, Holy Spirit, Guest Divine

1. Come, Ho-ly Spir-it, Guest di-vine, On these bap-tis-mal wa-ters shine, And teach our hearts, in high-est strain, To praise the Lamb for sin-ners slain.

2. We love Thy Name, we love Thy laws, And joy-ful-ly em-brace Thy cause; We love Thy cross, the shame, the pain, O Lamb of God for sin-ners slain.

3. We sink be-neath Thy mys-tic flood; O bathe us in Thy cleans-ing blood; We die to sin, and seek a grave With Thee be-neath the yield-ing wave.

4. And as we rise, with Thee to live, O let the Ho-ly Spir-it give Our God's a-noint-ing from a-bove, The breath of life, the fire of love. A-men.

Acts 2:38. Words, Adoniram Judson, 1832. Tune DUKE STREET, John Hatton, 1793.

360   Romans 6:3,4

All we who were baptized into Jesus Christ were baptized into his death. We were buried therefore with him through baptism into death: that like as Christ was raised from the dead through the glory of the Father, so we also might walk in newness of life.

I am Resolved

361

1. I am re-solved no long-er to lin-ger, Charmed by the world's de-light;
2. I am re-solved to go to the Sav-ior, Leav-ing my sin and strife;
3. I am re-solved to fol-low the Sav-ior, Faith-ful and true each day;
4. I am re-solved to en-ter the kingdom, Leav-ing the paths of sin;
5. I am re-solved, and who will go with me? Come, friends, with-out de-lay,

Things that are high-er, things that are no-bler, These have al-lured my sight.
He is the true one, He is the just one, He hath the words of life.
Heed what He say-eth, do what He will-eth, He is the liv-ing way.
Friends may op-pose me, foes may be-set me, Still will I en-ter in.
Taught by the Bi-ble, led by the Spir-it, We'll walk the heav'n-ly way.

I will has-ten to Him, Has-ten so glad and free,
I will has-ten, has-ten to Him, Has-ten glad and free,

Je - sus, great-est, high-est, I will come to Thee.
Je - sus, Je - sus,

Luke 15:18. Words, Palmer Hartsough, 1896. Tune RESOLUTION, James H. Fillmore, 1896.

362 Built on a Rock

1. Built on a rock the church doth stand, E - ven when
2. Not in our tem - ples made with hands God, the Al -
3. We are God's house of liv - ing stones, Built for His
4. Yet in this house, an earth - ly frame, Je - sus the

stee - ples are fall - ing; Crum-bled have spires in ev - 'ry
might - y, is dwell - ing; High in the heavens His tem - ple
own hab - i - ta - tion; He fills our hearts, His hum - ble
chil - dren is bless - ing; Hith - er we come to praise His

land, Bells still are chim - ing and call - ing;
stands, All earth - ly tem - ples ex - cell - ing;
thrones, Grant-ing us life and sal - va - tion;
Name, Faith in our Sav - ior con - fess - ing;

Call - ing the young and old to rest, Call - ing the souls of
Yet He who dwells in heaven a - bove Deigns to a - bide with
Were two or three to seek His face, He in their midst would
Je - sus to us His Spir - it sent, Mak - ing with us His

Matthew 16:18. Words, Nikolai F. S. Grundtvig, 1837; trans. Carl Doving, 1913; rev. Fred C. M. Hansen, 1958.
Copyright 1958. Text translation from *The Service Book and Hymnal*. Used by permission of Augsburg Publishing
House. Tune KIRKEN, Ludwig M. Lindeman, 1840. Arr. J.B., Copyright 1986, ACU Press.

men	dis - tressed,	Long - ing for	life ev - er - last - ing.
us	in love,	Mak - ing our	bod - ies His tem - ple.
show	His grace,	Bless - ings up - on them be - stow - ing.
cov - e - nant,	Grant - ing His	chil - dren the king - dom.

Matthew 16:13-18 · 363
1 Corinthians 3:10,11
Ephesians 2:19,20

Now when Jesus came into the parts of Caesarea Philippi, he asked his disciples, saying, "Who do men say that the Son of man is?" And they said, "Some say John the Baptist; some, Elijah; and others, Jeremiah, or one of the prophets." He said to them, "But who do you say that I am?" And Simon Peter answered and said, "You are the Christ, the Son of the living God." And Jesus answered and said to him, "Blessed are you, Simon Bar-Jonah: for flesh and blood has not revealed it to you, but my Father who is in heaven. And I also say to you, that you are Peter, and upon this rock I will build my church; and the gates of Hades shall not prevail against it."

According to the grace of God which was given unto me, as a wise masterbuilder, I laid a foundation; and another buildeth thereon. For other foundation can no man lay than that which is laid, which is Jesus Christ.

So then ye are no more strangers and sojourners, but ye are fellow-citizens with the saints, and of the household of God, being built upon the foundation of the apostles and prophets, Christ Jesus himself being the chief cornerstone.

364 Christ is Made the Sure Foundation

1. Christ is made the sure foun-da-tion, Christ the Head and
2. To our wor-ship where we call Thee, Come, O Lord of
3. Here vouch-safe to all Thy serv-ants What they ask of
4. Laud and hon-or to the Fa-ther, Laud and hon-or

Cor-ner Stone, Cho-sen of the Lord and pre-cious,
hosts, to-day: With Thy treas-ured lov-ing-kind-ness
Thee to gain, What they gain from Thee for-ev-er
to the Son, Laud and hon-or to the Spir-it,

Bind-ing all the Church in one: Ho-ly Zi-on's
Hear Thy peo-ple as they pray; And Thy full-est
With the bless-ed to re-tain, And here-aft-er
Ev-er Three and ev-er One, One in might, and

help for-ev-er, And her con-fi-dence a-lone.
ben-e-dic-tion Shed with-in these walls al-way.
in Thy glo-ry Ev-er-more with Thee to reign.
One in glo-ry, While un-end-ing a-ges run! A-men.

Ephesians 2:20. Words, from Latin Hymn *Urbs beata Jerusalem*, c. 700; trans. John Mason Neale, 1851; alt. Tune
REGENT SQUARE, Henry Smart, 1867.

The Church's One Foundation   **365**

1. The Church's one foun - da - tion Is   Je - sus Christ her   Lord;
2. E - lect from ev - 'ry   na - tion Yet   one o'er all the   earth;
3. Tho' with a scorn - ful   won - der Men   see her sore op - prest,
4. 'Mid toil and trib - u -   la - tion, And   tu - mult of her   war,

She   is His new cre - a - tion By   wa - ter and the   word;
Her   char - ter of sal - va - tion, One   Lord, one faith, one   birth;
By   schi - sms rent a - sun - der, By   her - e - sies dis - trest,
She   waits the con - sum - ma - tion Of   peace for ev - er - more;

From heav'n He came and   sought her To   be His ho - ly   bride;
One   ho - ly name she   bless - es, Par -   takes one ho - ly   food,
Yet   saints their watch are keep - ing, Their   cry goes up, "How long?"
Till   with the vi - sion   glo - rious Her   long - ing eyes are   blest,

With   His own blood He   bought her, And   for her life He   died.
And   to one hope she   press - es, With   ev - 'ry grace en -   dued.
And   soon the night of   weep - ing Shall   be the morn of   song.
And   the great church vic - to - rious Shall   be the church at   rest.

1 Corinthians 3:11. Words, Samuel J. Stone, 1866. Tune AURELIA, Samuel S. Wesley, 1864.

366 When We Meet in Sweet Communion

1. When we meet in sweet com-mun-ion Where the feast di - vine is spread;
2. "God so loved"—what won-drous meas-ure! Loved and gave the best of heav'n,
3. Feast di -vine, all else sur-pass-ing, Pre - cious blood for you and me,

Hearts are brought in clos - er un -ion While par - tak - ing of the bread.
Bought us with that match - less trea-sure, Yea, for us His life was giv'n.
While we sup, Christ gen - tly whis-pers;"Do this in my mem-o - ry."

Pre - cious feast all else sur - pass-ing, Won - drous love for you and me,

While we feast Christ gen - tly whis-pers: "Do this in my mem-o - ry."

1 Corinthians 11:24,25. Words and tune THE LORD'S SUPPER, Tillit Sidney Teddlie, 1922. Arr. J.B., Copyright 1986, ACU Press.

'Twas on That Night
367

1. 'Twas on that night when doomed to know The
2. And aft - er thanks and glo - ry giv'n To
3. "My bro - ken bod - y thus I give For
4. Then in His hands the cup He raised, And
5. "My blood I thus pour forth," He cries, "To

ea - ger rage of ev - 'ry foe, The night in which He
Him that rules the earth and heav'n, That sym - bol of His
you, for all: take, eat, and live; And oft the sa - cred
God a - new He thanked and praised, While kind - ness in His
cleanse the soul in sin that lies; Par - take: and when the

was be - trayed, The Sav - ior of the world took bread.
flesh He broke, And thus to all His fol - l'wers spoke:
feast re - new, That brings my won - drous love to view."
bos - om glowed, And from His lips sal - va - tion flowed.
cup ye pour, Re - mem - ber still my dy - ing hour."

Matthew 26:26-28. Words, John Morrison in *Scottish Paraphrases*, 1781; alt. Tune WINDHAM, Daniel Read, 1785.

1 Corinthians 10:16,17   368

The cup of blessing which we bless, is it not a communion of the blood of Christ? The bread which we break, is it not a communion of the body of Christ? Because there is one bread, we who are many, are one body.

369 Why Did My Savior Come to Earth

1. Why did my Sav-ior come to earth, And to the hum-ble go?
2. Why did He drink the bit-ter cup Of sor-row, pain and woe?
3. Till Je-sus comes I'll sing His praise, And then to glo-ry go,

Why did He choose a low-ly birth? Be-cause He loved me so!
Why on the cross be lift-ed up? Be-cause He loved me so!
And reign with Him thro' end-less days, Be-cause He loved me so!

He loved me so, He loved me so;
He loved, He loved me so, He loved, He loved me so;

He gave His pre-cious life for me, for me, Be-cause He loved me so.

John 10:17,18. Words and tune DAILEY, James Gerald Dailey, 1892.

Another Week

370

1. An-oth-er week with all its cares hath flown, An-oth-er day of rest and peace is here; Sweet day on which our wea-ried hearts are drawn In ho-ly fel-low-ship to Je-sus near.

2. Je-sus, our great High Priest, our Sac-ri-fice, Our Pass-o-ver, rich gift of love di-vine, With Thee we would in-to the ho-liest rise, Com-mun-ing with Thee in the bread and wine.

3. O what a feast in-ef-fa-ble is this, Thy ta-ble spread with more than an-gels' food! An-gels the high-est nev-er taste the bliss, The dear com-mun-ion of Thy flesh and blood.

4. May we as serv-ants joy to do Thy will, As sons the hon-or of Thy house main-tain, As sol-diers stand pre-pared for con-flict still, And count all suf-f'ring borne for Thee as gain.

Acts 20:7. Words, Gilbert Young Tickle. Tune TOULON, *Genevan Psalter,* 1551.

1 Corinthians 5:7,8

371

Purge out the old leaven, that you may be a new lump, even as you are unleavened.
For our passover also has been sacrificed, even Christ. Wherefore let us keep the
feast, not with old leaven, neither with the leaven of malice and wickedness, but
with the unleavened bread of sincerity and truth.

372   That Dreadful Night

1. That dread-ful night be - fore His death, The Lamb for sin - ner's slain,
2. To keep the feast, Lord, we have met, And to re - mem-ber Thee,

Did, al - most with His dy - ing breath, This sol - emn feast or - dain.
Help each re - deemed one to re - peat: For me He died, for me.

1 Corinthians 11:23. Words, Joseph Hart, 1759. Tune THE SOLEMN FEAST, Lloyd O. Sanderson, 1935.
Copyright 1963. Renewal. L. O. Sanderson, owner. All rights reserved.

373   Bread of the World

1. Bread of the world, in mer - cy bro - ken, Wine of the soul, in mer - cy shed,
2. Look on the heart by sor - row bro - ken, Look on the tears by sin - ners shed;

By whom the words of life were spo-ken, And in whose death our sins are dead.
And be Thy feast to us the to - ken, That by Thy grace our souls are fed.

John 6:51. Words, Reginald Heber, 1827. Tune EUCHARISTIC HYMN, John S. B. Hodges, 1868.

By Christ Redeemed, in Christ Restored 374

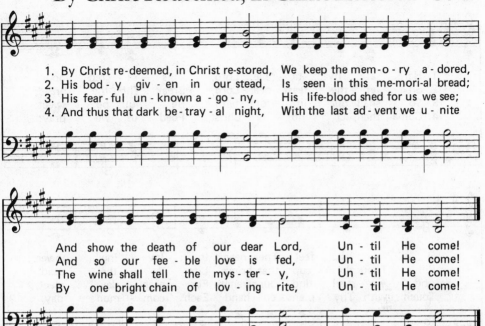

1. By Christ re-deemed, in Christ re-stored, We keep the mem-o-ry a-dored,
2. His bod-y giv-en in our stead, Is seen in this me-mori-al bread;
3. His fear-ful un-known a-go-ny, His life-blood shed for us we see;
4. And thus that dark be-tray-al night, With the last ad-vent we u-nite

And show the death of our dear Lord, Un-til He come!
And so our fee-ble love is fed, Un-til He come!
The wine shall tell the mys-ter-y, Un-til He come!
By one bright chain of lov-ing rite, Un-til He come!

1 Corinthians 11:26. Words, George Rawson, 1857. Tune TROYTE'S CHANT, No. 1, Arthur H. D. Troyte, 1860.

In Memory of the Savior's Love 375

1. In mem-'ry of the Sav-ior's love We keep the sa-cred feast,
2. By faith we take the bread of life With which our souls are fed,
3. Be-neath His ban-ner thus we sing The won-ders of His love;

Where ev-'ry hum-ble, con-trite heart Is made a wel-come guest.
The cup in to-ken of His blood That was for sin-ners shed.
And here an-tic-i-pate by faith The heav'n-ly feast a-bove.

1 Corinthians 10:16. Words, Thomas Cotterill, 1805. Tune WINCHESTER, OLD, Thomas Est's *Whole Book of Psalms*, 1592.

376 Here at Thy Table, Lord

1. Here at Thy table, Lord, This sacred hour,
O let us feel Thee near, In loving power;
Calling our thoughts away From self and sin.
As to Thy banquet hall We enter in.

2. Sit at the feast, dear Lord, Break Thou the bread;
Fill Thou the cup that brings Life to the dead;
That we may find in Thee, Pardon and peace;
And from all bondage win A full release.

3. So shall our life of faith Be full, be sweet;
And we shall find our strength For each day meet;
Fed by Thy living bread, All hunger past,
We shall be satisfied, And saved at last.

4. Come then, O holy Christ, Feed us, we pray;
Touch with Thy pierced hand Each common day;
Making this earthly life Full of Thy grace,
Till in the home of heav'n We find our place. A-men.

Mark 14:22-25. Words, May P. Hoyt. Tune BREAD OF LIFE, William F. Sherwin, 1877.

Here Before Thee, Savior

1. Here, be - fore Thee, Sav - ior, We would low - ly bow;
2. Grant this bread, now bro - ken, May a sym - bol be

Grant us now Thy pres - ence, Come, and bless us now.
Of Thy pre - cious bod - y Bruised on Cal - v'ry's tree;

In this sweet com - mun - ion May our souls be fed;
Grant this cup of bless - ing To our hearts may prove

In true con - se - cra - tion May we all be led.
One more tie that binds us Clos - er in Thy love. A - men.

Luke 22:19,20. Words and tune HUSTON, Frank C. Huston, 1906.

378   Come, Risen Lord

1. Come, ris - en Lord, and deign to be our guest; Nay, let us be Thy guests; the feast is Thine; Thy - self at Thine own board make man - i - fest In this com - mun - ion of the bread and wine.

2. We meet, as in that up - per room they met, Thou at the ta - ble, bless - ing, yet dost stand; "This is my bod - y"; so Thou giv - est yet: Still re - ceives the cup as from Thy hand.

3. One bod - y we, one bod - y who par - take, One Church u - nit - ed in com - mun - ion blest; One name we bear, one bread of life we break, With all Thy saints on earth and saints at rest.

4. One with each oth - er, Lord, for one in Thee, Who art one Sav - ior and one liv - ing Head; Then o - pen Thou our eyes, that we may see; Be known to us in break - ing of the bread.

1 Corinthians 10:17. Words, George W. Briggs, 1931. Tune SURSUM CORDA, Alfred M. Smith, 1941. Reprinted from *Songs of Praise*, Enlarged Edition, by permission of the Oxford University Press.

Lord of Our Highest Love

1. Lord of our high-est love! Let now Thy peace be giv'n;
2. Then, dear-est Lord, draw near While we Thy ta-ble spread,
3. Then as the loaf we break, Thine own rich bless-ing give;
4. Dear Lord! what mem-'ries crowd A-round the sa-cred cup!
5. O scenes of suf-f'ring love, E-nough our souls to win—

Fix all our tho'ts on things a-bove, Our hearts on Thee in heav'n.
And crown the feast with heav'n-ly cheer, Thy-self the liv-ing bread.
May all with lov-ing hearts par-take, And all new strength re-ceive.
The up-per room! Geth-sem-a-ne! Thy foes! Thy lift-ing up!
E-nough to melt our hearts and prove The an-ti-dote of sin.

1 John 2:2. Gilbert Young Tickle. Tune FRANCONIA, from Johann B. Koenig's *Harmonischer Liederschatz*, 1738; harm. W. H. Havergal, 1847.

Matthew 26:26-30

As they were eating, Jesus took bread, and blessed, and brake it; and he gave to the disciples, and said, "Take, eat; this is my body." And he took a cup, and gave thanks, and gave to them, saying, "Drink ye all of it; for this is my blood of the covenant, which is poured out for many unto remission of sins. But I say unto you, I shall not drink henceforth of this fruit of the vine, until that day when I drink it new with you in my Father's kingdom." And when they had sung a hymn, they went out into the mount of Olives.

381 Here, O My Lord, I See Thee

1. Here, O my Lord, I see Thee face to face; Here would I touch and han-dle things un-seen; Here grasp with firm-er hand th'e-ter-nal grace, And all my wea-ri-ness up-on Thee lean.

2. Here would I feed up-on the bread of God; Here drink with Thee the roy-al wine of heav'n; Here would I lay a-side each earth-ly load, Here taste a-fresh the calm of sin for-giv'n.

3. Feast aft-er feast thus comes and pass-es by; Yet, pass-ing, points to the glad feast a-bove— Giv-ing sweet fore-taste of the fes-tal joy, The Lamb's great bri-dal feast of bliss and love.

Revelation 3:20,21. Words, Horatius Bonar, 1855. Tune CONSOLATION; arr. from Felix Mendelssohn, 1833.

382 Sin Sorrow of Six Thousand Years

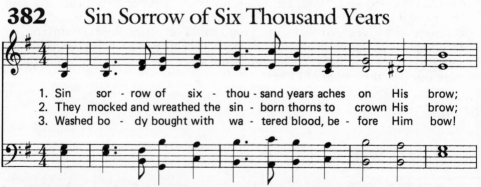

1. Sin sor-row of six-thou-sand years aches on His brow;

2. They mocked and wreathed the sin-born thorns to crown His brow;

3. Washed bo-dy bought with wa-tered blood, be-fore Him bow!

Romans 3:24,25. Words and tune THE LAMB OF GOD, George W. Ewing, 1982. Copyright 1986, ACU Press.

The wine - red blood - sweat stains His tears. Be - hold Him now!
They broke His flesh; the life poured down. Be - hold Him now!
In brok - en bread and life - filled cup, Be - hold Him now!

Till He Come

383

1. "Till He come:" O let the words Lin - ger on the trem-bling chords;
2. When the wea - ry ones we love En - ter on their rest a - bove,
3. See, the feast of love is spread: Drink the wine and break the bread—

Let the "lit - tle while" be - tween In their gold - en light be seen;
Seems the earth so poor and vast, All our life - joy o - ver-cast—
Sweet me-mo - rials— till the Lord Call us round His heav'n - ly board:

Let us think how heav'n and home Lie be - yond that "Till He come."
Hush! be ev - 'ry mur - mur dumb: It is on - ly "Till He come."
Some from earth, from glo - ry some, Sev-ered on - ly "Till He come." A-men.

1 Corinthians 11:26. Words, Edward H. Bickersteth, 1861. Tune HALLE, attr. to Franz Joseph Haydn.

384 Thy Supper, Lord, Before Us Spread

1. Thy sup-per, Lord, be-fore us spread, The cup be-side the
2. Thy sac-ri-fice was for our gain; To save us Thou didst
3. In fel-low-ship with Thee we feel That Thou art here, Thy
4. Now may the wor-ship we know here Re-mind us al-ways

bro-ken bread, Re-mind us of Thy life laid
bear the pain. Thy love is clear for all to
pres-ence real; For Thou hast ris-en and dost
Thou art near; Help us to live our lives each

down— The shame-ful cross, the thorn-y crown.
see; We bow in thank-ful prayer to Thee.
live With-in our hearts, new life to give.
day In love and faith, O Lord, we pray. A-men.

Matthew 28:20. Words, Joseph F. Green, 1961. Tune MAINZER, Joseph Mainzer, 1841; harm. Austin C. Lovelace, 1964. Copyright 1961, 1964, Broadman Press. All rights reserved. International copyright secured. Used by permission.

385   Hebrews 2:9

We behold him who hath been made a little lower than the angels, even Jesus, because of the suffering of death crowned with glory and honor, that by the grace of God he should taste of death for every man.

Let All Mortal Flesh Keep Silence 386

1. Let all mor-tal flesh keep si-lence, And with fear and
2. King of kings, yet born of Ma-ry, As of old on
3. Rank on rank the host of heav-en Spreads its van-guard
4. At His feet the six-winged ser-aph, Cher-u-bim, with

trem-bling stand; Pon-der noth-ing earth-ly-mind-ed,
earth He stood, Lord of lords, in hu-man ves-ture,
on the way, As the Light of light de-scend-eth,
sleep-less eye, Veil their fac-es to the pres-ence,

For with bless-ing in His hand, Christ our God to
In the bod-y and the blood, He will give to
From the realms of end-less day, That the powers of
As with cease-less voice they cry, Al-le-lu-ia,

earth de-scend-eth, Our full hom-age to de-mand.
all the faith-ful His own self for heaven-ly food.
hell may van-ish As the dark-ness clears a-way.
Al-le-lu-ia, Al-le-lu-ia, Lord most high! A-men.

Revelation 5:9,10. Words, from the Liturgy of St. James; trans. Gerard Moultrie, 1864. Tune PICARDY, Traditional
French Carol, c. 15th cent.

387 Father, We Thank Thee

1. Fa - ther, we thank Thee who hast plant - ed
2. Thou, Lord, didst make all for Thy pleas - ure,
3. Watch o'er Thy Church, O Lord, in mer - cy,
4. As grain, once scat - ter'd on the hill - sides,

Thy ho - ly name with - in our hearts.
Didst give man food for all his days.
Save it from ev - il, guard it still,
Was in this brok - en bread made one,

Knowl - edge and faith and life im - mor - tal
Giv - ing in Christ the Bread e - ter - nal;
Per - fect it in Thy love, u - nite it,
So from all lands Thy Church be gath - er'd

Je - sus Thy Son to us im - parts.
Thine is the power, be Thine the praise.
Cleansed and con - formed un - to Thy will.
In - to Thy king - dom by Thy Son. A - men.

John 11:52. Words, from the Didache, c. 110; trans. F. Bland Tucker, 1940. Words used by permission from *The Hymnal*, 1940. Copyright The Church Pension Fund. Tune RENDEZ A DIEU, Louis Bourgeois, 1543.

Beneath the Forms of Outward Rite **388**

1. Be - neath the forms of out - ward rite Thy sup - per, Lord, is spread
2. The bread is al - ways con - se - crate Which men di - vide with men;
3. The bless - ed cup is on - ly passed True mem - o - ry of Thee,
4. O Mas - ter, through these sym - bols shared, Thine own dear self im - part,

In ev - ery qui - et up - per room Where faint-ing souls are fed.
And ev - ery act of broth - er - hood Re - peats Thy feast a - gain.
When life a - new pours out its wine With rich suf - fi - cien - cy.
That in our dai - ly life may flame The pas - sion of Thy heart. A - men.

Corinthians 11:28. Words, James A. Blaisdell, d. 1957. Tune BELMONT, William Gardiner's
Sacred Melodies, 1815.

1 Corinthians 11:23-26 **389**

For I received of the Lord that which also I delivered unto you, that the Lord Jesus
in the night in which he was betrayed took bread; and when he had given thanks,
he brake it, and said, "This is my body which is for you: this do in remembrance
of me." In like manner also the cup, after supper, saying, "This cup is the new
covenant in my blood: this do, as often as ye drink it, in remembrance of me. For
as often as ye eat this bread, and drink the cup, ye proclaim the Lord's death till
he come."

390 How Sweet, How Heavenly

1. How sweet, how heav'n - ly is the sight, When those that love the Lord In one an - oth - er's peace de - light, And so ful - fill the word.
2. When each can feel his broth - er's sigh, And with him bear a part; When sor - row flows from eye to eye, And joy from heart to heart.
3. When, free from en - vy, scorn, and pride, Our wish - es all a - bove, Each can his broth - er's fail - ings hide, And show a broth - er's love.
4. When love in one de - light - ful stream Thro' ev - 'ry bos - om flows; When un - ion sweet and dear es - teem In ev - 'ry ac - tion glows.
5. Love is the gold - en chain that binds The hap - py souls a - bove; And he's an heir of heav'n who finds His bos - om glow with love.

1 John 4:7. Words, Joseph Swain, 1792. Tune BROWN, William B. Bradbury, 1844.

All Praise to Our Redeeming Lord   **391**

1. All praise to our re - deem - ing Lord, Who joins us
2. The gift which He on one be - stows, We all de -
3. He bids us build each oth - er up; And, gath - ered
4. We all par - take the joy of one; The com - mon
5. And if our fel - low - ship be - low In Je - sus

by His grace, And bids us, each to each re -
light to prove, The grace through ev - ery ves - sel
in - to one, To our high call - ing's glo - rious
peace we feel: A peace to world - ly minds un -
be so sweet, What height of rap - ture shall we

stored, To - geth - er seek His face.
flows In pur - est streams of love.
hope, We hand in hand go on.
known, A joy un - speak - a - ble.
know When round His throne we meet!   A - men.

1 Peter 4:10. Words, Charles Wesley, 1747. Tune ARMENIA, Sylvanus B. Pond, 1836.

392   In Christ There is No East or West

1. In Christ there is no east or west, In Him no south or north; But one great fel-low-ship of love Through-out the whole wide earth.

2. In Him shall true hearts ev-'ry-where Their high com-mu-nion find; His ser-vice is the gold-en cord Close bind-ing all man-kind.

3. Join hands, then, broth-er of the faith, What-e'er your race may be. Who serves my Fa-ther as a son Is sure-ly kin to me.

4. In Christ now meet both east and west, In Him meet south and north; All Christ-ly souls are one in Him Through-out the whole wide earth. A-men.

Romans 15:8-12. Words, John Oxenham, 1908. Used by permission of The American Tract Society.
Tune ST. PETER, Alexander R. Reinagle, 1836.

393   John 17:20,21

Neither for these only do I pray, but for them also that believe on me through their word; that they may all be one; even as thou, Father, art in me, and I in thee, that they also may be in us: that the world may believe that thou didst send me.

Blest Be the Tie

394

1. Blest be the tie that binds Our hearts in Chris - tian love; The fel - low - ship of kin - dred minds Is like to that a - bove.
2. Be - fore our Fa - ther's throne We pour our ar - dent pray'rs; Our fears, our hopes, our aims are one, Our com - forts and our cares.
3. We share our mu - tual woes, Our mu - tual bur - dens bear; And oft - en for each oth - er flows The sym - pa - thiz - ing tear.
4. When we a - sun - der part, It gives us in - ward pain; But we shall still be joined in heart, And hope to meet a - gain.
5. This glo - rious hope re - vives Our cour - age by the way; While each in ex - pec - ta - tion lives, And longs to see the day.
6. From sor - row, toil, and pain, And sin, we shall be free; And per - fect love and friend - ship reign Thro' all e - ter - ni - ty.

1 John 1:7. Words, John Fawcett, 1782. Tune DENNIS, Johann Georg Nägeli; arr. Lowell Mason, 1845.

395 My Brethren, Let Us Be as One

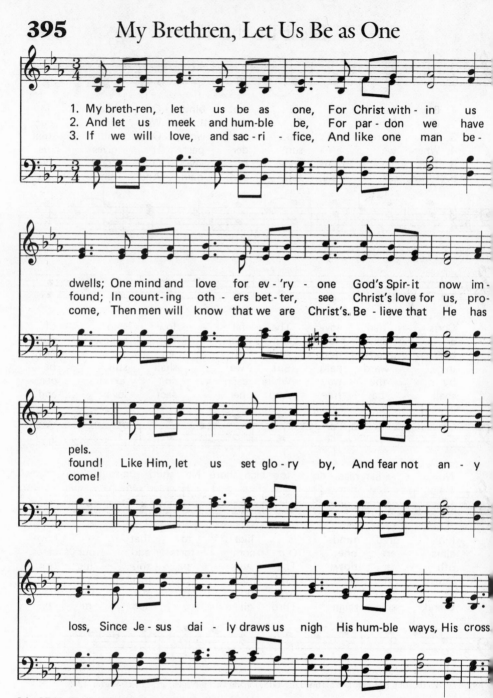

1. My breth-ren, let us be as one, For Christ with-in us
2. And let us meek and hum-ble be, For par-don we have
3. If we will love, and sac-ri - fice, And like one man be-

dwells; One mind and love for ev -'ry - one God's Spir-it now im-
found; In count-ing oth - ers bet - ter, see Christ's love for us, pro-
come, Then men will know that we are Christ's. Be - lieve that He has

pels.
found! Like Him, let us set glo - ry by, And fear not an - y
come!

loss, Since Je - sus dai - ly draws us nigh His hum-ble ways, His cross.

John 17:21. Words, Victor Vadney, 1983. Tune DANIELS, M. L. Daniels, 1984. Copyright ACU Press, 1985.

Eternal God, Whose Power Upholds 396

1. E - ter - nal God, whose power up - holds Both flower and flam - ing star,
2. O God of love, whose Spir - it wakes In ev - ery hu - man breast,
3. O God of truth, whom sci - ence seeks And rev - 'rent souls a - dore,
4. O God of beau - ty, oft re - vealed In dreams of hu - man art,
5. O God of right - eous - ness and grace, Seen in the Christ, Thy Son,

To whom there is no here nor there, No time, no near nor far,
Whom love, and love a - lone, can know, In whom all hearts find rest:
Who light - est ev - ery ear - nest mind Of ev - ery clime and shore:
In speech that flows to mel - o - dy, In ho - li - ness of heart:
Whose life and death re - veal Thy face, By whom Thy will was done:

No a - lien race, no for - eign shore, No child un-sought, un - known:
Help us to spread Thy gra - cious reign Till greed and hate shall cease,
Dis - pel the gloom of er - ror's night, Of ig - nor-ance and fear,
Teach us to ban all ug - li - ness That blinds our eyes to Thee,
In - spire Thy her - alds of good news To live Thy life di - vine,

O send us forth, Thy proph-ets true, To make all lands Thine own!
And kind - ness dwell in hu-man hearts, And all the earth find peace!
Un - til true wis - dom from a - bove Shall make life's path-way clear!
Till all shall know the love - li - ness Of lives made fair and free!
Till Christ is formed in all man-kind And ev - ery land is Thine! A-men.

Isaiah 40:28. Words, Henry Hallam Tweedy, 1929. Words used by permission of The Hymn Society of America.
Tune WELLINGTON SQUARE, Guy Warrack, 1931.

397 O Love, How Deep

1. O love, how deep, how broad, how high, How pass-ing
2. For us bap-tized, for us He bore His ho-ly
3. For us He prayed, for us He taught, For us His
4. For us to wick-ed men be-trayed, Scourged, mocked, in
5. For us He rose from death a-gain. For us He

thought and fan-ta-sy, That God, the Son of God should
fast, and hun-gered sore; For us temp-ta-tions sharp He
dai-ly works He wrought, By words and signs and ac-tions,
pur-ple robe ar-rayed, He bore the shame-ful cross and
went on high to reign; For us He sent His Spir-it

take Our mor-tal form for mor-tals' sake.
knew; For us the temp-ter o-ver-threw.
thus Still seek-ing not Him-self, but us.
death; For us gave up His dy-ing breath.
here To guide, to strength-en, and to cheer. A-men.

Acts 10:36-43. Words, Latin Hymn *O amor quam ecstaticus,* 15th cent.; trans. Benjamin Webb, 1854; alt. Tune DEUS TUORUM MILITUM, from *Grenoble Antiphoner,* 1753.

398 John 4:34,35

Jesus saith unto them, "My meat is to do the will of him that sent me, and to accomplish his work. Do you not say, 'There are yet four months and then come the harvest?' Behold, I say to you, lift up your eyes, and look on the fields, that they are white already for harvest."

Far and Near

1. Far and near the fields are teem-ing With the waves of rip-ened grain;
2. Send them forth with morn's first beaming, Send them in the noon-tide's glare;
3. O thou, whom thy Lord is send-ing, Gath-er now the sheaves of gold;

Far and near their gold is gleam-ing O'er the sun-ny slope and plain.
When the sun's last rays are gleam-ing, Bid them gath-er ev-'ry-where.
Heav'nward then at eve-ning wend-ing, Thou shalt come with joy un-told.

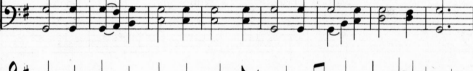

Lord of har-vest, send forth reap-ers! Hear us, Lord, To Thee we cry;

Send them now the sheaves to gath-er, Ere the har-vest time pass by.

John 4:35. Words, John O. Thompson, 1885. Tune CLEMM, J. B. O. Clemm, 1885.

400 Christ for the World We Sing

1. Christ for the world we sing; The world to
2. Christ for the world we sing; The world to
3. Christ for the world we sing; The world to
4. Christ for the world we sing; The world to

Christ we bring With lov - ing zeal—
Christ we bring With fer - vent prayer—
Christ we bring With one ac - cord—
Christ we bring With joy - ful song—

The poor and them that mourn, The faint and o - ver-borne,
The way - ward and the lost, By rest - less pas - sions tossed,
With us the work to share, With us re - proach to dare,
The new - born souls whose days, Re - claimed from er - ror's ways,

Sin - sick and sor - row-worn, For Christ to heal.
Re - deemed at count - less cost From dark de - spair.
With us the cross to bear, For Christ our Lord.
In - spired with hope and praise, To Christ be - long.

Galatians 1:3,4. Words, Samuel Wolcott, 1869. Tune ITALIAN HYMN, Felice de Giardini, 1769.

Soldiers of Christ, Arise

1. Sol - diers of Christ, a - rise   And   put   your ar - mor   on;
2. Strong in the Lord of   hosts   And   in   His might - y   pow'r;
3. Stand, then, in His great   might,   With   all   His strength en - dued;
4. Leave no un-guard-ed   place,   No   weak - ness of   the   soul;
5. That hav - ing all   things done,   And   all   your con - flicts   past,

1. a - rise,

1. Sol - diers of Christ, a - rise And put your ar - mor on;

Strong   in   the strength which   God   sup - plies,
Who   in   the strength of   Je - sus   trusts,
But   take, to   arm   you   for   the   fight,
Take   ev - 'ry vir - tue,   ev - 'ry   grace,
You   may o'er-come thro'   Christ   a - lone,

1.   Strong   in   the strength which   God sup - plies,

Strong in the strength which God sup - plies Thro' His   be - lov - ed   Son.
Who   in the strength of   Je - sus trusts, Is   more   than con-quer - or.
But   take, to arm   you   for the fight, The   pan - o - ply of   God.
Take   ev - 'ry vir - tue,   ev - 'ry grace, And   for - ti - fy the   whole.
You   may o'er- come thro'   Christ a - lone, And   stand   en - tire at   last.

Ephesians 6:11. Words, Charles Wesley, 1749. Tune KIRKWOOD, William B. Bradbury.

402 Christ is the World's True Light

1. Christ is the world's true Light, Its Cap-tain of sal - va - tion,
2. In Christ all ra - ces meet, Their an - cient feuds for - get - ting,
3. One Lord, in one great name U - nite us all who own Thee;

The Day - star clear and bright Of ev - ery man and na - tion;
The whole round world com - plete, From sun-rise to its set - ting,
Cast out our pride and shame That hin - der to en - throne Thee;

New life, new hope a - wakes, Wher - e'er men own His sway;
When Christ is throned as Lord, Men shall for - sake their fear,
The world has wait - ed long, Has trav - ailed long in pain;

Free-dom her bond - age breaks, And night is turned to day.
To plow-share beat the sword, To prun - ing hook the spear.
To heal its an - cient wrong, Come, Prince of Peace, and reign. A - men.

John 1:4. Words, George Wallace Briggs, 1931. Words from *Songs of Praise*, Enlarged Edition. Used by permission of Oxford University Press. Tune ST. JOAN, Percy E. B. Coller, 1941. Music Copyright, 1942, by The Church Pension Fund. Used by permission.

Stand Up, Stand Up for Jesus

403

1. Stand up, stand up for Je - sus! Ye sol - diers of the cross;
2. Stand up, stand up for Je - sus! The trump-et call o - bey;
3. Stand up, stand up for Je - sus! Stand in His strength a - lone;
4. Stand up, stand up for Je - sus! The strife will not be long;

Lift high His roy - al ban - ner, It must not suf - fer loss;
Forth to the might - y con - flict In this His glo - rious day;
The arm of flesh will fail you, Ye dare not trust your own;
This day the noise of bat - tle, The next the vic - tor's song;

From vic - t'ry un - to vic - t'ry His ar - my shall He lead,
Ye that are men now serve Him A - gainst un - num-bered foes;
Put on the gos - pel ar - mor, And watch-ing un - to prayer,
To him that o - ver - com - eth A crown of life shall be;

Till ev - 'ry foe is van - quished, And Christ is Lord in - deed.
Let cour - age rise with dan - ger, And strength to strength op - pose.
Where du - ty calls, or dan - ger, Be nev - er want - ing there.
He with the King of Glo - ry Shall reign e - ter - nal - ly.

Ephesians 6:13. Words, George Duffield, 1858. Tune WEBB, George J. Webb, 1837.

404   I Will Sing of My Redeemer

1. I will sing of my Re - deem - er And His won - drous
2. I will tell the won - drous sto - ry, How my lost es -
3. I will praise my dear Re - deem - er, His tri - um - phant
4. I will sing of my Re - deem - er And His heav'n - ly

love to me; On the cru - el cross He suf - fered,
tate to save, In His bound - less love and mer - cy,
power I'll tell, How the vic - to - ry He giv - eth
love for me; He from death to life hath brought me,

From the curse to set me free.
He the ran - som free - ly gave.   Sing, O sing of my Re -
O - ver sin and death and hell.
Son of God, with Him to be.

deem - er, With His blood He pur - chased me, On the

Titus 2:13,14. Words, Philip P. Bliss, c. 1876. Tune HYFRYDOL, Rowland H. Prichard, c. 1830.

cross He sealed my par - don, Paid the debt, and made me free.

Rise Up, O Men of God   405

1. Rise up, O men of God! Have done with less-er things; Give
2. Rise up, O men of God! His king-dom tar-ries long; Bring
3. Rise up, O men of God! The Church for you doth wait, Her
4. Lift high the cross of Christ! Tread where His feet have trod; As

heart and mind and soul and strength To serve the King of kings.
in the day of broth-er-hood And end the night of wrong.
strength un-e-qual to her task; Rise up, and make her great!
broth-ers of the Son of man, Rise up, O men of God! A-men.

2 Timothy 2:3,4. Words, William P. Merrill, 1911. Used by permission of *The Presbyterian Outlook*, Richmond, Virginia (U.S.A.). Tune FESTAL SONG, William H. Walter, 1894.

2 Timothy 1:6-8   406

Stir up the gift of God, which is in you . . . For God did not give us a spirit of fearfulness; but of power and love and discipline. Do not be ashamed therefore of the testimony of our Lord.

407 I Will Sing of My Redeemer

1. I will sing of my Re - deem - er, And His won - drous love for me;
2. I will tell the won-drous sto - ry, How my lost es - tate to save,
3. I will praise my dear Re - deem - er, His tri - um - phant pow'r I'll tell,
4. I will sing of my Re - deem - er And His heav'n - ly love to me;

On the cru - el cross He suf - fered, From the curse to set me free.
In His bound - less love and mer - cy, He the ran - som free - ly gave.
How the vic - to - ry He giv - eth O - ver sin, and death, and hell.
He from death to life hath brought me, Son of God, with Him to be.

Sing, O sing of my Re - deem - er! With His
Sing, O sing of my Re-deem-er, Sing, O sing of my Re-deem-er;

blood He pur-chased me; On the cross He sealed my
He purchased me, With His blood He purchased me. He sealed my pardon, On the

1 Peter 1:18,19. Words, Philip P. Bliss, 1876. Tune MY REDEEMER, James McGranahan, 1877.

par - don, Paid the debt and made me free.
cross He sealed my pardon, Paid the debt and made me free, and made me free.

I Love Thy Kingdom, Lord 408

1. I love Thy king - dom, Lord, The house of Thine a - bode, The
2. I love Thy Church, O God! Her walls be - fore Thee stand Dear
3. For her my tears shall fall, For her my prayers as - cend, To
4. Be - yond my high - est joy I prize her heaven-ly ways, Her
5. Sure as Thy truth shall last, To Zi - on shall be given The

Church our blest Re - deem-er saved With His own pre - cious blood.
as the ap - ple of Thine eye, And grav - en on Thy hand.
her my cares and toils be given, Till toils and cares shall end.
sweet com-mu - nion, sol - emn vows, Her hymns of love and praise.
bright-est glo - ries earth can yield, And bright - er bliss of heaven. A - men.

Matthew 16:18,19. Words, Timothy Dwight, 1800. Tune ST. THOMAS, Aaron Williams, 1763.

Ephesians 1:22,23 409

And he put all things in subjection under his feet, and gave him to be head over all things to the church, which is his body, the fulness of him that fills all in all.

410 I Love Thy Kingdom, Lord

1. I love Thy king - dom, Lord, The house of Thine a - bode,
2. For her my tears shall fall, For her my prayers as - cend;
3. Je - sus, Thou Friend di - vine, Our Sav - ior and our King!

The church our blest Re - deem - er saved With His own pre - cious blood;
To her my cares and toils be giv'n, Till toils and cares shall end;
Thy hand from ev - 'ry snare and foe Shall great de - liv - 'rance bring;

I love Thy church, O God! Her walls be - fore Thee stand,
Be - yond my high - est joy I prize her heav'n - ly ways,
Sure as Thy truth shall last, To Zi - on shall be giv'n

Dear as the ap - ple of Thine eye, And grav - en on Thy hand.
Her sweet com - mun - ion, sol - emn vows, Her hymns of love and praise.
The bright - est glo - ries earth can yield, And bright - er bliss of heav'n.

Matthew 16:18,19. Words, Timothy Dwight, 1800. Tune BEALOTH, from T.B. Mason's *Sacred Harp*, 1843.

Rescue the Perishing

411

1. Res - cue the per - ish - ing, Care for the dy - ing, Snatch them in pit - y from
2. Tho' they are slight-ing Him, Still He is wait - ing, Wait- ing the pen - i - tent
3. Down in the hu -man heart, Crushed by the tempter, Feel - ings lie bur - ied that
4. Res - cue the per - ish - ing, Du - ty de-mands it; Strength for thy la - bor the

sin and the grave; Weep o'er the err - ing one, Lift up the fall - en,
child to re - ceive; Plead with them ear-nest- ly, Plead with them gen-tly:
grace can re - store; Touched by a lov - ing hand, Wak- ened by kind - ness,
Lord will pro - vide; Back to the nar - row way Pa - tient - ly win them;

Tell them of Je - sus the Might - y to save.
He will for-give if they tru - ly be - lieve. Res - cue the per - ish - ing,
Chords that were bro - ken will vi - brate once more.
Tell the poor wan-d'rer a Sav - ior has died.

Care for the dy - ing; Je - sus is mer - ci - ful, Je - sus will save.

Proverbs 11:30. Words, Fanny J. Crosby, 1869. Tune RESCUE, William H. Doane, 1869.

412 Onward, Christian Soldiers

1. On - ward, Chris - tian sol - diers, March-ing as to war,
2. At the sign of tri - umph, Sa - tan's host doth flee;
3. Crowns and thrones may per - ish, King-doms rise and wane,
4. On - ward, then, ye peo - ple, Join our hap - py throng;

With the cross of Je - sus Go - ing on be - fore;
On, then, Chris - tian sol - diers, On to vic - to - ry;
But the church of Je - sus Con-stant will re - main;
Blend with ours your voic - es In the tri - umph - song;

Christ, the roy - al Mas - ter, Leads a - gainst the foe!
Hell's foun - da - tions quiv - er At the shout of praise:
Gates of hell can nev - er 'Gainst the church pre - vail;
Glo - ry, laud and hon - or Un - to Christ the King,

For - ward in - to bat - tle, See His ban - ners go!
Broth - ers, lift your voic - es, Loud your an - thems raise!
We have Christ's own prom - ise, And that can - not fail.
This thro' count - less a - ges Men and an - gels sing.

1 Timothy 6:12. Words, Sabine Baring-Gould, 1864. Tune ST. GERTRUDE, Arthur Sullivan, 1871.

Onward, Christian soldiers! Marching as to war,
With the cross of Jesus Going on before.

Savior, Teach Me, Day by Day 413

1. Savior, teach me, day by day, Love's sweet lesson to obey:
2. With a childlike heart of love, At Thy bidding may I move,
3. Teach me all Thy steps to trace, Strong to follow in Thy grace,
4. Love in loving finds employ, In obedience all her joy;

Sweeter lesson cannot be— Loving Him who first loved me.
Prompt to serve and follow Thee— Loving Him who first loved me.
Learning how to love from Thee— Loving Him who first loved me.
Ever new that joy will be— Loving Him who first loved me.

1 John 4:19. Words, Jane E. Leeson, 1842. Tune SEYMOUR, Carl Maria von Weber, 1825.

414   O Zion Haste, Thy Mission High

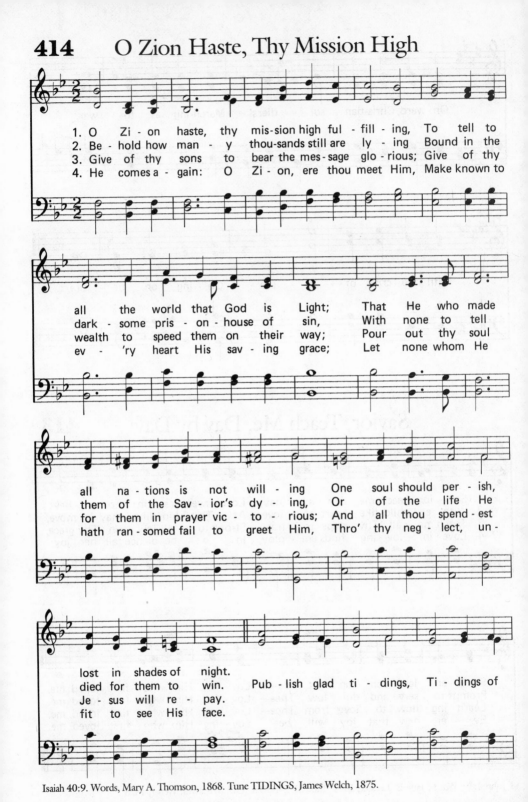

1. O Zi - on haste, thy mis-sion high ful - fill - ing, To tell to
2. Be - hold how man - y thou-sands still are ly - ing Bound in the
3. Give of thy sons to bear the mes - sage glo - rious; Give of thy
4. He comes a - gain: O Zi - on, ere thou meet Him, Make known to

all the world that God is Light; That He who made
dark - some pris - on - house of sin, With none to tell
wealth to speed them on their way; Pour out thy soul
ev - 'ry heart His sav - ing grace; Let none whom He

all na - tions is not will - ing One soul should per - ish,
them of the Sav - ior's dy - ing, Or of the life He
for them in prayer vic - to - rious; And all thou spend - est
hath ran - somed fail to greet Him, Thro' thy neg - lect, un -

lost in shades of night.
died for them to win. Pub - lish glad ti - dings, Ti - dings of
Je - sus will re - pay.
fit to see His face.

Isaiah 40:9. Words, Mary A. Thomson, 1868. Tune TIDINGS, James Welch, 1875.

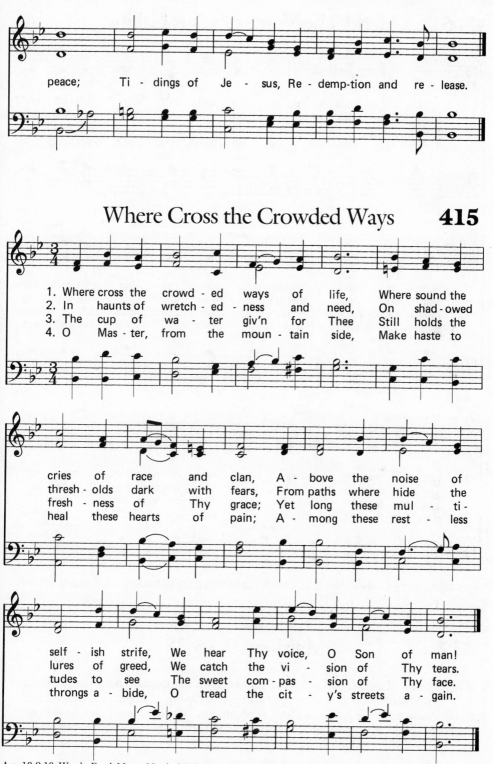

peace; Ti - dings of Je - sus, Re - demp-tion and re - lease.

Where Cross the Crowded Ways 415

1. Where cross the crowd - ed ways of life, Where sound the
2. In haunts of wretch - ed - ness and need, On shad - owed
3. The cup of wa - ter giv'n for Thee Still holds the
4. O Mas - ter, from the moun - tain side, Make haste to

cries of race and clan, A - bove the noise of
thresh - olds dark with fears, From paths where hide the
fresh - ness of Thy grace; Yet long these mul - ti -
heal these hearts of pain; A - mong these rest - less

self - ish strife, We hear Thy voice, O Son of man!
lures of greed, We catch the vi - sion of Thy tears.
tudes to see The sweet com - pas - sion of Thy face.
throngs a - bide, O tread the cit - y's streets a - gain.

Acts 18:9,10. Words, Frank Mason North, 1905. Tune GERMANY, attr. to Ludwig van Beethoven in William
Gardiner's *Sacred Melodies*, 1815.

Hark! The Voice of Jesus Calling

1. Hark! The voice of Je - sus call - ing: "Who will go and
2. While the souls of men are dy - ing, And the Mas - ter
3. If you can - not speak like an - gels, If you can - not
4. Glad - ly take the task He gives you; Let His work your

work to - day? Fields are white, the har - vest wait - ing—
calls for you, Let none hear you i - dly say - ing,
preach like Paul, You can tell the love of Je - sus,
pleas - ure be; An - swer quick - ly when He call - eth,

Who will bear the sheaves a - way? Who will bear the sheaves a - way?"
"There is noth - ing I can do. There is noth - ing I can do."
You can say, "He died for all." You can say, "He died for all."
"Here am I; O Lord, send me. Here am I; O Lord, send me."

John 9:4. Words, Daniel March, 1868. Tune UNSER LEBEN GLEICHT DER REISE, Swiss Melody, 1812.

417   ## Matthew 9:36-38

When he saw the multitudes, he was moved with compassion for them, because they were distressed and scattered, as sheep not having a shepherd. Then he said to his disciples, "The harvest indeed is plenteous, but the laborers are few. Pray therefore the Lord of the harvest, that he send forth laborers into his harvest."

Work, For the Night is Coming

418

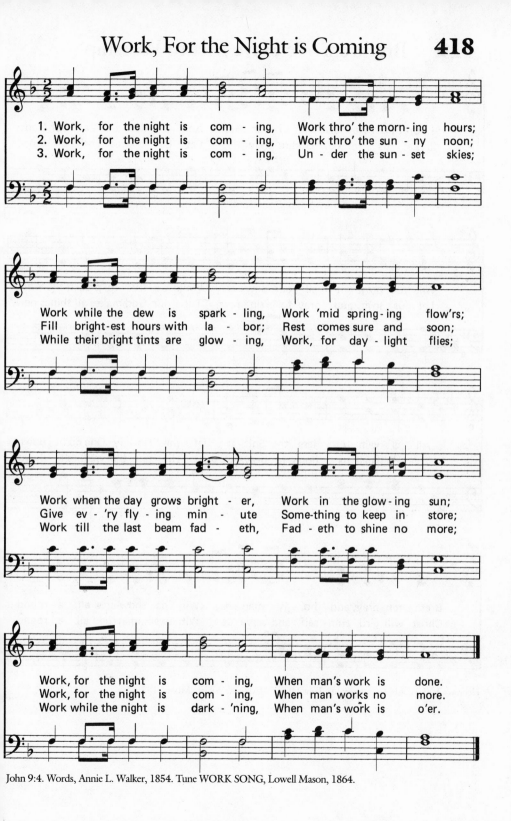

1. Work, for the night is com - ing, Work thro' the morn- ing hours;
2. Work, for the night is com - ing, Work thro' the sun - ny noon;
3. Work, for the night is com - ing, Un - der the sun - set skies;

Work while the dew is spark - ling, Work 'mid spring- ing flow'rs;
Fill bright-est hours with la - bor; Rest comes sure and soon;
While their bright tints are glow - ing, Work, for day - light flies;

Work when the day grows bright - er, Work in the glow- ing sun;
Give ev - 'ry fly - ing min - ute Some-thing to keep in store;
Work till the last beam fad - eth, Fad - eth to shine no more;

Work, for the night is com - ing, When man's work is done.
Work, for the night is com - ing, When man works no more.
Work while the night is dark - 'ning, When man's work is o'er.

John 9:4. Words, Annie L. Walker, 1854. Tune WORK SONG, Lowell Mason, 1864.

419 Brethren, We Have Met to Worship

1. Breth-ren we have met to wor-ship And a-dore the Lord our God;
2. Let us love our God su-preme-ly, Let us love each oth-er too;

Will you pray with all your pow-er, While we try to preach the Word?
Let us love and pray for sin-ners, Till our God makes all things new.

All is vain un-less the Spir-it Of the Ho-ly One comes down;
Then He'll call us home to heav-en, At His ta-ble we'll sit down;

Breth-ren, pray, and ho-ly man-na Will be show-ered all a-round.
Christ will gird Him-self, and serve us With sweet man-na all a-round.

Hebrews 2:12. Words, George Atkins. Tune HOLY MANNA, William Moore, 1825.

Brightly Beams Our Father's Mercy 420

1. Bright-ly beams our Fa-ther's mer-cy From His light - house ev - er - more,
2. Dark the night of sin has set-tled, Loud the an - gry bil - lows roar;
3. Trim your fee - ble lamp, my broth-er: Some poor sail - or tem-pest-tossed,

But to us He gives the keep - ing Of the lights a - long the shore.
Ea - ger eyes are watch-ing, long - ing, For the lights a - long the shore.
Try - ing now to make the har - bor, In the dark - ness may be lost.

Let the low - er lights be burn - ing! Send a gleam a - cross the wave!

some poor faint - ing, strug-gling sea - man You may res - cue, you may save.

Philippians 2:15,16. Words and tune LOWER LIGHTS, Philip P. Bliss, 1871.

421 Lead Me to Some Soul Today

Lead me to some soul to-day; O teach me, Lord, just what to say;

Friends of mine are lost in sin, And can-not find their way.

Few there are who seem to care, And few there are who pray;
who pray;

Melt my heart and fill my life: Give me one soul to - day.

Daniel 12:3. Words, Will H. Houghton, 1936. Tune LOVELESS, Wendell P. Loveless, 1936. Copyright 1936. Renewal 1964 extended by Hope Publishing Co., Carol Stream, Illinois, 60188. All rights reserved. Used by permission.

422 Daniel 12:3

And they that be wise shall shine as the brightness of the firmament; and they that turn many to righteousness as the stars for ever and ever.

Renew Thy Church

423

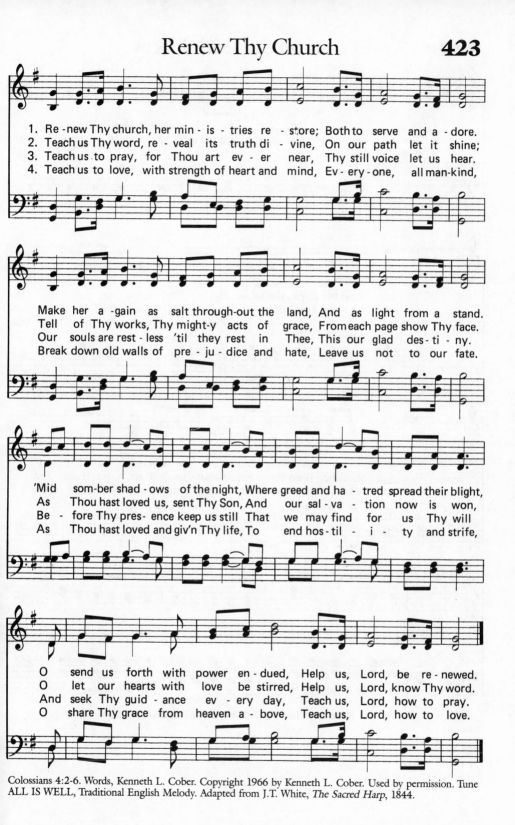

1. Re-new Thy church, her min-is-tries re-store; Both to serve and a-dore.
2. Teach us Thy word, re-veal its truth di-vine, On our path let it shine;
3. Teach us to pray, for Thou art ev-er near, Thy still voice let us hear.
4. Teach us to love, with strength of heart and mind, Ev-ery-one, all man-kind,

Make her a-gain as salt through-out the land, And as light from a stand.
Tell of Thy works, Thy might-y acts of grace, From each page show Thy face.
Our souls are rest-less 'til they rest in Thee, This our glad des-ti-ny.
Break down old walls of pre-ju-dice and hate, Leave us not to our fate.

'Mid som-ber shad-ows of the night, Where greed and ha-tred spread their blight,
As Thou hast loved us, sent Thy Son, And our sal-va-tion now is won,
Be-fore Thy pres-ence keep us still That we may find for us Thy will
As Thou hast loved and giv'n Thy life, To end hos-til-i-ty and strife,

O send us forth with power en-dued, Help us, Lord, be re-newed.
O let our hearts with love be stirred, Help us, Lord, know Thy word.
And seek Thy guid-ance ev-ery day, Teach us, Lord, how to pray.
O share Thy grace from heaven a-bove, Teach us, Lord, how to love.

Colossians 4:2-6. Words, Kenneth L. Cober. Copyright 1966 by Kenneth L. Cober. Used by permission. Tune ALL IS WELL, Traditional English Melody. Adapted from J.T. White, *The Sacred Harp*, 1844.

424 From All the Dark Places

1. From all the dark plac - es Of earth's hea - then rac - es,
2. The sun - light is glanc - ing O'er ar - mies ad - vanc - ing,
3. With shout - ing and sing - ing, And ju - bi - lant ring - ing,

O see how the thick shad-ows fly! The voice of sal - va - tion
To con - quer the king - doms of sin; Our Lord shall pos - sess them,
Their arms of re - bel - lion cast down, At last ev - 'ry na - tion

A - wakes ev - ery na - tion; "Come o - ver and help us," they cry.
His pres - ence shall bless them, His beau - ty shall en - ter them in.
The Lord of sal - va - tion Their King and Re - deem - er shall crown!

The kingdom is spreading, O tell ye the sto-ry, God's banner ex-alt-ed shall be!

Isaiah 11:9. Words, Mary B. C. Slade, 1873. Tune THE KINGDOM IS COMING, Rigdon M. McIntosh, 1873.

The earth shall be full of His knowledge and glory, And waters that cover the sea!

Hail to the Brightness

425

1. Hail to the bright-ness of Zi - on's glad morn-ing, Joy to the
2. Hail to the bright-ness of Zi - on's glad morn-ing, Long by the
3. See, from all lands, from the isles of the o - cean, Praise to Je -

lands that in dark-ness have lain! Hushed be the ac - cents of
proph-ets of Is - rael's fore - told; Hail to the mil - lions from
ho - vah as - cend-ing on high; Fall'n are the en - gines of

sor - row and mourn-ing, Zi - on in tri - umph be - gins her mild reign.
bond-age re - turn-ing! Gen - tiles and Jews the blest vi - sion be - hold.
war and com - mo-tion, Shouts of sal - va - tion are rend-ing the sky.

Isaiah 35:1,2. Words, Thomas Hastings, 1832. Tune WESLEY, Lowell Mason, 1833.

426 Sweetly, Lord, Have We Heard Thee

1. Sweet-ly, Lord, have we heard Thee call - ing, "Come, fol - low me!"
2. Tho' they lead o'er the cold, dark moun-tains, Seek - ing His sheep,
3. If they lead thro' the tem - ple ho - ly, Preach - ing the word;
4. By and by, thro' the shin - ing por - tals, Turn - ing our feet,

And we see where Thy foot-prints fall - ing Lead us to Thee.
Or a - long by Si - lo - am's foun-tains Help - ing the weak:
Or in homes of the poor and low - ly, Serv - ing the Lord.
We shall walk, with the glad im - mor - tals, Heav'n's gold - en street.

Foot - prints of Je - sus, that make the path - way glow;

We will fol - low the steps of Je - sus, wher - e'er they go.

1 Peter 2:21. Words, Mary B. C. Slade, 1871. Tune FOOTSTEPS, Asa B. Everett, 1871.

I Would Be True

427

1. I would be true, for there are those who trust me;
I would be pure, for there are those who care.
I would be strong, for there is much to suf - fer;
I would be brave, for there is much to dare,
I would be brave, for there is much to dare.

2. I would be friend of all, the foe, the friend - less;
I would be giv - ing, and for - get the gift.
I would be hum - ble, for I know my weak - ness;
I would look up, and laugh and love and lift,
I would look up, and laugh and love and lift.

Philippians 1:21. Words, Howard A. Walter, 1907. Tune PEEK, Joseph Y. Peek, 1909.

428   O Brother Man, Fold to Thy Heart

1. O broth-er man, fold to thy heart thy broth-er;
2. For he whom Je - sus loved has tru - ly spo - ken—
3. Fol - low with rev - erent steps the great ex - am - ple
4. Then shall all shack - les fall; the storm - y clang - or

Where pit - y dwells, the peace of God is there;
The ho - lier wor - ship which He deigns to bless
Of Him whose ho - ly work was do - ing good;
Of wild war mu - sic o'er the earth shall cease;

To wor - ship right - ly is to love each oth - er,
Re - stores the lost, and binds the spir - it bro - ken,
So shall the wide earth seem our Fa - ther's tem - ple,
Love shall tread out the bale - ful fire of an - ger,

Each smile a hymn, each kind - ly deed a prayer.
And feeds the wid - ow and the fa - ther - less.
Each lov - ing life a psalm of grat - i - tude.
And in its ash - es plant the tree of peace.

James 1:27. Words, John Greenleaf Whittier, 1848. Tune HENDERSON, O. C. Henderson. Harm., Rollie Blondeau.

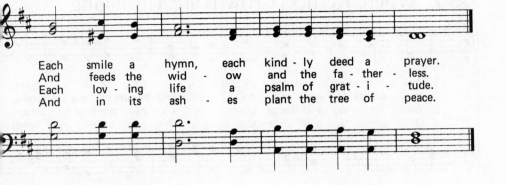

Each smile a hymn, each kind - ly deed a prayer.
And feeds the wid - ow and the fa - ther - less.
Each lov - ing life a psalm of grat - i - tude.
And in its ash - es plant the tree of peace.

Ephesians 4:25-32; 5:15-20   **429**

Wherefore putting away lying, speak every man truth with his neighbor: for we are members one of another. Be ye angry, and sin not: let not the sun go down upon your wrath: neither give place to the devil. Let him that stole steal no more: but rather let him labor, working with his hands the thing which is good, that he may have to give to him that needeth. Let no corrupt communication proceed out of your mouth, but that which is good to the use of edifying, that it may minister grace unto the hearers. And grieve not the Holy Spirit of God, whereby ye were sealed unto the day of redemption. Let all bitterness, and wrath, and anger, and clamor, and evil speaking, be put away from you, with all malice: and be ye kind one to another, tenderhearted, forgiving one another, even as God for Christ's sake hath forgiven you . . . Look therefore carefully how ye walk, not as unwise, but as wise; redeeming the time, because the days are evil. Wherefore be not foolish, but understand what the will of the Lord is. And be not drunken with wine, wherein is riot, but be filled with the Spirit; speaking one to another in psalms and hymns and spiritual songs, singing and making melody with your heart to the Lord; giving thanks always for all things in the name of our Lord Jesus Christ to God, even the Father.

430 Where Restless Crowds are Thronging

1. Where rest-less crowds are throng-ing A-long the cit-y ways,
2. In scenes of want and sor-row And haunts of fla-grant wrong,
3. With bomb-ing and fierce burn-ing Your peo-ple find no peace.
4. O Christ, be-hold your peo-ple; They press on ev-'ry hand!

Where pride and greed and tur-moil Con-sume the fe-vered days,
In homes where kind-ness fal-ters, And strife and fear are strong,
Help us to share their yearn-ing That sense-less death may cease.
Bring light to all the cit-ies Of our di-vid-ed land.

Where vain am-bi-tions ban-ish All thoughts of praise and prayer,
In bus-y streets of bar-ter, In lone-ly thor-ough-fare,
Break through our ease and com-fort, For-bid that we not care;
May all our bit-ter striv-ing Give way to vi-sions fair

The peo-ple's spir-its wa-ver: But you, O Christ, are there.
The peo-ple's spir-its lan-guish: But you, O Christ, are there.
And strength-en all our ef-forts, For you, O Christ, are there.
Of right-eous-ness and jus-tice, For you, O Christ, are there.

Mark 6:34. Words, Thomas C. Clark, 1953. Words Copyright 1954. Renewal 1982 by the Hymn Society of America, Texas Christian University, Fort Worth, Texas, 76129. Used by permission. Tune LLANGLOFFAN, Traditional Welsh Melody from David Evans' *Hymnau a Thônau*, 1865. From the *Revised Church Hymnary*, 1927, by permission of Oxford University Press.

O Holy City, Seen of John

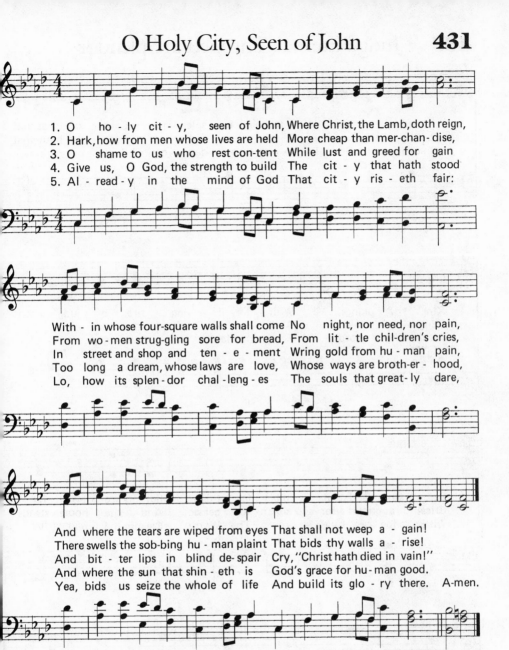

1. O ho - ly cit - y, seen of John, Where Christ, the Lamb, doth reign,
2. Hark, how from men whose lives are held More cheap than mer-chan-dise,
3. O shame to us who rest con-tent While lust and greed for gain
4. Give us, O God, the strength to build The cit - y that hath stood
5. Al - read - y in the mind of God That cit - y ris - eth fair:

With - in whose four-square walls shall come No night, nor need, nor pain,
From wo - men strug-gling sore for bread, From lit - tle chil-dren's cries,
In street and shop and ten - e - ment Wring gold from hu - man pain,
Too long a dream, whose laws are love, Whose ways are broth-er - hood,
Lo, how its splen-dor chal -leng - es The souls that great-ly dare,

And where the tears are wiped from eyes That shall not weep a - gain!
There swells the sob-bing hu - man plaint That bids thy walls a - rise!
And bit - ter lips in blind de-spair Cry, "Christ hath died in vain!"
And where the sun that shin - eth is God's grace for hu - man good.
Yea, bids us seize the whole of life And build its glo - ry there. A-men.

Revelation 22:1-5. Words, Walter Russell Bowie, 1909. Tune MORNING SONG, from John Wyeth's *Repository of Sacred Music, Part Second*, 1813.

Isaiah 1:16,17   432

Wash you, make you clean; put away the evil of your doings from before mine eyes; cease to do evil; learn to do well; seek justice, relieve the oppressed, judge the fatherless, plead for the widow.

433 Judge Eternal, Throned in Splendor

1. Judge e-ter-nal, throned in splen-dor, Lord of lords and
2. Still the wea-ry folk are pin-ing For the hour that
3. Crown, O God, Thine own en-deav-or; Cleave our dark-ness,

King of kings, With Thy liv-ing fire of judg-ment
brings re-lease; And the cit-y's crowd-ed clan-gor
with Thy sword; Feed the faint and hun-gry peo-ples

Purge this land of bit-ter things; Sol-ace all its
Cries a-loud for sin to cease; And the home-steads
With the rich-ness of Thy Word; Cleanse the bod-y

wide do-min-ion With the heal-ing of Thy wings.
and the wood-lands Plead in si-lence for their peace.
of this na-tion Through the glo-ry of the Lord. A-men.

1 Peter 2:9. Words, Henry S. Holland, d. 1918; alt. Tune RHUDDLAN, Traditional Welsh Melody.

O God of Earth and Altar

434

1. O God of earth and al - tar, Bow down and hear our cry;
2. From all that ter - ror teach - es, From lies of tongue and pen,

Our earth - ly rul - ers fal - ter, Our peo - ple drift and die;
From all the eas - y speech - es That com - fort cru - el men,

The walls of gold en - tomb us, The swords of scorn di - vide;
From sale and prof - a - na - tion Of hon - or and the sword,

Take not Thy thun - der from us, But take a - way our pride.
From sleep and from dam - na - tion, De - liv - er us, good Lord!

Hebrews 13:10-14. Words, Gilbert K. Chesterton, 1906. Tune LLANGLOFFAN, Traditional Welsh Melody
from David Evans' *Hymnau a Thônau*, 1865.

435 **O Beautiful for Spacious Skies**

1. O beau-ti-ful for spa-cious skies, For am-ber waves of grain,
2. O beau-ti-ful for pil-grim feet, Whose stern im-pas-sioned stress
3. O beau-ti-ful for pa-triot dream That sees be-yond the years

For pur-ple moun-tain maj-es-ties A-bove the fruit-ed plain;
A thor-ough-fare for free-dom beat A-cross the wil-der-ness;
Thine al-a-bas-ter cit-ies gleam Un-dimmed by hu-man tears;

A-mer-i-ca! A-mer-i-ca! God shed His grace on thee,
A-mer-i-ca! A-mer-i-ca! God mend thine ev-'ry flaw,
A-mer-i-ca! A-mer-i-ca! God shed His grace on thee,

And crown thy good with broth-er-hood From sea to shin-ing sea.
Con-firm thy soul in self con-trol, Thy lib-er-ty in law.
And crown thy good with broth-er-hood From sea to shin-ing sea.

Psalm 33:12. Words, Katherine Lee Bates, 1893. Tune MATERNA, Samuel A. Ward, c. 1885.

We are Called to be God's People   **436**

1. We are called to be God's peo - ple, Show-ing by our lives His grace,
2. We are called to be God's ser-vants, Work- ing in His world to - day;
3. We are called to be God's prophets, Spokesmen for the truth and right;

One in heart and one in spir - it, Sign of hope for all the race.
Tak - ing His own task up - on us, All His sa - cred words o - bey.
Stand-ing firm for god - ly jus - tice, Bring-ing e - vil in - to light.

Let us show how He has changed us, And re - made us as His own,
Let us rise, then, to His sum - mons, Ded - i - cate to Him our all,
Let us seek the cour-age need - ed, Our high call - ing to ful - fill,

Let us share our life to-geth - er As we shall a - round His throne.
That we may be faith - ful ser - vants, Quick to an - swer now His call.
That man-kind may know the bless - ing Of the do - ing of God's will.

John 17:21. Words, Thomas A. Jackson, 1973. Copyright 1975 Broadman Press. All rights reserved. Used by permission. Tune AUSTRIAN HYMN, Franz Joseph Haydn, 1797.

437   # When the Trumpet of the Lord

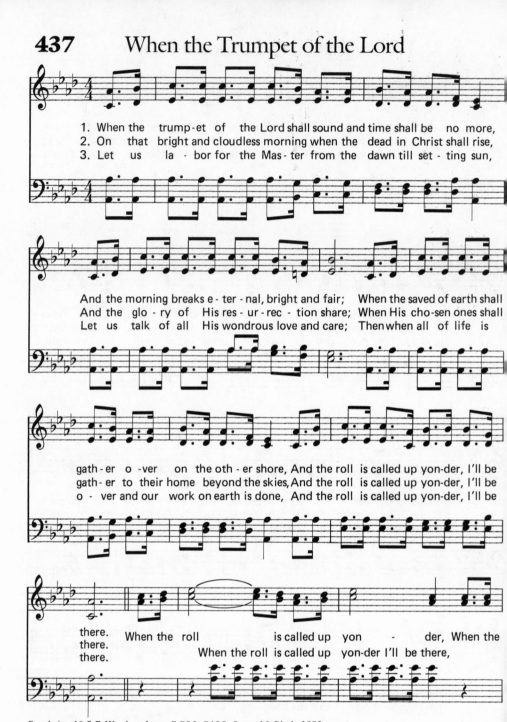

1. When the trump-et of the Lord shall sound and time shall be no more,
2. On that bright and cloudless morning when the dead in Christ shall rise,
3. Let us la - bor for the Mas- ter from the dawn till set - ting sun,

And the morning breaks e - ter - nal, bright and fair; When the saved of earth shall
And the glo - ry of His res - ur - rec - tion share; When His cho-sen ones shall
Let us talk of all His wondrous love and care; Then when all of life is

gath - er o -ver on the oth - er shore, And the roll is called up yon-der, I'll be
gath- er to their home beyond the skies, And the roll is called up yon-der, I'll be
o - ver and our work on earth is done, And the roll is called up yon-der, I'll be

there.   When the roll   is called up yon - der, When the
there.
there.   When the roll is called up yon-der I'll be there,

Revelation 10:5-7. Words and tune ROLL CALL, James M. Black, 1893.

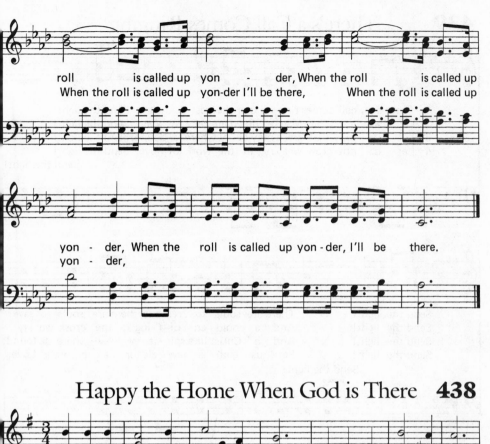

roll   is called up yon - der, When the roll   is called up
When the roll is called up yon-der I'll be there,   When the roll is called up

yon - der, When the   roll is called up yon - der, I'll be   there.
yon - der,

Happy the Home When God is There   **438**

1. Hap-py the home when God is   there   And love fills ev - ery-one,
2. Hap-py the home where God's strong love   Is start-ing to ap - pear,
3. Hap-py the home where prayer is   heard   And praise is ev - ery-where,
4. Lord, let us in   our homes a - gree   This bless-ed peace to gain;

When with u - ni - ted work and prayer The Mas-ter's will is done.
Where all the chil - dren hear His fame   And par-ents hold Him dear.
Where par-ents love the sa - cred Word And its true wis - dom share.
U - nite our hearts in love to Thee, And love to all will reign. A-men.

2 Timothy 1:5. Words, Henry Ware, Jr.; alt. Bryan Jeffery Leech, 1976. Text revision Copyright 1976 by Fred Bock Music Co. All rights reserved. Used by permission. Tune ST. AGNES, John B. Dykes, 1866.

There's a Call Comes Ringing

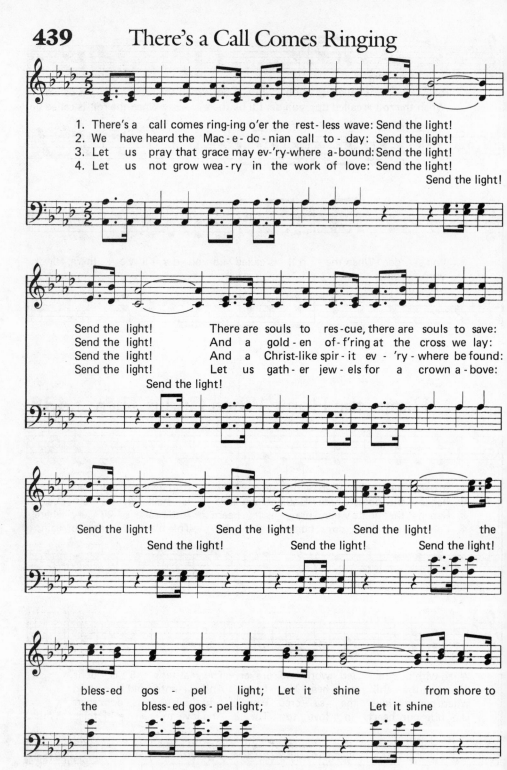

1. There's a call comes ring-ing o'er the rest- less wave: Send the light!
2. We have heard the Mac-e-do-nian call to-day: Send the light!
3. Let us pray that grace may ev-'ry-where a-bound: Send the light!
4. Let us not grow wea-ry in the work of love: Send the light!

Send the light!

Send the light! There are souls to res-cue, there are souls to save:
Send the light! And a gold-en of-f'ring at the cross we lay:
Send the light! And a Christ-like spir-it ev - 'ry - where be found:
Send the light! Let us gath-er jew-els for a crown a-bove:

Send the light!

Send the light! Send the light! Send the light! the
Send the light! Send the light! Send the light!

bless-ed gos - pel light; Let it shine from shore to
the bless-ed gos - pel light; Let it shine

Acts 16:8-10. Words and tune McCABE, Charles H. Gabriel, 1890.

shore!   Send the   light!   the bless - ed
from shore to shore!   Send the light!   the

gos - pel   light; Let it   shine   for ev - er - more.
bless-ed gospel light;   Let it shine   for ev - er-more.

O Day of God, Draw Nigh   440

1. O   day   of   God, draw   nigh   In   beau-ty and in   power;
2. Bring   to   our trou - bled   minds,   Un - cer-tain and a - fraid,
3. Bring   jus - tice to   our   land,   That   all   may dwell se - cure,
4. Bring   to   our world of   strife   Thy   sov - ereign word of   peace,
5. O   day   of   God, draw   nigh   As   at   cre - a - tion's   birth;

Come with Thy time - less judge-ment now To match our pres-ent hour.
The   qui - et   of   a   stead-fast faith, Calm of   a   call o - beyed.
And   fine - ly build for   days to come Foun- da - tions that en - dure.
That   war may haunt the earth no more And des - o - la - tion cease.
Let   there be light a - gain, and set   Thy judg-ments in the earth. A-men.

1 Peter 2:11,12. Words, Robert B. Y. Scott, 1937. Copyright. Words used by permission of R. B. Y. Scott. Tune
ST. MICHAEL, from *Genevan Psalter*, 1551.

441   O Master, Let Me Walk With Thee

1. O Mas-ter, let me walk with Thee In low-ly paths of serv-ice free; Tell my Thy se-cret, help me bear The strain of toil, the fret of care.

2. Help me the slow of heart to move By some clear, win-ning word of love; Teach me the way-ward feet to stay, And guide them in the home-ward way.

3. Teach me Thy pa-tience; still with Thee In clos-er, dear-er com-pa-ny, In work that keeps faith sweet and strong, In trust that tri-umphs o-ver wrong.

4. In hope that sends a shin-ing ray Far down the fu-ture's broad-ening way, In peace that on-ly Thou canst give, With Thee, O Mas-ter, let me live. A-men.

Philippians 4:13. Words, Washington Gladden, 1879. Tune MARYTON, H. Percy Smith, 1874.

Fight the Good Fight

442

1. Fight the good fight with all your might; Christ is your
2. Run the straight race through God's good grace, Lift up your
3. Cast care a - side, up - on your Guide Lean, and His
4. Faint not, nor fear, His arms are near, He chang - es

strength and Christ your right; Lay hold on life, and
eyes, and seek His face; Life with its way be -
mer - cy will pro - vide; Lean, and the trust - ing
not, and you are dear; On - ly be - lieve, and

it shall be Your joy and crown e - ter - nal - ly.
fore us lies: Christ is the path, and Christ the prize.
soul shall prove Christ is its life, and Christ its love.
you shall see That Christ is all e - ter - nal - ly.

1 Timothy 6:12. Words, John S.B. Monsell, 1863. Tune PENTECOST, William Boyd, 1864.

443 Sowing in the Morning

1. Sow-ing in the morn-ing, sow-ing seeds of kind-ness, Sow-ing in the noon-tide
2. Sow-ing in the sun-shine, sow-ing in the shad-ows, Fear-ing nei-ther clouds nor
3. Go then e-ven weep-ing, sow-ing for the Mas-ter, Tho' the loss sus-tained our

and the dew-y eves; Wait-ing for the har-vest and the time of reap-ing,
win-ter's chill-ing breeze; By and by the har-vest, and the la-bor end-ed,
spir-it oft-en grieves; When our weeping's o-ver, He will bid us wel-come,

We shall come re-joic-ing, bring-ing in the sheaves. Bring-ing in the sheaves,

bring-ing in the sheaves, We shall come re-joic-ing, Bring-ing in the sheaves;

Bring-ing in the sheaves, We shall come re-joic-ing,
Bring-ing in the sheaves, Bring-ing in the sheaves.

Psalm 126:5,6. Words, Knowles Shaw, 1874. Tune BRINGING IN THE SHEAVES, George A. Minor, 1879.

Immortal Love, Forever Full 444

1. Im - mor - tal Love, for - ev - er full, For -
2. We may not climb the heaven - ly steeps To
3. But warm, sweet, ten - der, e - ven yet A
4. The heal - ing of His seam - less dress Is
5. Through Him the first fond prayers are said, Our

ev - er flow - ing free, For - ev - er shared, for -
bring the Lord Christ down; In vain we search the
pres - ent help is He; And faith has still its
by our beds of pain; We touch Him in life's
lips of child - hood frame; The last low whis - pers

ev - er whole, A nev - er - ebb - ing sea!
low - est deeps, For Him no depths can drown.
Ol - i - vet, And love its Gal - i - lee.
throng and press, And we are whole a - gain.
of our dead Are bur - dened with His name.

Matthew 28:20. Words, John Greenleaf Whittier, 1866. Tune SERENITY, William V. Wallace, 1856; arr. Uzziah C. Burnap, 1878.

Isaiah 42:1-3 445

Behold, my servant, whom I uphold; my chosen, in whom my soul delights: I have put my Spirit upon him; he will bring forth justice to the nations. He will not cry, nor lift up his voice, nor cause it to be heard in the street. A bruised reed will he not break, and a dimly burning wick will he not quench: he will bring forth justice in truth.

446 O Jesus, My Savior

1. O Jesus, my Savior, with Thee I am blest,
2. Oh, who's like my Savior, He's Salem's bright King;
3. I'm happy, I'm happy, oh, won-drous ac - count!

My life and sal - va - tion, my joy and my rest:
He smiles and He loves me and helps me to sing:
My joys are im - mor - tal, I stand on the mount:

Thy name be my theme, and Thy love be my song;
I'll praise Him, I'll praise Him with notes loud and clear,
I gaze on my treas - ure and long to be there,

Thy grace shall in - spire both my heart and my tongue.
While riv - ers of pleas - ure my spir - it shall cheer.
With Je - sus and an - gels and kin - dred so dear.

1 Timothy 1:15-17. Words, Anonymous; arr. Tune I LOVE THEE, Jeremiah Ingall's *Christian Harmony*, 1805.

Glorious Things of Thee are Spoken 447

1. Glo-rious things of Thee are spo-ken, Zi - on, cit - y of our God!
2. See, the streams of liv - ing wa - ters, Springing from e - ter - nal love,
3. Sav - ior, since of Zi - on's cit - y, I, thro' grace, a mem-ber am,

He whose word can - not be bro - ken Formed thee for His own a - bode:
Well sup - ply Thy sons and daugh-ters, And all fear of want re - move:
Let the world de - ride or pit - y, I will glo - ry in Thy name.

On the Rock of A - ges found - ed, What can shake Thy sure re - pose?
Who can faint while such a riv - er Ev - er flows their thirst t'as-suage?
Fad - ing is the world-ling's pleas-ure, All his boast - ed pomp and show;

With sal - va - tion's walls sur-round-ed, Thou may'st smile at all Thy foes.
Grace, which, like the Lord the Giv - er, Nev - er fails from age to age.
Sol - id joys and last - ing treas-ure None but Zi - on's chil-dren know.

Psalm 48:1,2. Words, John Newton, 1779. Tune AUSTRIAN HYMN, Franz Joseph Haydn, 1797.

448 Lift Up, Lift Up Your Voices Now

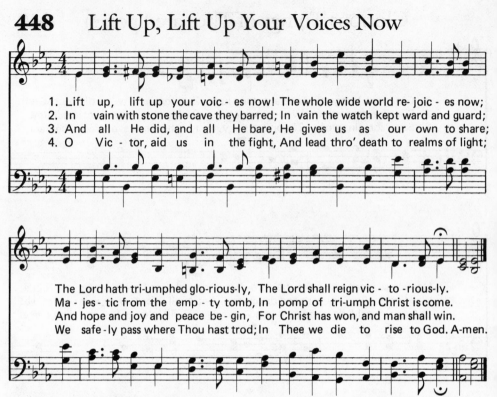

1. Lift up, lift up your voic - es now! The whole wide world re- joic - es now;
2. In vain with stone the cave they barred; In vain the watch kept ward and guard;
3. And all He did, and all He bare, He gives us as our own to share;
4. O Vic - tor, aid us in the fight, And lead thro' death to realms of light;

The Lord hath tri-umphed glo-rious-ly, The Lord shall reign vic - to -rious-ly.
Ma - jes- tic from the emp - ty tomb, In pomp of tri-umph Christ is come.
And hope and joy and peace be- gin, For Christ has won, and man shall win.
We safe -ly pass where Thou hast trod; In Thee we die to rise to God. A-men.

Psalm 24:7-10. Words, from Charles L. Hutchins' *The Church Hymnal*, 1892. Tune WALTHAM, John Baptiste Calkin, 1872.

449 Revelation 12:10,11

And I heard a great voice in heaven, saying, "Now is come the salvation, and the power, and the kingdom of our God, and the authority of his Christ: for the accuser of our brethren is cast down, who accuseth them before our God day and night. And they overcame him because of the blood of the Lamb, and because of the word of their testimony; and they loved not their life even unto death."

For All the Saints

450

1. For all the saints, who from their la - bors rest,
2. Thou wast their Rock, their For - tress and their Might;
3. O may Thy sol - diers, faith - ful, true and bold,
4. And when the strife is fierce, the war - fare long,
5. The gold - en eve - ning bright-ens in the west,
6. But lo! there breaks a yet more glo - rious day:

Who Thee by faith be - fore the world con - fessed, Thy
Thou, Lord, their Cap - tain in the well - fought fight; And
Fight as the saints who no - bly fought of old, And
Steals on the ear the dis - tant tri - umph song, And
Soon, soon to faith - ful war - riors com - eth rest; Sweet
The saints tri - um - phant rise in bright ar - ray; The

name, O Je - sus, be for - ev - er blest. Al -
Thou, in dark - ness drear, their one true Light. Al -
win with them the vic - tor's crown of gold. Al -
hearts are brave a - gain, the arms are strong, Al -
is the calm of Par - a - dise the blest: Al -
King of glo - ry pass - es on His way: Al -

- le - lu - ia, Al - le - lu - ia!

Hebrews 11:13. Words, William W. How, 1864. Tune SINE NOMINE, Ralph Vaughan Williams, 1906.
Music from *The English Hymnal*, 1906, by permission of Oxford University Press.

451 My God, I Love Thee

1. My God, I love Thee: not be-cause I hope for heav'n there - by;
2. And griefs and tor-ments num-ber less, And sweat of a - go - ny,
3. Not with the hope of gain-ing aught; Not seek-ing a re - ward:

Nor yet be-cause if I love not I must for ev - er die.
E'en death it - self; and all for me Who was Thine en - e - my.
But as Thy-self hast lov - ed me, O ev - er - lov - ing Lord!

But, O my Je - sus, Thou didst me Up - on the cross em - brace;
Not for the hope of win-ning heav'n, Nor of es - cap - ing hell;
E'en so I love Thee, and will love, And in Thy praise will sing;

For me didst bear the nails and spear, And man - i - fold dis - grace.
Then why, O bless - ed Je - sus Christ, Should I not love Thee well?
Sole - ly be - cause Thou art my God And my e - ter - nal King?

Psalm 40:1-3. Words, attr. to Francis Xavier, 1546; trans. Edward Caswall, 1849. Tune KINGSFOLD, English Folk Tune. Copyright 1906 from *The English Hymnal* by permission of Oxford University Press. Arr. J.B., Copyright 1986, ACU Press.

Where Charity and Love Prevail 452

1. Where char-i-ty and love pre-vail, There God is ev-er found; Brought here to-geth-er by Christ's love, By love we thus are bound.
2. With grate-ful joy and ho-ly fear, God's char-i-ty we learn; Let us with heart and mind and soul Now love God in re-turn.
3. Let us re-call that in our midst Dwells Christ, God's ho-ly Son; As mem-bers of all con-ten-tions cease. Be God's the glo-ry that we seek; Be His our on-ly peace.
4. Let strife a-mong us be un-known; Let all con-ten-tions cease. Be God's the glo-ry that we seek; Be His our on-ly peace.
5. For love ex-cludes no race or clan That names the Sav-ior's name; His fam-i-ly em-bra-ces all Whose Fa-ther is the same.
6. We now for-give each oth-er's faults As we our own con-fess, That we may love each oth-er well In Chris-tian gen-tle-ness.

Ephesians 4:1-3. Words, Latin Hymn *Ubi caritas et amor,* c. 9th cent.; trans. Omer Westendorf, 1961. From *The People's Mass Book.* Copyright 1961, 1962, World Library Publications. Used by permission. Tune TWENTY-FOURTH, in John Wyeth's *Repository of Sacred Music, Part Second,* 1813; attr. to Lucius Chapin. Arr. J.B., Copyright 1986, ACU Press.

453 My Jesus, I Love Thee

1. My Je - sus, I love Thee, I know Thou art mine; For Thee all the fol - lies
2. I love Thee, be-cause Thou hast first lov-ed me, And purchased my par-don
3. In man-sions of glo - ry and end-less de - light, I'll ev - er a - dore Thee

of sin I re - sign; My gra-cious Re-deem - er, my Sav - ior art Thou;
on Cal - va - ry's tree; I love Thee for wear - ing the thorns on Thy brow;
in heav-en so bright; I'll sing with the glit - ter-ing crown on my brow,

If ev - er I loved Thee, my Je - sus, 'tis now.

1 John 4:19. Words, William R. Featherstone, c. 1862. Tune GORDON, Adoniram J. Gordon, 1876.

454 1 John 4:9,10,19

Herein was the love of God manifested in our case, that God sent his only begotten Son into the world that we might live through him. Herein is love, not that we loved God, but that he loved us, and sent his Son to be the propitiation for our sins. We love, because he first loved us.

There is a Name I Love to Hear

455

1. There is a name I love to hear, I love to sing its worth;
2. It tells me of a Sav-ior's love, Who died to set me free;
3. It tells me what my Fa-ther hath In store for ev - 'ry day,
4. It tells of One whose lov - ing heart Can feel my deep - est woe,

It sounds like mu - sic in mine ear, The sweet-est name on earth.
It tells me of His pre-cious blood, The sin - ner's per - fect plea.
And though I tread a dark-some path, Yields sun-shine all the way.
Who in each sor - row bears a part, That none can bear be - low.

Oh, how I love Je - sus, Oh, how I love Je - sus,

Oh, how I love Je - sus, Be - cause He first loved me.

Acts 4:12. Words, Frederick Whitfield, 1855. Tune O HOW I LOVE JESUS, American Folk Hymn, 19th cent.

456   # We are One in the Spirit

1. We are one in the Spir-it, we are one in the Lord,
2. We will walk with each oth-er, we will walk hand in hand,
3. We will work with each oth-er, we will work side by side,
4. All praise to the Fa-ther, from whom all things come,

We are one in the Spir-it, we are one in the Lord,
We will walk with each oth-er, we will walk hand in hand,
We will work with each oth-er, we will work side by side,
And all praise to Christ Je-sus, His on-ly Son,

And we pray that our u-ni-ty may one day be re-stored:
And to-geth-er we'll spread the news that God is in our land:
And we'll guard each man's dig-ni-ty and save each man's pride:
And all praise to the Spir-it who makes us one:

And they'll know we are Chris-tians by our love, by our love,

and they'll know we are Chris-tians by our love.

John 13:35. Words, Peter Scholtes. Copyright 1966 by F.E.L. Publications, Ltd., 1925 Pontius Avenue, Los Angeles, CA 90025. Performance rights licensed through ASCAP. Further reproduction, even words only, not permitted without F.E.L.'s permission. (and tune ST. BRENDAN'S)

O for a Soul

1. O for a soul a-glow with love, With love for God and man;
2. A soul so large that all man-kind Can be em-braced there-in.
2. A soul so great that God a-lone Can ac-tu-ate its will;

Re-joic-ing ev-'ry pass-ing day To fol-low God's own plan!
The high, the low, the good, the bad, Be count-ed all a-kin.
That ev-'ry pulse shall beat for Him, His pur-pose to ful-fill.

1 John 4:19-21. Words and tune AGAPE, William J. Kirkpatrick.

Matthew 5:43-48
Ephesians 5:1,2

458

You have heard that it was said, "You shall love your neighbor, and hate your enemy." But I say to you, "Love your enemies, and pray for them that persecute you; that you may be sons of your Father who is in heaven: for he makes his sun to rise on the evil and the good, and sends rain on the just and the unjust. For if you love them that love you, what reward do you have? Do not even the publicans do the same? And if you salute your brethren only, what do you do more than others? Do not even the Gentiles do the same? You therefore shall be perfect, as your heavenly Father is perfect."

Be ye therefore imitators of God, as beloved children; and walk in love, even as Christ also loved you, and gave himself up for us, an offering and a sacrifice to God.

459

It Only Takes a Spark

1. It on-ly takes a spark to get a fire go-ing,
2. What a won-drous time is spring when all the trees are bud-ding;
3. I wish for you, my friends, this hap-pi-ness that I've found,

And soon all those a-round can warm up in its glow-ing;
The birds be-gin to sing, the flow-ers start their bloom-ing;
You can de-pend on Him, It mat-ters not where you're bound;

That's how it is with God's love; Once you've ex-
That's how it is with God's love; Once you've ex-
I'll shout it from the moun-tain top, I want my

per-i-enced it, You spread His love to ev-'ry-one; You
per-i-enced it, You want to sing, it's fresh like spring, You
world to know; The Lord of love has come to me, I

Acts 8:4. Words and tune PASS IT ON, Kurt Kaiser, 1969. Copyright 1969 by Lexicon Music, Inc. International copyright secured. All rights reserved. Used by permission.

want to pass it on.
want to pass it on.

want to pass it on.

To Love Some One More Dearly **460**

1. To love someone more dear-ly ev - 'ry day, To help a wan- d'ring
2. To fol- low truth as blind men long for light, To do my best from
3. And then my Sav - ior by and by to meet, When faith hath made her

child to find his way, To pon-der o'er a no - ble tho't and pray,
dawn of day till night, To keep my heart fit for His ho - ly sight,
task on earth com - plete, And lay my hom-age at the Mas - ter's feet,

And smile when evening falls, And smile when evening falls: This is my task.
And an-swer when He calls, And answer when He calls: This is my task.
With - in the jas - per walls, With-in the jas - per walls: This crowns my task.

3 John, verse 4. Words, st. 1 and 2, Maude Louise Ray, 1903; st. 3, F. H. Pickup, 1913. Third stanza Copyright
1913 by Lorenz Publishing Co. Renewal secured. Used by permission. Tune MY TASK, Emma Hindle Ashford.

461 Jesus My Lord Will Love Me Forever

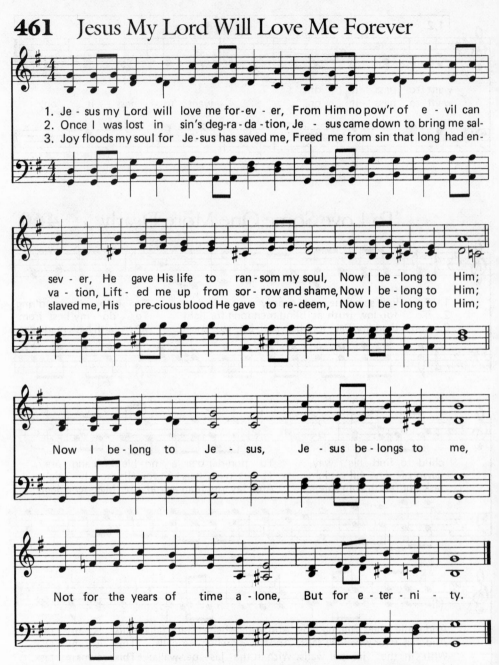

1. Je - sus my Lord will love me for-ev - er, From Him no pow'r of e - vil can
2. Once I was lost in sin's deg-ra - da - tion, Je - sus came down to bring me sal-
3. Joy floods my soul for Je -sus has saved me, Freed me from sin that long had en-

sev - er, He gave His life to ran - som my soul, Now I be - long to Him;
va - tion, Lift - ed me up from sor - row and shame, Now I be - long to Him;
slaved me, His pre-cious blood He gave to re-deem, Now I be - long to Him;

Now I be - long to Je - sus, Je - sus be - longs to me,

Not for the years of time a - lone, But for e - ter - ni - ty.

Romans 14:8. Words, Norman J. Clayton, 1943. Tune ELLSWORTH, Norman J. Clayton, 1943. Copyright 1938, 1943. Renewed 1966, 1971, by Norman Clayton Publishing Co., owner. Used by permission.

Walking in Sunlight

462

1. Walk-ing in sun-light all of my jour-ney, O-ver the mountains, thro' the deep vale;
2. Shad-ows a-round me, shad-ows a-bove me, Nev-er con-ceal my Sav-ior and Guide;
3. In the bright sun-light, ev-er re-joic-ing, Pressing my way to man-sions a-bove;

Je-sus had said, "I'll nev-er for-sake thee," Promise di-vine that nev-er can fail.
He is the light, in Him is no dark-ness, Ev-er I'm walk-ing close to His side.
Singing His prais-es, glad-ly I'm walk-ing, Walking in sun-light, sun-light of love.

Heav-en-ly sun-light, heav-en-ly sun-light, Flood-ing my soul with glo-ry di-vine,

Hal-le-lu-jah! I am re-joic-ing, Sing-ing His prais-es, Je-sus is mine!

John 8:12. Words, Henry J. Zelley, 1899. Tune HEAVENLY SUNLIGHT, George H. Cook, 1899.

463   There is Sunshine in My Soul

1. There is sun-shine in my soul to-day, More glo-ri-ous and bright
2. There is mu-sic in my soul to-day, A car-ol to my King,
3. There is spring-time in my soul to-day, For when the Lord is near,
4. There is glad-ness in my soul to-day, And hope and praise and love,

Than glows in an-y earth-ly sky, For Je-sus is my light.
And Je-sus, lis-ten-ing, can hear The songs I can-not sing.
The dove of peace sings in my heart, The flow'rs of grace ap-pear.
For bless-ings which He gives me now, For joys laid up a-bove.

O there's sun - shine, bless-ed sun - shine,
O there's sun-shine in my soul, bless-ed sun-shine in my soul,

While the peace-ful, hap-py mo-ments roll;   When
hap-py mo-ments roll;

John 8:12. Words, Eliza Edmunds Hewitt, 1887. Tune SUNSHINE, John R. Sweney, 1887.

Je - sus shows His smil - ing face, There is sun-shine in my soul.

Philippians 1:3,4,6; 4:4-7,10,13   **464**
Psalm 92:1,2,4

I thank my God upon all my remembrance of you, always in every supplication of mine on behalf of you all making my supplication with joy . . . being confident of this very thing, that he who began a good work in you will perfect it until the day of Jesus Christ . . . Rejoice in the Lord always; again I will say, Rejoice. Let your forbearance be known unto all men. The Lord is at hand. In nothing be anxious; but in everything by prayer and supplication with thanksgiving let your requests be made known unto God. And the peace of God, which passeth all understanding, shall guard your hearts and your thoughts in Christ Jesus. . . . I rejoice in the Lord greatly . . . I can do all things in him that strengtheneth me.

It is a good thing to give thanks unto the Lord,
And to sing praises unto thy name, O Most High;
To show forth thy lovingkindness in the morning
And thy faithfulness every night.
For thou, Lord, hast made me glad through thy work:
I will triumph in the works of thy hands.

465 There's Within My Heart a Melody

1. There's with-in my heart a mel-o-dy; Je-sus
2. All my life was wrecked by sin and strife, Dis-cord
3. Feast-ing on the rich-es of His grace, Rest-ing
4. Tho' some-times He leads thro' wa-ters deep, Tri-als
5. Soon He's com-ing back to wel-come me Far be-

whis-pers sweet and low, "Fear not, I am with thee,
filled my heart with pain, Je-sus swept a-cross the
'neath His shel-t'ring wing, Al-ways look-ing on His
fall a-cross the way, Tho' some-times the path seems
yond the star-ry sky; I shall wing my flight to

peace, be still," In all of life's ebb and flow.
bro-ken strings, Stirred the slumb'ring chords a-gain.
smil-ing face, That is why I shout and sing.
rough and steep, See His foot-prints all the way.
worlds un-known, I shall reign with Him on high.

Je-sus, Je-sus, Je-sus, Sweet-est name I know,

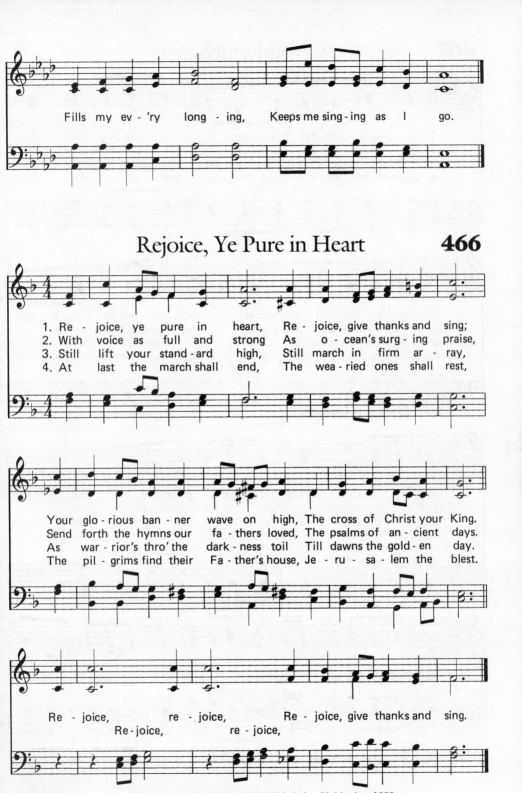

Fills my ev-'ry long-ing, Keeps me sing-ing as I go.

Rejoice, Ye Pure in Heart 466

1. Re - joice, ye pure in heart, Re - joice, give thanks and sing;
2. With voice as full and strong As o - cean's surg - ing praise,
3. Still lift your stand - ard high, Still march in firm ar - ray,
4. At last the march shall end, The wea - ried ones shall rest,

Your glo - rious ban - ner wave on high, The cross of Christ your King.
Send forth the hymns our fa - thers loved, The psalms of an - cient days.
As war - rior's thro' the dark - ness toil Till dawns the gold - en day.
The pil - grims find their Fa - ther's house, Je - ru - sa - lem the blest.

Re - joice, re - joice, Re - joice, give thanks and sing.
Re - joice, re - joice,

Galatians 5:22. Words, Edward H. Plumtre, 1865. Tune MARION, Arthur H. Messiter, 1889.

467 # A Wonderful Savior

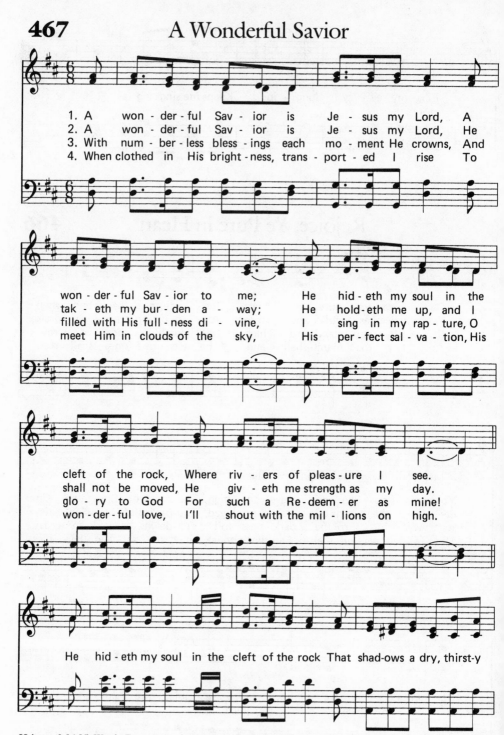

1. A won-der-ful Sav-ior is Je-sus my Lord, A
2. A won-der-ful Sav-ior is Je-sus my Lord, He
3. With num-ber-less bless-ings each mo-ment He crowns, And
4. When clothed in His bright-ness, trans-port-ed I rise To

won-der-ful Sav-ior to me; He hid-eth my soul in the
tak-eth my bur-den a - way; He hold-eth me up, and I
filled with His full-ness di - vine, I sing in my rap-ture, O
meet Him in clouds of the sky, His per-fect sal-va-tion, His

cleft of the rock, Where riv-ers of pleas-ure I see.
shall not be moved, He giv-eth me strength as my day.
glo-ry to God For such a Re-deem-er as mine!
won-der-ful love, I'll shout with the mil-lions on high.

He hid-eth my soul in the cleft of the rock That shad-ows a dry, thirst-y

Hebrews 2:14,15. Words, Fanny J. Crosby, 1890. Tune KIRKPATRICK, William J. Kirkpatrick, 1890.

land; He hid-eth my life in the depths of His love, And cov-ers me

there with His hand, And cov-ers me there with His hand.

Children of the Heavenly King 468

1. Chil-dren of the heav'n-ly King, As ye jour-ney, sweet-ly sing;
2. Shout, ye ran-somed ones and blest! You on Je-sus' throne shall rest:
3. Lift your eyes, ye sons of light! Zi-on's cit-y is in sight:
4. Fear not, breth-ren, joy-ful stand On the bor-ders of your land;
5. Lord, o-be-dient-ly we go, Glad-ly leav-ing all be-low:

Sing your Sav-ior's wor-thy praise, Glo-rious in His works and ways.
There your seat is now pre-pared, There your glo-ry and re-ward.
There our end-less home shall be, There our Lord we soon shall see.
Je-sus Christ, your Fa-ther's Son, Bids you un-dis-mayed go on.
On-ly, Lord, our Lead-er be, That we still may fol-low Thee.

Isaiah 35:10. Words, John Cennick, 1712. Tune PLEYEL'S HYMN, Ignace J. Pleyel, 1791.

469 There's a Glad New Song

1. There's a glad new song ring-ing in my heart, Such as an - gels would sing a - bove, And the whole day long it doth joy im - part; 'Tis the song of re-deem - ing love.
2. When my soul was lost in a star - less night Where my feet nev - er ceased to rove, At a dread-ful cost Je - sus brought me light, All be - cause of re-deem - ing love.
3. When at last I stand with the heav'n-ly choir In the light of the throne a - bove, On the gold - en strand I shall nev - er tire Of the song of re-deem - ing love.

Of His love I shall ev - er sing Till a - bove I be - hold the King; Thro' e-

Of His love Till a - bove

1 Peter 1:18,19. Words and tune REDEEMING LOVE, Albert C. Fisher, c. 1940. Copyright 1956. Renewal 1984 Broadman Press. All rights reserved. Used by permission.

ter - ni - ty my glad song shall be Of the Sav - ior's re-deem-ing love.

Morning Has Broken

470

1. Morn-ing has bro - ken Like the first morn - ing, Black- bird has
2. Sweet the rain's new fall Sun - lit from heav - en, Like the first
3. Mine is the sun - light! Mine is the morn - ing Born of the

spo - ken Like the first bird. Praise for the sing - ing!
dew - fall On the first grass. Praise for the sweet - ness
one light E - den saw play! Praise with e - la - tion,

Praise for the morn - ing! Praise for them, spring-ing Fresh from the Word!
Of the wet gar - den, Sprung in com-plete -ness Where His feet pass.
Praise ev - 'ry morn - ing, God's re - cre - a - tion Of the new day!

Lamentations 3:22,23. Words, Eleanor Farjeon, 1931. Copyright by permission of David Higham Associates, Ltd., London. Tune BUNESSAN, traditional Gaelic melody. Arr. J.B., Copyright 1986, ACU Press.

471 What a Wonderful Change in My Life

1. What a won-der-ful change in my life has been wrought Since
2. I have ceased from my wand-'ring and go - ing a-stray, Since
3. There's a light in the val - ley of death now for me, Since
4. I shall go there to dwell in that cit - y, I know, Since

Je - sus came in - to my heart! I have light in my soul
Je - sus came in - to my heart! And my sins, which were man-
Je - sus came in - to my heart! And the gates of the Cit-
Je - sus came in - to my heart! And I'm hap - py, so hap-

for which long I have sought, Since Je-sus came in-to my heart!
y, are all washed a - way, Since Je-sus came in-to my heart!
y be - yond I can see, Since Je-sus came in-to my heart!
py, as on - ward I go, Since Je-sus came in-to my heart!

Since Je - sus came in - to my heart, Since
Since Je - sus came in, came in - to my heart, Since

2 Corinthians 5:17. Words, Rufus H. McDaniel, 1914. Tune McDANIEL, Charles H. Gabriel, 1914. Copyright 1914. Renewal secured 1942. By permission of Word Music, Winona Lake, Indiana.

Je - sus came in-to my heart, Floods of joy o'er my soul like the
Je - sus came in, came in - to my heart,

sea bil - lows roll, Since Je - sus came in - to my heart.

Titus 3:3-7 472

For we also once were foolish, disobedient, deceived, serving divers lusts and
pleasures, living in malice and envy, hateful, hating one another. But when the
kindness of God our Savior, and his love toward man appeared, not by works done
in righteousness, which we did ourselves, but according to his mercy he saved us,
through the washing of regeneration and renewing of the Holy Spirit, which he
poured out upon us richly, through Jesus Christ our Savior; that, being justified
by his grace, we might be made heirs according to the hope of eternal life.

473 ## Sing On, Ye Joyful Pilgrims

1. Sing on, ye joy-ful pil - grims, Nor think the mo - ments long; My
2. Sing on, ye joy-ful pil - grims, While here on earth we stay; Let
3. Sing on, ye joy-ful pil - grims: The time will not be long, Till

faith is heav'n-ward ris - ing With ev - 'ry tune - ful song; Lo!
songs of home and Je - sus Be - guile each fleet - ing day; Sing
in our Fa - ther's king - dom We swell a no - bler song, Where

on the mount of bless - ing, The glo - rious mount, I stand; And
on the grand old sto - ry Of His re - deem - ing love, The
those we love are wait - ing To greet us on the shore; We'll

look - ing o - ver Jor - dan, I see the prom - ised land.
ev - er - last - ing cho - rus That fills the realms a - bove.
meet be - yond the riv - er, Where surg - es roll no more.

Hebrews 13:15. Words, Carrie M. Wilson, 1886. Tune SING ON, John R. Sweney, 1886.

474 Rejoice, the Lord is King

1. Re - joice, the Lord is King! Your Lord and King a - dore!
2. The Lord the Sav - ior reigns, The God of truth and love:
3. His king - dom can - not fail; He rules o'er earth and heaven;
4. Re - joice in glo - rious hope! Our Lord the Judge shall come,

Man - kind, give thanks and sing, And tri - umph ev - er - more.
When He had purged our stains, He took His seat a - bove.
The keys of death and hell To Christ the Lord are given.
And take His ser - vants up To their e - ter - nal home.

Lift up your heart! lift up your voice!

Re - joice! a - gain I say, re - joice! A - men.

Revelation 1:17,18. Words, Charles Wesley, 1746. Tune DARWALL'S 148, John Darwall, 1770.

Peace, Perfect Peace

475

1. Peace, per - fect peace, in this dark world of sin:
2. Peace, per - fect peace, by throng-ing du - ties pressed:
3. Peace, per - fect peace, with sor - rows surg - ing round:
4. Peace, per - fect peace, with loved ones far a - way:
5. Peace, per - fect peace, our fu - ture all un - known:
6. It is e - nough; earth's strug - gles soon shall cease,

The blood of Je - sus whis - pers peace with - in.
To do the will of Je - sus— this is rest.
On Je - sus' bos - om naught but calm is found.
In Je - sus' keep - ing we are safe, and they.
Je - sus we know, and He is on the throne.
And Je - sus call us to heav'n's per - fect peace.

Philippians 4:7. Words, Edward H. Bickersteth, 1875. Tune PAX TECUM, George T. Caldbeck, 1878.

Philippians 4:6,7

476

In nothing be anxious but in everything by prayer and supplication with thanksgiving let your requests be made known unto God. And the peace of God, which passeth all understanding, shall guard your hearts and your thoughts in Christ Jesus.

477 Only in Thee

1. On-ly in Thee, O Sav - ior mine, Dwell-eth my soul in peace di -vine,
2. On-ly in Thee a ra - diance bright, Shines like a bea - con in the night,
3. On-ly in Thee, when days are drear, When nei-ther sun nor stars ap - pear,
4. On-ly in Thee, dear Sav - ior, slain, Los- ing Thy life my own to gain,

Peace, that the world, tho' all com - bine, Nev -er can take from me.
Guid - ing my pil - grim bark a - right, O - ver life's track - less sea.
Still I can trust and feel no fear, Sing when I can - not see.
Trust-ing, I'm cleansed from ev - 'ry stain; Thou art my on - ly plea.

Pleas-ures of earth, so seem-ing-ly sweet, Fail at the last my long-ings to
On - ly in Thee, when trou-bles mo - lest, When with temp-ta-tion I am op-
On - ly in Thee, what - ev - er be - tide, All of my need is free-ly sup-
On - ly in Thee, my heart will de - light, Till in that land where cometh no

meet; On - ly in Thee my bliss is com-plete, On-ly, dear Lord, in Thee!
pressed, There is a sweet pa - vil - ion of rest, On-ly, dear Lord, in Thee!
plied, There is no hope nor help-er be - side, On-ly, dear Lord, in Thee!
night Faith will be lost in heav-en-ly sight, On-ly, dear Lord, in Thee!

John 16:33. Words, Thomas O. Chisholm, 1905. Tune MONOS, Charles H. Gabriel, 1905.

Prince of Peace! Control My Will 478

1. Prince of peace! con-trol my will, Bid this strug-gling heart be still;
2. Thou hast bought me with Thy blood, O-pened wide the gate of God;
3. May Thy will, not mine, be done; May Thy will; and mine be one;
4. Sav-ior, at Thy feet I fall; Thou my Life, my God, my All;

Bid my fears and doubt-ings cease— Hush my spir-it in-to peace.
Peace I ask, but peace must be, Lord, in be-ing one with Thee.
Chase these doubtings from my heart; Now Thy per-fect peace im-part.
Let Thy hap-py serv-ant be One for ev-er-more with Thee. A-men.

John 14:27. Words, Mary A. S. Barber, 1838. Tune HATFIELD, W. T. Porter.

Savior, Grant Me Rest and Peace 479

1. Sav-ior, grant me rest and peace, Let my trou-bled dreamings cease;
2. I would trust my all with Thee, All my cares and sor-rows flee,
3. I would seek Thy serv-ice, Lord, Lean-ing on Thy prom-ise-word;

With the chim-ing mid-night bell, Teach my heart that "all is well."
Till the break-ing light shall tell, Night is past and "all is well."
Let my hour-ly la-bors tell I am Thine, and "all is well." A-men.

John 14:1. Words, Mrs. L. M. Beal Bateman, 19th cent. Tune BATEMAN, James H. Fillmore, 1882.

480   **In the Cross of Christ I Glory**

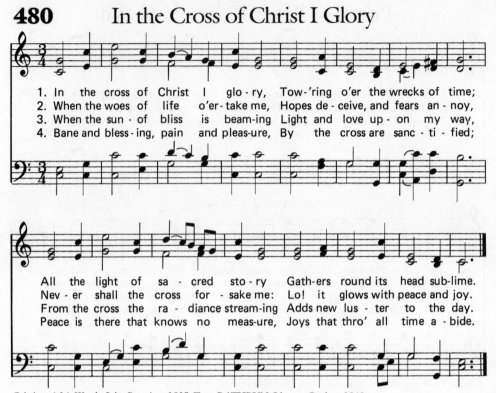

1. In   the cross of   Christ   I   glo - ry,   Tow-'ring o'er the wrecks of time;
2. When the woes of   life   o'er-take me, Hopes de - ceive, and fears an - noy,
3. When the sun · of   bliss   is   beam-ing Light and love up - on my way,
4. Bane and bless - ing, pain   and pleas-ure, By   the cross are sanc - ti - fied;

All the light of   sa - cred   sto - ry   Gath-ers round its   head sub-lime.
Nev - er shall the cross for - sake me: Lo! it   glows with peace and joy.
From the cross the   ra - diance stream-ing Adds new lus - ter to   the day.
Peace is there that knows no   meas-ure, Joys that thro' all   time a - bide.

Galatians 6:14. Words, John Bowring, 1825. Tune RATHBUN, Ithamar Conkey, 1849.

481   **Ephesians 2:14-18**

For he is our peace, who made both one, and broke down the middle wall of
partition, having abolished in his flesh the enmity, even the law of commandments
contained in ordinances; that he might create in himself of the two one new man,
so making peace; and might reconcile them both in one body unto God through
the cross, having slain the enmity thereby: and he came and preached peace to you
that were far off, and peace to them that were nigh: for through him we both have
our access in one Spirit unto the Father.

There is a Place of Quiet Rest

1. There is a place of qui-et rest, Near to the heart of God,
2. There is a place of com-fort, sweet, Near to the heart of God,
3. There is a place of full re-lease, Near to the heart of God,

A place where sin can-not mo-lest, Near to the heart of God.
A place where we our Sav-ior meet, Near to the heart of God.
A place where all is joy and peace, Near to the heart of God.

O Je-sus, blest Re-deem-er, Sent from the heart of God,

Hold us who wait be-fore Thee Near to the heart of God.

Isaiah 26:3. Words and tune McAFEE, Cleland B. McAfee, 1901.

483 Nearer, Still Nearer

1. Near - er, still near - er, close to Thy heart, Draw me, my
2. Near - er, still near - er, noth - ing I bring, Naught as an
3. Near - er, still near - er, Lord, to be Thine; Sin, with its
4. Near - er, still near - er, while life shall last, Till safe in

Sav - ior, so pre - cious Thou art; Fold me, O fold me
of - f'ring to Je - sus my King, On - ly my sin - ful,
fol - lies, I glad - ly re - sign, All of its pleas - ures,
glo - ry my an - chor is cast; Thro' end - less a - ges,

close to Thy breast, Shel - ter me safe in that ha - ven of
now con - trite heart; Grant me the cleans - ing Thy blood doth im -
pomp and its pride; Give me but Je - sus, my Lord cru - ci -
ev - er to be Near - er, my Sav - ior, still near - er to

rest, Shel - ter me safe in that ha - ven of rest.
part, Grant me the cleans - ing Thy blood doth im - part.
fied, Give me but Je - sus, my Lord cru - ci - fied.
Thee, Near - er, my Sav - ior, still near - er to Thee.

Psalm 119:151. Words and tune MORRIS, Leila N. Morris, 1898.

Not too slow

1. Pur - er in heart, O God, Help me to be; May I de - vote my life
2. Pur - er in heart, O God, Help me to be; Teach me to do Thy will
3. Pur - er in heart, O God, Help me to be; That I Thy ho - ly face

Whol - ly to Thee; Watch Thou my way - ward feet, Guide me with
Most lov - ing - ly; Be Thou my Friend and Guide, Let me with
One day may see; Keep me from se - cret sin, Reign Thou my

coun - sel sweet; Pur - er in heart, Help me to be.
Thee a - bide; Pur - er in heart, Help me to be.
soul with - in; Pur - er in heart, Help me to be. A - men.

1 John 3:3. Words, Fannie E. Davison, 1877. Tune PURER IN HEART, James H. Fillmore, 1877.

1 Peter 1:15-19

485

As he who called you is holy, be ye yourselves also holy in all manner of living; because it is written, "Ye shall be holy, for I am holy." And if ye call on him as Father, who without repect of persons judgeth according to each man's work, pass the time of your sojourning in fear: knowing that ye were redeemed, not with corruptible things; but with precious blood, as of a lamb without blemish and without spot, even the blood of Christ.

486   Jesus Rose of Sharon

1. Je - sus, Rose of Shar - on, bloom with-in my heart; Beau - ties of Thy
2. Je - sus, Rose of Shar - on, sweet - er far to see Than the fair-est
3. Je - sus, Rose of Shar - on, balm for ev - 'ry ill, May Thy ten-der
4. Je - sus, Rose of Shar - on, bloom for ev - er - more; Be Thy glo - ry

truth and ho - li - ness im - part, That wher-e'er I go my life may
flow'rs of earth could ev - er be, Fill my life com - plete - ly, adding
mer - cy's heal - ing pow'r dis - til For af - flict-ed souls of wea-ry,
seen on earth from shore to shore, Till the na - tions own Thy sov-'reign-

shed a - broad Fra - grance of the knowl-edge of the love of God.
more each day Of Thy grace di - vine and pu - ri - ty, I pray.
bur-dened men, Giv - ing need - y mor-tals health and hope a - gain.
ty com-plete, Lay their hon - ors down and wor-ship at Thy feet.

Je - sus,   Rose of Shar - on,
Bless-ed Je - sus,   Rose of Shar - on,

Titus 2:11,12. Words, Isa A. Guirey, 1922. Tune SHARON, Charles H. Gabriel, 1922. Copyright by permission of Word Music, Winona Lake, Indiana.

Bloom in ra-diance and in love with-in my heart.

Take Time to Be Holy **487**

1. Take time to be ho - ly, Speak oft with thy Lord; A - bide in Him
2. Take time to be ho - ly, The world rush-es on; Spend much time in
3. Take time to be ho - ly, Let Him be thy Guide; And run not be-
4. Take time to be ho - ly, Be calm in thy soul; Each tho't and each

al - ways, And feed on His word; Make friends of God's chil - dren;
se - cret With Je - sus a - lone; By look - ing to Je - sus,
fore Him, What - ev - er be - tide; In joy or in sor - row,
mo - tive Be - neath His con - trol; Thus led by His Spir - it

Help those who are weak; For - get - ting in noth-ing His bless-ing to seek.
Like Him thou shalt be; Thy friends in thy con-duct His like-ness shall see.
Still fol - low thy Lord; And, look - ing to Je - sus, Still trust in His word.
To foun-tains of love, Thou soon shalt be fit - ted For serv - ice a - bove.

Hebrews 12:14. Words, William D. Longstaff, 1882. Tune HOLINESS, George C. Stebbins, 1890.

488   More Holiness Give Me

1. More ho-li-ness give me, More striv-ings with-in, More pa-tience in
2. More grat-i-tude give me, More trust in the Lord, More pride in His
3. More pu-ri-ty give me, More strength to o'er-come, More free-dom from

suf-f'ring, More sor-row for sin, More faith in my Sav-ior,
glo-ry, More hope in His word, More tears for His sor-rows,
earth-stains, More long-ings for home; More fit for the king-dom,

More sense of His care, More joy in His serv-ice, More pur-pose in prayer.
More pain at His grief, More meek-ness in tri-al, More praise for re-lief.
More use-ful I'd be, More bless-ed and ho-ly, More, Sav-ior, like Thee.

Colossians 3:12. Words and tune MY PRAYER, Philip P. Bliss, 1873.

489   Purer Yet and Purer

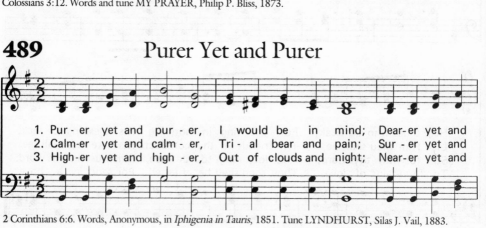

1. Pur-er yet and pur-er, I would be in mind; Dear-er yet and
2. Calm-er yet and calm-er, Tri-al bear and pain; Sur-er yet and
3. High-er yet and high-er, Out of clouds and night; Near-er yet and

2 Corinthians 6:6. Words, Anonymous, in *Iphigenia in Tauris*, 1851. Tune LYNDHURST, Silas J. Vail, 1883.

dear - er,   Ev - 'ry du - ty   find;   Hop - ing still and trust - ing
sur - er,   Peace at last to   gain;   Suf - f'ring still and do - ing,
near - er,   Ris - ing to the   light;   Oft these ear - nest long - ings

God with-out a   fear,   Pa - tient - ly be - liev - ing   He will make all clear.
To His will re - signed,   And to God sub - du - ing   Heart and will and mind.
Swell with-in my breast;   Yet their in - ner mean-ing   Ne'er can be ex - prest.

Matthew 5:3-10   **490**

Blessed are the poor in spirit: for theirs is the kingdom of heaven.
Blessed are they that mourn: for they shall be comforted.
Blessed are the meek: for they shall inherit the earth.
Blessed are they that hunger and thirst after righteousness: for they shall
    be filled.
Blessed are the merciful: for they shall obtain mercy.
Blessed are the pure in heart: for they shall see God.
Blessed are the peacemakers: for they shall be called sons of God.
Blessed are they that have been persecuted for righteousness' sake: for theirs
    is the kingdom of heaven.

491 O for a Heart to Praise My God

1. O for a heart to praise my God, A heart from
2. A heart re - signed, sub - mis - sive, meek, My great Re -
3. O for a low - ly, con - trite heart, Con - fid - ing,
4. Thy Spir - it, gra - cious Lord, im - part; Di - rect me

sin set free! A heart that al - ways feels the
deem - er's throne, Where on - ly Christ is heard to
true and clean, Which nei - ther life nor death can
from a - bove; May Thy dear name be near my

blood So free - ly shed for me.
speak, Where Je - sus reigns a - lone.
part From Him that dwells with - in.
heart; That dear, best name is Love. A - men.

Psalm 9:1. Words, Charles Wesley, 1742. Tune ARMENIA, Sylvanus B. Pond, 1836.

492 1 Peter 3:15

Sanctify in your hearts Christ as Lord: being ready always to give answer to every man that asketh you a reason concerning the hope that is in you, yet with meekness and fear.

How Firm a Foundation

1. How firm a foun-da-tion, ye saints of the Lord, Is laid for your
2. "Fear not, I am with thee, O be not dis-mayed; I, I am thy
3. "When thro' the deep wa-ters I cause thee to go, The riv-ers of
4. "When thro' fi-ery tri-als thy path-way shall lie, My grace, all-suf-
5. "E'en down to old age all my peo-ple shall prove My sov-'reign, e-
6. "The soul that on Je-sus hath leaned for re-pose, I will not, I

faith in His ex-cel-lent word! What more can He say than to
God, and will still give thee aid; I'll strength-en thee, help thee, and
sor-row shall not o-ver-flow; For I will be with thee thy
fi-cient, shall be thy sup-ply; The flame shall not hurt thee: I
ter-nal, un-change-a-ble love; And when hoar-y hairs shall their
will not de-sert to his foes; That soul, tho' all hell should en-

you He has said, You who un-to Je-sus for ref-uge have fled?
cause thee to stand, Up-held by My gra-cious, om-nip-o-tent hand.
trou-bles to bless, And sanc-ti-fy to thee thy deep-est dis-tress.
on-ly de-sign Thy dross to con-sume, and thy gold to re-fine.
tem-ples a-dorn, Like lambs they shall still in my bos-om be borne.
deav-or to shake, I'll nev-er, no, nev-er, no, nev-er for-sake."

2 Timothy 2:19. Words, John Rippon's *Selection of Hymns*, 1787. Tune FOUNDATION, William Caldwell's *Union Harmony*, 1837.

494 ## Faith of Our Fathers

1. Faith of our fa - thers! liv - ing still In spite of dun - geon,
2. Our fa - thers, chained in pris - ons dark, Were still in heart and
3. Faith our our fa - thers! we will love Both friend and foe in

fire and sword; O how our hearts beat high with joy
con - science free; How sweet would be their chil - dren's fate
all our strife; And preach thee too, as love knows how,

When-e'er we hear that glo - rious word!
If they, like them, could die for thee! Faith of our fa - thers,
By kind - ly words and vir - tuous life.

ho - ly faith, We will be true to thee till death.

Hebrews 11:13. Words, Frederick W. Faber, 1849. Tune ST. CATHERINE, Henri F. Hemy, 1864.

We Saw Thee Not

495

1. We saw Thee not when Thou didst come To this poor world of sin and death;
2. We saw Thee not when lift-ed high, A- mid that wild and sav-age crew;
3. We gazed not in the o-pen tomb, Where once Thy mangled bod-y lay;
4. We walked not with the cho-sen few, Who saw Thee from the earth as-cend;

Nor yet be-held Thy cot-tage home, In that de-spis-ed Naz-a-reth;
Nor heard we that im-plor-ing cry, "For-give, they know not what they do!"
Nor saw Thee in that "up-per room," Nor met Thee on the o-pen way;
Who raised to heav'n their wond'ring view, Then low to earth all pros-trate bend;

But we be-lieve Thy foot-steps trod Its streets and plains, Thou Son of God:
But we be-lieve the deed was done, That shook the earth and veiled the sun;
But we be-lieve that an-gels said, "Why seek the liv-ing with the dead?"
But we be-lieve that hu-man eyes Be-held that jour-ney to the skies;

But we be-lieve Thy foot-steps trod Its streets and plains, Thou Son of God.
But we be-lieve the deed was done, That shook the earth and veiled the sun.
But we be-lieve that an-gels said, "Why seek the liv-ing with the dead?"
But we be-lieve that hu-man eyes Be-held that jour-ney to the skies.

1 Corinthians 15:20. Words, Anne Richter, 1834; recast by John H. Gurney, 1851. Tune SHAW, Knowles Shaw.

496

We Would See Jesus

1. We would see Je - sus, for the shad - ows length - en
2. We would see Je - sus, the great Rock foun - da - tion,
3. We would see Je - sus: oth - er lights are pal - ing,
4. We would see Je - sus: this is all we're need - ing;

A - cross the lit - tle land - scape of our life;
On which our feet were set with sov - 'reign grace;
Which for long years we have re - joiced to see;
Strength, joy, and will - ing - ness come with the sight;

We would see Je - sus, our weak faith to strength-en
Nor life, nor death, with all their ag - i - ta - tion,
The bless - ings of our pil - grim - age are fail - ing:
We would see Je - sus, dy - ing, ris - en, plead - ing:

For the last wea - ri - ness, the fi - nal strife.
Can thence re - move us, if we see His face.
We would not mourn them, for we go to Thee.
Then wel - come, day, and fare - well, mor - tal night!

John 12:20,21. Words, Anna B. Warner, 1852. Tune CONSOLATION, adpt. from Felix Mendelssohn's *Songs Without Words*, 1834.

'Tis So Sweet to Trust in Jesus

497

1. 'Tis so sweet to trust in Je - sus, Just to take Him at His word,
2. O how sweet to trust in Je - sus, Just to trust His cleans - ing blood,
3. Yes, 'tis sweet to trust in Je - sus, Just from sin and self to cease,
4. I'm so glad I learned to trust Thee, Pre - cious Je - sus, Sav - ior, Friend;

Just to rest up - on His prom - ise, Just to know, "Thus saith the Lord."
Just in sim - ple faith to plunge me 'Neath the heal - ing, cleans - ing flood.
Just from Je - sus sim - ply tak - ing Life and rest, and joy and peace.
And I know that Thou art with me, Wilt be with me to the end.

Je - sus, Je - sus, how I trust Him! How I've proved Him o'er and o'er!

Je - sus, Je - sus, pre - cious Je - sus! O for grace to trust Him more!

Ephesians 1:12. Words, Louisa M. R. Stead, 1882. Tune TRUST IN JESUS, William J. Kirkpatrick, 1882.

498 Encamped Along the Hills of Light

1. En - camped a - long the hills of light, Ye Chris - tian sol - diers, rise,
2. His ban - ner o - ver us is love, Our sword the Word of God;
3. To him that o - ver - comes the foe White rai - ment shall be giv'n;

And press the bat - tle ere the night Shall veil the glow - ing skies.
We tread the road the saints a - bove With shouts of tri - umph trod.
Be - fore the an - gels he shall know His name con - fessed in heav'n;

A - gainst the foe in vales be - low Let all our strength be hurled;
By faith they, like a whirlwind's breath, Swept on o'er ev - 'ry field;
Then on - ward from the hills of light, Our hearts with love a - flame;

Faith is the vic - to - ry, we know, That o - ver - comes the world.
The faith by which they con - quered death Is still our shin - ing shield.
We'll van - quish all the hosts of night, In Je - sus' con - qu'ring name.

1 John 5:4. Words, John H. Yates, 1891. Tune SANKEY, Ira D. Sankey, 1891.

Faith is the vic - to - ry! Faith is the vic - to - ry!
Faith is the vic - to - ry! Faith is the vic - to - ry!

O glo - ri - ous vic - to - ry That o - ver - comes the world.

Have Faith in God, My Heart 499

1. Have faith in God, my heart, Trust and be un - a - fraid;
2. Have faith in God, my mind, Though oft thy light burns low;
3. Have faith in God, my soul, His cross for - ev - er stands;
4. Lord Je - sus, make me whole; Grant me no rest - ing place,

God will ful - fill in ev - ery part Each prom - ise He has made.
God's mer - cy holds a wis - er plan Than thou canst ful - ly know.
And nei - ther life nor death can pluck His chil - dren from His hands.
Un - til I rest, heart, mind, and soul, The cap - tive of Thy grace. A - men.

1 Peter 1:7. Words, Bryn Austin Rees, 1951. Copyright by Bryn Austin Rees. Used by permission.
Tune FRANCONIA, Johann B. König's *Harmonischer Liederschatz*, 1738; arr. William H. Havergal, 1847.

500 Jesus is All the World to Me

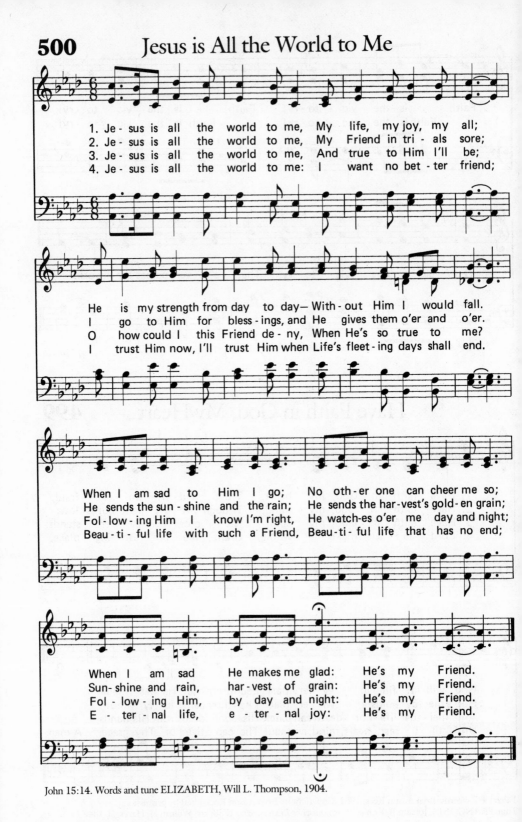

1. Je - sus is all the world to me, My life, my joy, my all;
2. Je - sus is all the world to me, My Friend in tri - als sore;
3. Je - sus is all the world to me, And true to Him I'll be;
4. Je - sus is all the world to me: I want no bet - ter friend;

He is my strength from day to day— With - out Him I would fall.
I go to Him for bless - ings, and He gives them o'er and o'er.
O how could I this Friend de - ny, When He's so true to me?
I trust Him now, I'll trust Him when Life's fleet - ing days shall end.

When I am sad to Him I go; No oth - er one can cheer me so;
He sends the sun - shine and the rain; He sends the har - vest's gold - en grain;
Fol - low - ing Him I know I'm right, He watch - es o'er me day and night;
Beau - ti - ful life with such a Friend, Beau - ti - ful life that has no end;

When I am sad He makes me glad: He's my Friend.
Sun - shine and rain, har - vest of grain: He's my Friend.
Fol - low - ing Him, by day and night: He's my Friend.
E - ter - nal life, e - ter - nal joy: He's my Friend.

John 15:14. Words and tune ELIZABETH, Will L. Thompson, 1904.

Forth in Thy Name

501

1. Forth in Thy name, O Lord, I go, My dai - ly
2. The task Thy wis - dom hath as - signed, O let me
3. Thee may I set at my right hand, Whose eyes my
4. For Thee de - light - ful - ly em - ploy What-e'er Thy

la - bor to pur - sue, Thee, on - ly Thee, re - solved to
cheer - ful - ly ful - fill: In all my works Thy pres - ence
in - most sub - stance see, And la - bor on at Thy com -
boun - teous grace hath giv'n, And run my course with e - ven

know In all I think, or speak, or do.
find, And prove Thy good and per - fect will.
mand, And of - fer all my works to Thee.
joy, And close - ly walk with Thee to heav'n. A - men.

Colossians 3:17. Words, Charles Wesley, 1749. Tune SONG XXXIV, Orlando Gibbons, 1623. Arr. J.B., Copyright 1986, ACU Press.

Colossians 3:17,23,24

502

Whatever you do, in word or in deed, do all in the name of the Lord Jesus, giving thanks to God the Father through him. Whatever you do, work heartily, as to the Lord, and not to men; knowing that from the Lord you will receive the recompense of the inheritance: you serve the Lord Christ.

503 Take Up Your Cross

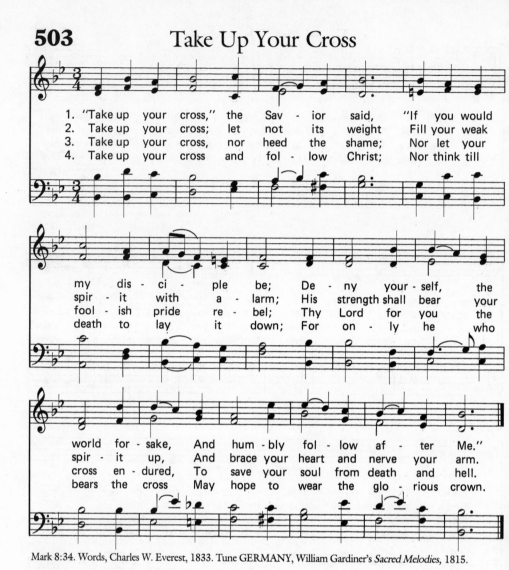

1. "Take up your cross," the Sav - ior said, "If you would
2. Take up your cross; let not its weight Fill your weak
3. Take up your cross, nor heed the shame; Nor let your
4. Take up your cross and fol - low Christ; Nor think till

my dis - ci - ple be; De - ny your - self, the
spir - it with a - larm; His strength shall bear your
fool - ish pride re - bel; Thy Lord for you the
death to lay it down; For on - ly he who

world for - sake, And hum - bly fol - low af - ter Me."
spir - it up, And brace your heart and nerve your arm.
cross en - dured, To save your soul from death and hell.
bears the cross May hope to wear the glo - rious crown.

Mark 8:34. Words, Charles W. Everest, 1833. Tune GERMANY, William Gardiner's *Sacred Melodies*, 1815.

504 I'm Not Ashamed to Own My Lord

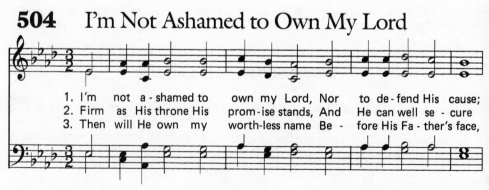

1. I'm not a - shamed to own my Lord, Nor to de - fend His cause;
2. Firm as His throne His prom - ise stands, And He can well se - cure
3. Then will He own my worth - less name Be - fore His Fa - ther's face,

2 Timothy 1:12. Words, Isaac Watts, 1707. Tune AZMON, Carl Gläser; arr. Lowell Mason, 1839.

Main - tain the hon - ors of His word, The glo - ry of His cross.
What I've com - mit - ted to His hands, Till the de - ci - sive hour.
And in the new Je - ru - sa - lem Ap - point for me a place.

O for a Faith That Will Not Shrink **505**

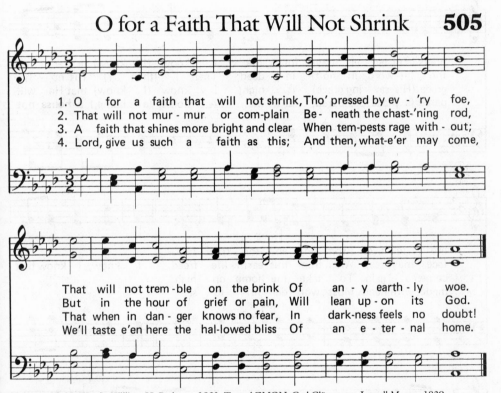

1. O for a faith that will not shrink, Tho' pressed by ev - 'ry foe,
2. That will not mur - mur or com-plain Be - neath the chast-'ning rod,
3. A faith that shines more bright and clear When tem-pests rage with - out;
4. Lord, give us such a faith as this; And then, what-e'er may come,

That will not trem - ble on the brink Of an - y earth - ly woe.
But in the hour of grief or pain, Will lean up - on its God.
That when in dan - ger knows no fear, In dark-ness feels no doubt!
We'll taste e'en here the hal-lowed bliss Of an e - ter - nal home.

Hebrews 10:38. Words, William H. Bathurst, 1831. Tune AZMON, Carl Gläser; arr. Lowell Mason, 1839.

1 John 5:4,5 **506**

For whatsoever is begotten of God overcometh the world: and this is the victory that hath overcome the world, even our faith. And who is he that overcometh the world, but he that believeth that Jesus is the Son of God.

507 I Know That My Redeemer Lives

1. I know (I know) that my Re-deem-er lives, And ev-er
2. He wills (He wills) that I should ho-ly be, In word, in
3. I know (I know) that un-to sin-ful men His sav-ing
4. I know (I know) that o-ver yon-der stands A place pre-

prays (and ev-er prays) for me; I know (I know) e-ter-nal
tho't, (in word, in tho't) in deed; Then I (then I) His ho-ly
grace (His sav-ing grace) is nigh; I know (I know) that He will
pared (a place pre-pared) for me; A home, (a home,) a house not

life He gives, From sin and sor-row free.
face may see, When from this earth-life freed. I know, I know that
come a-gain To take me home on high.
made with hands, Most won-der-ful to see.

my Re-deem-er lives, I know, I know e-ter-nal life He gives;

Job 19:25. Words arr. from Job 19:25 by Fred A. Fillmore, 1917. Copyright 1944, renewal by The Gospel Advocate Co., owner.

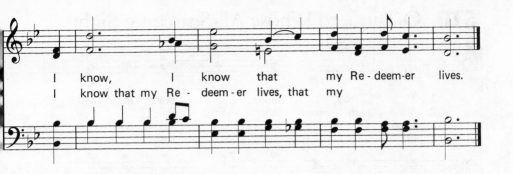

I know, I know that my Re - deem-er lives.
I know that my Re - deem - er lives, that my

My Times are in Thy Hand **508**

1. "My times are in Thy hand:" My God, I wish them there; My
2. "My times are in Thy hand," What - ev - er they may be; Pleas-
3. "My times are in Thy hand:" Why should I doubt or fear? My
4. "My times are in Thy hand," Je - sus, the Cru - ci - fied! The

life, my friends, my soul, I leave En - tire - ly to Thy care.
ing or pain - ful, dark or bright, As best may seem to Thee.
Fa - ther's hand will nev - er cause His child a need-less tear.
hand my cru - el sins had pierced Is now my guard and guide.

Psalm 31:15. Words, W. F. Lloyd, 1824. Tune ALDERSGATE, G. P. Merrick.

2 Timothy 1:12 **509**

I am not ashamed; for I know him whom I have believed, and I am persuaded that
he is able to guard that which I have committed unto him against that day.

510 O Thou, to Whose All-Searching Sight

1. O Thou, to whose all-search-ing sight The
2. If in this dark-some wild I stray, Be
3. When ris-ing floods my soul o'er-flow, When
4. Sav-ior, wher-e'er thy steps I see, Daunt-

dark-ness shin-eth as the light: Search, prove my heart, it
Thou my light, be Thou my way; No foes, no vi-o-
sinks my heart in waves of woe, Je-sus, Thy time-ly
less, un-tired, I fol-low Thee; O let Thy hand sup-

yearns for Thee; O burst these bonds and set it free!
lence I fear, No fraud, while Thou, my God, art near.
aid im-part, And raise my head, and cheer my heart.
port me still, And lead me to Thy ho-ly hill! A - men.

Psalm 139:12. Words, Nicolaus von Zinzendorf, 1721. Tune ROCKINGHAM (MASON), Lowell Mason, 1830.

511 Something Beautiful

Some-thing beau-ti-ful, Some-thing good; All my con-fu-sion

Ephesians 2:1-5. Words, Gloria Gaither, 1971. Tune SOMETHING BEAUTIFUL, William J. Gaither.

He un-der-stood; All I had to of-fer Him was bro-ken-ness and

strife, But He made some-thing beau-ti-ful of my life.

1 Timothy 1:12-17   **512**

I thank him that enabled me, even Christ Jesus our Lord, for that he counted me
faithful, appointing me to his service; though I was before a blasphemer, and a
persecutor, and injurious: howbeit I obtained mercy, because I did it ignorantly in
unbelief; and the grace of our Lord abounded exceedingly with faith and love which
is in Christ Jesus. Faithful is the saying and worthy of all acceptance, that Christ
Jesus came into the world to save sinners; of whom I am chief: howbeit for this
cause I obtained mercy, that in me as chief might Jesus Christ show forth all his
longsuffering, for an example to them that should thereafter believe on him unto
eternal life. Now unto the King eternal, immortal, invisible, the only God, be honor
and glory, for ever and ever. Amen.

513 When We Walk With the Lord

1. When we walk with the Lord In the light of His Word, What a glo-ry He
2. Not a shad-ow can rise, Not a cloud in the skies, But His smile quickly
3. Not a bur-den we bear, Not a sor-row we share, But our toil He doth
4. But we nev-er can prove The de-lights of His love Un-til all on the
5. Then in fel-low-ship sweet We will sit at His feet, Or we'll walk by His

sheds on our way! While we do His good will, He a-bides with us still,
drives it a-way; Not a doubt nor a fear, Not a sigh nor a tear,
rich-ly re-pay; Not a grief nor a loss, Not a frown nor a cross,
al-tar we lay; For the fa-vor He shows, And the joy He be-stows,
side in the way; What He says we will do, Where He sends we will go—

And with all who will trust and o-bey.
Can a-bide while we trust and o-bey.
But is blest if we trust and o-bey.   Trust and o-bey, for there's
Are for those who will trust and o-bey.
Nev-er fear, on-ly trust and o-bey.

no oth-er way To be hap-py in Je-sus, but to trust and o-bey.

John 8:31. Words, John H. Sammis, 1887. Tune TRUST AND OBEY, Daniel B. Towner, 1887.

Simply Trusting Every Day

1. Sim - ply trust - ing ev - ery day, Trust - ing through a storm - y way;
2. Bright - ly doth His Spir - it shine In - to this poor heart of mine;
3. Sing - ing if my way is clear, Pray - ing if the path be drear;
4. Trust - ing Him while life shall last, Trust - ing Him till earth be past;

E - ven when my faith is small, Trust - ing Je - sus— that is all.
While He leads I can - not fall, Trust - ing Je - sus— that is all.
If in dan - ger, for Him call, Trust - ing Je - sus— that is all.
Till with - in the jas - per wall, Trust - ing Je - sus— that is all.

Trust - ing as the mo - ments fly, Trust - ing as the days go by;

Trust - ing Him what - e'er be - fall, Trust - ing Je - sus— that is all.

Psalm 37:5. Words, Edgar P. Stites, 1876. Tune TRUSTING JESUS, Ira D. Sankey, 1876.

515 Without Him I Could Do Nothing

1. With - out Him I could do noth - ing, With - out Him
2. With - out Him I would be dy - ing, With - out Him

I'd sure - ly fail; With - out Him I would be
I'd be en - slaved; With - out Him life would be

drift - ing Like a ship with - out a sail.
hope - less But with Je - sus, thank God, I'm saved.

Je - sus, O Je - sus! Do you know Him to -

Philippians 3:8. Words and tune WITHOUT HIM, Mylon R. LeFevre, 1963. Copyright 1963 by The LeFevres. International copyright secured. All rights reserved. Used by permission.

day? You can't turn Him a - way; O Je - sus, O

Je - sus! With - out Him how lost I would be.

John 8: 12,24,31,32,36 **516**

I am the light of the world: he that followeth me shall not walk in the darkness, but shall have the light of life. Except ye believe that I am he, ye shall die in your sins. If ye abide in my word, then are ye truly my disciples; and ye shall know the truth, and the truth shall make you free. If therefore the Son shall make you free, ye shall be free indeed.

517　　　I Heard an Old, Old Story

1. I heard an old, old sto-ry, How a Sav-ior came from glo-ry,
2. I heard a-bout His heal-ing, Of His cleans-ing pow'r re-veal-ing,
3. I heard a-bout a man-sion He has built for me in glo-ry,

How He gave His life on Cal-va-ry To save a wretch like me;
How He made the lame to walk a-gain And caused the blind to see;
And I heard a-bout the streets of gold Be-yond the crys-tal sea;

I heard a-bout His groan-ing, Of His pre-cious blood's a-ton-ing,
And then I cried "Dear Je-sus, Come and heal my bro-ken spir-it,"
A-bout the an-gels sing-ing, And the old re-demp-tion sto-ry,

Then I re-pent-ed of my sins, And won the vic-to-ry.
And some-how Je-sus came and bro't To me the vic-to-ry.
And some sweet day I'll sing up there The song of vic-to-ry.

John 16:33. Words and tune HARTFORD, E. M. Bartlett, 1939. Copyright 1939 by E. M. Bartlett. Copyright 1967 by Mrs. E. M. Bartlett. Renewal. Assigned to Albert E. Brumley and Sons. Used by permission.

O vic-to-ry in Je-sus, My Sav-ior, for-ev-er, He

sought me and bought me With His re-deem-ing blood; He

loved me ere I knew Him And all my love is due Him, He

plunged me to vic-to-ry, Be-neath the cleans-ing flood.

518 Trying to Walk in the Steps

1. Try - ing to walk in the steps of the Sav - ior, Try - ing to fol - low our
2. Press - ing more close-ly to Him who is lead - ing, When we are tempt-ed to
3. Walk - ing in foot-steps of gen - tle for-bear-ance, Foot-steps of faith-ful-ness,
4. Try - ing to walk in the steps of the Sav - ior, Up-ward, still up-ward we'll

Sav - ior and King; Shap - ing our lives by His bless - ed ex - am - ple,
turn from the way; Trust-ing the arm that is strong to de - fend us,
mer - cy and love; Look-ing to Him for the grace free - ly prom - ised,
fol - low our Guide; When we shall see Him,"the King in His beau - ty,"

Hap-py, how hap-py, the songs that we bring.
Hap-py, how hap-py, our prais - es each day. How beau-ti - ful to walk in the
Hap-py, how hap-py, our jour - ney a - bove!
Hap-py, how hap-py, our place at His side!

steps of the Sav - ior, Step-ping in the light, Step-ping in the light; How

1 Peter 2:21. Words, Eliza Edmunds Hewitt. Tune ICHNOS, William J. Kirkpatrick.

beau-ti - ful to walk in the steps of the Sav-ior, Led in paths of light!

John 1:1-13   **519**

In the beginning was the Word, and the Word was with God, and the Word was God. The same was in the beginning with God. All things were made by him; and without him was not any thing made that was made.

In him was life; and the life was the light of men. And the light shineth in darkness; and the darkness comprehended it not. There was a man sent from God, whose name was John. The same came for a witness, to bear witness of the Light that all men through him might believe. He was not that Light, but was sent to bear witness of that Light. There was a true Light, which lighteth every man that cometh into the world.

He was in the world, and the world was made by him, and the world knew him not. He came unto his own, and his own received him not. But as many as received him, to them gave he power to become the sons of God, even to them that believe on his name: which were born, not of blood, nor of the will of the flesh, nor of the will of man, but of God.

And the Word became flesh, and dwelt among us (and we beheld his glory, glory as of the only begotten from the Father), full of grace and truth.

520 Hold Thou My Hand

1. Hold Thou my hand: so weak I am, and help-less, I dare not
2. Hold Thou my hand, and clos-er, clos-er draw me To Thy dear
3. Hold Thou my hand, that when I reach the mar-gin Of that lone

take one step with-out Thine aid; Hold Thou my hand, for then, O
self— my hope, my joy, my all; Hold Thou my hand, lest hap-ly
riv-er Thou didst cross for me, A heav'n-ly light may flash a-

lov-ing Sav-ior, No dread of ill shall make my soul a-fraid.
I should wan-der; And miss-ing Thee, my trem-bling feet should fall.
long its wa-ters, And ev-'ry wave like crys-tal bright shall be.

John 10:28. Words, Fanny J. Crosby, 1880. Tune MAIN, Hubert P. Main, 1881.

521 Isaiah 43:2,3

When thou passest through the waters, I will be with thee; and through the rivers, they shall not overflow thee: when thou walkest through the fire, thou shalt not be burned, neither shall the flame kindle upon thee. For I am the Lord thy God, the Holy One of Israel, thy Savior.

Come Down, Lord

522

1. Come down, Lord, my son is ill, wracked with fe-ver the live-long day. He is life to me, if you will, drive death a-way, drive death a-way. Lord, do not come to my house, I'm un-worth-y, speak and the prom-ise is sealed. For when your word, O God, is spok-en, he shall be healed, he shall be healed.

2. Come down, Lord, my soul is ill, wracked with an-guish the live-long day. All my sor-row-ing will be still, if You but say, if You but say. Lord, do not come to my house, I'm un-worth-y, speak and the prom-ise is sealed. For when your word, O God, is spok-en, I shall be healed, I shall be healed.

3. Come down, Lord, the world is ill, wracked with blood-shed the live-long day. Man must strug-gle for peace un-til You show the way, You show the way. Lord, do not come to our house, we're un-worth-y, speak and the prom-ise is sealed. For then your word, O God, is spok-en, we shall be healed, we shall be healed.

Luke 7:2-10. Words and Tune COME DOWN, LORD, Miriam Therese Winter. Copyright 1965 by Medical Mission Sisters, Philadelphia, PA. Reprinted by permission of Vanguard Music Corp., 1595 Broadway, New York, NY 10019. Further reproduction prohibited. Arr. J.B.

523 Teach Me Your Way, O Lord

1. Teach me Your way, O Lord, Teach me Your way!
2. When I am sad at heart, Teach me Your way!
3. When doubts and fears a - rise, Teach me Your way!
4. Long as my life shall last, Teach me Your way!

Your guid - ing grace af - ford— Teach me Your way!
When earth - ly joys de - part, Teach me Your way!
When storm-clouds fill the skies, Teach me Your way!
Wher - e'er my lot be cast, Teach me Your way!

Help me to walk a - right, More by faith, less by sight;
In hours of lone - li - ness, In times of dire dis - tress,
Shine through the wind and rain, Through sor - row, grief and pain;
Un - til the race is run, Un - til the jour - ney's done,

Lead me with heaven - ly light— Teach me Your way!
In fail - ure or suc - cess, Teach me Your way!
Make now my path - way plain— Teach me Your way!
Un - til the crown is won, Teach me Your way! A - men.

Psalm 25:4,5. Words and tune CAMACHA, B. Mansell Ramsey. Used by permission of George Taylor, The Cross Printing Works, Stainland, Halifax.

Take the Name of Jesus With You **524**

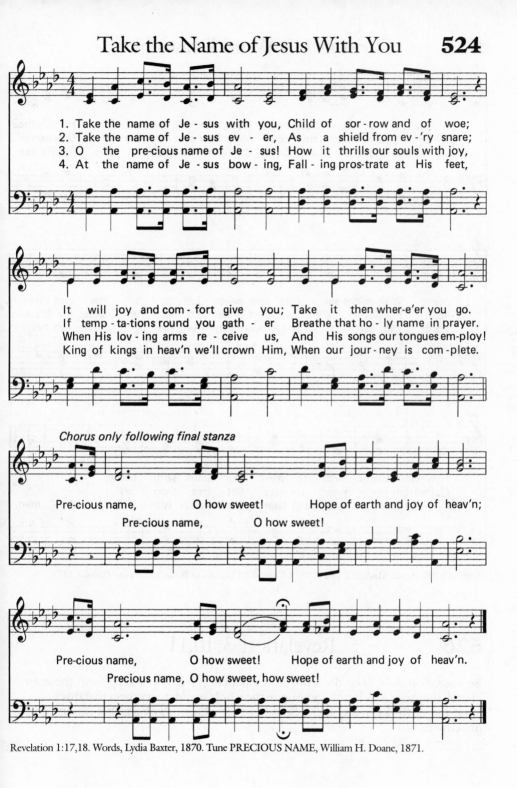

1. Take the name of Je - sus with you, Child of sor - row and of woe;
2. Take the name of Je - sus ev - er, As a shield from ev -'ry snare;
3. O the pre-cious name of Je - sus! How it thrills our souls with joy,
4. At the name of Je - sus bow - ing, Fall - ing pros-trate at His feet,

It will joy and com - fort give you; Take it then wher-e'er you go.
If temp - ta-tions round you gath - er Breathe that ho - ly name in prayer.
When His lov - ing arms re - ceive us, And His songs our tongues em-ploy!
King of kings in heav'n we'll crown Him, When our jour - ney is com - plete.

Chorus only following final stanza

Pre-cious name, O how sweet! Hope of earth and joy of heav'n;
Pre-cious name, O how sweet!

Pre-cious name, O how sweet! Hope of earth and joy of heav'n.
Precious name, O how sweet, how sweet!

Revelation 1:17,18. Words, Lydia Baxter, 1870. Tune PRECIOUS NAME, William H. Doane, 1871.

525   Christ in His Word Draws Near

1. Christ in His word draws near; Hush, moan-ing voice of fear, He bids thee
2. Ris - ing a - bove thy care, Meet Him as in the air, O wear-y
3. From the bright sky a - bove, Clad in His robes of love, 'Tis He, our

cease; With songs sin - cere and sweet Let us a - rise and meet
heart; Put on joy's sa - cred dress; Lo, as He comes to bless,
Lord! Dim earth it - self grows clear, As His light draw - eth near;

Him who comes forth to greet Our souls with peace.
Quite from thy wear - i - ness Set free thou art.
O let us hush and hear His ho - ly word. A - men.

Psalm 119:105. Words, Thomas T. Lynch, 1854. Tune SERUG, Samuel Wesley's *European Psalmist*, 1872.

526   Revelation 3:10,11

Because thou didst keep the word of my patience, I also will keep from the hour of trial, that hour which is to come upon the whole world, to try them that dwell upon the earth. I come quickly: hold fast that which thou hast, that no one take thy crown.

Take Thou My Hands and Lead Me   **527**

1. Take Thou my hands and lead me A - long life's way, Un -
2. With - in Thy grace so ten - der I would a - bide. Thy
3. I may not glimpse Thy foot - prints, Nor feel Thy pow'r, Yet

til earth's night is ban - ished By ra - diant day. I
per - fect peace my por - tion What - e'er be - tide. I
Thou dost draw me goal - ward Tho' dark the hour. Then,

would not take a sin - gle step A - part from Thee; Where
kneel, dear Lord, be - fore Thee, Be - liev - ing - ly. Thy
take my hands and lead me, Thro' storm - swept night, Till

Thou dost walk or tar - ry, There let me be.
help - less child would trust Though it can - not see.
earth's de - vious ways have end - ed In heav'ns pure de - light. A - men.

Matthew 6:13. Words, Julie Hausmann, 1862; trans. Martha D. Lange. Tune SO NIMM DENN MEINE HÄNDE, Friedrich Silcher, 1842.

528 Dying With Jesus

1. Dy-ing with Je-sus, by death reck-oned mine; Liv-ing with
2. Nev-er a tri-al that He is not there, Nev-er a
3. Nev-er a weak-ness that He doth not feel, Nev-er a

Je-sus, a new life di-vine; Look-ing to Je-sus till
bur-den that He doth not bear, Nev-er a sor-row that
sick-ness that He can-not heal; Mo-ment by mo-ment, in

glo-ry doth shine, Mo-ment by mo-ment, O Lord, I am Thine.
He doth not share, Mo-ment by mo-ment, I'm un-der His care.
woe or in weal, Je-sus, my Sav-ior, a-bides with me still.

Mo-ment by mo-ment I'm kept in His love; Mo-ment by

Colossians 3:3. Words, Daniel W. Whittle, 1893. Tune WHITTLE, May Whittle Moody, 1893.

mo - ment I've life from a - bove; Look - ing to Je - sus till

glo - ry doth shine; Mo - ment by mo - ment, O Lord, I am Thine.

Lord Jesus, Think on Me **529**

1. Lord Je - sus, think on me, And purge a - way my sin;
2. Lord Je - sus, think on me, With care and woe op - prest;
3. Lord Je - sus, think on me, A - mid the bat - tle's strife;
4. Lord Je - sus, think on me, Nor let me go a - stray;
5. Lord Je - sus, think on me, When flows the tem - pest high:
6. Lord Je - sus, think on me, That, when the flood is past,

From earth-born pas - sions set me free, And make me pure with - in.
Let me Thy lov - ing serv - ant be, And taste Thy prom - ised rest.
In all my pain and mis - er - y Be Thou my health and life.
Through darkness and per - plex - i - ty Point Thou the heaven - ly way.
When on doth rush the en - e - my O Sav - ior, be Thou nigh.
I may th' e - ter - nal bright - ness see, And share Thy joy at last. A - men.

Jonah 2:7. Words, Synesius of Cyrene, d. 430; trans. Allen William Chatfield, 1876. Tune SOUTHWELL, William
Damon, *The Psalms of David in English Meter*, 1579.

530 Anywhere With Jesus

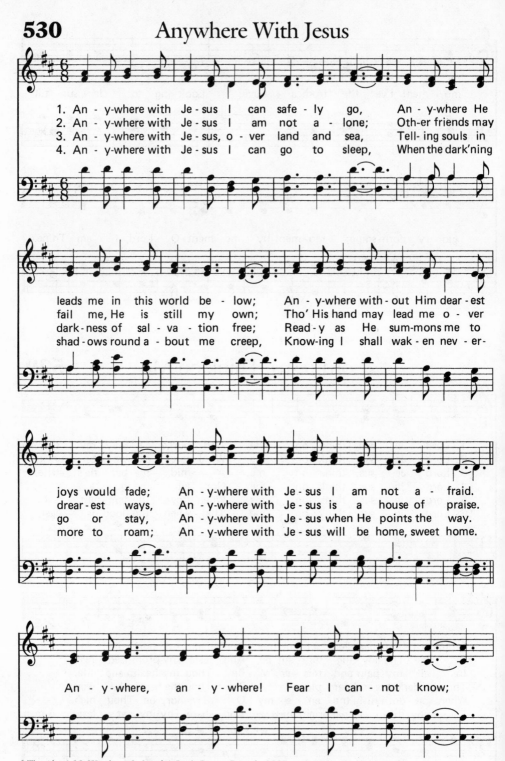

1. An - y-where with Je - sus I can safe - ly go,
   An - y-where He leads me in this world be - low;
   An - y-where with-out Him dear - est joys would fade;
   An - y-where with Je - sus I am not a - fraid.

2. An - y-where with Je - sus I am not a - lone;
   Oth-er friends may fail me, He is still my own;
   Tho' His hand may lead me o - ver drear - est ways,
   An - y-where with Je - sus is a house of praise.

3. An - y-where with Je - sus, o - ver land and sea,
   Tell- ing souls in dark - ness of sal - va - tion free;
   Read - y as He sum-mons me to go or stay,
   An - y-where with Je - sus when He points the way.

4. An - y-where with Je - sus I can go to sleep,
   When the dark'ning shad - ows round a - bout me creep,
   Know-ing I shall wak - en nev - er-more to roam;
   An - y-where with Je - sus will be home, sweet home.

An - y-where, an - y - where! Fear I can - not know;

2 Timothy 4:18. Words, st. 1, 2 and 4, Jessie Brown Pounds, 1887; st. 3, Helen C. Alexander Dixon, c. 1915. Tune SECURITY, Daniel B. Towner, 1887.

An - y - where with Je - sus I can safe - ly go.

My Soul, Be On Thy Guard **531**

1. My soul, be on thy guard; Ten thou-sand foes a - rise; The
2. O watch and fight and pray; The bat - tle ne'er give o'er; Re -
3. Ne'er think the vic - tory won, Nor lay thine ar - mor down; The
4. Fight on, my soul, till death Shall bring thee to thy God; He'll

hosts of sin are press - ing hard To draw thee from the skies.
new it bold - ly ev - ery day, And help di - vine im - plore.
work of faith will not be done Till thou ob - tain the crown.
take thee, at thy part - ing breath, To His di - vine a - bode.

1 Corinthians 16:13. Words, George Heath, 1781. Tune LABAN, Lowell Mason, 1830.

Revelation 3:12 **532**

He that overcometh, I will make him a pillar in the temple of my God, and he shall go out thence no more: and I will write upon him the name of my God, and the name of the city of my God, the new Jerusalem, which cometh down out of heaven from my God, and mine own new name.

533 My Jesus, As Thou Wilt

1. My Jesus, as Thou wilt! O may Thy will be mine;
2. My Jesus, as Thou wilt! If need-y here and poor,
3. My Jesus, as Thou wilt! Tho' seen through man-y a tear,
4. My Jesus, as Thou wilt! All shall be well with me;

In - to Thy hand of love I would my all re - sign;
Give me Thy peo - ple's bread, Their por - tion rich and sure;
Let not my star of hope Grow dim or dis - ap - pear;
Each chang-ing fu - ture scene I glad - ly trust with Thee;

Thro' sor - row and thro' joy, Con - duct me as Thine own,
The man - na of Thy word, Let my soul feed up - on,
Since Thou on earth hast wept And sor - rowed oft a - lone,
Straight to my home a - bove I trav - el calm - ly on,

And help me still to say, "My Lord, Thy will be done."
And, if all else should fail, "My Lord, Thy will be done."
If I must weep with Thee, "My Lord, Thy will be done."
And sing, in life or death, "My Lord, Thy will be done."

Psalm 143:10. Words, Benjamin Schmolke, 1704; trans. Jane Borthwick, 1854. Tune JEWETT, Carl Maria von Weber, 1820; arr. Joseph P. Holbrook, 1862.

Jesus, Savior, Pilot Me

534

1. Je - sus, Sav - ior, pi - lot me O - ver life's tem -pes-tuous sea;
2. As a moth - er stills her child, Thou canst hush the o - cean wild;
3. When at last I near the shore, And the fear - ful break-ers roar

Un - known waves be -fore me roll, Hid - ing rock and treach'rous shoal;
Bois-t'rous waves o - bey Thy will When Thou say'st to them, "Be still;"
'Twixt me and the peace-ful rest, Then, while lean - ing on Thy breast,

Chart and com - pass came from Thee: Je - sus, Sav - ior, pi - lot me.
Won-drous Sov - 'reign of the sea, Je - sus, Sav - ior, pi - lot me.
May I hear Thee say to me, "Fear not, I will pi - lot thee."

Mark 4:39. Words, Edward Hopper, 1871. Tune PILOT, John E. Gould, 1871.

Revelation 2:10,11   **535**

Fear not the things which thou art about to suffer. Be thou faithful unto death,
and I will give thee the crown of life. He that hath an ear, let him hear what the
Spirit saith to the churches. He that overcometh shall not be hurt of the second death.

536 Jesus, I My Cross Have Taken

1. Je - sus, I my cross have tak - en, All to leave and fol - low Thee;
2. Let the world de - spise and leave me, It has left my Sav - ior too;
3. Know, my soul, Thy full sal - va - tion, Rise o'er sin, and fear, and care;
4. Go, then, earth - ly fame and treas - ure! Come, dis - as - ter, scorn, and pain!

I am poor, de - spised, for - sak - en, Thou from hence my all shalt be.
Hu - man hearts and looks de-ceive me, Thou art not, like man, un-true;
Joy to find, in ev - 'ry sta - tion, Some-thing still to do or bear;
In Thy serv - ice, pain is pleas - ure; With Thy fa - vor, loss is gain;

Per - ish ev - 'ry fond am - bi - tion, All I've sought and hoped and known;
And, while Thou shalt smile up - on me, God of wis - dom, love, and might,
Think what Spir - it dwells with-in thee, Think what Fa-ther's smiles are thine,
I have called Thee "Ab - ba, Fa-ther;" I have stayed my heart on Thee;

Yet how rich is my con - di - tion, God and heav'n are still my own.
Foes may hate, and friends may shun me; Show Thy face, and all is bright.
Think that Je - sus died to win thee: Child of heav'n, canst thou re - pine?
Storms may howl, and clouds may gath-er, All must work for good to me.

Mark 10:28. Words, Henry F. Lyte, 1824. Tune ELLESDIE, attr. to Wolfgang A. Mozart; from Joshua Leavitt's *The Christian Lyre*, 1831.

I Know Not Why

537

1. I know not why God's won-drous grace To me He hath made known,
2. I know not how the Spir-it moves, Con-vinc-ing men of sin,
3. I know not what of good or ill May be re-served for me,
4. I know not when my Lord may come, At night, or noon-day fair,

Nor why un-wor-thy, Christ in love Re-deemed me for His own.
Re-veal-ing Je-sus through the word, Cre-at-ing faith in Him.
Of wea-ry ways or gold-en days, Be-fore His face I see.
Nor if I'll walk the vale with Him, Or "meet Him in the air."

But "I know whom I have be-liev-ed, And am per-suad-ed that He is

a-ble To keep that which I've com-mit-ted Un-to Him a-gainst that day."

2 Timothy 1:12. Words, Daniel W. Whittle, 1883. Tune EL NATHAN, James McGranahan, 1883.

538 In the Hour of Trial

1. In the hour of trial, Jesus, plead for me,
Lest by base denial I depart from Thee;
When Thou seest me waver, With a look recall,
Nor for fear nor favor Suffer me to fall.

2. With forbidden pleasures Would this vain world charm,
Or its sordid treasures Spread to work me harm;
Bring to my remembrance Sad Gethsemane,
Or, in darker semblance, Cross-crowned Calvary.

3. Should Thy mercy send me Sorrow, toil and woe,
Or should pain attend me On my path below,
Grant that I may never Fail Thy hand to see;
Grant that I may ever Cast my care on Thee.

Luke 22:32. Words, James Montgomery, 1834. Tune PENITENCE, Spencer Lane, 1875.

While On the Sea

539

1. While on the sea hear the ter-ri-ble roar-ing;
2. Save me, O mer-ci-ful Fa-ther, for-give me;
3. I have no strength left to aid on my jour-ney;

See how the boat of my life rolls with me;
How as my life with its end-ing I see.
Help me to reach that fair land past the sea;

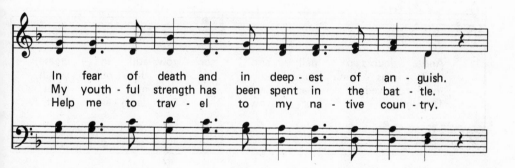

In fear of death and in deep-est of an-guish.
My youth-ful strength has been spent in the bat-tle.
Help me to trav-el to my na-tive coun-try.

Lord, hear my prayer, watch my soul on the sea.
Lord, now I beg You, have mer-cy on me.
Lord, now I beg You, have mer-cy on me.

Psalm 107:29. Words, Anonymous Ukrainian Poem; trans. Stephen Bilak; versed by Jack Boyd, 1974.
Tune UKRAINE, Ukrainian Folk Melody. Translation Copyright 1974, ACU Press.

540 Lead Us, O Father

1. Lead us, O Fa - ther, in the paths of peace;
2. Lead us, O Fa - ther, in the paths of truth;
3. Lead us, O Fa - ther, in the paths of right;
4. Lead us, O Fa - ther, to Thy heaven - ly rest,

With - out Thy guid - ing hand we go a - stray,
Un - helped by Thee, in er - ror's maze we grope,
Blind - ly we stum - ble when we walk a - lone,
How - ev - er rough and steep the path may be,

And doubts ap - pall, and sor - rows still in - crease;
While pas - sion stains and fol - ly dims our youth,
In - volved in shad - ows of a mor - tal night;
Through joy or sor - row, as Thou deem - est best,

Lead us through Christ, the true and liv - ing Way.
And age comes on un - cheered by faith and hope.
On - ly with Thee we jour - ney safe - ly on.
Un - til our lives are per - fect - ed in Thee. A - men.

Psalm 43:3. Words, William H. Burleigh, 1859. Tune LANGRAN, James Langran, 1861.

One Step at a Time

541

1. One step at a time, dear Sav - ior: I can - not take an - y - more;
2. One step at a time, dear Sav - ior: I am not walk-ing by sight;
3. One step at a time, dear Sav - ior: O guard my fal - ter-ing feet!
4. One step at a time, dear Sav - ior: Thou know-est all of my fear;

The flesh is so weak and hope - less: I know not what is be - fore.
Keep step with my soul, dear Sav - ior: I walk by faith in Thy might.
Keep hold of my hand, dear Sav - ior, Till I my jour - ney com-plete.
One word from Thy heart, dear Sav - ior, And heav-en's man-sions ap - pear.

One step at a time, dear Sav - ior, Till faith grows stronger in Thee; One
in Thee;

step at a time, dear Sav - ior, Till hope grows strong-er in me.

1 Peter 2:21. Words, T. J. Shelton. Tune ROSECRANS, James H. Rosecrans.

542 Remember Me, O Mighty One

1. When storms a-round are sweep-ing, When lone my watch I'm keep-ing,
2. When walk-ing on life's o - cean, Con - trol its rag - ing mo - tion;
3. When weight of sin op - press - es, When dark de - spair dis - tress - es;

'Mid fires of e - vil fall-ing, 'Mid tempt-ers' voic - es call - ing,
When from its dan - gers shrink-ing, When in its dread deeps sink - ing,
All through the life that's mor - tal, And when I pass death's por - tal,

Re-mem-ber me, O might-y One! Re-mem-ber me, O might-y One!

Psalm 25:6. Words, anonymous. Tune REMEMBER ME, arr. from Johanna Kinkel, c. 1858.

543 Awake, My Soul, Stretch Every Nerve

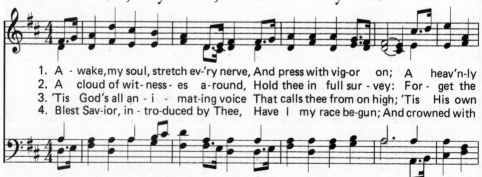

1. A - wake, my soul, stretch ev-'ry nerve, And press with vig-or on; A heav'n-ly
2. A cloud of wit-ness-es a-round, Hold thee in full sur - vey: For - get the
3. 'Tis God's all an - i - mat-ing voice That calls thee from on high; 'Tis His own
4. Blest Sav-ior, in - tro-duced by Thee, Have I my race be-gun; And crowned with

Hebrews 12:1,2. Words, Philip Doddridge, 1755. Tune CHRISTMAS, George Frederick Handel, 1728;
adpt. David Weyman's *Melodia Sacra*, 1815.

race de-mands Thy zeal, And an im-mor-tal crown, And an im-mor-tal crown.
steps al - read - y trod, And on-ward urge thy way, And on-ward urge thy way.
hand pre-sents the prize To thine as - pir - ing eye, To thine as - pir - ing eye.
vic - t'ry, at Thy feet I'll lay my hon-ors down, I'll lay my hon-ors down.

When Day's Shadows Lengthen 544

1. When day's shad-ows length - en, Je - sus, be Thou near;
2. Then the night grows dark - est, And the stars are pale,
3. So no fears shall chill me On that un - known shore,
4. Bless - ed war - fare o - ver, End-less rest a - lone;

Par - don, com - fort, strength - en, Chase a - way my fear;
When the foe - men gath - er, In death's mist - y vale,
For in death He con - quered, And can die no more;
Tears no more, nor sor - row, Nei - ther sigh nor moan,

Love and hope be deep - ened, Faith, more strong and clear.
Be Thou Sword and Buck - ler, Be Thou Shield and Mail.
His hand guards and guides me, To the heav'n - ly door.
But a song of tri - umph Round a - bout the throne.

Revelation 7:15-17. Words, Frederick G. Lee, 1867. Tune MONTANI, Traditional Melody;
arr. Nicola A. Montani, 1920.

545   When Upon Life's Billows

1. When up-on life's bil-lows you are tem - pest - tossed, When you are dis-
2. Are you ev - er bur-dened with a load of care? Does the cross seem
3. When you look at oth - ers with their lands and gold, Think that Christ has
4. So, a - mid the con-flict, wheth-er great or small, Do not be dis-

cour - aged, think-ing all is lost, Count your many blessings, name them
heav - y you are called to bear? Count your many blessings, ev - 'ry
prom-ised you His wealth un - told; Count your many blessings, mon-ey
cour - aged, God is o - ver all; Count your many blessings, an - gels

one by one, And it will sur - prise you what the Lord hath done.
doubt will fly, And you will be sing - ing as the days go by.
can - not buy Your re-ward in heav - en, nor your home on high.
will at - tend, Help and com-fort give you to your jour - ney's end.

Count your bless-ings, name them one by one; Count your
Count your man-y bless-ings, name them one by one; Count your man-y

Ephesians 1:3. Words, Johnson Oatman, Jr., 1897. Tune BLESSINGS, Edwin O. Excell, 1897.

bless-ings, see what God hath done; Count your bless-ings,
bless-ings, see what God hath done; Count your man-y bless-ings,

name them one by one; Count your man-y bless-ings, see what God hath done.

Am I a Soldier of the Cross **546**

1. Am I a sol - dier of the cross, A fol-lower of the Lamb,
2. Must I be car - ried to the skies On flower-y beds of ease,
3. Are there no foes for me to face? Must I not stem the flood?
4. Sure I must fight, if I would reign: In - crease my cour - age, Lord;
5. Thy saints in all this glo - rious war Shall con-quer, though they die;
6. When that il - lus - trious day shall rise, And all Thy ar - mies shine

And shall I fear to own His cause, Or blush to speak His name?
While oth - ers fought to win the prize, And sailed through blood-y seas?
Is this vile world a friend to grace, To help me on to God?
I'll bear the toil, en - dure the pain, Sup - port - ed by Thy word.
They see the tri - umph from a - far, By faith they bring it nigh.
In robes of vic - tory through the skies, The glo - ry shall be Thine.

1 Corinthians 16:13. Words, Isaac Watts, 1724. Tune ARLINGTON, Thomas A. Arne, 1762.

547

Be Still, My Soul

1. Be still, my soul: the Lord is on thy side; Bear patient-
2. Be still, my soul: thy God doth undertake To guide the
3. Be still, my soul: the hour is hastening on When we shall

ly the cross of grief or pain: Leave to thy God to
future as He has the past. Thy hope, thy confi-
be forever with the Lord, When disappointment,

order and provide; In ev'ry change He faithful will re-
dence let nothing shake; All now mysterious shall be bright at
grief, and fear are gone, Sorrow forgot, love's purest joys re-

main. Be still, my soul: thy best, thy heavenly Friend
last. Be still, my soul: the waves and winds still know
stored. Be still, my soul: when change and tears are past,

Psalm 46:10. Words, Katharina von Schlegel, 1752; trans. Jane Borthwick, 1855. Tune FINLANDIA, Jean Sibelius, 1899. Copyright melody by permission of Breitkopf & Härtel, Weisbaden. All rights reserved. Arr. of music copyright 1933 by Presbyterian Board of Christian Education; renewed, 1961. Used by permission of the Westminster Press.

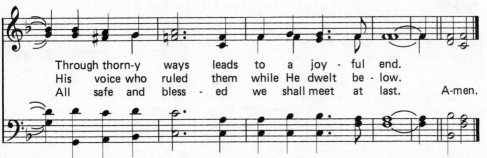

Through thorn-y ways leads to a joy - ful end.
His voice who ruled them while He dwelt be - low.
All safe and bless - ed we shall meet at last. A-men.

Give to the Winds Thy Fears **548**

1. Give to the winds your fears; Hope and be un - dis - mayed;
2. Through waves and clouds and storms, He gent - ly clears your way;
3. Leave to His sov - ereign sway To choose and to com - mand;
4. Let us in life, in death, Your stead - fast truth de - clare,

God bears your sighs and counts your tears, God shall lift up your head.
Wait for His time; so shall this night Soon end in joy - ous day.
So, won-d'ring, you shall own His way, How wise, how strong His hand!
And pub - lish with our lat - est breath Your love and guard-ian care. A-men.

Psalm 37:5. Words, Paul Gerhardt, 1653; trans. John Wesley, 1739. Tune ST. BRIDE, Samuel Howard, 1762.

549 Out of the Depths I Cry to You

1. Out of the depths I cry to you; O Fa-ther, hear me call-ing. In-cline your ear to my dis-tress In spite of my re-bel-ling. Do not re-gard my sin-ful deeds. Send me the grace my spir-it needs; With-out it I am noth-ing.

2. All things you send are full of grace; You crown our lives with fa-vor. All our good works are done in vain With-out our Lord and Sav-ior. We praise the God who gives us faith And saves us from the grip of death; Our lives are in His keep-ing.

3. It is in God that we shall hope, And not in our own mer-it. We rest our fears in His good Word And trust His Ho-ly Spir-it. His prom-ise keeps us strong and sure; We trust the ho-ly sig-na-ture In-scribed up-on our tem-ples.

4. My soul is wait-ing for the Lord As one who longs for morn-ing; No watch-er waits with great-er hope Than I for His re-turn-ing. I hope as Is-rael in the Lord; He sends re-demp-tion through His Word. We praise Him for His mer-cy.

Psalm 130:1. Words, Martin Luther, 1523; trans. Gracia Grindal, 1978. Copyright 1978 *Lutheran Book of Worship*. By permission of Augsburg Publishing House. Tune AUS TIEFER NOT, Martin Luther, 1524. Arr. J.B., Copyright 1986, ACU Press.

Jesus Lives and So Shall I

550

1. Je - sus lives, and so shall I; Death, thy sting is gone for - ev - er. He who deigned for me to die Lives the bands of death to sev - er. He shall raise me with the just: Je - sus is my hope and trust.

2. Je - sus lives, and God ex - tends Grace to each re - turn - ing sin - ner. Reb - els He re - ceives as friends, And ex - alts to high - est hon - or. God is true as He is just: Je - sus is my hope and trust.

3. Je - sus lives, and by His grace Vic - tory o'er my pas - sions giv - ing, I will cleanse my heart and ways, Ev - er to His glo - ry liv - ing. Rais - ing all the weak from dust: Je - sus is my hope and trust.

4. Je - sus lives, and death be - comes But my en - try in - to glo - ry. Cour - age, then, my soul, for thou Hast a crown of life be - fore thee; Thou shalt find thy hopes were just: Je - sus is my hope and trust. A - men.

Hebrews 2:14. Words, Christian F. Gellert, 1757; trans. J. D. Long, 1826. Tune JESUS, MEINE ZUVERSICHT, Johann Crüger's *Praxis Pietatis Melica*, 1653.

551   Shall We Gather at the River

1. Shall we gath - er at the riv - er, Where bright an - gel feet have trod,
2. On the mar - gin of the riv - er, Wash - ing up its sil - ver spray,
3. Ere we reach the shin - ing riv - er, Lay we ev - 'ry bur - den down;
4. Soon we'll reach the sil - ver riv - er, Soon our pil - grim-age will cease;
5. At the smil - ing of the riv - er, Mir - ror of the Sav - ior's face,

With its crys - tal tide for - ev - er Flow-ing by the throne of God?
We will walk and wor-ship ev - er, All the hap - py, gold - en day.
Grace our spir - its will de - liv - er, And pro - vide a robe and crown.
Soon our hap - py hearts will quiv - er With the mel - o - dy of peace.
Saints whom death will nev-er sev - er Lift their songs of sav - ing grace.

Yes, we'll gath-er at the riv - er, The beau-ti-ful, the beau-ti-ful riv - er,

Gath-er with the saints at the riv - er, That flows by the throne of God.

Revelation 22:1. Words and tune HANSON PLACE, Robert Lowry, 1864.

I Know That My Redeemer Lives

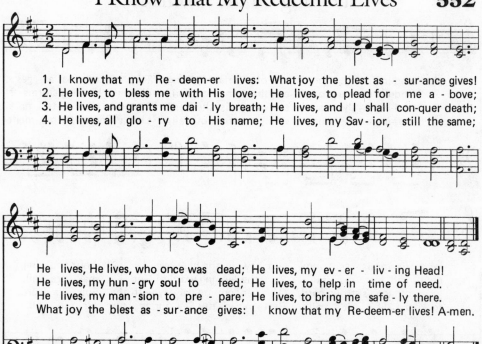

1. I know that my Re-deem-er lives: What joy the blest as - sur-ance gives!
2. He lives, to bless me with His love; He lives, to plead for me a - bove;
3. He lives, and grants me dai - ly breath; He lives, and I shall con-quer death;
4. He lives, all glo - ry to His name; He lives, my Sav - ior, still the same;

He lives, He lives, who once was dead; He lives, my ev - er - liv - ing Head!
He lives, my hun - gry soul to feed; He lives, to help in time of need.
He lives, my man - sion to pre - pare; He lives, to bring me safe - ly there.
What joy the blest as - sur-ance gives: I know that my Re-deem-er lives! A-men.

Job 19:25. Words, Samuel Medley, 1775. Tune TRURO, Thomas Williams' *Psalmodia Evangelica*, 1789.

1 Peter 1:3-5   553

Blessed be the God and Father of our Lord Jesus Christ, who according to his great mercy begat us again unto a living hope by the resurrection of Jesus Christ from the dead, unto an inheritance incorruptible, and undefiled, and that fadeth not away, reserved in heaven for you, who by the power of God are guarded through faith unto a salvation ready to be revealed in the last time.

554 Standing on the Promises

1. Stand-ing on the prom-is-es of Christ my King, Thro' e-ter-nal a-ges
2. Stand-ing on the prom-is-es that can-not fail, When the howling storms of
3. Stand-ing on the prom-is-es of Christ the Lord, Bound to Him e-ter-nal-
4. Stand-ing on the prom-is-es I can-not fall, Lis-t'ning ev-'ry mo-ment

let His prais-es ring; Glo-ry in the high-est, I will shout and sing,
doubt and fear as-sail, By the liv-ing word of God I shall pre-vail,
ly by love's strong cord, O-ver-com-ing dai-ly with the Spir-it's sword,
to the Spir-it's call, Rest-ing in my Sav-ior as my all in all,

Stand-ing on the prom-is-es of God. Stand - ing, stand - ing,
Standing on the promises, standing on the promises,

Stand-ing on the prom-is-es of God my Sav-ior; Stand - ing,
Stand-ing on the prom-is-es,

2 Corinthians 1:20. Words and tune PROMISES, R. Kelso Carter, 1886.

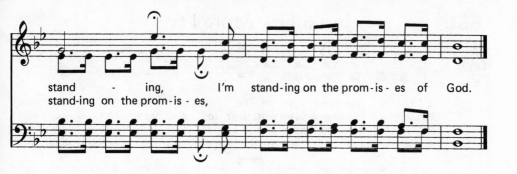

stand - ing, I'm stand-ing on the prom-is - es of God.
stand-ing on the prom-is - es,

Here We Are but Straying Pilgrims   **555**

1. Here we are but stray-ing pil - grims; Here our path is oft - en dim;
2. Here our feet are of - ten wea - ry On the hills that throng our way;
3. Here our souls are of - ten fear - ful Of the pil -grim's lurk-ing foe;

But to cheer us on our jour - ney, Still we sing this way-side hymn:
Here the tem - pest dark - ly gath - ers, But our hearts with - in us say:
But the Lord is our de - fend - er, And He tells us we may know:

Yon-der o - ver the roll-ing riv - er, Where the shining mansions rise, Soon will be our

home for ev - er, And the smile of the bless-ed Giv - er Gladdens all our long-ing eyes.

Revelation 22:3-5. Words, I. N. Carman, c. 1865. Tune PERKINS, W. O. Perkins, c. 1865.

556 Just a Few More Days

1. Just a few more days to be filled with praise, And to tell the old, old sto-ry; Then, when twi-light falls, and my Sav-ior calls, I shall go to Him in glo-ry.

2. Just a few more years with their toil and tears, And the jour-ney will be end-ed; Then I'll be with Him, where the tide of time With e-ter-ni-ty is blend-ed. I'll ex-change my cross for a

3. Tho' the hills be steep and the val-leys deep, With no flow'rs my way a-dorn-ing; Tho' the night be lone and my rest a stone, Joy a-waits me in the morn-ing.

4. What a joy 'twill be when I wake to see Him for whom my heart is burn-ing! Nev-er-more to sigh, nev-er-more to die— For that day my heart is yearn-ing.

star-ry crown, Where the gates swing out-ward nev-er; At His feet I'll

John 14:3. Words and tune WHERE THE GATES SWING OUTWARD NEVER, Charles H. Gabriel, 1920.
Copyright 1920. Renewal 1948. By permission of Word Music, Winona Lake, Indiana.

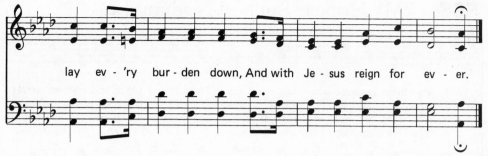

lay ev - 'ry bur - den down, And with Je - sus reign for ev - er.

I Know That My Redeemer Lives   557

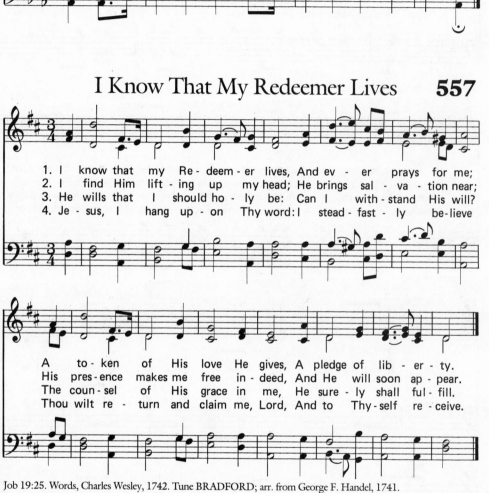

1. I know that my Re - deem - er lives, And ev - er prays for me;
2. I find Him lift - ing up my head; He brings sal - va - tion near;
3. He wills that I should ho - ly be: Can I with - stand His will?
4. Je - sus, I hang up - on Thy word: I stead - fast - ly be - lieve

A to - ken of His love He gives, A pledge of lib - er - ty.
His pres - ence makes me free in - deed, And He will soon ap - pear.
The coun - sel of His grace in me, He sure - ly shall ful - fill.
Thou wilt re - turn and claim me, Lord, And to Thy - self re - ceive.

Job 19:25. Words, Charles Wesley, 1742. Tune BRADFORD; arr. from George F. Handel, 1741.

558 My Hope is Built on Nothing Less

1. My hope is built on noth-ing less Than Je-sus' blood and right-eous-ness;
2. When darkness veils His love-ly face, I rest in His un-chang-ing grace;
3. His oath, His cov-e-nant, His blood, Sup-port me in the whelm-ing flood;
4. When He shall come with trum-pet sound, O may I then in Him be found,

I dare not trust the sweet-est frame, But whol-ly lean on Je-sus' name.
In ev-'ry high and storm-y gale, My an-chor holds with-in the veil.
When all a-round my soul gives way, He then is all my hope and stay.
Dressed in His right-eous-ness a-lone, Fault-less to stand be-fore the throne.

On Christ, the Sol-id Rock, I stand; All oth-er ground is

sink-ing sand, All oth-er ground is sink-ing sand.

1 Corinthians 3:11. Words, Edward Mote, 1834. Tune SOLID ROCK, William B. Bradbury, 1863.

Sweet Hour of Prayer

Psalm 65:2. Words, William W. Walford, 1845. Tune SWEET HOUR, William B. Bradbury, 1861.

560 'Tis the Blessed Hour of Prayer

1. 'Tis the bless-ed hour of prayer, when our hearts low-ly bend,
2. 'Tis the bless-ed hour of prayer, when the Sav-ior draws near,
3. 'Tis the bless-ed hour of prayer, when the tempt-ed and tried
4. At the bless-ed hour of prayer, trust-ing Him, we be-lieve

And we gath-er to Je-sus, our Sav-ior and Friend;
With a ten-der com-pas-sion His chil-dren to hear;
To the Sav-ior who loves them their sor-row con-fide;
That the bless-ing we're need-ing we'll sure-ly re-ceive;

If we come to Him in faith, His pro-tec-tion to share,
When He tells us we may cast at His feet ev-'ry care,
With a sym-pa-thiz-ing heart He re-moves ev-'ry care;
In the full-ness of this trust we shall lose ev-'ry care;

What a balm for the wea-ry! O how sweet to be there! Bless-ed hour of prayer,

John 16:23. Words, Fanny J. Crosby, 1880. Tune BLESSED HOUR, William H. Doane, 1880.

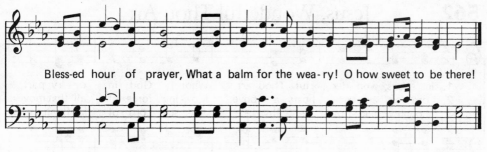

Bless-ed hour of prayer, What a balm for the wea-ry! O how sweet to be there!

From Every Stormy Wind That Blows 561

1. From ev - ery storm - y wind that blows, From ev - ery
2. There is a place where Je - sus sheds The oil of
3. There is a scene where spir - its blend, Where friend holds
4. Ah! there on ea - gle wings we soar, Where sin and

swell - ing tide of woes, There is a calm, a sure re - treat:
glad - ness on our heads; A place than all be - side more sweet:
fel - low - ship with friend; Though sun - dered far, by faith they meet
sense mo - lest no more; And heaven comes down our souls to greet,

'Tis found be - neath the mer - cy seat.
It is the blood - bought mer - cy seat.
A - round one com - mon mer - cy seat.
And glo - ry crowns the mer - cy seat. A - men.

Psalm 123:1,2. Words, Hugh Stowell, 1828. Tune RETREAT, Thomas Hastings, 1842.

562   Jesus, Wonderful Thou Art

1. Je - sus, won - der - ful Thou art, Whol - ly God in ev - 'ry part,
2. Lord of an - gel hosts a - bove, Mov - ing force of all that moves,
3. Though we can - not see Thy face, Je - sus, Lord of far-flung space,

Yet Thou know-est ev - 'ry heart, Dwell in us to - day.
First - born, King, Thy name is love, Dwell in us to - day.
While Thou rul - est ev - 'ry place, Dwell in us to - day. A - men.

Colossians 1:13-17. Words, Forrest M. McCann, 1973. Tune DAVIS, Bill W. Davis, 1973. Words and tune
Copyright 1974 by ACU Press.

563   Father of Mercy

1. Fa - ther of Mer - cy, We bow be - fore Thee;
2. We seek Thee, Fa - ther; Re - veal Thy glo - ry.
3. Lay hands up - on us, O ris - en Je - sus.
4. Com - fort - ing Spir - it, Come and in - dwell us.

Bless us, O bless us, And hear our prayer.
Strength-en, O strength-en, The vi - sion that we share.
Touch us, O touch us; Our con-fi-dence in - crease.
Breathe now, O breathe now, The prom-ise of Thy peace. A - men.

2 Corinthians 1:3. Words, st. 1 Anonymous; st. 2,3,4 George William Walton, 1985. Tune SEMELE; arr. from
George Frederick Handel.

Father, Hear the Prayer We Offer 564

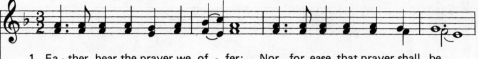

1. Fa - ther, hear the prayer we of - fer: Nor for ease that prayer shall be,
2. Not for ev - er by still wa - ters   Would we i - dly, qui - et   stay;
3. Be our strength in hours of weak - ness,   In   our wan-d'rings be our   guide;
4. Let our path be bright or drear - y,   Storm or sun-shine be   our   share;

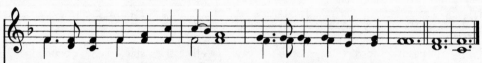

But for strength, that we may ev - er   Live our lives cour-age-ous - ly.
But would smite the liv - ing foun-tains   From the rocks a - long our   way.
Thro' en-deav - or, fail - ure, dan-ger,   Fa - ther, be Thou at our   side.
May our souls in hope un - wea - ry   Make Thy work our ceaseless prayer. A - men.

Psalm 18:31,32. Words, Love M. Willis, 1856. Tune ST. SYLVESTER, John B. Dykes, 1862.

Matthew 6:9-13 565

Our Father which art in heaven
Hallowed be thy name.
Thy kingdom come;
Thy will be done,
On earth as it is in heaven.
Give us this day our daily bread.
And forgive us our debts,
As we forgive our debtors.
And lead us not into temptation,
But deliver us from evil:
For thine is the kingdom and the power and the glory, for ever. Amen.

566

God of Our Fathers

1. God of our fa - thers, whose al - might - y hand
2. Thy love di - vine hath led us in the past;
3. From war's a - larms, from dead - ly pest - i - lence,
4. Re - fresh Thy peo - ple on their toil - some way;

Leads forth in beau - ty all the star - ry band
In this free land by Thee our lot is cast;
Be Thy strong arm our ev - er sure de - fense;
Lead us from night to nev - er - end - ing day;

Of shin - ing worlds in splen - dor thro' the skies,
Be Thou our rul - er, guard - ian, guide and stay,
Thy true re - lig - ion in our hearts in - crease,
Fill all our lives with love and grace di - vine,

Our grate - ful songs be - fore Thy throne a - rise.
Thy word our law, Thy path our cho - sen way.
Thy boun - teous good - ness nour - ish us in peace.
And glo - ry, laud and praise be ev - er Thine. A - men.

Psalm 46:7. Words, Daniel C. Roberts, 1876. Tune NATIONAL HYMN, George W. Warren, 1892.

What a Friend We Have in Jesus 567

1. What a Friend we have in Je - sus, All our sins and griefs to bear!
2. Have we tri - als and temp - ta - tions? Is there trou-ble an - y - where?
3. Are we weak and heav-y - la - den, Cum-bered with a load of care?

What a priv - i - lege to car - ry Ev - 'ry-thing to God in prayer!
We should nev-er be dis - cour - aged: Take it to the Lord in prayer;
Pre - cious Sav-ior, still our ref - uge— Take it to the Lord in prayer;

O what peace we oft - en for - feit, O what need-less pain we bear,
Can we find a friend so faith - ful, Who will all our sor-rows share?
Do thy friends de-spise, for - sake thee? Take it to the Lord in prayer;

All be-cause we do not car - ry Ev - 'ry-thing to God in prayer.
Je - sus knows our ev - 'ry weak - ness: Take it to the Lord in prayer.
In His arms He'll take and shield thee; Thou wilt find a sol - ace there.

John 15:15. Words, Joseph Scriven, 1855. Tune CONVERSE, Charles C. Converse, 1868.

568   Father Almighty, Bless Us

1. Fa - ther al - might - y,   bless us with Thy bless-ing; An - swer in
2. Shep-herd of souls, who bring-est all   who seek Thee To pas-tures
3. Fa - ther of mer - cy, from Thy watch and keep - ing   No place can

love Thy chil - dren's sup-pli - ca - tion; Hear now our prayer, the
green be - side the peace-ful wa - ters, Ten - der - est guide, in
part, nor hour of time re - move us; Give us Your good, and

spo - ken and un - spo - ken; Hear us, our Fa - ther.
ways of cheer - ful du - ty Lead us, good Shep - herd.
save us from our e - vil, In - fi - nite Spir - it. A-men.

Psalm 141:1,2. Words, *Berwick Hymnal,* 1886. Tune FLEMMING, Friedrich F. Flemming.

569   Dear Lord and Father of Mankind

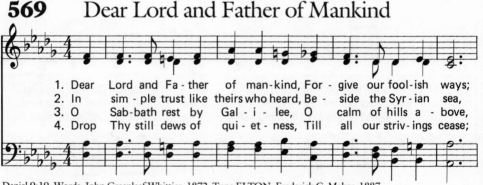

1. Dear Lord and Fa - ther of man - kind, For - give our fool-ish ways;
2. In sim - ple trust like theirs who heard, Be - side the Syr - ian sea,
3. O Sab-bath rest by Gal - i - lee, O calm of hills a - bove,
4. Drop Thy still dews of qui - et - ness, Till all our striv-ings cease;

Daniel 9:19. Words, John Greenleaf Whittier, 1872. Tune ELTON, Frederick C. Maker, 1887.

Re - clothe us in our right - ful mind, In pur - er lives
The gra - cious call - ing of the Lord, Let us, like them,
Where Je - sus knelt to share with Thee The si - lence of
Take from our souls the strain and stress, And let our or -

Thy serv - ice find, In deep - er rev - 'rence, praise.
with - out a word, Rise up and fol - low Thee.
e - ter - ni - ty, In - ter - pret - ed by love!
dered lives con - fess The beau - ty of Thy peace. A - men.

Psalm 25:1-6   570

Unto thee, O Lord, do I lift up my soul.
O my God, I trust in thee:
    let me not be ashamed;
    let not mine enemies triumph over me.
Yea, let none that wait on thee be ashamed:
Let them be ashamed which transgress without cause.
Shew me thy way, O Lord;
Teach me thy paths.
Lead me in thy truth, and teach:
    for thou art the God of my salvation;
    on thee do wait all the day.
Remember, O Lord, thy tendermercies,
    and thy lovingkindnesses;
    for they have been ever of old.

571   Dear Master, in Whose Life I See

1. Dear Mas - ter, in whose life I see All that I
2. Though what I dream and what I do In my weak

would, but fail to be, Let Thy clear light for -
days are al - ways two, Help me, op - pressed by

ev - er shine, To shame and guide this life of mine.
things un - done, O Thou, whose deeds and dreams were one! A - men.

1 Peter 2:21. Words, John Hunter, 1889. Tune HURSLEY, adpt. from *Katholisches Gesangbuch*, 1774.

572   Jesus, Meek and Gentle

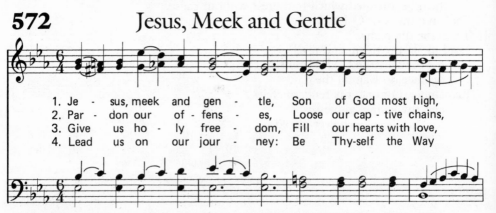

1. Je - sus, meek and gen - tle, Son of God most high,
2. Par - don our of - fens - es, Loose our cap - tive chains,
3. Give us ho - ly free - dom, Fill our hearts with love,
4. Lead us on our jour - ney: Be Thy-self the Way

Ephesians 3:14-19. Words, George R. Prynne, 1856. Tune DOWSTON CASTLE, Clarence Hudson, 19th cent.

Pity - ing, lov - ing Sav - ior, Hear Thy chil - dren's cry.
Break down ev - 'ry i - dol Which our soul de - tains.
Draw us, ho - ly Je - sus, To the realms a - bove.
Thro' ter - res - trial dark - ness To ce - les - tial day.

Closer to Thee 573

1. Clos - er to Thee, near to Thy side, Clos - er, dear Lord,
2. Clos - er to Thee, near to Thy breast, Clos - er, to Thee;
3. Clos - er to Thee, hap - py and free, Grant me, O Lord,

I would a - bide; Hold me in Thy em - brace, 'Neath ev - 'ry
Lord, let me rest; Guide me when I would stray, Keep me from
ev - er to be; Hear me in ev - 'ry cry, Stand near when

smile of grace, Grant me, Thy child, a place Clos - er to Thee.
sin each day, Draw me, dear Lord, I pray, Clos - er to Thee.
I must die, Then take me home on high, Clos - er to Thee.

Hebrews 4:14-16. Words and tune TAYLOR, Austin Taylor, 1911.

574

I Need Thee Every Hour

1. I need Thee ev-'ry hour, Most gra - cious Lord; No ten-der voice like Thine
2. I need Thee ev-'ry hour: Stay Thou near by; Temptations lose their pow'r
3. I need Thee ev-'ry hour, In joy or pain; Come quick-ly and a-bide,
4. I need Thee ev-'ry hour, Most Ho - ly One; O make me Thine in-deed,

Can peace af - ford.
When Thou art nigh. I need Thee, O I need Thee; Ev-'ry hour I
Or life is vain.
Thou bless - ed Son!

need Thee! O bless me now, my Sav-ior: I come to Thee! A-men.

Philippians 4:19. Words, Annie S. Hawks, 1872. Tune NEED, Robert Lowry, 1872.

575

My Lord, My Truth, My Way

1. My Lord, my Truth, my Way, My sure, un - err - ing Light,
2. My Wis - dom and my Guide, My Coun - sel - or Thou art;
3. Teach me the hap - py art In all things to de - pend

John 14:6. Words, Charles Wesley. Tune KINGSLEY, George Kingsley.

On Thee my fee - ble steps I stay, Which Thou wilt guide a - right.
O nev - er let me leave Thy side, Or from Thy paths de - part!
On Thee: O nev - er, Lord, de - part, But love me to the end!

O for a Closer Walk With God 576

1. O for a clos - er walk with God, A calm and heav'n - ly frame,
2. Where is the bless - ed - ness I knew When first I saw the Lord?
3. The dear - est i - dol I have known, What-e'er that i - dol be,
4. So shall my walk be close with God, Calm and se - rene my frame;

A light to shine up - on the road That leads me to the Lamb!
Where is the soul - re - fresh - ing view Of Je - sus and His word?
Help me to tear it from Thy throne, And wor - ship on - ly Thee.
So pur - er light shall mark the road That leads me to the Lamb.

Genesis 5:24. Words, William Cowper, 1772. Tune BEATITUDE, John B. Dykes, 1875.

Ephesians 5:8-10 577

You were once darkness, but are now light in the Lord: walk as children of light (for the fruit of the light is in all goodness and righteousness and truth), proving what is well-pleasing to the Lord; and have no fellowship with the unfruitful works of darkness, but rather even reprove them.

578 Be Thou My Vision

1. Be Thou my vi - sion, O Lord of my heart;
2. Be Thou my wis - dom, and Thou my true Word;
3. Rich - es I heed not, nor man's emp - ty praise;
4. High King of heav - en, my vic - to - ry won,

Naught be all else to me, save that Thou art;
I ev - er with Thee and Thou with me, Lord;
Thou mine in - her - i - tance, now and al - ways;
May I reach heav'n's joys, O bright heav - en's Sun!

Thou my best thought, by day and by night,
Thou my great Fa - ther, and I Thy true son,
Thou and Thou on - ly, first in my heart,
Heart of my own heart, what - ev - er be - fall,

Wak - ing or sleep - ing, Thy pres - ence my light.
Thou in me dwell - ing, and I with Thee one.
High King of heav - en, my trea - sure Thou art.
Still by my vi - sion, O Rul - er of all. A - men.

1 Corinthians 1:30. Words, Anonymous Irish Poem, c. 8th cent.; trans. Mary E. Byrne, 1905; versed by Eleanor H. Hull, 1912. Tune SLANE, Traditional Irish Melody. Arr. J.B., Copyright 1974, ACU Press.

Be With Me Lord

1. Be with me, Lord, I can - not live with-out Thee, I dare not
2. Be with me, Lord, and then if dan-gers threat - en, If storms of
3. Be with me, Lord! No oth - er gift or bless - ing Thou couldst be-
4. Be with me, Lord, when lone - li - ness o'er-takes me, When I must

try to take one step a - lone, I can - not bear the loads of
tri - al burst a - bove my head, If lash - ing seas leap ev - 'ry-
stow could with this one com-pare— A con-stant sense of Thy a -
weep a - mid the fires of pain, And when shall come the hour of

life, un - aid - ed, I need Thy strength to lean my - self up - on.
where a - bout me, They can - not harm, or make my heart a - fraid.
bid - ing pres - ence, Wher- e'er I am, to feel that Thou art near.
"my de - part - ure" For "worlds un-known," O Lord, be with me then.

Matthew 28:20. Words, Thomas O. Chisholm. Tune SANDERSON, Lloyd O. Sanderson, 1935.

Hebrews 13:5,6

God himself hath said:
I will in no wise fail thee,
Neither will in any wise forsake thee.
So that with good courage we say:
The Lord is my helper;
I will not fear:
What shall man do unto me?

581 God of Grace and God of Glory

1. God of grace and God of glo - ry, On Thy peo - ple pour Thy power; Crown Thine an - cient Church - 's sto - ry; Bring her bud to glo - rious flower. Grant us wis - dom, Grant us cour - age, For the fac - ing of this
2. Lo! the hosts of e - vil round us Scorn Thy Christ, as - sail His ways! Fears and doubts too long have bound us; Free our hearts to work and praise. Grant us wis - dom, Grant us cour - age, For the liv - ing of these
3. Cure Thy chil - dren's war - ring mad - ness, Bend our pride to Thy con - trol; Shame our wan - ton, self - ish glad - ness, Rich in things and poor in soul. Grant us wis - dom, Grant us cour - age, Lest we miss Thy king - dom's
4. Set our feet on loft - y plac - es; Gird our lives that they may be Ar - mored with all Christ - like grac - es In the fight to set men free. Grant us wis - dom, Grant us cour - age, That we fail not man nor
5. Save us from weak res - ig - na - tion To the e - vils we de - plore; Let the search for Thy sal - va - tion Be our glo - ry ev - er - more. Grant us wis - dom, Grant us cour - age, Serv - ing Thee whom we a -

1 Peter 5:10. Words, Harry Emerson Fosdick, 1830. Copyright used by permission of Elinor Fosdick Downs.
Tune CWM RHONDDA, John Hughes, 1907. Copyright used by permission of Mrs. Dilys S. Webb,
Glamorganshire, England.

hour,   For the fac - ing   of this hour.
days,   For the liv - ing   of these days.
goal,   Lest we miss Thy   king - dom's goal.
Thee,   That we fail not   man nor Thee!
dore,   Serv - ing Thee whom we a - dore. A - men.

Father, Hear Thy Children's Call   **582**

1. Fa - ther, hear Thy chil - dren's call; Hum - bly at Thy feet we fall,
2. Christ, be- neath Thy cross we blame All our life of sin and shame;
3. Sick, we come to Thee for cure; Guilt - y, seek Thy mer - cy sure;
4. Blind, we pray that we may see; Bound, we pray to be made free;
5. By Thy love that bids Thee spare, By the heav'n Thou dost pre-pare,

Prod - i - gals, con - fess - ing all: We be-seech Thee, hear us.
Pen - i - tent, we breathe Thy name: We be-seech Thee, hear us.
E - vil, long to be made pure: We be-seech Thee, hear us.
Stained, we pray for sanc - ti - ty: We be-seech Thee, hear us.
By Thy prom - is - es to prayer: We be-seech Thee, hear us. A - men.

Psalm 102:1. Words, Thomas B. Pollock, 1870. Tune GOWER'S LITANY, John H. Gower, 1890.

583 Lead, Kindly Light

1. Lead, kind-ly Light, a-mid th'en-cir-cling gloom, Lead Thou me
2. I was not ev - er thus, nor prayed that Thou Shouldst lead me
3. So long Thy pow'r has blest me, sure it still Will lead me

on; The night is dark, and I am far from home; Lead Thou me
on; I loved to choose and see my path; but now Lead Thou me
on O'er moor and fen, o'er crag and tor-rent, till The night is

on. Keep Thou my feet; I do not ask to see
on. I loved the gar - ish day, and spite of fears,
gone. And with the morn those an - gel fac - es smile,

The dis - tant scene—one step e - nough for me.
Pride ruled my will: Re - mem-ber not past years.
Which I have loved long since, and lost a - while. A-men.

Psalm 43:3. Words, John Henry Newman, 1833. Tune LUX BENIGNA, John B. Dykes, 1865.

My Faith Looks Up to Thee

584

1. My faith looks up to Thee, Thou Lamb of Cal - va - ry,
2. May Thy rich grace im - part Strength to my faint - ing heart,
3. While life's dark maze I tread, And griefs a - round me spread,
4. When ends life's tran - sient dream, When death's cold, sul - len stream

Sav - ior di - vine! Now hear me while I pray, Take all my
My zeal in - spire; As Thou hast died for me, O may my
Be Thou my guide; Bid dark - ness turn to day, Wipe sor - row's
Shall o'er me roll; Blest Sav - ior, then, in love, Fear and dis -

guilt a - way, O let me from this day Be whol - ly Thine!
love to Thee Pure, warm, and change - less be, A liv - ing fire!
tears a - way, Nor let me ev - er stray From Thee a - side.
trust re - move; O bear me safe a - bove, A ran - somed soul! A - men.

Hebrews 12:2. Words, Ray Palmer, 1830. Tune OLIVET, Lowell Mason, 1832.

Romans 5:1,2

585

Being therefore justified by faith, we have peace with God through our Lord Jesus Christ; through whom also we have had our access by faith into this grace wherein we stand; and we rejoice in hope of the glory of God.

586 God the Almighty One

1. God the al - might - y One! wise - ly or - dain - ing
2. God the all mer - ci - ful! earth hath for - sak - en
3. God the all right - eous One! man hath de - fied Thee;

Judg - ments un - search - a - ble, fam - ine and sword;
Thy ways of bless - ed - ness, slight - ed Thy Word;
Yet to e - ter - ni - ty stand - eth Thy Word;

O - ver the tu - mult of war Thou art reign - ing:
Bid not Thy wrath in its ter - rors a - wak - en:
False - hood and wrong shall not tar - ry be - side Thee:

Give to us peace in our time, O Lord! A - men.

Isaiah 32:18. Words, st. 1 and 2, Henry F. Chorley, 1842; st. 3, John Ellerton, 1870. Tune RUSSIAN HYMN, Alexis F. Lvov, 1833.

Guide Me, O Thou Great Jehovah **587**

1. Guide me, O Thou great Je-ho-vah, Pil-grim through this
2. O-pen now the crys-tal foun-tain, Whence the heal-ing
3. When I tread the verge of Jor-dan, Bid my anx-ious

bar-ren land; I am weak, but Thou art might-y; Hold me with Thy
stream doth flow; Let the fire and cloud-y pil-lar Lead me all my
fears sub-side; Bear me through the swell-ing cur-rent, Land me safe on

power-ful hand; Bread of heav-en, Bread of heav-en, Feed me
jour-ney through; Strong de-liv-er-er, strong de-liv-er-er, Be Thou
Ca-naan's side; Songs of prais-es, songs of prais-es I will

till I want no more, Feed me till I want no more.
still my strength and shield, Be Thou still my strength and shield.
ev-er give to Thee, I will ev-er give to Thee. A-men.

Psalm 48:14. Words, William Williams, 1745; trans., st. 1, Peter Williams, 1771; st. 2 and 3, William Williams, 1772. Tune CWM RHONDDA, John Hughes, 1907. Music Copyright used by permission of Mrs. Dilys S. Webb, Glamorganshire, England.

588 I Come to the Garden Alone

1. I come to the gar-den a - lone, While the dew is
2. He speaks, and the sound of His voice Is so sweet the
3. I'd stay in the gar-den with Him Though the night a-

still on the ros - es; And the voice I hear fall - ing on my ear,
birds hush their sing - ing; And the mel - o - dy that He gave to me
round me be fall - ing; But He bids me go; through the voice of woe,

The Son of God dis - clos - es.
With - in my heart is ring - ing. And He walks with me, and He
His voice to me is call - ing.

talks with me, And He tells me I am His own, And the joy we

John 20:18. Words and tune GARDEN, C. Austin Miles, 1912. Copyright by permission of Word Music, Winona Lake, Indiana.

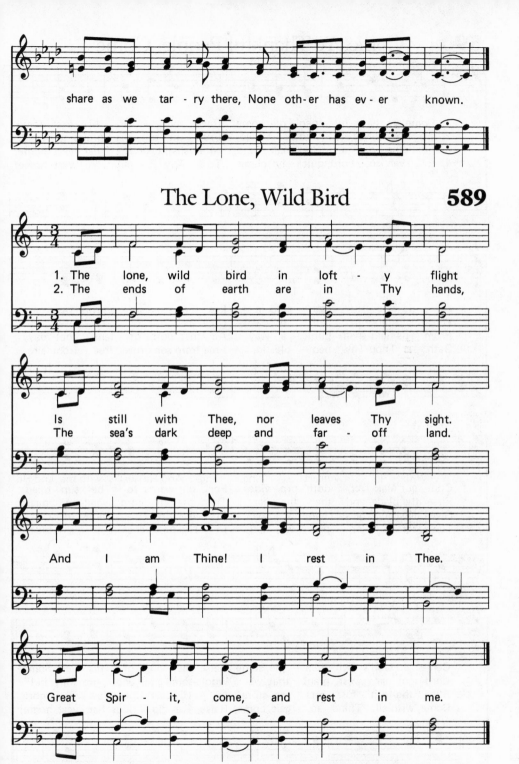

share as we tar - ry there, None oth- er has ev - er known.

The Lone, Wild Bird   **589**

1. The lone, wild bird in loft - y flight
2. The ends of earth are in Thy hands,

Is still with Thee, nor leaves Thy sight.
The sea's dark deep and far - off land.

And I am Thine! I rest in Thee.

Great Spir - it, come, and rest in me.

Psalm 104:16,17. Words, Henry Richard McFadyen, 1925; alt. 1968. Copyright 1927 by *The Homiletic Review*, used by permission. Tune PROSPECT, Southern Folk Hymn in William Walker's *Southern Harmony*, 1854. Arr. J.B., Copyright 1986, ACU Press.

590 Come, Ye Thankful People, Come

1. Come, ye thank-ful peo - ple, come, Raise the song of har - vest - home!
2. We our-selves are God's own field, Fruit un - to His praise to yield,
3. For the Lord our God shall come, And shall take His har - vest home;
4. E - ven so, Lord, quick - ly come To Thy fi - nal har - vest - home!

All is safe - ly gath - ered in Ere the win - ter storms be - gin:
Wheat and tares to - geth - er sown, Un - to joy or sor - row grown:
From His field shall purge a - way All that doth of - fend that day;
Gath - er Thou Thy peo - ple in, Free from sor - row, free from sin;

God, our Mak - er, doth pro - vide For our wants to be sup - plied:
First the blade, and then the ear, Then the full corn shall ap - pear:
Give His an - gels charge at last In the fire the tares to cast,
There, for ev - er pu - ri - fied, In Thy pres - ence to a - bide:

Come to God's own tem - ple, come, Raise the song of har - vest home!
Lord of har - vest, grant that we Whole-some grain and pure may be!
But the fruit - ful ears to store In His gar - ner ev - er - more.
Come, with all Thine an - gels, come, Raise the glo - rious har - vest home!

Matthew 13:39. Words, Henry Alford, 1844. Tune ST. GEORGE'S WINDSOR, George J. Elvey, 1858.

Father, Whate'er of Earthly Bliss 591

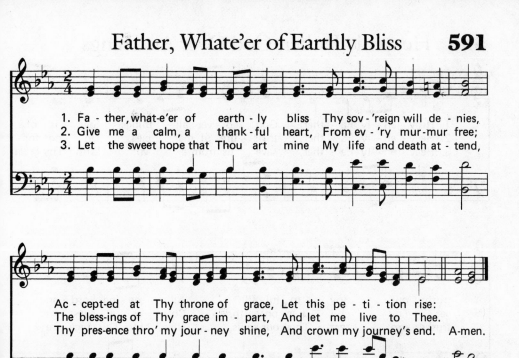

1. Fa - ther, what-e'er of earth - ly bliss Thy sov - 'reign will de - nies,
2. Give me a calm, a thank - ful heart, From ev - 'ry mur-mur free;
3. Let the sweet hope that Thou art mine My life and death at - tend,

Ac - cept-ed at Thy throne of grace, Let this pe - ti - tion rise:
The bless-ings of Thy grace im - part, And let me live to Thee.
Thy pres-ence thro' my jour - ney shine, And crown my journey's end. A-men.

Psalm 119:67. Words, Anne Steele, 1760. Tune NAOMI, Hans G. Nägeli, 1836; arr. Lowell Mason, 1836.

2 Corinthians 4:16-18   592

We faint not; but though our outward man is decaying, yet our inward man is renewed day by day. For our light affliction, which is for the moment, worketh for us more and more exceedingly an eternal weight of glory; while we look not at the things which are seen, but at the things which are not seen: for the things which are seen are temporal; but the things which are not seen are eternal.

593 Heavenly Father, God Over All Things

1. Heav-en-ly Fa-ther, God o-ver all things, Spir-it of truth, our joy to ful-fill. All-see-ing Lord and eve-ry-where pre-sent, Stay Thou a-mong us, show us Thy will.
2. Heav-en-ly Fa-ther, treas-ure of mer-cies, Do not for-get Thy chil-dren on earth. Come as a guest and live in our poor hearts, Bless us and cleanse us, show us our worth.
3. Heav-en-ly Fa-ther, save us from e-vil; With Thy great truths pro-tect Thou our souls. Now, by Thy grace, re-store our true pleas-ure; Save us, our Fa-ther, save and con-sole.

Romans 9:5. Words, Ukranian Folk Hymn, trans. Stephen Bilak, versed by J.B., 1973. Tune BILAK, Ukranian Folk Tune. Arr. J.B., Copyright 1986, ACU Press.

594   Jeremiah 10:6,7,10

There is none like unto thee, O Lord; thou art great, and thy name is great in might. Who should not fear thee, O king of the nations? For to thee doth it appertain; forasmuch as among all the wise men of the nations, and in all their royal estate, there is none like unto thee. The Lord is the true God, and an everlasting King.

Come, Thou Fount of Every Blessing   **595**

1. Come, Thou Fount of ev - ery bless-ing, Tune my heart to sing Thy grace;
2. Here I raise my Eb - e - ne - zer; Hith - er by Thy help I'm come;
3. O to grace how great a debt - or Dai - ly I'm con-strained to be!

Streams of mer - cy, nev - er ceas - ing, Call for songs of loud - est praise.
And I hope, by Thy good pleas - ure, Safe - ly to ar - rive at home.
Let Thy good-ness, like a fet - ter, Bind my wan-dering heart to Thee:

Teach me ev - er to a - dore Thee; May I still Thy good-ness prove;
Je - sus sought me when a stran - ger, Wan-dering from the fold of God;
Nev - er let me wan - der from Thee, Nev - er leave the God I love;

While the hope of end-less glo - ry Fills my heart with joy and love.
He, to res - cue me from dan-ger, In - ter-posed His pre-cious blood.
Here's my heart, O take and seal it, Seal it for Thy courts a - bove. A-men.

Ephesians 1:3. Words, Robert Robinson, 1758. Tune NETTLETON, Traditional American Melody, John Wyeth's *Repository of Sacred Music*, 1813. *Note: "Ebenezer" (st. 2), see 1 Samuel 7:12.*

596 How I Praise Thee, Precious Savior

1. How I praise Thee, pre - cious Sav-ior, That Thy love laid hold of me;
2. Emp-tied that Thou should-est fill me, A clean ves - sel in Thy hand;
3. Wit - ness - ing Thy pow'r to save me, Set - ting free from self and sin;
4. Je - sus, fill now with Thy Spir-it Hearts that full sur - ren-der know;

Thou hast saved and cleansed and filled me That I might Thy chan-nel be.
With no pow'r but as Thou giv - est Gra-cious-ly with each command.
Thou who bought me to pos - sess me, In Thy ful-ness, Lord, come in.
That the streams of liv - ing wa - ter From our in - ner man may flow.

Chan-nels on - ly, bless-ed Mas - ter, But with all Thy won-drous pow'r

Flow-ing through us, Thou canst use us Ev- 'ry day and ev- 'ry hour.

2 Timothy 2:21. Words, Mary E. Maxwell, 1910. Tune CHANNELS, Ada R. Gibbs, 1910.

Have Thine Own Way

1. Have Thine own way, Lord, Have Thine own way! Thou art the
2. Have Thine own way, Lord, Have Thine own way! Search me and
3. Have Thine own way, Lord, Have Thine own way! Wound-ed and
4. Have Thine own way, Lord, Have Thine own way! Hold o'er my

Pot - ter; I am the clay. Mold me and make me
try me, Mas-ter, to - day! Whit - er than snow, Lord,
wea - ry, Help me, I pray! Pow - er, all pow - er,
be - ing Ab - so - lute sway! Fill with Thy Spir - it

Aft - er Thy will, While I am wait - ing, Yield-ed and still.
Wash me just now, As in Thy pres - ence Hum-bly I bow.
Sure - ly is Thine! Touch me and heal me, Sav - ior di - vine!
Till all shall see Christ on - ly, al - ways, Liv - ing in me!

Isaiah 64:8. Words, Adelaide A. Pollard, 1902. Tune ADELAIDE, George C. Stebbins, 1907.

Isaiah 64:8; 2 Corinthians 3:18   598

Now, O Lord, thou art our Father; we are the clay, and thou our potter; and we all are the work of thy hand.

We all, with unveiled face beholding as in a mirror the glory of the Lord, are transformed into the same image from glory to glory, even as from the Lord the Spirit.

599 I Am Thine, O Lord

1. I am Thine, O Lord, I have heard Thy voice, And it told Thy
2. Con - se - crate me now to Thy serv - ice, Lord, By the pow'r of
3. O the pure de - light of a sin - gle hour That be - fore Thy
4. There are depths of love that I can - not know Till I cross the

love to me; But I long to rise in the arms of faith,
grace di - vine; Let my soul look up with a stead-fast hope,
throne I spend, When I kneel in prayer, and with Thee, my God,
nar - row sea; There are heights of joy that I may not reach

And be clos - er drawn to Thee.
And my will be lost in Thine. Draw me near - er,
I com - mune as friend with friend!
Till I rest in peace with Thee. near - er, near - er,

near - er, bless-ed Lord, To the cross where Thou hast died; Draw me near - er,

Hebrews 10:22. Words, Fanny J. Crosby, 1875. Tune I AM THINE, William H. Doane, 1875.

near - er, near - er, bless-ed Lord, To Thy pre - cious, bleed - ing side.

A Charge to Keep I Have 600

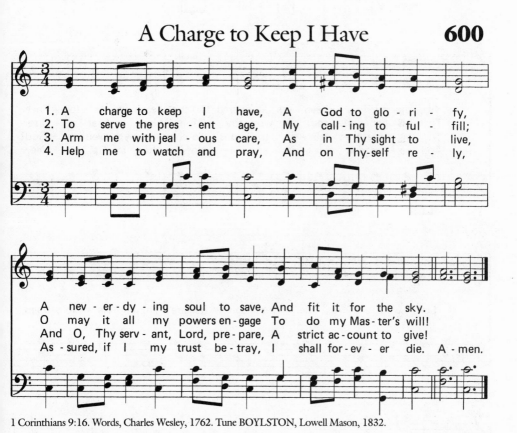

1. A charge to keep I have, A God to glo - ri - fy,
2. To serve the pres - ent age, My call - ing to ful - fill;
3. Arm me with jeal - ous care, As in Thy sight to live,
4. Help me to watch and pray, And on Thy-self re - ly,

A nev - er - dy - ing soul to save, And fit it for the sky.
O may it all my powers en - gage To do my Mas - ter's will!
And O, Thy serv - ant, Lord, pre - pare, A strict ac - count to give!
As - sured, if I my trust be - tray, I shall for - ev - er die. A - men.

1 Corinthians 9:16. Words, Charles Wesley, 1762. Tune BOYLSTON, Lowell Mason, 1832.

1 Peter 4:10,11 601

As each one has received a gift, minister it among yourselves, as good stewards of the manifold grace of God: if any speaks, speaking as it were oracles of God; if any man ministers, ministering as of the strength which God supplies: that in all things God may be glorified through Jesus Christ, whose is the glory and the dominion for ever and ever. Amen.

602   Are Ye Able?

1. "Are ye a - ble," said the Mas - ter, "To be cru - ci - fied with me?"
2. Are ye a - ble to re - mem - ber, When a thief lifts up his eyes,
3. Are ye a - ble when the shad - ows Close a - round you with the sod,
4. Are ye a - ble? Still the Mas - ter Whis - pers down e - ter - ni - ty,

"Yea," the sturd - y dream - ers an - swered, "To the death we fol - low Thee."
That his par - doned soul is wor - thy Of a place in par - a - dise?
To be - lieve that spir - it tri - umphs, To com - mend your soul to God?
And he - ro - ic spir - its an - swer Now, as then, in Gal - i - lee.

Lord, we are a - ble. Our spir - its are Thine. Re - mold them,

make us, Like Thee, di - vine. Thy guid - ing ra - diance A - bove us shall

Mark 10:38,39. Words, Earl Marlatt, 1926. Words used by permission of Earl B. Marlatt. Tune BEACON HILL, Harry S. Mason, 1924.

be A bea - con to God, To love, and loy - al - ty. A - men.

Take My Life, O Father, Mold It 603

1. Take my life, O Fa - ther, mold it In o - be - dience to Thy will;
2. Fa - ther, keep it pure and low - ly, Strong and brave, yet free from strife,
3. Ev - er let Thy might sur - round it; Strength - en it with pow'r di - vine,

And as rip - 'ning years un - fold it, Keep it true and child-like still.
Turn - ing from the paths un - ho - ly Of a vain or sin - ful life.
Till Thy cords of love have bound it, Fa - ther, whol - ly un - to Thine.

All to Thee, all to Thee, Con - se - cra - ted, Lord, to Thee.

1 Peter 1:14,15. Words, Anonymous. Tune TELEIOS, Philip P. Bliss in Sankey's *Gospel Hymns, Nos. 1-6 Complete*, 1894.

604 All to Jesus I Surrender

1. All to Je - sus I sur-ren - der, All to Him I free - ly give;
2. All to Je - sus I sur-ren - der, Hum - bly at His feet I bow;
3. All to Je - sus I sur-ren - der, Lord, I give my - self to Thee;

I will ev - er love and trust Him, In His pres - ence dai - ly live.
World - ly pleas-ures all for - sak - en, Take me, Je - sus, take me now.
Fill me with Thy love and pow - er, Let Thy bless-ing fall on me.

I sur-ren-der all, I sur-ren-der all;
I sur-ren-der all, I sur-ren-der all;

All to Thee, my bless - ed Sav - ior, I sur - ren - der all.

Galatians 2:20. Words, Judson W. Van de Venter, 1896. Tune I SURRENDER ALL, Winfield S. Weeden, 1896.

Take Thou Our Minds

1. Take Thou our minds, dear Lord, we hum-bly pray;
2. Take Thou our hearts, O Christ, they are Thine own;
3. Take Thou our wills, Most High! Hold Thou full sway;
4. Take Thou our-selves, O Lord, heart, mind, and will;

Give us the mind of Christ each pass-ing day;
Come Thou with-in our souls and claim Thy throne;
Have in our in-most souls Thy per-fect way;
Through our sur-ren-dered souls Thy plans ful-fill.

Teach us to know the truth that sets us free;
Help us to shed a-broad Thy death-less love;
Guard Thou each sa-cred hour from self-ish ease;
We yield our-selves to Thee— time, tal-ents, all;

Grant us in all our thoughts to hon-or Thee.
Use us to make the earth like heaven a-bove.
Guide Thou our or-dered lives as Thou dost please.
We hear, and hence-forth heed, Thy sov-ereign call. A-men.

Matthew 22:37. Words, William H. Foulkes, 1918. Tune HALL, Calvin W. Laufer, 1918.

606 **Savior, Like a Shepherd Lead Us**

1. Sav - ior, like a shep-herd lead us; Much we need Thy ten-d'rest care;
2. We are Thine; do Thou be- friend us; Be the Guard-ian of our way;
3. Thou hast prom-ised to re - ceive us, Poor and sin - ful though we be;
4. Ear - ly let us seek Thy fa - vor, Ear - ly let us do Thy will;

In Thy pleas-ant pas-tures feed us, For our use Thy folds pre - pare:
Keep Thy flock, from sin de - fend us, Seek us when we go a - stray:
Thou hast mer-cy to re - lieve us, Grace to cleanse, and pow'r to free:
Bless-ed Lord and on - ly Sav - ior, With Thy love our bos - oms fill:

Bless-ed Je - sus, Bless-ed Je - sus, Thou hast bought us, Thine we are;
Bless-ed Je - sus, Bless-ed Je - sus, Hear, O hear us when we pray;
Bless-ed Je - sus, Bless-ed Je - sus, Ear - ly let us turn to Thee;
Bless-ed Je - sus, Bless-ed Je - sus, Thou hast loved us, love us still;

Bless-ed Je - sus, Bless-ed Je - sus, Thou hast bought us, Thine we are.
Bless-ed Je - sus, Bless-ed Je - sus, Hear, O hear us when we pray.
Bless-ed Je - sus, Bless-ed Je - sus, Ear - ly let us turn to Thee.
Bless-ed Je - sus, Bless-ed Je - sus, Thou hast loved us, love us still.

John 10:11. Words, *Hymns for the Young*, 1836; attr. to Dorothy A. Thrupp. Tune BRADBURY, William B. Bradbury, 1859.

Open My Eyes, That I May See

607

1. O-pen my eyes, that I may see Glimp-ses of truth Thou hast for me;
2. O-pen my ears, that I may hear Voi - ces of truth Thou send-est clear;
3. O-pen my mouth, and let me bear Glad - ly the warm truth ev -'ry-where;

Place in my hands the won-der-ful key That shall un - clasp, and
And while the wave - notes fall on my ear, Ev - 'ry-thing false will
O - pen my heart, and let me pre-pare Love with Thy chil - dren

set me free. Si - lent - ly now I wait for Thee, Read - y, my God, Thy
dis - a--pear. Si - lent - ly now I wait for Thee, Read - y, my God, Thy
thus to share. Si - lent - ly now I wait for Thee, Read - y, my God, Thy

will to see: O-pen my eyes, il - lu - mine me, Sav - ior di - vine!
will to see: O-pen my ears, il - lu - mine me, Sav - ior di - vine!
will to see: O - oen my heart, il - lu - mine me, Sav - ior di - vine!

Psalm 119:18. Words and tune SCOTT, Clara H. Scott, 1895.

608 Take My Life, and Let it Be

1. Take my life, and let it be Con-se-cra-ted, Lord, to Thee.
2. Take my voice, and let me sing Al-ways, on-ly, for my King.
3. Take my will, and make it Thine; It shall be no long-er mine.

Take my mo-ments and my days; Let them flow in cease-less praise.
Take my lips, and let them be Filled with mes-sag-es from Thee.
Take my heart, it is Thine own; It shall be Thy roy-al throne.

Take my hands, and let them move At the im-pulse of Thy love.
Take my sil-ver and my gold; Not a mite would I with-hold.
Take my love; my Lord, I pour At Thy feet its trea-sure-store.

Take my feet, and let them be Swift and beau-ti-ful for Thee.
Take my in-tel-lect, and use Ev-ery power as Thou shalt choose.
Take my-self, and I will be Ev-er, on-ly, all for Thee. A-men.

Romans 12:1. Words, Frances R. Havergal, 1874. Tune MESSIAH, Louis J. F. Herold; arr. George Kingsley, 1839.

Savior, Thy Dying Love

609

Not too slow

1. Sav - ior, Thy dy - ing love Thou gav - est me;
2. At the blest mer - cy - seat, Plead - ing for me,
3. Give me a faith - ful heart— Like - ness to Thee—
4. All that I am and have— Thy gifts so free—

Nor should I aught with - hold, Dear Lord, from Thee:
My fee - ble faith looks up, Je - sus, to Thee:
That each de - part - ing day, Hence - forth may see
In joy, in grief, thro' life, Dear Lord, for Thee!

In love my soul would bow, My heart ful - fill its vow,
Help me the cross to bear, Thy won - drous love de - clare,
Some work of love be - gun, Some deed of kind - ness done,
And when Thy face I see, My ran - somed soul shall be,

Some of - f'ring bring Thee now, Some - thing for Thee.
Some song to raise, or prayer, Some - thing for Thee.
Some wan - d'rer sought and won, Some - thing for Thee.
Thro' all e - ter - ni - ty, Some - thing for Thee.

Galatians 5:6. Words, Sylvanus D. Phelps, 1862. Tune SOMETHING FOR THEE, Robert Lowry, 1871.

610 We Give Thee But Thine Own

1. We give Thee but Thine own, What - e'er the gift may be;
2. May we Thy boun-ties thus As stew-ards true re - ceive,
3. And we be - lieve Thy word, Tho' dim our faith may be,

All that we have is Thine a - lone, A trust, O Lord, from Thee.
And glad - ly, as Thou bless-est us, To Thee, our first-fruits give.
What - e'er for Thine we do, O Lord, We do it un - to Thee.

1 Chronicles 29:14. Words, William W. How, 1858. Tune SCHUMANN, Mason and Webb's *Cantica Laudis*, 1850.

611 My God, My Father, Though I Stray

1. My God, my Fa - ther, tho' I stray Far from my home, on life's rough way,
2. Tho' dark my path, and sad my lot, Let me be still and mur - mur not,
3. Re - new my will from day to day; Blend it with Thine, and take a - way
4. Then, when on earth I breathe no more The prayer oft mixed with tears be - fore,

O teach me from my heart to say, "Thy will be done!"
Or breathe the prayer di - vine - ly taught, "Thy will be done!"
All that now makes it hard to say, "Thy will be done!"
I'll sing up - on a hap - pier shore, "Thy will be done!" A - men.

Philippians 3:10,11. Words, Charlotte Elliott, 1834; alt. Tune HANFORD, Arthur S. Sullivan, 1874.

Still With Thee, O My God

612

1. Still with Thee O my God, I would de-
2. With Thee when dawn comes in And calls me
3. With Thee a - mid the crowd That throngs the
4. With Thee when day is done, And eve - ning
5. With Thee when dark - ness brings The sig - nal
6. With Thee, in Thee, by faith A - bid - ing,

sire to be, By day, by night, at home, a -
back to care, Each day re - turn - ing to be -
bus - y mart, To hear Thy voice, where men are
calms the mind; The set - ting as the ris - ing
of re - pose, Calm in the shad - ow of Thy
I would be; By day, by night, in life, in

broad, I would be still with Thee.
gin With Thee, my God, in prayer.
loud, Speak soft - ly to my heart.
sun With Thee my heart would find.
wings, Mine eye - lids I would close.
death I would be still with Thee.

Psalm 139:17,18. Words, James D. Burns, 1857. Tune PROSOPON, M. L. Daniels, 1984. Copyright ACU Press.

613

More Love to Thee

Not too slow

1. More love to Thee, O Christ, More love to Thee! Hear Thou the
2. Once earth-ly joy I craved, Sought peace and rest; Now Thee a-
3. Then shall my lat-est breath Whis-per Thy praise; This be the

prayer I make On bend-ed knee; This is my ear-nest plea:
lone I seek: Give what is best; This all my prayer shall be:
part-ing cry My heart shall raise; This still my prayer shall be:

More love, O Christ, to Thee, More love to Thee, More love to Thee!

Philippians 1:9. Words, Elizabeth Prentiss, 1856. Tune MORE LOVE TO THEE, William H. Doane, 1870.

614

Jesus Calls Us

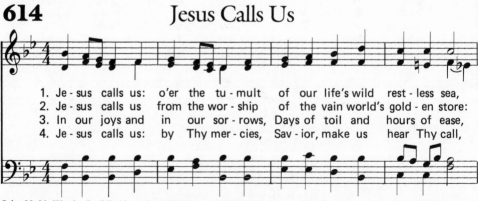

1. Je-sus calls us: o'er the tu-mult of our life's wild rest-less sea,
2. Je-sus calls us from the wor-ship of the vain world's gold-en store:
3. In our joys and in our sor-rows, Days of toil and hours of ease,
4. Je-sus calls us: by Thy mer-cies, Sav-ior, make us hear Thy call,

John 21:22. Words, Cecil F. Alexander, 1852. Tune BURFORD, Leonard Burford. Copyright 1974, ACU Press.

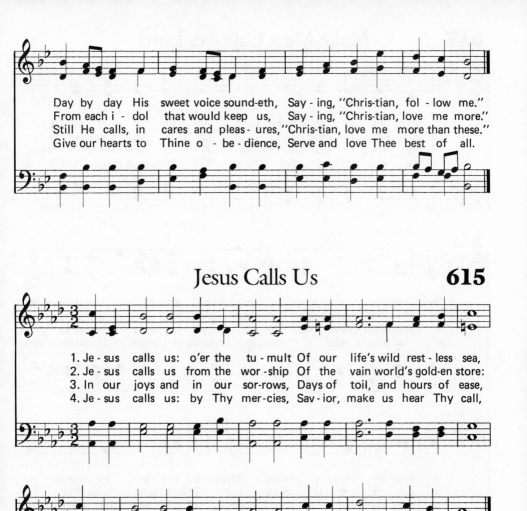

Day by day His sweet voice sound-eth, Say - ing, "Chris-tian, fol - low me."
From each i - dol that would keep us, Say - ing, "Chris-tian, love me more."
Still He calls, in cares and pleas - ures, "Chris-tian, love me more than these."
Give our hearts to Thine o - be - dience, Serve and love Thee best of all.

Jesus Calls Us   615

1. Je - sus calls us: o'er the tu - mult Of our life's wild rest - less sea,
2. Je - sus calls us from the wor - ship Of the vain world's gold-en store:
3. In our joys and in our sor - rows, Days of toil, and hours of ease,
4. Je - sus calls us: by Thy mer-cies, Sav - ior, make us hear Thy call,

Day by day His sweet voice sound-eth, Say - ing, "Chris-tian, fol-low me."
From each i - dol that would keep us, Say - ing, "Chris-tian, love me more."
Still He calls, in cares and pleas-ures, "Chris-tian, love me more than these."
Give our hearts to Thine o - be - dience, Serve and love Thee best of all.

John 21:22. Words, Cecil F. Alexander, 1852. Tune GALILEE, William H. Jude, 1887.

Matthew 10:37,38   616

He that loveth father or mother more than me is not worthy of me; and he that loveth son or daughter more than me is not worthy of me. And he that doth not take his cross and follow after me, is not worthy of me.

617 Make Me a Captive, Lord

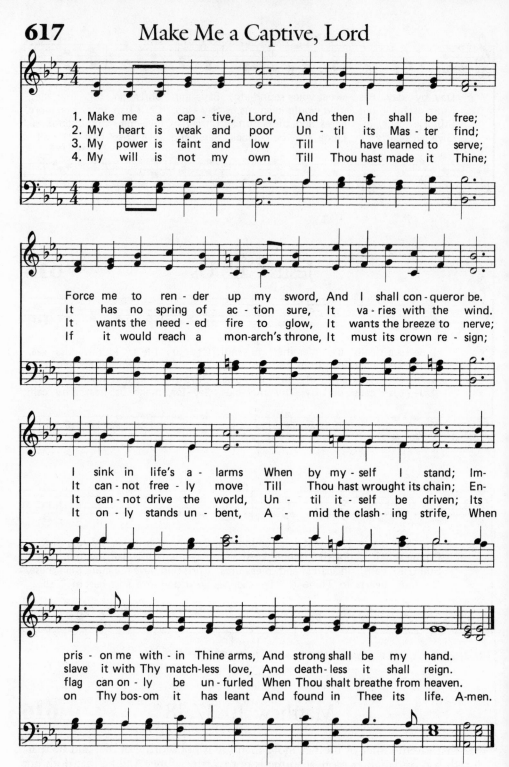

1. Make me a cap - tive, Lord, And then I shall be free;
2. My heart is weak and poor Un - til its Mas - ter find;
3. My power is faint and low Till I have learned to serve;
4. My will is not my own Till Thou hast made it Thine;

Force me to ren - der up my sword, And I shall con - queror be.
It has no spring of ac - tion sure, It va - ries with the wind.
It wants the need - ed fire to glow, It wants the breeze to nerve;
If it would reach a mon - arch's throne, It must its crown re - sign;

I sink in life's a - larms When by my - self I stand; Im-
It can - not free - ly move Till Thou hast wrought its chain; En-
It can - not drive the world, Un - til it - self be driven; Its
It on - ly stands un - bent, A - mid the clash - ing strife, When

pris - on me with - in Thine arms, And strong shall be my hand.
slave it with Thy match - less love, And death - less it shall reign.
flag can on - ly be un - furled When Thou shalt breathe from heaven.
on Thy bos - om it has leant And found in Thee its life. A-men.

Ephesians 3:1. Words, George Matheson, 1890. Tune DIADEMATA, George J. Elvey, 1868.

Into the Heart of Jesus

618

1. In - to the heart of Je - sus, deep - er and deep - er I go,
2. In - to the will of Je - sus, deep - er and deep - er I go,
3. In - to the cross of Je - sus, deep - er and deep - er I go,
4. In - to the joy of Je - sus, deep - er and deep - er I go,

Seek - ing to know the rea - son why He should love me so,
Pray - ing for grace to fol - low, seek - ing His way to know,
Fol - low - ing thro' the gar - den, fac - ing the dread - ed foe,
Ris - ing with soul en - rap - tured far from the world be - low;

Why He should stoop to lift me up from the mir - y clay,
Bow - ing in full sur - ren - der low at His bless - ed feet,
Drink - ing the cup of sor - row, sob - bing with bro - ken heart:
Joy in the place of sor - row, peace in the midst of pain,

Sav - ing my soul, mak - ing me whole, Tho' I had wan - dered a - way.
Bid - ding Him take, break me and make, Till I am mold - ed and meet.
"O Sav - ior, help! dear Sav - ior, help! Grace for my weak - ness im - part."
Je - sus will give, Je - sus will give; He will up - hold and sus - tain.

1 Corinthians 15:10. Words and tune DEEPER AND DEEPER, Oswald J. Smith, 1915. Copyright 1915. Renewal 1933 extended by Hope Publishing Co., Carol Stream, Illinois, 60188. All rights reserved. Used by permission.

619 O Love That Wilt Not Let Me Go

1. O Love that wilt not let me go,
2. O Light that fol-lowest all my way,
3. O Joy that seek-est me through pain,
4. O Cross that lift-est up my head,

I rest my wea-ry soul in Thee;
I yield my flick-ering torch to Thee;
I can-not close my heart to Thee;
I dare not ask to hide from Thee;

I give Thee back the life I owe, That
My heart re-stores its bor-rowed ray, That
I trace the rain-bow through the rain, And
I lay in dust life's glo-ry dead, And

in Thine o-cean depths its flow May rich-er, full-er be.
in Thy sun-shine's glow its day May bright-er, fair-er be.
feel the prom-ise is not vain That morn shall tear-less be.
from the ground there blos-soms red, Life that shall end-less be.

John 13:1. Words, George Matheson, 1882. Tune ST. MARGARET, Albert L. Peace, 1884.

O Jesus, I Have Promised

620

1. O Jesus, I have prom-ised To serve Thee to the end; Be Thou for ev-er near me, My Mas-ter and my Friend: I shall not fear the bat-tle If Thou art by my side, Nor wan-der from the path-way If Thou wilt be my Guide.

2. O let me feel Thee near me: The world is ev-er near; I see the sights that daz-zle, The tempt-ing sounds I hear; My foes are ev-er near me, A-round me and with-in; But, Je-sus, draw Thou near-er, And shield my soul from sin.

3. O Je-sus, Thou hast prom-ised To all who fol-low Thee, That where Thou art in glo-ry There shall Thy serv-ant be; And Je-sus, I have prom-ised To serve Thee to the end: O give me grace to fol-low My Mas-ter and my Friend.

Revelation 2:10,11. Words, John E. Bode, 1866. Tune ANGEL'S STORY, Arthur H. Mann, 1881.

621 Jesus, Thy Boundless Love to Me

1. Je-sus, Thy bound-less love to me No thought can reach, no tongue de-clare; O knit my thank-ful heart to Thee, And reign with-out a ri-val there! Thine whol-ly, Thine a-lone, I'd live, My-self to Thee en-tire-ly give.

2. O Love, how cheer-ing is Thy ray! All fear be-fore Thy pres-ence flies; Care, an-guish, sor-row, melt a-way, Wher-e'er Thy heal-ing beams a-rise: O Je-sus, noth-ing may I see, Noth-ing de-sire, or seek, but Thee!

3. In suf-fering be Thy love my peace; In weak-ness be Thy love my power; And when the storms of life shall cease, O Je-sus, in that sol-emn hour, In death as life be Thou my guide, And save me, who for me hast died. A-men.

Ephesians 3:19. Words, Paul Gerhardt, 1653; trans. John Wesley, 1739. Tune ST. CATHERINE, Henri F. Hemy, 1864; adpt. James G. Walton, 1874.

Lord, Speak to Me

622

1. Lord, speak to me that I may speak In liv-ing ech-oes of Thy tone; As Thou hast sought, so let me seek Thine err-ing chil-dren, lost and lone.

2. O strength-en me, that while I stand Firm on the Rock and strong in Thee, I may stretch out a lov-ing hand To wres-tlers with the trou-bled sea.

3. O teach me, Lord, that I may teach The pre-cious things Thou dost im-part; And wing my words that they may reach The hid-den depths of many a heart.

4. O fill me with Thy full-ness, Lord, Un-til my ver-y heart o'er-flow; In kin-d'ling thought and glow-ing word, Thy love to tell, Thy praise to show.

2 Timothy 2:2. Words, Frances R. Havergal, 1872. Tune HOLLEY, George Hews, 1835.

2 Timothy 2:1,2

623

You therefore, my child, be strengthened in the grace that is in Christ Jesus. And the things which you have heard from me among many witnesses, the same commit to faithful men, who shall be able to teach others also.

624
O to Be Like Thee

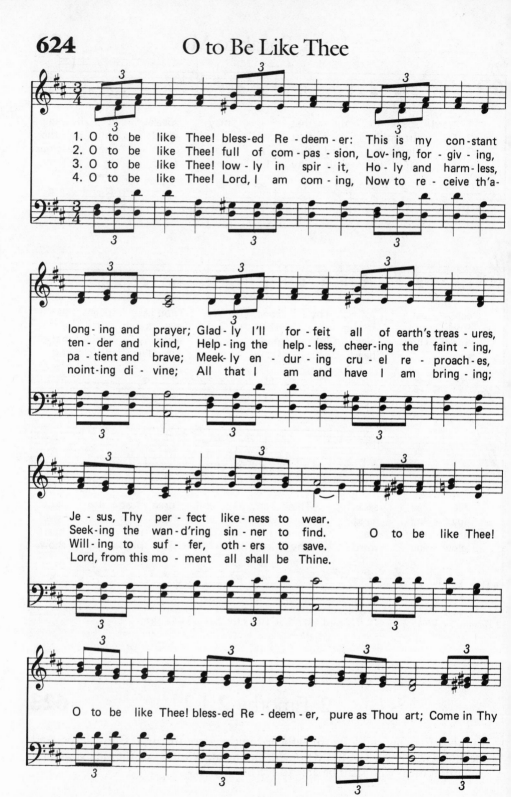

1. O to be like Thee! bless-ed Re-deem-er: This is my con-stant
2. O to be like Thee! full of com-pas-sion, Lov-ing, for-giv-ing,
3. O to be like Thee! low-ly in spir-it, Ho-ly and harm-less,
4. O to be like Thee! Lord, I am com-ing, Now to re-ceive th'a-

long-ing and prayer; Glad-ly I'll for-feit all of earth's treas-ures,
ten-der and kind, Help-ing the help-less, cheer-ing the faint-ing,
pa-tient and brave; Meek-ly en-dur-ing cru-el re-proach-es,
noint-ing di-vine; All that I am and have I am bring-ing;

Je-sus, Thy per-fect like-ness to wear.
Seek-ing the wan-d'ring sin-ner to find.   O to be   like Thee!
Will-ing to suf-fer, oth-ers to save.
Lord, from this mo-ment all shall be Thine.

O to be   like Thee! bless-ed Re-deem-er, pure as Thou art; Come in Thy

Romans 8:19. Words, Thomas O. Chisholm, 1897. Tune RONDINELLA, William J. Kirkpatrick, 1897.

sweet-ness, come in Thy full-ness; Stamp Thine own im - age deep on my heart.

Walk in the Light 625

1. Walk in the light! so shalt thou know That fel - low-
2. Walk in the light! and thou shalt find Thy heart made
3. Walk in the light! and thou shalt own Thy dark - ness
4. Walk in the light! and thine shall be A path, though

ship of love His Spir - it on - ly can be -
tru - ly His, Who dwells in cloud - less light en -
passed a - way, Be - cause that light hath on thee
thorn - y, bright: For God, by grace, shall dwell in

stow, Who reigns in light a - bove.
shrined, In whom no dark - ness is.
shone, In which is per - fect day.
thee, And God Him - self is light. A - men.

1 John 1:7. Words, Bernard Barton, 1826. Tune MANOAH, Henry W. Greatorex's *Collection of Church Music,*
1851.

626 More About Jesus

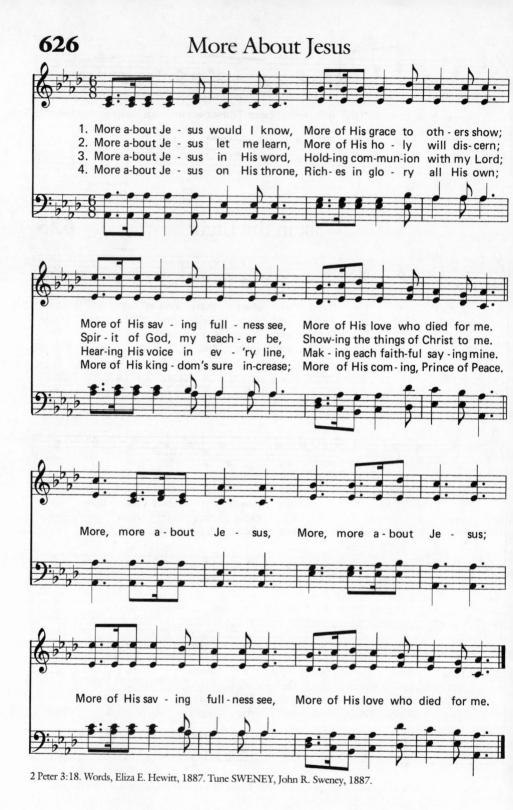

1. More a-bout Je - sus would I know, More of His grace to oth - ers show;
2. More a-bout Je - sus let me learn, More of His ho - ly will dis-cern;
3. More a-bout Je - sus in His word, Hold-ing com-mun-ion with my Lord;
4. More a-bout Je - sus on His throne, Rich- es in glo - ry all His own;

More of His sav - ing full - ness see, More of His love who died for me.
Spir - it of God, my teach - er be, Show-ing the things of Christ to me.
Hear-ing His voice in ev - 'ry line, Mak - ing each faith-ful say - ing mine.
More of His king - dom's sure in-crease; More of His com - ing, Prince of Peace.

More, more a - bout Je - sus, More, more a - bout Je - sus;

More of His sav - ing full-ness see, More of His love who died for me.

2 Peter 3:18. Words, Eliza E. Hewitt, 1887. Tune SWENEY, John R. Sweney, 1887.

Jesus, Keep Me Near the Cross

627

1. Je - sus, keep me near the cross: There a pre - cious foun - tain,
2. Near the cross, a trem - bling soul, Love and mer - cy found me;
3. Near the cross! O Lamb of God, Bring its scenes be - fore me;

Free to all, a heal - ing stream, Flows from Cal - v'ry's moun - tain.
There the Bright and Morn - ing Star Sheds its beams a - round me.
Help me walk from day to day With its shad - ow o'er me.

In the cross, in the cross, Be my glo - ry ev - er,

Till my rap - tured soul shall find Rest be - yond the riv - er.

John 19:25. Words, Fanny J. Crosby, 1869. Tune NEAR THE CROSS, William H. Doane, 1869.

628 ## Would You Live for Jesus?

1. Would you live for Je - sus and be al - ways pure and good?
2. Would you have Him make you free, and fol - low at His call?
3. Would you in His king - dom find a place of con - stant rest?

Would you walk with Him with - in the nar - row road? Would you have Him
Would you know the peace that comes by giv - ing all? Would you have Him
Would you prove Him true each prov - i - den - tial test? Would you in His

bear your bur - den, car - ry all your load? Let Him have His
save you, so that you need nev - er fall? Let Him have His
serv - ice la - bor al - ways at your best? Let Him have His

way with thee.
way with thee. His pow'r can make you what you ought to be; His
way with thee.

Acts 22:10. Words and tune NUSBAUM, Cyrus S. Nusbaum, 1898.

blood can cleanse your heart and make you free; His love can fill your soul, and

you will see 'Twas best for Him to have His way with thee.

Must Jesus Bear the Cross Alone? 629

1. Must Je-sus bear the cross a-lone, And all the world go free?
2. The con-se-crat-ed cross I'll bear Till He shall set me free,
3. O pre-cious cross! O glo-rious crown! O res-ur-rec-tion day!

No, there's a cross for ev-'ry one, And there's a cross for me.
And then go home my crown to wear, For there's a crown for me.
Ye an-gels from the stars, come down And bear my soul a-way.

Matthew 16:24. Words, Thomas Shepherd, 1693, and others. Tune MAITLAND, George N. Allen, 1844.

630 **I'm Pressing On**

1. I'm press-ing on the up-ward way, New heights I'm gain-ing ev-'ry day;
2. My heart has no de-sire to stay Where doubts a-rise and fears dis-may;
3. I want to live a-bove the world, Tho' Sa-tan's darts at me are hurled;
4. I want to scale the ut-most height, And catch a gleam of glo-ry bright;

Still pray-ing as I on-ward bound, "Lord, plant my feet on high-er ground."
Tho' some may dwell where these abound, My prayer, my aim is high-er ground.
For faith has caught the joy-ful sound, The song of saints on high-er ground.
But still I'll pray till heav'n I've found, "Lord, lead me on to high-er ground."

Lord, lift me up and let me stand, By faith, on heav-en's ta-ble-land,

A high-er plane than I have found; Lord, plant my feet on high-er ground.

Philippians 3:14. Words, Johnson Oatman, Jr., 1898. Tune HIGHER GROUND, Charles H. Gabriel, 1898.

Lord Jesus, I Long to Be

631

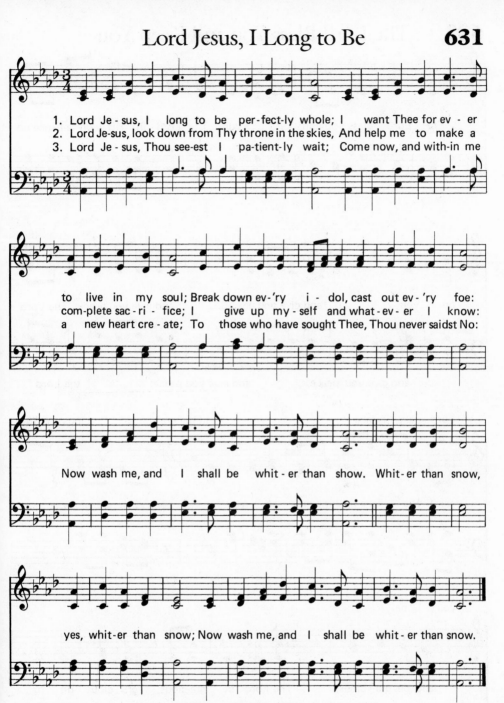

1. Lord Je-sus, I long to be per-fect-ly whole; I want Thee for ev - er
2. Lord Je-sus, look down from Thy throne in the skies, And help me to make a
3. Lord Je-sus, Thou see-est I pa-tient-ly wait; Come now, and with-in me

to live in my soul; Break down ev-'ry i - dol, cast out ev-'ry foe:
com-plete sac-ri - fice; I give up my-self and what-ev-er I know:
a new heart cre-ate; To those who have sought Thee, Thou never saidst No:

Now wash me, and I shall be whit-er than show. Whit-er than snow,

yes, whit-er than snow; Now wash me, and I shall be whit-er than snow.

Psalm 51:7. Words, James L. Nicholson, 1872. Tune FISCHER, William G. Fischer, 1872.

632   The Lord Bless You and Keep You

Numbers 6:24-26. Words, paraphrase of Numbers 6:24-26 with seven-fold Amen. Tune LUTKIN, Peter Lutkin.

1 Thessalonians 5:23,24   **633**

The God of peace himself sanctify you wholly; and may your spirit and soul and body be preserved entire, without blame at the coming of our Lord Jesus Christ. Faithful is he who calls you, who will also do it.

634

O Thou, in Whose Presence

1. O Thou, in whose pres - ence my soul takes de - light,
2. Where dost Thou, dear Shep - herd, re - sort with Thy sheep,
3. O why should I wan - der, an a - lien from Thee,
4. Re - store, my dear Sav - ior, the light of Thy face;
5. He looks! and ten thou - sands of an - gels re - joice,

On whom in af - flic - tion I call, My com - fort by day and my
To feed them in pas - tures of love? Say, why in the val - ley of
Or cry in the des - ert for bread? Thy foes will re - joice when my
Thy soul - cheer - ing com - fort im - part; And let the sweet to - kens of
And myr - i - ads wait for His word; He speaks! and e - ter - ni - ty,

song in the night, My hope, my sal - va - tion, my all!
death should I weep, Or a - lone in this wil - der - ness rove?
sor - rows they see, And smile at the tears I have shed.
par - don - ing grace Bring joy to my des - o - late heart.
filled with His voice, Re - ech - oes the praise of the Lord. A - men.

Song of Solomon 1:7. Words, Joseph Swain, 1791. Tune WYETH, John Wyeth's *Repository of Sacred Music, Part Second*, 1814.

Tarry With Me

635

1. Tar - ry with me, O my Sav - ior, For the day is pass - ing by;
2. Deep-er, deep - er grow the shad-ows, Pal - er now the glow-ing west;
3. Tar - ry with me, O my Sav - ior; Lay my head up - on Thy breast

See, the shades of eve - ning gath - er, And the night is draw-ing nigh.
Swift the night of death ad - vanc - es: Shall it be the night of rest?
Till the morn - ing; then a - wake me, Morn-ing of e - ter - nal rest.

Tar - ry with me, bless - ed Sav - ior; Leave me not till morn-ing light;

For I'm lone - ly here with - out Thee: Tar - ry with me thro' the night.

Isaiah 65:17-20. Words, Caroline Sprague Smith, 1852. Tune REST, Knowles Shaw.

636
Nearer, My God, to Thee

1. Near - er, my God, to Thee, Near - er to Thee! E'en tho' it
2. Tho' like a wan - der - er, The sun gone down, Dark - ness be
3. There let the way ap - pear Steps un - to heav'n; All that Thou
4. Or, if on joy - ful wing, Cleav - ing the sky, Sun, moon, and

be a cross That rais - eth me; Still all my song shall be,
o - ver me, My rest a stone; Yet in my dreams I'd be
send - est me, In mer - cy giv'n; An - gels to beck - on me
stars for - got, Up - ward I fly; Still all my song shall be,

Near - er, my God, to Thee, Near - er, my God, to Thee, Near - er to Thee!

Genesis 28:16. Words, Sarah F. Adams, 1840. Tune BETHANY, Lowell Mason, 1856.

637
Cast Thy Burden on the Lord

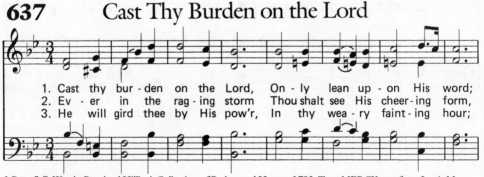

1. Cast thy bur - den on the Lord, On - ly lean up - on His word;
2. Ev - er in the rag - ing storm Thou shalt see His cheer - ing form,
3. He will gird thee by His pow'r, In thy wea - ry faint - ing hour;

1 Peter 5:7. Words, Rowland Hill's *A Collection of Psalms and Hymns*, 1783. Tune MERCY, arr. from Louis M. Gottschalk, 1854.

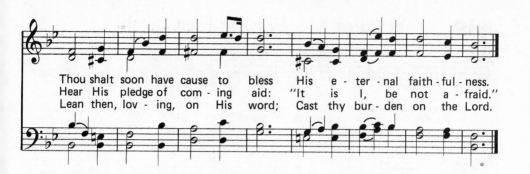

Thou shalt soon have cause to bless His e - ter - nal faith - ful - ness.
Hear His pledge of com - ing aid: "It is I, be not a - fraid."
Lean then, lov - ing, on His word; Cast thy bur - den on the Lord.

Cast Thy Burden Upon the Lord **638**

Cast thy bur - den up - on the Lord; and He shall sus - tain thee: He

ne - ver will suf - fer the right-eous to fall; He is at thy right hand. Thy

mer - cy, Lord, is great, and far a - bove the heavens. Let

none be made a - shamed that wait up - on___ Thee!

1 Peter 5:7. Words, Psalm 55:22. Tune ELIJAH, Felix Mendelssohn, 1846.

639 Yes, For Me, For Me He Careth

1. Yes, for me, for me He car - eth With a
   broth - er's ten - der care; Yes, with me, with me He
   shar - eth Ev - 'ry bur - den, ev - 'ry care; Yes, o'er
   me, o'er me He watch - eth, Cease - less watch - eth

2. Yes, for me He stand - eth plead - ing, At the
   mer - cy - seat a - bove, Ev - er for me in - ter-
   ced - ing, Con - stant in un - tir - ing love; Yes, in
   me a - broad He shed - deth Joys un - earth - ly,

3. Yes, in me, in me He dwell - eth— I in
   Him, and He in me; And my emp - ty soul He
   fill - eth, Here and through e - ter - ni - ty; Thus I
   wait for His re - turn - ing, Sing - ing all the

John 16:33. Words, Horatius Bonar, 1844. Tune MERIMNA, M.L. Daniels, 1984. Copyright 1986, ACU Press.

night   and   day;   Yes,   e'en   me,   e'en   me   He
love   and   light;   And   to   cov - er   me   He
way   to   heav'n;   Such   the   joy - ful   song   of

snatch - eth   From   the   per - ils   of   the   way.
spread - eth   His   pa - ter - nal   wing   of   might.
morn - ing,   Such   the   tran - quil   song   of   ev'n.

Matthew 6:25,26,28,33,34   **640**

Be not anxious for your life, what you shall eat, or what you shall drink; nor yet for your body, what you shall put on. Is not the life more than the food, and the body than the clothing? Look at the birds of the heaven, that they neither sow, nor reap, nor gather into barns; and your heavenly Father feeds them . . . And why are you anxious concerning clothing? Consider the lilies of the field, how they grow; they neither toil nor spin: yet I tell you, even Solomon in all his glory was not arrayed like one of these . . . Seek first the kingdom of God and his righteousness; and all these things shall be added to you. Do not be anxious about tomorrow; tomorrow will be anxious about itself. Each day's evil is sufficient for the day.

641 Still, Still With Thee

1. Still, still with Thee, when pur - ple morn - ing break - eth,
2. A - lone with Thee, a - mid the mys - tic shad - ows,
3. When sinks the soul, sub - dued by toil to slum - ber,
4. So shall it be at last, in that bright morn - ing

When the bird wa - keth, and the shad - ows flee;
The sol - emn hush of na - ture new - ly born;
Its clos - ing eye looks up to Thee in prayer;
When the soul wa - keth, and life's shad - ows flee;

Fair - er than morn - ing, love - li - er than day - light,
A - lone with Thee in breath-less ad - o - ra - tion,
Sweet the re - pose be - neath Thy wings o'er - shad - ing,
Oh, in that hour, fair - er than day - light dawn - ing,

Dawns the sweet con - scious-ness, I am with Thee.
In the calm dew and fresh - ness of the morn.
But sweet - er still, to wake and find Thee there.
Shall rise the glo - rious thought I am with Thee.

Psalm 139:17,18. Words, Harriet Beecher Stowe, 1855. Tune METASOU, Ira D. Sankey, *Sacred Songs and Solos*.

Does Jesus Care?

1. Does Je - sus care when my heart is pained Too   deep-ly for mirth and song,
2. Does Je - sus care when my way is dark With a name - less dread and fear?
3. Does Je-sus care when I've tried and failed To re-sist some temp-ta-tion strong?
4. Does Je - sus care when I've said "good-by" To the dear-est on earth to me,

As the bur -dens press, and the cares distress, And the way grows weary and long?
As the day-light fades in-to deep night shades, Does He care e-nough to be near?
When for my deep grief I find no re- lief, Tho' my tears flow all the night long?
And my sad heart aches till it near-ly breaks— Is it aught to Him? Does He see?

O yes, He cares, I know He cares, His   heart is touched with my grief;

When the days are wea-ry, the long nights drear-y, I know my Sav-ior cares.
He cares.

Matthew 11:28-30. Words, Frank E. Graeff, 1901. Tune MY SAVIOR CARES, J. Lincoln Hall, 1901.

643 Under His Wings

1. Un - der His wings I am safe - ly a - bid-ing; Though the night
2. Un - der His wings, what a ref - uge in sor-row! How the heart
3. Un - der His wings, O what pre - cious en - joy-ment! There will I

deep - ens and tem - pests are wild, Still I can trust Him: I
yearn-ing - ly turns to His rest! Oft - en when earth has no
hide till life's tri - als are o'er; Shel - tered, pro - tect - ed, no

know He will keep me; He has re - deemed me and I am His child.
balm for my heal-ing, There I find com - fort, and there I am blest.
e - vil can harm me; Rest - ing in Je - sus I'm safe ev - er - more.

Un-der His wings, un - der His wings, Who from His love can sev - er?

Psalm 17:8. Words, William O. Cushing, c. 1896. Tune HINGHAM, Ira D. Sankey, 1896.

Un-der His wings my soul shall a - bide, Safe-ly a - bide for ev - er.

Children of the Heavenly Father 644

1. Chil - dren of the heaven - ly Fa - ther Safe - ly
2. God His own doth tend and nour - ish; In His
3. Nei - ther life nor death shall ev - er From the
4. Though He giv - eth or He tak - eth, God His

in His bos - om gath - er; Nest - ling bird nor star in
ho - ly courts they flour - ish. From all e - vil things He
Lord His chil - dren sev - er; Un - to them His grace He
chil - dren ne'er for - sak - eth; His the lov - ing pur - pose

heav - en Such a ref - uge e'er was giv - en.
spares them; In His might - y arms He bears them.
show - eth, And their sor - rows all He know - eth.
sole - ly To pre - serve them pure and ho - ly. A - men.

Romans 8:35-39. Words, Karolina W. Sandell-Berg, 1855; trans. Ernst W. Olson, 1925. Copyright Board of
Publication, Lutheran Church in America. Tune TRYGGARE KAN INGEN VARA, Swedish Folk Melody.

645   # My Shepherd Will Supply My Need

1. My shep-herd will sup-ply my need; Je-ho-vah
2. When I walk through the shades of death Thy pres-ence
3. The sure pro-vi-sions of my God At-tend me

is His name: In pas-tures fresh He makes me feed, Be-
is my stay; One word of Thy sup-port-ing breath Drives
all my days; O may Thy house be my a-bode, And

side the liv-ing stream. He brings my wan-d'ring spir-it
all my fears a-way. Thy hand, in sight of all my
all my work be praise. There would I find a set-tled

back, When I for-sake His ways; And leads me,
foes, Doth still my ta-ble spread; My cup with
rest, While oth-ers go and come; No more a

Psalm 23:1. Words, Psalm 23, paraphrased Isaac Watts, 1719. Tune RESIGNATION, William Walker's *Southern Harmony*, 1855.

for His mer - cy's sake, In paths of truth and grace.
bless - ings o - ver - flows, Thine oil a - noints my head.
stran - ger, nor a guest, But like a child at home.

When Peace Like a River 646

1. When peace like a riv - er at - tend - eth my way, When sor - rows like
2. My sin— O the bliss of this glo - ri - ous tho't— My sin, not in
3, And, Lord, haste the day when the faith shall be sight, The clouds be rolled

sea - bil - lows roll; What - ev - er my lot, Thou hast taught me to say,
part but the whole, Is nailed to the cross and I bear it no more:
back as a scroll, The trump shall re - sound and the Lord shall de - scend,

"It is well, it is well with my soul." It is well
Praise the Lord, praise the Lord, O my soul!
"E - ven so"— it is well with my soul. It is well

with my soul (with my soul), It is well, it is well with my soul.

Isaiah 66:12. Words, Horatio G. Spafford, 1873. Tune VILLE DU HAVRE, Philip P. Bliss, 1876.

647 Safe in the Arms of Jesus

1. Safe in the arms of Je - sus, Safe on His gen - tle breast,
2. Safe in the arms of Je - sus, Safe from cor-rod - ing care,
3. Je - sus, my heart's dear ref - uge, Je - sus has died for me;

There by His love o'er - shad - ed, Sweet - ly my soul shall rest.
Safe from the world's temp - ta - tions, Sin can-not harm me there.
Firm on the Rock of A - ges, Ev - er my trust shall be.

Hark! 'tis the voice of an - gels, Borne in a song to me,
Free from the blight of sor - row, Free from my doubts and fears;
Here let me wait with pa - tience, Wait till the night is o'er;

O - ver the fields of glo - ry, O - ver the jas - per sea:
On - ly a few more tri - als, On - ly a few more tears:
Wait till I see the morn - ing Break on the gold - en shore:

2 Corinthians 5:17. Words, Fanny J. Crosby, 1870. Tune BRACHIONI, William H. Doane, 1870.

Safe in the arms of Je - sus, Safe on His gen - tle breast,

There by His love o'er - shad - ed, Sweet - ly my soul shall rest.

John 10:27-30; Revelation 7:16,17 **648**

My sheep hear my voice, and I know them, and they follow me: and I give to them
eternal life; and they shall never perish, and no one shall snatch them out of my
hand. My Father, who has given them to me, is greater than all; and no one is able
to snatch them out of the Father's hand. I and the Father are one.

They shall hunger no more, neither thirst any more; neither shall the sun strike
upon them, nor any heat: for the Lamb that is in the midst of the throne shall be
their shepherd, and shall guide them to fountains of waters of life: and God shall
wipe away every tear from their eyes.

649 In Heavenly Love Abiding

1. In heav'n-ly love a - bid - ing, No change my heart shall fear;
2. Wher - ev - er He may guide me, No want shall turn me back;
3. Green pas - tures are be - fore me, Which yet I have not seen;

And safe is such con - fid - ing, For noth - ing chang - es here.
My Shep - herd is be - side me, And noth - ing can I lack.
Bright skies will soon be o'er me, Where the dark clouds have been.

The storm may roar with - out me, My heart may low be laid,
His wis - dom ev - er wak - eth, His sight is nev - er dim;
My hope I can - not meas - ure, My path to life is free;

But God is round a - bout me, And can I be dis - mayed?
He knows the way He tak - eth, And I will walk with Him.
My Sav - ior has my treas - ure, And He will walk with me
(1.) And can I be dis - mayed?

Hebrews 13:8. Words, Anna L. Waring, 1850. Tune SEASONS, arr. from Felix Mendelssohn, Op.59.

Christ Will Me His Aid Afford — **650**

1. Christ will me His aid af-ford, Nev-er to fall, nev-er to fall;
2. I can fol-low all the way, Hear-ing Him call, hear-ing Him call;
3. Though a ves-sel I may be, Bro-ken and small, bro-ken and small,
4. When I reach the crys-tal sea, Voic-es will call, voic-es will call;

While I find my pre-cious Lord Sweet-er than all, sweet-er than all.
Find-ing Him, from day to day, Sweet-er than all, sweet-er than all.
Yet His bless-ings fall on me, Sweet-er than all, sweet-er than all.
But my Sav-ior's voice will be Sweet-er than all, sweet-er than all.

Je-sus is now, and ev-er will be, Sweet-er than all the world to me,

Since I heard His lov-ing call, Sweet-er than all, sweet-er than all.

Revelation 7:17. Words, Johnson Oatman, Jr. Tune SWEETER THAN ALL, J. Howard Entwisle, 1900.

651 All the Way My Savior Leads Me

1. All the way my Sav-ior leads me: What have I to ask be-side?
2. All the way my Sav-ior leads me, Cheers each wind-ing path I tread,
3. All the way my Sav-ior leads me: O the full-ness of His love!

Can I doubt His ten-der mer-cy, Who thro' life has been my Guide?
Gives me grace for ev-'ry tri-al, Feeds me with the liv-ing bread;
Per-fect rest to me is prom-ised In my Fa-ther's house a-bove;

Heav'n-ly peace, di-vin-est com-fort, Here by faith in Him to dwell!
Tho' my wea-ry steps may fal-ter, And my soul a-thirst may be,
When my spir-it, clothed im-mor-tal, Wings its flight to realms of day,

For I know, what-e'er be-fall me, Je-sus do-eth all things well;
Gush-ing from the Rock be-fore me, Lo! a spring of joy I see;
This my song thro' end-less a-ges: Je-sus led me all the way!

Deuteronomy 31:6. Words, Fanny J. Crosby, 1875. Tune ALL THE WAY, Robert Lowry, 1875.

For I know, what-e'er be - fall me, Je - sus do - eth all things well.
Gush-ing from the Rock be - fore me, Lo! a spring of joy I see.
This my song thro' end-less a - ges: Je - sus led me all the way!

When This Passing World is Done **652**

1. When this pass-ing world is done, When has sunk yon glar-ing sun,
2. When I stand be - fore the throne, Dressed in beau - ty not my own,
3. When the praise of heav'n I hear, Loud as thun-ders to the ear,
4. E'en on earth, as thro' a glass, Dark - ly let Thy glo - ry pass;

When I stand with Christ on high, Look - ing o'er life's his - to - ry—
When I see Thee as Thou art, Love Thee with un - sin-ning heart—
Loud as man - y wa - ters' noise, Sweet as harp's me - lo-dious voice—
Make for - give - ness feel so sweet; Make Thy Spir - it's help so meet;

Then, Lord, shall I ful - ly know, Not till then, how much I owe.
(v.4): E'en on earth, Lord, make me know Some-thing of how much I owe.

1 Corinthians 13:12. Words, Robert M. McCheyne, c. 1840. Tune SPANISH HYMN, Traditional Spanish Melody;
arr. Benjamin Carr, 1826.

653   God Sent His Son

1. God sent His Son, they called Him Je - sus; He came to love, heal, and for - give; He lived and died to buy my par - don, An emp - ty grave is there to prove my Sav - ior lives.

2. How sweet to hold a new - born ba - by, And feel the pride, and joy He gives; But great - er still the calm as - sur - ance, This child can face un - cer - tain days be - cause He lives.

3. And then one day I'll cross the riv - er; I'll fight life's fi - nal war with pain; And then as death gives way to vic - t'ry, I'll see the lights of glo - ry and I'll know He lives.

Be - cause He lives I can face to - mor - row; Be - cause He lives

Revelation 1:17,18. Words, Gloria & William J. Gaither, 1971. Tune RESURRECTION, William J. Gaither, 1971. Copyright 1971, William J. Gaither. All rights reserved. Used by permission.

all fear is gone; Be-cause I know He holds the fu-ture, And life is worth the liv-ing just be-cause He lives.

1 Thessalonians 4:14-18   **654**

If we believe that Jesus died and rose again, even so them also that are fallen asleep in Jesus will God bring with him. For this we say unto you by the word of the Lord, that we that are alive, that are left unto the coming of the Lord, shall in no wise precede them that are fallen asleep. For the Lord himself shall descend from heaven, with a shout, with the voice of the archangel, and with the trump of God; and the dead in Christ shall rise first; then we that are alive, that are left, shall together with them be caught up in the clouds, to meet the Lord in the air: and so shall we ever be with the Lord. Wherefore comfort one another with these words.

655 On a Hill Far Away

1. On a hill far a-way stood an old rug-ged cross, The em-blem of
2. O that old rug-ged cross, so de-spised by the world, Has a won-drous at-
3. In that old rug-ged cross, stained with blood so divine, A won - drous
4. To the old rug-ged cross I will ev - er be true, Its shame and re-

suf - f'ring and shame; And I love that old cross where the dear-est and best
trac - tion for me; For the dear Lamb of God left His glo - ry a - bove,
beau - ty I see; For 'twas on that old cross Je - sus suf-fered and died,
proach glad-ly bear; Then He'll call me some day to my home far a - way,

For a world of lost sin -ners was slain.
To bear it to dark Cal - va - ry. So I'll cher-ish the old rug - ged
To par - don and sanc-ti - fy me.
Where His glo - ry for ev - er I'll share. So I'll cher-ish the cross, the

cross, Till my tro-phies at last I lay down; I will cling to the
old rug-ged cross,

Acts 2:22-24. Words and tune OLD RUGGED CROSS, George Bennard, 1913. Copyright 1941, renewal. By permission of Word Music, Winona Lake, Indiana.

old rug-ged cross, And ex-change it some day for a crown.
cross, the old rug-ged cross,

Jesus, Thy Name I Love   **656**

1. Je - sus, Thy name I love, All oth - er names a - bove,
2. Thou, bless - ed Son of God, Hast bought me with Thy blood,
3. Soon Thou wilt come a - gain: I shall be hap - py then,

Je - sus, my Lord! O Thou art all to me; Noth - ing to
Je - sus, my Lord! How might - y is Thy love, All oth - er
Je - sus, my Lord! Then Thine own face I'll see, Then I shall

please I see, Noth - ing a - part from Thee, Je - sus, my Lord!
loves a - bove, Love that I dai - ly prove, Je - sus, my Lord!
like Thee be, Then ev - er - more with Thee, Je - sus, my Lord!

Philippians 2:9. Words, James G. Deck, 1853. Tune LYTE, Joseph P. Holbrook.

657 Jesus Saves Forever

1. Je - sus saves for - ev - er, I shall not be moved; He will leave me nev-er,
2. On His grace re - ly - ing, I shall not be moved; For His love un - dy - ing,
3. With the Church I'm go-ing, I shall not be moved; Christ to lost ones showing,
4. From the Word e-ter - nal I shall not be moved; From its truth su-per-nal

I shall not be moved; Just like a tree that's plant-ed by the wa - ter,

I shall not be moved. I shall not be, I shall not be moved;

I shall not be, I shall not be moved; Just like a

tree that's plant-ed by the wa - ter, I shall not be moved.

Psalm 92:12-15. Words, Edward Boatner; arr. Baylus B. McKinney, 1927. Tune I SHALL NOT BE MOVED,
Traditional Melody; arr. Baylus B. McKinney, 1927. Copyright Robert H. Coleman.

When All My Labors and Trials Are O'er 658

1. When all my la - bors and tri - als are o'er, And I am safe on that
2. When, by the gift of His in - fi - nite grace, I am ac - cord-ed in
3. Friends will be there I have loved long a - go; Joy like a riv - er a-

beau - ti - ful shore, Just to be near the dear Lord I a - dore
heav - en a place, Just to be there and to look on His face
round me will flow; Yet just a smile from my Sav - ior I know

Will thro' the a - ges be glo - ry for me. O that will be
O that will

glo - ry for me, Glo - ry for me, glo - ry for me; When by His
be glo - ry for me, Glo - ry for me, glo - ry for me;

grace I shall look on His face, That will be glo - ry, be glo - ry for me.

1 Peter 1:6-9. Words and tune GLORY SONG, Charles H. Gabriel, 1900.

659 There's a Land That is Fairer Than Day

1. There's a land that is fair-er than day, And by faith we can
2. We shall sing on that beau-ti-ful shore The me-lo-di-ous
3. To our boun-ti-ful Fa-ther a-bove We will of-fer our

see it a-far; For the Fa-ther waits o-ver the way, To pre-
songs of the blest; And our spir-its shall sor-row no more— Not a
trib-ute of praise For the glo-ri-ous gift of His love, And the

pare us a dwell-ing place there.   In the sweet   by and
sigh for the bless-ing of rest.
bless-ings that hal-low our days.   In the sweet

by,   We shall meet on that beau-ti-ful shore;   In the
by and by,   by and by;

sweet   by and by,   We shall meet on that beau-ti-ful shore.
In the sweet   by and by,

Revelation 22:3-5. Words, Sanford F. Bennett, 1868. Tune SWEET BY AND BY, Joseph P. Webster, 1868.

Face to Face

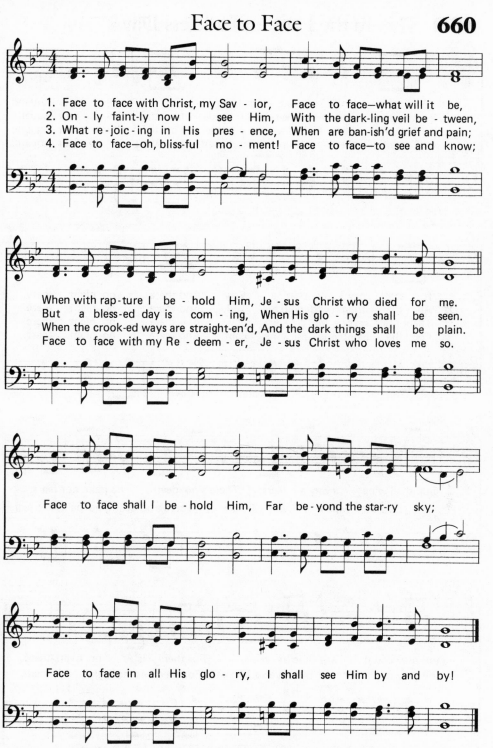

1. Face to face with Christ, my Sav - ior, Face to face—what will it be,
2. On - ly faint-ly now I see Him, With the dark-ling veil be - tween,
3. What re - joic - ing in His pres - ence, When are ban-ish'd grief and pain;
4. Face to face—oh, bliss-ful mo - ment! Face to face—to see and know;

When with rap-ture I be - hold Him, Je - sus Christ who died for me.
But a bless-ed day is com - ing, When His glo - ry shall be seen.
When the crook-ed ways are straight-en'd, And the dark things shall be plain.
Face to face with my Re - deem - er, Je - sus Christ who loves me so.

Face to face shall I be - hold Him, Far be - yond the star-ry sky;

Face to face in all His glo - ry, I shall see Him by and by!

1 John 3:2. Words, Carrie E. Breck, 1898. Tune FACE TO FACE, Grant Colfax Tullar, 1898.

661   In the Land of Fadeless Day

1. In the land of fade-less day   Lies the cit-y four-square;
2. All the gates of pearl are made   In the cit-y four-square;
3. And the gates shall nev-er close   To the cit-y four-square;
4. There they need no sun-shine bright,   In the cit-y four-square;

It shall nev-er pass a-way,   And there is no night there.
All the streets with gold are laid,   And there is no night there.
There life's crys-tal riv-er flows,   And there is no night there.
For the Lamb is all the light,   And there is no night there.

God shall wipe a-way all tears;   There's no death, no pain, nor fears;

God shall wipe a-way all tears;   There's no death, no pain, nor fears;

And they count not time by years,   For there is no night there.

And they count not time by years, by years, For there is no night there.

Revelation 21:16. Words, John R. Clements, 1899. Tune NO NIGHT THERE, Hart P. Danks, 1899.

Beyond the Sunset

1. Be - yond the sun - set, O bliss - ful morn - ing, When with our
2. Be - yond the sun - set no clouds will gath - er, No storms will
3. Be - yond the sun - set a hand will guide me To God, the
4. Be - yond the sun - set, O glad re - un - ion, With our dear

Sav - ior heav'n is be - gun; Earth's toil-ing end - ed, O glo - rious
threat - en, no fears an - noy; O day of glad - ness, O day un -
Fa - ther, whom I a - dore; His glo-rious pres - ence, His words of
loved ones who've gone be - fore; In that fair home-land we'll know no

dawn - ing, Be - yond the sun - set, when day is done.
end - ing, Be - yond the sun - set, e - ter - nal joy!
wel - come, Will be my por - tion on that fair shore.
part - ing; Be - yond the sun - set for ev - er - more.

Revelation 22:5. Words, Virgil B. Brock, 1936. Tune BROCK, Blanche Kerr Brock, 1936.

Revelation 21:1-4

And I saw a new heaven and a new earth: for the first heaven and the first earth are passed away; and the sea is no more. And I saw the holy city, new Jerusalem, coming down out of heaven from God, made ready as a bride adorned for her husband. And I heard a great voice out of the throne saying, "Behold, the tabernacle of God is with men, and he shall dwell with them, and they shall be his peoples, and God himself shall be with them, and be their God: and he shall wipe away every tear from their eyes; and death shall be no more; neither shall there be mourning, nor crying, nor pain, any more: the first things are passed away."

664 There is a Habitation

1. There is a hab-i-ta-tion, Built by the liv-ing God,
2. A cit-y with foun-da-tions, Firm as th'e-ter-nal throne;
3. No night is there, no sor-row, No death, and no de-cay;
4. With-in its pearl-y por-tals, An-gel-ic ar-mies sing,

For all of ev-'ry na-tion Who seek that grand a-bode.
Nor wars nor des-o-la-tions Shall ev-er move a stone.
No yes-ter-day, no mor-row— But one e-ter-nal day.
With glo-ri-fied im-mor-tals, The prais-es of its King.

O Zi-on, Zi-on, I long thy gates to see;
O Zi-on, love-ly Zi-on, O love-

O Zi-on, Zi-on, When shall I dwell in thee?
ly Zi-on, love-ly Zi-on,

Hebrews 12:22-24. Words, L.H. Jameson. Tune ROSECRANS, James Holmes Rosecrans.

To Canaan's Land I'm on My Way

1. To Ca-naan's land I'm on my way, Where the soul (of man) nev-er dies;
2. A rose is bloom-ing there for me, Where the soul (of man) nev-er dies;
3. My life will end in death-less sleep, Where the soul (of man) nev-er dies;
4. I'm on my way to that fair land, Where the soul (of man) nev-er dies;

My dark-est night will turn to day, Where the soul (of man) nev-er dies.
And I will spend e-ter-ni-ty, Where the soul (of man) nev-er dies.
And ev-er-last-ing joys I'll reap, Where the soul (of man) nev-er dies.
Where there will be no part-ing hand, And the soul (of man) nev-er dies.

No sad fare-wells, No tear-dimmed eyes,
Dear friends, there'll be no sad fare-wells, There'll be no tear-dimmed eyes,

Where all is love, And the soul nev-er dies.
Where all is peace and joy and love, And the soul of man nev-er dies.

Revelation 21:4. Words and tune GOLDEN, William M. Golden, 1914.

On Jordan's Stormy Banks

1. On Jor-dan's storm-y banks I stand, And cast a wish-ful eye
2. O'er all those wide-ex-tend-ed plains Shines one e-ter-nal day;
3. When shall I reach that hap-py place, And be for-ev-er blest?
4. Filled with de-light, my rap-tured soul Would here no long-er stay;

To Ca-naan's fair and hap-py land, Where my pos-ses-sions lie.
There God the Son for-ev-er reigns And scat-ters night a-way.
When shall I see my Fa-ther's face, And in His bos-om rest?
Tho' Jor-dan's waves a-round me roll, Fear-less I'd launch a-way.

I am bound for the prom-ised land, I am bound for the prom-ised land;

O who will come and go with me? I am bound for the prom-ised land.

Hebrews 4:9. Words, Samuel Stennett, 1787. Tune, PROMISED LAND, American Folk Hymn; arr. Rigdon M. McIntosh, 1895.

On Jordan's Stormy Banks

667

1. On Jordan's storm-y banks I stand, And cast a wish-ful eye
2. O'er all those wide-ex-tend-ed plains Shines one e-ter-nal day;
3. When shall I reach that hap-py place, And be for ev-er blest?
4. Filled with de-light, my rap-tured soul Would here no long-er stay;

To Canaan's fair and hap-py land, Where my pos-ses-sions lie.
There God, the Sun, for ev-er reigns, And scat-ters night a-way.
When shall I see my Fa-ther's face, And in His bos-om rest?
Tho' Jordan's waves a-round me roll, Fear-less I'd launch a-way.

We will rest in the fair and hap-py land, by and by, Just a-

cross on the ev-er-green shore, Sing the song of
ev-er-green shore,

Mo-ses and the Lamb, by and by, And dwell with Je-sus ev-er-more.

Hebrews 4:9. Words, Samuel Stennett, 1787. Tune EVERGREEN SHORE, Tullius C. O'Kane, 1877.

668 The Sands of Time

1. The sands of time are sink - ing, The dawn of heav - en breaks;
2. O Christ, He is the foun - tain, The deep, sweet well of love;
3. With mer - cy and with judg - ment My web of time He wove,
4. The King there in His beau - ty With - out a veil is seen;

The sum - mer morn I've sighed for, The fair, sweet morn a - wakes;
The streams on earth I've tast - ed, More deep I'll drink a - bove;
And aye the dews of sor - row Were bright-ened by His love;
It were a well - spent jour - ney, Tho' sev'n deaths lay be - tween;

Dark, dark hath been the mid - night, But day - spring is at hand,
There to an o - cean full - ness His mer - cy doth ex - pand,
I'll bless the hand that guid - ed, I'll bless the heart that planned,
The Lamb with His fair ar - my Doth on Mount Zi - on stand,

And glo - ry, glo - ry dwell - eth In Im - man - uel's land.
And glo - ry, glo - ry dwell - eth In Im - man - uel's land.
When throned where glo - ry dwell - eth In Im - man - uel's land.
And glo - ry, glo - ry dwell - eth In Im - man - uel's land.

Revelation 14:1. Words, Anne R. Cousin, 1857. Tune RUTHERFORD, Chretien d'Urhan, 1834; arr. Edward F. Rimbault, 1867. *Note: "seven deaths" (st. 4), i.e. the greatest of perils. See Psalm 23:4.*

Sing the Wondrous Love

669

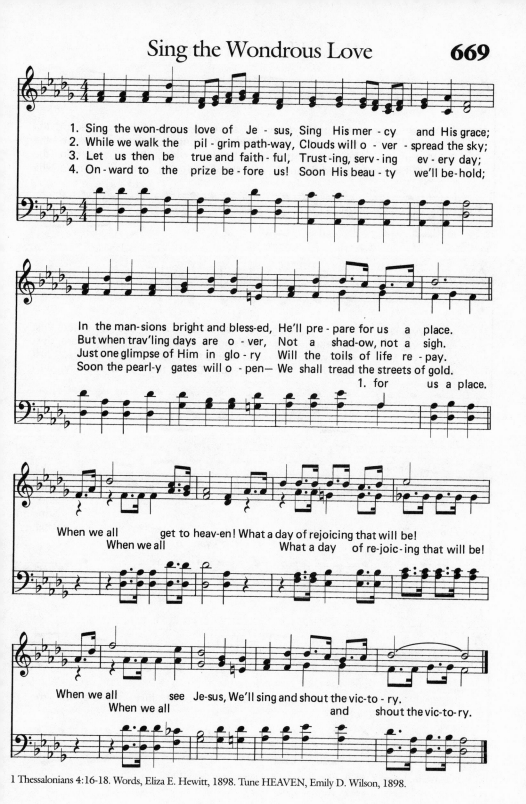

1 Thessalonians 4:16-18. Words, Eliza E. Hewitt, 1898. Tune HEAVEN, Emily D. Wilson, 1898.

670 I've a Home Prepared

1. I've a home pre - pared where the saints a - bide, Just o - ver in the
2. I am on my way to those man - sions fair, Just o - ver in the
3. What a joy - ful thought that my Lord I'll see, Just o - ver in the
4. With the blood-washed throng I will shout and sing, Just o - ver in the

glo - ry - land; And I long to be by my Sav - ior's side, Just
glo - ry - land; There to sing God's praise, and His glo - ry share, Just
glo - ry - land; And with kin - dred saved, there for - ev - er be, Just
glo - ry - land; Glad ho - san - nas to Christ, the Lord and King, Just

o - ver in the glo - ry - land. Just o - ver in the glo - ry - land,
o - ver, o - ver

I'll join the hap-py an - gel band, Just o - ver in the
yes, join

Psalm 26:8. Words, James W. Acuff, 1906. Tune DEAN, Emmett S. Dean, 1906.

glo-ry - land; Just o - - ver in the glo - ry - land, There
o - ver, o - ver

with the might-y host I'll stand, just o-ver in the glo-ry - land.
yes, with

Asleep in Jesus 671

1. A - sleep in Je - sus! bless-ed sleep, From which none ev-er wakes to weep!
2. A - sleep in Je - sus! O how sweet To be for such a slum-ber meet!
3. A - sleep in Je - sus! peace-ful rest, Whose wak-ing is su-preme-ly blest!
4. A - sleep in Je - sus! O for me May such a bliss-ful ref - uge be!

A calm and un - dis - turbed re - pose, Un-bro-ken by the last of foes.
With ho - ly con - fi - dence to sing, That death hath lost its ven-omed sting.
No fear, no woe, shall dim that hour That man-i - fests the Sav - ior's pow'r.
Se - cure - ly shall my ash - es lie, And wait the sum-mons from on high.

1 Thessalonians 4:13,14. Words, Margaret Mackay, 1832. Tune REST, William B. Bradbury.

672 Sing to Me of Heaven

1. Sing to me of heav-en, sing that song of peace, From the toils that bind me it will bring re-lease; Bur-dens will be lift-ed that are press-ing so, Show-ers of great bless-ing o'er my heart will flow. Sing to me of heav-en, let me fond-ly dream Of its gold-en glo-ry, of its

2. Sing to me of heav-en, ten-der-ly and low, Till the shad-ows o'er me rise and swift-ly go; When my heart is wea-ry, when the day is long, Sing to me of heav-en, sing that old, sweet song. Sing to me of heav-en, let me fond-ly dream Of its gold-en glo-ry,

pearl - y   gleam; Sing to   me   when shad-ows of the   eve - ning   fall,
of its pearl-y gleam;   Sing to me when shad-ows   of the eve-ning fall,

Sing to   me   of   heav - en, Sweet - est   song   of   all.
Sing to me of heav - en, Sing   the   sweet - est song of   all.

Brief Life is Here Our Portion   **673**

1. Brief life is   here   our   por - tion; Brief   sor - row, short - lived   care:
2. O   sweet and bless - ed   coun - try, The   home of God's e -   lect;
3. The   morn-ing shall   a - wak - en, The   shad - ows shall de -   cay,
4. There God, our King and Por - tion, In   full - ness of His   grace,

The life that knows no   end - ing, The   tear - less life is   there.
O   sweet and bless - ed   coun - try, That   ea - ger hearts ex - pect!
And each true-heart-ed   serv - ant Shall shine as   doth the   day.
Shall we be - hold for   ev - er, And   wor - ship face to   face.

Revelation 21:3,4. Words, Bernard of Cluny, *De contemptu mundi*, c. 1140; trans. John M. Neale, 1849. Tune
ST. ALPHEGE, Henry J. Gauntlett, 1852.

AUTHOR-COMPOSER INDEX

INDEX OF TUNES

SCRIPTURE INDEX

TOPICAL INDEX

FIRST LINE INDEX